Pursuing
Food Security

International Political Economy Yearbook, Volume 3
W. Ladd Hollist and F. LaMond Tullis, Series Editors

Pursuing Food Security

Strategies and Obstacles
in Africa, Asia,
Latin America,
and the Middle East

edited by
W. Ladd Hollist
& F. LaMond Tullis

Lynne Rienner Publishers • Boulder & London

Published in the United States of America in 1987 by
Lynne Rienner Publishers, Inc.
948 North Street, Boulder, Colorado 80302

Library of Congress Cataloging-in-Publication Data

Pursuing food security.

  (International political economy yearbook,
ISSN 8755-8335 ; v. 3)
    Bibliography: p.
    Includes index.
    1. Food supply—Developing countries—
Congresses.   2. Agriculture—Economic aspects—
Developing countries—Congresses.   I. Hollist,
W. Ladd, 1947–   II. Tullis, F. LaMond, 1935–
III. Series.
HF1410.I579   Vol. 3   337'.05 s   87-4524
[HD9018.D44]   [338.1'9'1724]

ISBN 1-55587-032-5 (lib. bdg.)
ISBN 1-55587-033-3 (pbk.)

Printed and bound in the United States of America

The paper used in this publication meets
the requirements of the American National Standard
for Permanence of Paper for Printed Library
Materials Z39.48-1984. ∞

To a world in which food security for everyone
may become as real as it is ideal

Contents

Tables and Figures

Tables

Figures

Acknowledgments

We thank the Milton R. Merrill Chair and the Department of Political Science at Utah State University for sponsoring the conference that ultimately led to this book.

For more than forty years, Milton R. Merrill served Utah State University as a teacher, a scholar, and as an administrator. During his career he was head of the political science and history departments, dean of the College of Business and Social Sciences, and, in 1959, he became Utah State University's first vice-president. Active in public affairs, Professor Merrill was a longtime member of the Logan City Board of Education. He was also a member of the Council of the American Political Science Association.

Although Professor Merrill's achievements as an administrator and participant in public affairs were outstanding, he was best known as a superb and inspiring teacher by the thousands of students who attended his classes.

When he retired as academic vice-president and returned to teaching as professor emeritus in 1969, Professor Merrill's friends, associates, and former students envisioned a project to honor him on the occasion of his retirement. A national committee was formed, led by M. Judd Harmon and Phillip A. Bullen, to raise funds to establish the Milton R. Merrill Chair of Political Science that would bring distinguished political scientists and other scholars to Utah State University.

The initial response and continued support by contributors to the Merrill Chair Fund have made it possible to establish Utah State University's first and only endowed chair. The fund has brought a series of distinguished educators and public figures to the Utah State University campus and has greatly benefited students, faculty, and the general community. Seven manuscripts have resulted from conferences and research sponsored by the fund.

We express sincere appreciation to the participants at the Utah State University conference whose work with ours is here presented. And we thank faculty members and students at Utah State University whose questions and comments provoked additional serious thinking of the arguments and analyses that are presented here.

We also thank the David M. Kennedy Center for International Studies at Brigham Young University for supporting the preparation of the final manuscript.

Ultimately, human experience and scholars' efforts to understand it combine to produce a book such as this. Accordingly, we voice concern for the human condition by inquiring into the questions of food security in developing nations, and we express appreciation to those from lesser-developed countries who have shared their experiences with us and who have, therefore, made our analyses possible. We join with them in hoping for a world in which food security for everyone may become as real as it is ideal. It is to that idea that we dedicate this book.

Preface

In launching the *International Political Economy Yearbook* series, we stated that our intention was to promote dialogue. To this end we suggested that the Yearbook "remain open to new ideas and insights," and that "it ought not to become the 'property' of any one theoretical perspective or normative persuasion." We did ask that every contribution to the Yearbook "clearly explicate premises, concepts, and values." (See W. Ladd Hollist and F. LaMond Tullis, *An International Political Economy,* Boulder, Colorado: Westview Press, 1985: 9.)

In this volume we seek to promote debate concerning strategies and obstacles that confront the developing nations' pursuit of food security. Contributors, all respected scholars, were selected because they advance reasonable but different theoretical and normative views concerning food security. Many, but admittedly not all, perspectives are represented. For example, some North American economists may rightly contend that their views are not amply represented. Whatever one's views may be, however, the urgency of the task at hand—pursuing food security for all people—and the consistency with which past efforts have proven inadequate, require that we offer our best thinking while remaining open to views that challenge our perspectives.

Scholars have long noted impediments to its achievement in Latin America. Several African and Asian studies scholars with whom we have interacted[1] have amply shown that insights, theories, and explanations appropriate to understanding rural development issues in Latin America are inadequate for comprehending many of the world's other lesser-developed regions. In this volume, we have continued our cross-hemispheric comparisons because we are confident that they will add significantly to an understanding of obstacles to rural development and related national food security issues.

To that end we brought together renowned scholars of rural development and international political economy whose studies have focused on food security issues (a biographical sketch of each participant may be found in the list of contributors). Opportunity to do so within the context of an international conference arose when Ladd Hollist was appointed visiting Milton R. Merrill Professor of Political Science at Utah State University. As many of that university's faculty and several of its departments have long been active in research and outreach programs to promote rural development throughout the globe, it was natural that the university would be interested in hosting such a conference.[2] We are grateful for the graciousness of its faculty and administration and for the willingness of the Milton R. Merrill Chair trustees to fund the conference which met in Logan from May 2 to 4, 1985.

Of the several objectives to which rural development should aspire, none is more basic than food security. Food security is achieved either by producing food or by acquiring the resources necessary to purchase it. No surer sign of failed rural development exists than the widespread persistence of rural poverty, hunger, and even starvation—clear signs that millions of people neither grow enough food nor acquire enough money to purchase it from food-surplus producers. As food security in many countries has remained an elusive ideal, we focused the conference on impediments to its achievement in Africa, Asia, Latin America, and the Middle East.

We realize, of course, that rural development is a complex process in any setting, and that diverse obstacles have combined to thwart the attainment of food security in many less-developed countries. Floods, droughts, population pressures, and other "acts of God" have combined to contribute—each in its own way—to food shortages, most recently in Africa. "Acts of people" are equally or more devastating. Inappropriate technologies, government policies of cheap food for urban laborers, credit preferences to producers of cash crops for export, a bias for urban industrialization over rural development, and inadequate support for needed rural infrastructure have negatively affected rural development, particularly in the production and distribution of basic foodstuffs for the poor and "ultra poor." Without ignoring such factors as adversely affecting a developing nation's ability to feed itself adequately, we desired to explore features of the international political economy that may combine with domestic policies and natural conditions to increase a country's misfortunes and its people's afflictions in relation to food security. We chose to explore two sides of an argument: first, that many less-developed countries' relations with the international economy severely strain their capacities to feed their rural and urban poor, thereby contributing to national food insecurities; second, and obversely, that the international economy has opened opportunities for developing nations to enhance their food security, and that insofar as impediments exist they are largely of domestic origin, quite unrelated to the external political economy.

On the whole, the first argument claims that the unfavorable terms of trade available to developing countries for food exports and imports, foreign demand for specialty and processed foods that are too high-priced for mass consumption, and the influx of transnational agribusinesses with their export emphasis and reliance on capital-intensive and labor-displacing technologies tend to undermine basic food production and thus, usually, food security for the masses. The second argument holds that regional specialization in comparative advantage production technologies not only offers the best hope for developing countries to actually develop, but for the lowest population quintiles to have any long-term prospects of improving the quality of their lives. International markets, international trade, and foreign investment are therefore given considerable plaudits in this perspective.

To explore the general meaningfulness of these and related conflicting international political economy arguments we sought participants for our conference whose published works had rigorously analyzed and argued these and related claims. In short, we sought respected scholars with dissimilar perspectives on the causes of food insecurity in Africa, Latin America, South Asia and

China, and the Middle East. We were delighted that they accepted our invitation. Among those who came were Keith B. Griffin and John W. Mellor. Perhaps no other scholars are better known for their work on rural development, although they approach the issues that we chose to consider from notably different perspectives. As we requested, they assumed a general or global view of rural development and food security. As evidenced in their chapters and in the associated discussions in Part 1 of this book, they set the agenda for the three days of our conference.

Papers on food crises in Africa, again from different vantages, were prepared by Cheryl Christensen, by Michael F. Lofchie, and by Keith B. Griffin. These papers comprise Part 2 of this volume.

What of factors contributing to food insecurity in South Asia? Bringing their knowledge to this question were F. Tomasson Jannuzi, a longtime U.S. observer of South Asian rural development, and Ronald J. Herring, whose book *Land to the Tiller: The Political Economy of Agrarian Reform in South Asia* has received much commentary and had provoked our interest. At about the same time as the conference at Utah State University, Keith B. Griffin presented a paper at an open forum at Brigham Young University entitled "The Chinese Economy After Mao." The insights it provides about rural development in China since Mao's death proved especially pertinent to the issues addressed at our conference in Logan. We are grateful that Griffin has allowed that work to be included in this volume. These papers by Jannuzi, Herring, and Griffin comprise Part 3.

Given our personal interest in food security in Latin America, we were particularly pleased that Alain de Janvry, whose arguments in his book *The Agrarian Question and Reformism in Latin America* had long challenged our thinking, agreed to participate. His paper and ours appear as Part 4.

When we began this project we knew very little about the challenges that threaten food security in the Middle East and North Africa. We therefore sought a scholar who could succinctly unravel the complex dynamics that surround food problems in those regions. Colleagues repeatedly recommended that we invite Alan Richards, who accepted and contributed an understanding born of in-depth research on rural development there. His work appears as Part 5.

Quite predictably, the conference fielded excellent papers. Nevertheless, intense discussions in the workshop sessions challenged every author's arguments.[3] Not only did the contributors criticize and debate each other's work, but various of Utah State University's excellent scholars added their own insights and vigorously stated their arguments. It is not surprising that when the conference concluded, each author chose to revise his or her work in consideration of important issues and insights that had been raised. These revised papers, and some of the debates, comprise this book. We consider that the issues addressed are essential to any understanding of why food security has remained such an elusive ideal in much of Africa, Latin America, South Asia and China, and the Middle East.

Ladd Hollist
LaMond Tullis

NOTES

1. See W. Ladd Hollist, "Dependency Transformed: Brazilian Agriculture in Historical Perspective"; F. LaMond Tullis, "The Current View on Rural Development: Fad or Breakthrough in Latin America"; and F. LaMond Tullis and W. Ladd Hollist, eds., *Food, the State, and International Political Economy*.

2. For many years Utah State University has sought to promote rural development and food security throughout the world. Few U.S. universities have been more consistently involved in such activity. USU scientists have researched how best to augment agricultural productivity and total output in numerous countries. USU's development experts—scientists; technicians; social, economic, and political analysts—and students have shared their knowledge about disease control, sanitation, water purification, irrigation, pest control, resource management, marketing, finance, and much more. In 1986 alone Utah State University administered in excess of $6 million in contracts designed to contribute to the development of less-developed countries, principally in Africa and Latin America.

3. Were it possible, we would publish much of that dialogue here. However, we are limited to including only the comments made in response to Keith B. Griffin's paper "World Hunger and the World Economy" and to John Mellor's paper "Opportunities in the International Economy for Meeting the Food Requirements of the Developing Countries," as well as a response by Keith B. Griffin, in Part 1 of this book.

1

W. Ladd Hollist
F. LaMond Tullis

Pursuing Food Security

"Food security" is sometimes equated, at a national level, with "food self-sufficiency." That is not necessarily the meaning we have in mind. Some nations with food-production deficits enjoy considerable national food security. They import to satisfy their population's food consumption needs. The volume and nature of these countries' exports, which produce the income to pay for food imports, allow some food-deficit nations to enjoy considerable food security (for example, Japan). Such security probably will continue as long as the political economy of producing nations encourages food exports (for example, the United States). On the other hand, some countries have national food self-sufficiency but export so much food that many of their own citizens go hungry (for example, Brazil). Then, of course, some nations neither produce enough food nor have an import capability to satisfy consumption needs. There, chronic hunger is abundant. Thus, national food security is not to be understood simply as national food self-sufficiency but whether people, on the whole, are able to consume a minimum diet, the production sources of which are reasonably secure. While we have given the term food security a more expansive definition than is usual, in practical applications one will not go far wrong in assuming that it does refer principally to food self-sufficiency. The rural poor—most of the world's hungry—are not likely to eat well unless they produce their own food in adequate amounts.

All societies have their health and nutrition-related afflictions. In affluent countries of Europe and North America these are heart and lung disease, cancer, drug addiction (legal and illegal), obesity, and diseases incident to old age. Among the causes are life-style, including excess consumption of food and beverages, and the fact that because of pervasive medical intervention people in those countries tend to live long enough for their bodies to wear out. By contrast, for many hundreds of millions living in the developing countries of Africa, South Asia, Latin America, and the Middle East the afflictions are more basic.[1] They derive from the shortage, not the abundance, of food. Food short-

1

ages and related nutritional diseases that are devastating to mind and body are part of the daily experience of the third of humanity whose lives begin and end in the "developing" world.

People secure in their food entitlements consume what is necessary to enjoy a vigorous life. As many as 750 million people in developing countries consume but 90 percent of that amount, and it is estimated that 340 million of these are "acutely undernourished," eating but 80 percent or less of a minimum nutritional standard.[2] For millions of people, life's daily routines reflect a constant worry about and search for ways to provide sufficient food for themselves and their families. Frequently, neither worry nor effort produces satisfaction. Nutrition-related disease and early death result; malnutrition both takes and denigrates human life. In a world in which a "Green Revolution" of advanced technologies and hybrid seeds now combine to produce such prodigious harvests[3] that much of the food produced can neither be consumed, stored, nor sold, why is there so much hunger?

Poverty, not global food insufficiency or the inability to produce more food (even in food-short Africa), assures that millions of rural and shantytown people in developing countries cannot either buy or grow sufficient food for their needs. Why is this so? One reason lies in how societies are structured. In Chapter 2, Keith B. Griffin contends that the social and economic inequities, reflected in unequal patterns of national income distribution, and the political institutions that sustain them are root causes of poverty and therefore of malnutrition among the poor. One policy implication is clear: Restructure society by replacing the existing political/economic elite with an alternative social, political, and economic order that is more agreeable to an equitable distribution of the national income and the eradication of poverty and hunger. A difficult order, indeed, that only a few nations have tried and fewer still have successfully delivered.

In addition to inappropriate social inequalities, contributors to this volume point out other factors that hinder the elimination of hunger in today's world of actual and potential food abundance: counterproductive, if not actually malicious, government policies that favor urban areas at the expense of rural areas; too much emphasis on agricultural production for export; excess reliance on food imports (including food aid); and excessively foreign-financed, debt-creating industrialization. Mutually reinforcing relationships frequently exist among these domestic and international factors that make their cumulative effect more detrimental than a simple sum of their individual impacts.

All this calls for reform.[4] One of the impediments to reform has been the resiliency of old institutions and the elites who back them. They have been unwilling to accommodate new social forces and a new distribution of the national income. Doubting that social, political, and economic reforms with sufficient force to significantly enhance people's food security in developing countries will be forthcoming, John W. Mellor, in Chapter 3, advocates a distinctive market strategy to increase food production and to expand the number of people who can benefit from it. Mellor assumes that many people are hungry because the right people do not grow enough food in the right way. Although he acknowledges that Griffin may be correct in his view about the structural causes of hunger, Mellor seeks a politically accomplishable remedy. He argues that a technology-based strategy designed to promote increased food production by all rural groups, particularly by the peasantry—using land and labor resources already in hand and doing so in ways that enhance employment opportunities—will lessen hunger.

With more food grown and more money in circulation among more people, the distribution of national income will be more equitable, Mellor contends, and therefore poor people will be more able to buy food. Working within the system may ultimately undermine it and promote purposeful structural and other reforms, but social and political reforms prior to helpful technological innovations are not a prerequisite to reducing the incidence of hunger through specific kinds of increased food production, Mellor argues. This is especially true for Africa, he observes, where in recent years per capita food production has declined annually by 1.2 percent.

The right kind of increased food production may be achieved, Mellor states, by introducing appropriate agricultural technology (including hybrid seeds, fertilizer, and irrigation), electric power, and suitable transportation and communication systems to bring foodstuffs inexpensively to consumers. In this strategy, public institutions are charged with ensuring that these inputs and associated infrastructure are consistently and predictably provided to the *small* farmer as well as to others. It is hoped that improved food production will enhance the amount of food available locally; expanded employment will increase poor people's purchasing power; food-deficit countries will need to import less food, thereby saving foreign exchange for other critical international transactions; and the unit price of food to the local consumer will be lowered, thereby permitting poor people to consume more of it. In this model, expanded production triggered by the direct and indirect multiplier effects of technological change will not only increase the purchasing power of the poor but also increase their employment opportunities. The heart of the strategy is to implement cost-reducing technologies in areas where underutilized rural labor may be productively employed and reasonably remunerated.

Critics of Mellor's technological approach to reducing poverty and hunger are many. They observe that the very reason small farmers are now shortchanged is because of the preferences that existing social and economic elites have for other ways of doing things, among them their heavy emphasis on export agriculture, a subject that almost all the contributing authors address. Beyond this, many new technologies introduced have been "inappropriate" and counterproductive to the ends Mellor advocates, another significant problem that the contributing authors explore.

But suppose Mellor's proposal were promising if the right set of conditions prevailed. We might then benefit from inquiring into those conditions, into what obstacles to their realization yet prevail, and into how those obstacles might be removed. That, in part, is our purpose here; accordingly, domestic and international factors that affect the possibilities of structural and techno-logical approaches to reducing hunger—the Griffin and the Mellor ap-proaches—constitute the bulk of this work.

Although a review of the table of contents will reveal that this book is or-ganized into geographical sections, it will come as no surprise that our substan-tive focus is thematic. What internal and external restraints are at work in the various regions that cause some people to go hungry? How are these restraints different or similar? How can they be overcome?

Black Africa is the world's most food-deficit region as well as its hungriest. In Chapter 4 Cheryl Christensen addresses the question of why this crisis has occurred and what needs to be done if we hope to reverse the ominous trends. Two major challenges confront Africa. First, the countries have been unable to respond to natural shocks associated with catastrophes such as cyclical drought. A typical feast/famine cycle follows. After drought and associated food shortages occur, prices rise, the rains return, farmers invest their energies in response to opportunity and economic incentives, and food supplies grow. The increased food supply generally results in a lowering of consumer food prices. As a result, producer incentives are inadequate to stimulate further growth in food production. Compensating action by African governments has been at best negligible and has often hurt. Thus, neither the marketplace nor govern-ments have been able to adjust to changes induced by natural catastrophes. Sec-ond, most nations of sub-Saharan Africa have been unable to maintain a level of exports that would allow importation of food, capital, and technological inputs that might stimulate overall economic growth.

Christensen shows that for black African nations to increase their ability to promote food production and to buy food imports sufficient to meet their im-mediate and near-term food needs, they must change certain practices. They must "get their prices right" so that economic returns to producers will be suffi-cient to encourage substantially increased production of domestically consum-able food. Moreover, the countries must increase institutional support to moti-vate a large supply response to increased producer prices. Such support should include credit at reasonable rates, better transportation facilities for de-livery of produce to markets, and general improvements in the marketing system.

The practices of parastatals—governmental agencies that set prices for, purchase, and resell agricultural commodities—must be changed. Policies that impede efficiency and competency must be abolished (or the parastatals aban-doned) in the need to give more consistent stimuli to food production. Moreover, certain governmental expenditures need to be curbed. For ex-ample, job guarantees (frequently in unproductive sectors) to college graduates and the promotion of inefficient public enterprises need to be reduced. Exports should be taxed as a revenue-gathering mechanism, monetary devaluation should occur, and the kinds and amounts of imports should be regulated according to their contribution to economic development. In short, for food production to increase, Christensen shows that African governments' fiscal, monetary, and pricing policies must change.

Beyond discussing the appropriateness of these policy recommendations is an even more difficult consideration. Assuming that such policies would increase food production if adopted, what chance is there that they will be adopted? Christensen laments that her agenda for policy changes may not be politically possible. At present an appropriate coalition able to carry out such reforms does not exist within any of these African nations. Powerful special interests, including the holders of land and capital, oppose such changes. Beyond that the matter is even more complicated. Parallel markets, "black" markets, and smuggling, outside the control of policymakers, abound. Given such institutions, the outcome of reform policies, even if enacted, is uncertain.

The difficulties of understanding the possibilities of reform do not end simply with a discussion of the imponderables of domestic policies. Christensen notes that for new internal policies, even if adopted, to have the desired impact on food production, international adjustments must also occur—rescheduling of African foreign debt, increasing foreign exchange earnings for African nations through improved commodity prices, and further response to the need for external aid. The mutually reinforcing relationship of domestic and international variables further complicates the dilemma.

The importance of appropriate government policy in achieving increased food production and food security in Africa is further evidenced in Keith B. Griffin's case study of Ethiopia (Chapter 6). In 1982, Griffin headed a team of consultants to Ethiopia who recommended that the government direct its attention to developing the agricultural sector, then and still in 1987 the weakest sector in the economy, as the best way to enhance overall economic development. The team recommended that the seasonally surplus labor force be mobilized to carry out much-needed projects, that more land be put under cultivation, that yields be increased by labor-intensive land improvement projects and improved irrigation, that the quantity and productivity of basic farm implements be improved, that small businesses be stimulated to process agricultural products before export, and that the government get its prices right. The group recommended investment in infrastructure, particularly transportation and communication developments, geared to assist the agricultural sector. Food rationing was recommended to lessen already acute hunger and starvation.

The team's members also questioned the productivity of existing state farms whose products tended to be used to feed the army and other government employees. They noted the high overhead costs, excessive mechanization, labor shortages, overcentralized management, and apparent disregard for appropriate financial decisions in these operations. The team challenged industry to become more oriented toward the service of agriculture, that is, to emphasize the processing of agricultural commodities, the production of farm implements, and the provision of simple consumer goods that the majority of the population who reside and work in the rural areas might consume.

As anyone who has tracked the plight of the Ethiopian people will note, neither these nor hardly any other policies intended to benefit rural people have been adopted. Instead, the government has systematically diverted its resources to its armed forces. It has concentrated on organizing a Workers Party to sustain itself rather than addressing the pressing problems faced by its constituents. The government has ruthlessly prosecuted the civil war, apparently seeking to starve its opposition into submission.

Elsewhere, John W. Mellor has noted the success in the Punjab region of India of the technology-driven strategy he advocates.[5] In Chapter 7, F. Tomasson Jannuzi examines the impacts of such strategies in the Permanent Settlement Region of India and Bangladesh. Concluding that the productivity effects of new agricultural technologies have been important there, he nevertheless notes that the gains that might have been achieved have been limited or perhaps reversed when these technologies have been introduced in regions of great social inequality. He specifically argues that the spread effects of such technologies in this region have been limited, and that these technological innovations have been distributed in a manner that reflects and reinforces existing inequalities and in ways that do not address hunger issues at all.

With Jannuzi, Mellor's critics agree in principle that had an *appropriate* technology-based strategy been implemented, food security likely would have been enhanced in developing countries. They note, however, that in practice, especially in areas of great social inequality and grossly unequal distribution of productive assets, the introduction of new technologies often has proven counterproductive to the reduction of hunger. Usually the new methods have been obtained through the import of expensive technologies, not local research. The cost of the technology typically has been high relative to the ability of the food producers to employ it. Moreover, the cost savings of the so-called Green Revolution technology have generally depended upon economies of scale, requiring application of the technology to relatively large plots of fertile land. Also, mechanization of production, with displacement of rural labor, often has accompanied the adoption of this technology.

Consequently, even when cost savings in food production have been achieved, the overall ability of the poor rural laborer to consume food has improved little and in many cases has even declined. The poor have not become more able than before the technology was employed to successfully bid for the food supply. This inadequate local demand for increased foodstuffs and other agricultural commodities often has tended to be accompanied by stronger demand and accompanying higher prices offered in external markets. Agricultural producers who are able to employ these new technologies respond to this external demand, bringing much desired foreign exchange. Under such circumstances, any increases in the locally available food supply that an appropriately applied technology might have produced tend to be lost.

More particularly, Jannuzi observes that in Bangladesh the unequal relationship between rent-receiving landlords and the tillers of the land remains little altered since its colonial origins. He examines the "agrarian reform" known as the Zamindari abolition, noting that the rhetoric of the reform was more extravagant than the reforms themselves. He asserts that through it all the landlords retained their rights to the land. Consequently, the benefits of increased productivity in food and agriculture in the Permanent Settlement Region continue to be unevenly enjoyed, to the disadvantage of small farmers, tenants, sharecroppers, and landless laborers. If the socioeconomic conditions had been different, productivity gains might have been more widely beneficial and the incidence of hunger thereby reduced in line with a reduction in relative and absolute poverty. Similar social and political constraints on rural development within Latin American countries are presented in Chapters 10 and 11 by Alain de Janvry and W. Ladd Hollist. Ronald J. Herring examines such obstacles within Sri Lanka (Chapter 8).

Regardless of the rightness of solutions to existing food crises, including Mellor's emphasis on appropriate technologies and improved production strategies and the policy packages suggested by Christensen and Griffin, political and social factors often block their implementation. Griffin seems to be right when he argues that famines often are not short-term economic phenomena but the outcome of long-term political, social, and economic choices that are contrary to the attainment of food security (Chapters 2 and 6).

Strategies intended to enhance food security are further constrained by external factors. With an eye to such factors, Michael F. Lofchie characterizes the food crisis in Africa in terms of plummeting per capita food production related to the way African governments' policies interface with international variables (Chapter 5). He takes particular note of a troubling symptom of the crisis—a skyrocketing demand for food imports. Exports from the agricultural sector have stagnated and foreign exchange earnings required to purchase food have therefore fallen sharply. Moreover, the stagnation of agricultural exports bodes poorly for the import of medical and educational supplies, petroleum products, transportation equipment, and consumer goods. Also, the inability to import contributes to Africa's inadequate industrial performance. In view of these developments, Lofchie notes that Africa faces a cruel choice. Should it allocate foreign exchange reserves to acquire additional food imports to avert starvation, or should it invest in industry to avoid higher rates of politically threatening urban unemployment?

With this as background, Lofchie argues that the colonial period in Africa left a heritage of export-oriented production of primary agricultural commodities, and that this dependence on export agriculture is at the heart of Africa's contemporary crisis. The export bias has consistently resulted in the neglect of food production. Furthermore, what technological innovations and investments have been made in African agriculture have been concentrated in the export sector. The government-controlled pricing system has also reinforced the export bias to the detriment of domestic food producers.

The severity of the food crisis in Africa has been heightened as international market conditions have moved against African exports. World demand for these exports has waned as substitutes have been found and as protectionist pressures in importing countries have mounted. Prices have been very volatile, inducing new competitors to enter during periods of relative high prices, an occurrence that has been devastating to the less competitive African export producers during periods of downturn. The overall trend is clear: The ability of African agricultural exports to provide a consistent and adequate supply of foreign exchange to buy needed imports has been continually eroded.

The propensity to emphasize export agriculture with similar negative impacts on food security is evident in other developing countries. In Chapter 8, Ronald J. Herring documents the vulnerability of Sri Lankan food security to volatile shifts in the international economy. On the one hand, the case of Sri Lanka has often been cited as an innovative instance in which food security has been largely achieved even though incomes have remained among the lowest in the world. On the other hand, that success story has recently soured as the international economy has experienced recession; Sri Lanka's welfare policies have consequently been altered.

Herring notes that prior to 1977 the state generously supported food, education, health, and other welfare programs. Its welfare programs were so encompassing and generally successful in lessening hunger and providing basic human needs that the government achieved some notoriety as a "model" for other extremely poor nations. The financing of these programs depended upon revenues received from levies on exports. However, since the early 1970s, the terms of trade for Sri Lanka have deteriorated, with obvious negative effects upon the economy in general and the welfare programs in particular. While its export earnings declined, world food prices gradually increased. Consequently, food rations in Sri Lanka fell and local food prices rose.

Confronted with these crises, the state welfare regime lost favor; its policies were criticized as "premature welfarism" by the regime's successors and the international community. The succeeding regime has emphasized a liberalization strategy, cutting food subsidies, courting foreign investment and aid, relaxing import controls, pursuing ambitious public works programs, and otherwise following the recommendations of the International Monetary Fund (IMF). Through it all, the Sri Lankan economy has deepened its relationship with the international economy while reducing, although not eliminating, welfare expenditures. Deeper welfare cuts appear to be inevitable. Herring concludes that the result is clear: The calorie intake levels of the bottom 20 percent of the households have undergone serious deterioration. Again, external factors severely constrain internal policy options, often with negative effects on food security.

In Chapter 11 W. Ladd Hollist analyzes the food crisis that has steadily worsened in Brazil over the past twenty years. Recognizing the negative impact of government policies on food security, particularly from 1965 to 1985, he also notes that external factors are heavily implicated. In Brazil, the per capita production of basic foodstuffs that are the staples of the poor—rice, beans, and manioc—have steadily declined. By contrast, export-oriented production of soya beans, frozen orange juice concentrate, chicken, and similar cash crops have increasingly captured government-sponsored subsidies (credit, research expenditures, technological innovations, price incentives) that otherwise could have been employed to stimulate the production of basic foodstuffs. Moreover, sugarcane production has increased as the alcohol program designed to provide substitute fuels for automobiles, trucks, and industry has flourished. The continuing drive to further industrialize and the dramatic need to service an enormous external debt continue to stimulate growth of agricultural exports to supply much needed foreign exchange. The opportunity costs include reduced food production, displacement of rural laborers, declining incomes for the poor, and severely threatened food security.

In Chapter 12, F. LaMond Tullis demonstrates how one of the abuses of health in the advanced market economies, cocaine use, contributes to hunger in coca-producing and -exporting countries. He documents that coca is a major export crop in Bolivia and Peru, approaching 20 percent of gross domestic product (GDP) in Bolivia and nearly as much in Peru, and that its production negatively affects food security in these two countries. Food production is down, and the cost of food, including food imports, is up as a consequence of incentives to produce and market coca; these are dramatically stronger than incentives to produce food. Poor people unable to become integrated into the cocaine economy have seen their nutritional standards fall dramatically.

Changes in the international economy of cocaine seem essential if coca production is to decline in favor of food production. For example, drug-law enforcement efforts could be emphasized to the point that the risks of production and marketing become sufficiently severe to stimulate shifts in crop patterns. As more coca farmers come on-line, competition may increase and coca prices may decline, thereby reducing production incentives of that crop over food crops. Cocaine and similar drugs might be legalized in the United States and Europe, thereby cutting deeply into growers' profits. Designer drugs (substitutes) may make the growing of coca less essential to the drug industry. In the absence of such changes, coca production will persist and food security will continue to be negatively affected.

Internal factors (such as government policies and inappropriately unequal distribution of wealth) and external factors (such as terms of trade, export biases, and foreign-owed debt) affect food security. Together they form a complex tapestry of reinforcing pressures that complicate the struggle against poverty and hunger. Chapters by Alain de Janvry and Alan Richards consider the dynamic interplay of these factors in Latin America, and the Middle East and North Africa.

In Chapter 10, de Janvry examines the impacts on agriculture of two major policy packages that have been tried in post-World War II Latin America:

import-substitution industrialization (ISI) and neoliberalism (NL). These two policy packages vary in how they define relationships between producers and consumers within Latin America on the one hand and the international economy on the other. Neither policy has proven beneficial to domestic food producers or poor food consumers. Under ISI, branches of industry were given protection through tariffs and quantitative import restrictions. Subsidies were granted to imported capital goods through overvalued exchange rates. Agricultural commodities vulnerable to cheap imports were not protected, whereas exportable agricultural products were taxed by the overvalued exchange rate. Also, industrial inputs for agriculture were made relatively more expensive by these policies.

In terms of food security, the results, de Janvry demonstrates, have been unfortunate. In agriculture, unfavorable prices and distortions in favor of capital led to both stagnation of output and massive labor displacement. Desired economies of scale were not achieved, and protectionist policies contributed to mounting inefficiencies. Over time, the ISI policy resulted in declining economic growth and worsening "social disarticulation." Social disarticulation occurs when the geographic and social location of markets for final goods is abroad or in the expenditures of profits and rents, not wages. As economic growth does not depend upon demand for wage goods, inequality grows and labor continues to be purchased cheaply. Poverty deepens, national food security suffers, and hunger grows among increasing numbers of impoverished people.

Beginning in the late 1960s and early 1970s, ISI policies were abandoned in most Latin American countries. Whereas the persistence of poverty had been and could continue to be ignored, governments were pressured to invigorate economic growth. They adopted a policy package that de Janvry labels neoliberal authoritarianism (NA). The intent of the neoliberal policies was to open these economies to the free, international movement of capital and consumer products. To that end, international comparative advantages influenced resource allocations within these economies. Balance-of-payments deficits were financed through international borrowing and devaluations. State interventions, be it in the form of outright ownership of production units, price setting, or subsidizing both production and consumption, were curbed.

De Janvry shows how the neoliberal policies were expected to eliminate the negative effects of cheap food policies and protectionist policies that advocates of the neoliberal perspective considered a prime cause of agricultural stagnation. By reallocating resources to internationally competitive sectors, imports of commodities once inefficiently produced locally would increase. Agriculture would then respond to price incentives, adopting new technologies and increasing food production. And with flexible prices in free markets, the gains from technological change would be passed on to consumers as falling prices; agriculture would be launched on a process of falling costs and falling prices.

Whatever the positive effects (economic growth) may have been, neo-liberal policies have not lessened poverty nor heightened food security, de Janvry concludes. The relative position of small farmers who produce most basic foodstuffs has worsened as incentives increasingly have favored large farmers who grow agricultural commodities for export and food for the palates and pocketbooks of the wealthy. The supply of labor has increased as capital-intensive technologies have displaced labor. Unemployment and underemployment have increased and real wages for rural labor have declined.

Moreover, neoliberal policies have produced a debt crisis in several Latin American countries. In response, many of these countries have rediscovered agriculture as a source of foreign exchange. The predictable consequence has been that the long-standing bias for export crops has been strengthened at the expense of food crops. Again, small farmers and landless laborers have borne much of the burden of the debt crisis.

For the countries of the Middle East and North Africa (MENA), the food problem is one of a growing imbalance between consumption and domestic production. This "food gap," Richards argues in Chapter 13, continues to grow as demand[6] increases while local food production stagnates or declines.

Faced with this growing food gap, governments have opted to import food. This choice has been acceptable for many reasons. Domestic production, often dependent upon erratic rainfall, has long been unstable. The barter terms of trade have favored the export of oil and the import of food; foreign exchange has been abundant. Tastes of urban consumers have shifted away from locally produced grains. Moreover, for several reasons food imports have been politically attractive. Governments have been able to provide needed food supplies in urban areas; they have successfully avoided disruptions that drought and decreased local production would have caused; and they have insulated themselves against the possibility that farmers might withhold foodstuffs from the market in an attempt to challenge cheap food policies.

Predictably, Richards continues, this ability to acquire sufficient food via imports has allowed the already urban-biased governments to neglect or even abuse their rural areas. What assistance has been forthcoming to the agricultural sector has been funneled almost exclusively to the large farms that are often owned by urban-based landlords.[7] For example, MENA governments have supported the development of irrigation, but have located that public sector investment in the relatively well-off farms. Moreover, government subsidies for other modern agricultural inputs (seeds, fertilizer, and tractors) generally have gone to these more affluent farmers. Credit has been similarly concentrated. In short, the rich farmers have had much greater access to the state than have the poor farmers. Still, state support of agriculture has been meager; rural concerns have not been a high priority.

Richards argues that even at best the urban-biased, food-import policies of the MENA nations, coupled with policies of limited, unequal investment in agriculture, have not served the majority of the people well. The benefits of these policies have been further eroded as the international economy has moved against these nations. Foreign-exchange earnings have declined significantly, and the capacity to import food has suffered. A period of austerity has ensued.

In response, these governments have placed renewed emphasis on export crops to increase foreign exchange, with predictable negative effects on domestic food production. Richards notes that the region's nearest market— the European Economic Community (EEC), with the addition of Greece, Spain, and Portugal—has become less inclined to import export crops from the MENA countries because of its own problems of food overabundance. The ability of MENA governments to continue even their limited investment in domestic agriculture has declined, with retrenchment in public investment hitting particularly hard the projects intended to benefit small farmers in areas of rain-fed agriculture.

Thus, once again, government policies, social structure, and potentially disadvantageous linkages with the international economy combine to threaten food security. Even if we grant the potential of technology-based strategies for increasing food production and supply, we cannot ignore these obstacles to their success. Any strategy intended to promote food security in developing countries must address these economic, political, social, and international issues.

The goal of this book is not only to catalogue political, social, economic, and international reasons why strategies intended to achieve food security in developing countries have fallen short but also to examine strategies that may prove beneficial. We have already broached some of the strategies advocated in this volume, and there are others. For example, in Chapter 9 Griffin analyzes development strategies in the People's Republic of China before and after Mao. He concludes that agriculture organized on principles of communal farming has brought food security to the Chinese people, and that departures from this pattern may bring unexpected, undesirable consequences. In Chapter 11, Hollist explores the potential benefits of and prospects for Mellor-like proposals and land reform in Brazil. As previously mentioned, policy strategies for reducing hunger in Africa are advanced by Christensen, Lofchie, and Griffin. Strategies that would be required to lessen the negative effects of international factors upon food security are explored by Griffin, Lofchie, Herring, Hollist, Tullis, and Richards.

We do not claim to have definitive policy answers. We offer, however, a serious consideration of political, social, economic, and international impediments to food security in the developing countries, and we engage in the debate regarding what strategies ought to be pursued. We hope that many others will join in a search for responsible and humane ways to help assure that all people have an adequate opportunity to be secure in their food supplies. If, as we have argued, poverty is at the root of hunger, it is clear that hunger cannot be eliminated in the absence of rural economic development, and rural economic development cannot affect the incidence of hunger significantly if its product and benefits are not widely shared.

NOTES

1. See World Bank, *Poverty and Hunger: Issues and Options for Food Security in Developing Countries,* pp. 1-6.

2. Ibid. The People's Republic of China is not counted as a developing country in these estimates.

3. See "Scientific Advances Lead to Era of Food Surplus Around World," *New York Times,* 9 September 1986.

4. The literature on social, economic, and political reforms and associated policy perspectives on rural development and food policy is substantial. Contributors to this volume have raised their viewpoints in a number of forums. See, for example, Cheryl Christensen, "World Hunger: A Structural Approach"; Alain de Janvry, *The Agrarian Question and Reformism in Latin America*; Keith B. Griffin, *The Political Economy of Agrarian Change*; Ronald J. Herring, *Land to the Tiller: The Political Economy of Agrarian Reform in South Asia*; F. Tomasson Jannuzi and James T. Peach, *The Agrarian Structure of Bangladesh: An Impediment to Development*; Michael F. Lofchie, ed., *Agricultural Development in Africa*; John W. Mellor, *The New Economics of Growth: A Strategy for India and the Developing World*; Alan Richards and Philip Martin, eds., *Migration, Mechanization, and Agricultural Labor Markets in Egypt*; and F. LaMond Tullis, *Lord and Peasant in Peru: A Paradigm of Political and Social Change.*

5. See Mellor, *The New Economics of Growth.*

6. Richards argues that sources of increased food demand include fast-paced population growth and even faster income growth. This growing consumer demand has spurred agricultural production, although inadequately, in the region. Food production between 1961 and 1977 grew 2.5 percent per year. Agricultural growth has depended mostly on technologies that have increased yields, with the addition of new agricultural lands contributing some. In the future, growth will depend progressively more on increasing yields, as most cultivable land in the region is now in production. See Richards and Martin, eds. *Migration, Mechanization, and Agricultural Labor Markets in Egypt,* Chapter 12.

7. In conference discussions Richards noted that Turkey has had a different experience. There the state continually tried to reduce the power of large landlords. As a result, small farms are the rule in most productive areas of Turkey. The benefits of the Green Revolution have been widely shared in Turkey, whereas in other parts of the Middle East and North Africa the benefits have been more concentrated.

Part 1
World Food Security

2

Keith B. Griffin

World Hunger and the World Economy

Let us begin with two propositions. First, there is no world food problem, but there is a problem of hunger in the world. Food and hunger are, of course, related, and it is tempting to argue that an increase in food output will lead to a reduction in hunger, malnutrition, and starvation. But, alas, the connection is not so straightforward or so simple. Indeed, many cases may be found in which hunger has increased, or failed to diminish, despite a rise in per capita food supplies.

Second, even if there were a direct connection between the availability of food and the incidence of hunger, it does not follow that each region, country, or continent should aim to be self-sufficient in basic foodstuffs. Presumably, nobody would suggest that the city-states of Hong Kong and Singapore would be better off or better fed if they produced fewer manufactured goods and more rice, or that Saudi Arabia and Botswana should switch from oil and mineral extraction to farming, or even, perhaps, that Cuba should reduce its production of sugar and concentrate on growing more cereals and beans. Generally what matters in countries such as these is the resource endowment people enjoy, the opportunities that exist for profitable international trade, and the overall rate of growth of domestic product per capita.

On the whole, economic growth has been encouraging, even in the recent years of oil price explosions and global recession. During the period 1970 to 1982, gross domestic product (GDP) per capita increased 3.2 percent a year in China and India (the two largest Third World countries), 0.8 percent in what the World Bank describes as the thirty-two "other low-income economies" and 3 percent in the sixty "middle-income economies."[1] Of course, some countries did much better than others, but only in the twenty-three low-income economies of sub-Saharan Africa was there a general tendency for per capita GDP to fall. During the period 1970 to 1983, the rate of decline was about 1.1 percent a year, and in consequence, production per capita today is little different from what it was a quarter-century ago.[2] The situation in these twenty-three

17

countries evidently is very serious, but from a global perspective it may be some consolation to know that the low-income economies of sub-Saharan Africa account for less than one-tenth of the population of all low-income countries combined. Seen from this angle the scale of the problem, in terms of the number of people affected, is thus relatively small.

PATTERNS OF GROWTH IN FOOD PRODUCTION

Turning from growth of total product to growth in the agricultural sector, the picture is broadly the same. That is, there has been a sustained increase in world output of agricultural products since 1960. Most of the major groups of countries and geographical areas of the world have participated in this increase. Only in India and in the "other low-income economies" has agricultural production per capita failed to rise (see Table 2.1). Elsewhere there has been expansion, with the "middle-income economies," followed by China, leading the way. It is slightly worrying, however, that in a number of Third World countries the performance of the agricultural sector in the 1970s and early 1980s appears to have been worse than it was in the 1960s. Growth of agricultural output per capita slowed down in the middle-income countries, in India, and in the "other low-income economies," whereas it accelerated sharply in China, the United States, and several of the other industrial market-economy countries.

There is no evidence that food is becoming increasingly scarce in the world. On the contrary, the data indicate that for the world as a whole the amount of food produced continues to rise, and it is safe to assume that never in history has the physical supply of food per capita been greater than in the last ten or twenty years. If humanity continues to suffer from hunger—and we are now witnessing the worst famines in forty years—the explanation cannot be in terms of a global inadequacy of food.

Moreover, the rise in food production is not confined to the advanced industrial economies, capitalist and socialist. We hear much about the high-

Table 2.1   Average Annual Percentage Rate of Growth of Agricultural Product per Capita

	1960–70	1970–82	1960–82
Low-income economies	−0.1	0.4	0.2
India	−0.4	−0.5	−0.5
China	−0.7	1.4	0.4
Others	0.2	−0.3	−0.1
Middle-income economies	0.9	0.6	0.7
High-income oil exporters	n.a.	0.6	n.a.
Industrial market economies	0.3	1.1	0.7

Source: World Bank, *World Development Report 1984* (New York, Oxford University Press, 1984).

calorie diets in the Soviet Union and Eastern Europe[3] and about the "food mountains" in the West, but few people seem to realize that food has become relatively abundant in many parts of the Third World, too. In China, food output per capita increased about 1.4 percent a year in the decade of the 1970s. In the rest of the world, the increase was about 0.4 percent a year (see Table 2.2). In India there was a sharp fall in nonfood agricultural production, and consequently, as we have seen, there was a poor performance in the agricultural sector as a whole, but food production per capita has expanded rapidly since 1970 at 0.8 percent a year. Those who believe that the solution to hunger is to put "food first" should be cheered by India's example,[4] but the sad truth is that the average nutritional status of the Indian population has not improved since the late 1960s.[5] The so-called Green Revolution in India, "while it has indeed dramatically improved yields in particular crops (e.g., wheat) in particular regions (e.g., the northwest), has not led to any acceleration in the overall rate of growth in agriculture,"[6] nor, I might add, to any reduction in hunger. Yet in 1986, paradoxically, India is an exporter of food grains.

In the middle-income economies, too, food output per capita has grown rapidly since 1970 at 0.9 percent a year, and, as in India, food production has expanded much more swiftly than the rest of the agricultural sector. Only in the low-income economies other than China and India, and above all in sub-Saharan Africa, has per capita food production declined. Even there, however, the decline is associated not with a bias against food production for domestic consumption and in favor of cash crop production for export, but with a generally poor economic performance as reflected in negative growth per capita of GDP, investment, exports, manufacturing, and agriculture.[7]

This brief survey of some of the readily available facts suggests that hunger is not caused primarily by inadequate production of food, nor can it be cured, except in the long run, merely by increasing production further. There are exceptions, of course, and I have emphasized the situation in sub-Saharan Africa, but the number of people living in poor countries in which food production

Table 2.2   Average Annual Percentage Rate of Growth of Food Output Per Capita

	1960–70	1970–80
China	n.a.	1.4[a]
Low-income economies (excluding China)	0.2	−0.3
India	n.a.	0.8[a]
Middle-income economies	0.7	0.9
All developing countries (excluding China)	0.4	0.4
Industrial market economies	1.3	1.1
Nonmarket industrial economies	2.2	0.9
Total world (excluding China)	0.8	0.5

[a] 1971–1980

Sources: World Bank, World Development Report 1982 (New York, Oxford University Press, 1982), Table 5.1, p. 41; Food and Agriculture Organization (FAO), *Socio-economic Indicators Relating to the Agricultural Sector and Rural Development* (Rome, 1984), Table 16, p. 51.

per capita has declined accounts for only a small fraction of the world's population.[8] And the number of people in those countries who are hungry is a smaller
fraction still. It seems clear, therefore, that a commodity-oriented analysis of
hunger will not take us very far. Instead, we need to focus on people and on the
factors that determine the amount of food they consume. The volume of food
production may be part of the answer, but in most circumstances it is unlikely
to constitute the principal explanation.

INCIDENCE OF HUNGER

A number of attempts have been made to calculate the extent of malnutrition.
One of the best studies was prepared by the World Bank, in which the authors
estimated calorie deficits by income groups for the whole of Latin America,
Asia, the Middle East, and Africa. They concluded that in 1965 approximately
840 million people, or 56 percent of the population of the regions studied, had
diets deficient by 250 or more calories a day.[9] The Food and Agriculture Organization (FAO) undertook a study using a similar methodology except that the
analysis was conducted at the country level rather than at the level of large regions. This refinement resulted in an estimate for 1972 to 1974 of 455 million
people suffering from insufficient protein-energy supply, or about 25 percent
of the Third World's population.[10]

Studies such as these can be and have been criticized,[11] and I believe the
criticisms are justified in that there is a tendency both to exaggerate nutritional
requirements and to understate the extent to which poor people manage by
one way or another to acquire enough to eat. But there can be little doubt that
there are today several hundreds of millions of people who must make do on
poor and monotonous diets, who suffer various forms of malnutrition to a
greater or lesser degree, and who in a distressingly large number of cases are
dying from starvation and associated diseases. The exact number of people suffering from hunger is unimportant; it is enough to know that the number is
huge.

Anyone who has thought about the matter knows that hunger is not distributed evenly or randomly throughout a society; it is largely (but not exclusively) a rural phenomenon and within the rural areas is concentrated among
the poor. That is, hunger tends to be associated with particular classes and occupational groups: landless agricultural laborers; small tenant cultivators; deficit
farmers with too little land to be self-sufficient and who consequently must supplement their incomes with part-time, off-farm jobs; pastoralists living on or
beyond the fringes of the arable land; and fisherpeople and petty artisans supplying traditional goods and services in traditional ways.

The fundamental cause of hunger, then, is the poverty of specific groups of
people, not a general shortage of food. In simple terms, what distinguishes the
poor from the rest of us is that they do not have sufficient purchasing power or

effective demand to enable them to acquire enough to eat. More generally, the heart of the problem is the relationship of particular groups of people to food, not food itself. This relationship is governed by what Amartya Sen calls "entitlement systems," that is, the set of relations embodied in a society's laws, customs, and conventions that determines the ability of people to command access to food.[12]

One is "entitled" to food through the application of one's own labor, through trade, through production, through the return on one's assets, or through transfer or gift. Unfortunately, the bundle of entitlements of many people, either chronically or episodically, is not large enough to permit adequate nutrition. This may be so for a variety of reasons. For example, the productivity of one's own labor may be permanently low because of primitive technology and inadequate investment, or productivity may fall precipitously for a period of time because, say, of epidemic disease. Employment opportunities in a particular locality may be scarce and they could decline further as a result of the introduction of labor-saving equipment. As an alternative, the daily wage rate could be too low for adequate subsistence, and in certain times of the year or in periods of crisis the real wage could fall further as a result of a decline in the demand for labor or a rise in the price of food. Similarly, the command over food of small farmers producing cash crops will depend on the sales price of their outputs. This in turn could be determined by the purchasing policy of state marketing boards, a government's exchange-rate policy, the level of world prices, short-term fluctuations in a country's international terms of trade, and other factors.

The ownership of land, livestock, and other productive assets, as well as jewelry and other forms of savings, are part of the entitlement system. Indeed, the extent to which a household can transform assets into food often determines whether starvation occurs. One of the most common features of famine conditions is distress sales of assets by already poor households. In periods of drought, landowning cultivators of small holdings, for instance, starve partly because their reduced output leads to a direct decline in food consumption, partly because their reduced output leads to a decline in cash income and hence in market purchasing power, and partly because distress sales lead to a fall in the price of land and consequently in the rate at which their assets can be transformed into food. An analogous situation faces the pastoralists. A drought causes a reduction in the number of livestock. More important, however, it forces herdsmen to sell their animals and this, in turn, leads to a sharp fall in the price of cattle and hence in the value of the herdsman's assets. "The pastoralist, hit by drought, [is] decimated by the market mechanism."[13] Pastoralists' assets decline in quantity and in unit value; their ability to command grain in the market vanishes, and they starve.

This approach to the analysis of world hunger naturally directs our attention to the distribution of income and wealth; to organizational mechanisms that supplement income in determining entitlements to food (such as rationing systems); and to institutional arrangements concerned with property rights that govern access to productive assets, the most important of which are land and water rights.

There is considerable evidence from a number of countries, not conclusive but sufficiently well documented to be taken seriously, that the incidence of poverty among certain groups, above all in the rural areas, has failed to decline significantly even where growth in per capita production has occurred.[14] In such countries hunger has persisted despite greater average prosperity. I am referring here not to those countries in sub-Saharan Africa and elsewhere where per capita growth has been negative, but to the more typical Third World countries that have enjoyed an unprecedented rise in average income per capita. Asia contains several examples, and one of these is India.

As Michael Lipton says, "what is truly amazing . . . is that, by general agreement, despite India's long period of steady and unprecedented real growth . . . of output-per-person, there has been no *substantial* fall in the proportions of persons in absolute poverty, upon any plausible and constant definition of those terms; nor in the extent to which, on average, those persons fall short of the poverty line."[15] A recent series of ten studies sponsored by the International Labor Organization reaches a similar conclusion for much of South and Southeast Asia. After reviewing research on Bihar, the Punjab, Kerala, and West Bengal in India and on Pakistan, Nepal, Bangladesh, Thailand, Sri Lanka, and the island of Java in Indonesia, the organizers of the project conclude that

> there has been no major shift in extent and nature of poverty in rural Asia between the early 1960s and the mid- or late-1970s. . . . In no case has there been a dramatic breakthrough in the reduction of rural poverty. In several cases there [has] been a reduction in poverty levels between the early and late 1970s but this only resulted in bringing back poverty to the levels prevailing in the early 1960s. In only two cases—Thailand and the Punjab—has there been a reduction in poverty compared to the 1960s but even here levels of poverty remain high and, especially in the Punjab, the margin of reduction was not great.[16]

A similar story could be told about parts of Latin America and the Middle East. In Egypt, for instance, between 1958 and 1978, the number of rural poor increased by nearly 2 million and the proportion of the rural population below the poverty line increased from 22.5 to 25 percent.[17] This was associated with, and partially caused by, a rise in the incidence of landlessness from 40 percent of agricultural households in 1961 to 45 percent in 1972.[18] Again, in Morocco, real household consumption of the poorest 20 percent of the population fell sharply in the 1960s in both rural and urban areas,[19] and it is highly likely that this process continues to the present, at least in the rural areas, if only because of the sharp negative trend in agricultural production per capita that began around 1970.

The persistence of inequality, poverty, and hunger is caused not so much by the absence of growth as by the characteristics of the growth that has occurred. That is, in most Third World countries growth has been accompanied, first, by rising landlessness;[20] second, by greater reliance of the poor on casual, non-permanent employment; and third, by increased unemployment or a reduction in the number of days worked per person per year.[21] In other words, a significant number of small landowning peasants and tenants has been converted into a wage-earning class of casual agricultural laborers. This implies, fourth, that the asset base of the rural poor has suffered considerable erosion, in the sense that a declining proportion of the poor has assured access to productive assets—and of those who continue to have access, the quantity and hence the average value of their assets is falling.[22]

To make matters worse, fifth, the real daily wage rate of this growing number of wage earners appears either to have remained stagnant (as in India as a whole[23]) or to have fallen (as in Bangladesh, Nepal, and the Philippines[24]). Cases of higher real wages (such as in Thailand or, in some periods, Pakistan) appear to be exceptions to the general rule. As a result of these various processes, sixth, landless households have tended to experience a fall in their real yearly incomes. A careful study of India by Pranab Bardhan, for example, shows that the annual wage income of agricultural labor households fell by 16 percent in real terms between 1964/65 and 1974/75. Moreover, of the fifteen states studied, in only one (Uttar Pradesh) did real incomes rise; in the other fourteen they fell between 1 percent (in Karnataka) and 44 percent (in Orissa).[25]

Finally, it should be remembered that the poor and the hungry often are the victims of political, social, and economic discrimination. In some countries discrimination is based on caste (India), in others on language (Sri Lanka) or race (as in Andean South America), in still others on tribal origin (as in parts of Africa) or on religion (as in the suppression of Muslims in the Philippines). The effect of discrimination in the labor market is to restrict occupational mobility, and to augment the supply of those forced to seek low-wage employment. Particularly when discrimination is combined with a high degree of land concentration, as often is the case, large landowners and other employers acquire oligopsonistic power in determining wage rates.[26] When discrimination is superimposed on rigid social and class stratification and a low average productivity of labor, widespread hunger is almost certain to result.

Moreover, output growth in such a system may actually increase rather than reduce poverty and hunger. This could occur if a landlord-biased growth process results in the introduction of labor-displacing machinery such as tractors and combines;[27] or if technical change is accompanied by the eviction of tenants and a rise in landlessness; or if small peasants are driven out of cultivation because the powerful irrigation pumps owned or controlled by large landowners lower the water table so much that the traditional irrigation techniques used by small farmers cease to be effective;[28] or if large landowners persuade the government to raise the official support price of food grains and thereby impoverish wage earners and small deficit farmers who purchase grain in the market;[29] or if village artisans are displaced by heavily protected, mass-

produced urban manufactured goods.[30] These are not mere theoretical possibilities—all have happened repeatedly in many countries. Indeed, a careful
statistical study in West Bengal has shown that the probability of an agricultural
labor household falling below the poverty line, and hence risking hunger, is
significantly greater if the household happens to be located in a district where
agricultural production has grown at a faster rate![31]

Just as hunger can persist and even increase in a country in which growth
is taking place, so too can famine and starvation occur even when there has
been no decline in the availability of food. In fact, a startling finding of Amartya
Sen's research is that in a number of major famines—the great Bengal famine
of 1943, the Bangladesh famine of 1974, and the Ethiopian famines of 1972-
1974—there was no significant fall in the supply of food grains.[32] Acute hunger
was caused not by a sharp drop in production but by a rapid change in the distribution of income.[33] Moreover, even in those cases in which hunger was caused
by a fall in output, as in the Kampuchean famine of 1979,[34] we will not get very
far in analyzing the extent and incidence of starvation by focusing on time
series data for production. The cause of hunger, as Sen reminds us, is a shortage
of income rather than an overall shortage of food,[35] and some households have
a much greater shortage of income than others.

INTERNATIONAL LINKAGES

In a world of sovereign nation-states, the government of each country must assume the larger part of the responsibility for ensuring that everyone under its
administrative authority has enough to eat. This responsibility is an inescapable
consequence of the way the world is presently organized. Indeed, if a government is consistently unable to guarantee its own people enough to eat, it is
doubtful that the minimum condition for statehood exists. Perhaps the world
should be organized differently; perhaps we need powerful supranational organizations that can overrule national governments; but, for the time being, at
least, we shall have to accept the world as it is and not pretend otherwise.

This does not imply that hunger is exclusively a national phenomenon or
solely a national responsibility. Clearly, there are international forces at work
that affect the geography of hunger. These forces should not and have not been
ignored. Certainly economists have written a great deal about the major economic issues and policy questions—the pattern of international trade, direct
investment by transnational corporations and other flows of private capital,
concessionary loans and grants (including food aid), international stockpiles
of grains and commodity-price stabilization schemes. I do not propose to review these lengthy discussions here. Rather, I treat three relatively neglected
topics: the role of Western ideas and ideology, the transfer of Western technology, and the nature of the state in the Third World.

Before turning to these three neglected topics, I mention a bit dogmatically my views on two international linkages I intend to pass over—foreign aid and direct investment. Foreign aid, whether loans or grants, whether in cash or in kind (such as food), has done little or nothing on average to accelerate the long-run rate of growth of Third World countries. It has done even less to reduce inequality in the distribution of income within the recipient countries and consequently has had no discernible impact on reducing the incidence of hunger and malnutrition.[36] In the short run, during famine conditions, emergency relief aid obviously has a role to play. That role could be played more effectively, moreover, if international stockpiles of grain were available and under the direct control of the relief agencies. Stockpiles of grain under the control of the European Economic Community and the U.S. government are less easily mobilized quickly in an emergency because their use is subject to political calculation and cumbersome bureaucratic delays.

If aid is largely ineffective in reducing world hunger, it is likely that direct investment by transnational corporations will be even less relevant. Indeed, if government policy is biased against the poor and the hungry, it is inconceivable that foreign investors could counteract that bias; more likely, they would reinforce it. On the other hand, if a government were pursuing a "basic needs" strategy of development, it is likely that the opportunities for profitable investment in that country by transnational corporations would diminish.[37] The reason for this is that the superiority of transnational over local firms lies in their marketing skills for sophisticated products, the provision of mass-produced Western-designed consumer durables, and the development of advanced capital-intensive technology. These are services that are not likely to be required in large volume in countries where the alleviation of hunger has top priority.

Western Ideas and Ideology

There are, of course, many Western ideas, and there is more than one Western ideology. Marxism, for example, is a product of the West, not of the East. The dominant ideology in the West, however, is capitalism, and it is this ideology of free enterprise, free trade, and free movement of capital[38] that has shaped the international order and that has been recommended whenever possible to the countries of the Third World. If it is true, as is often claimed, that democratic socialism is about equality, then it is equally true that modern capitalism is about production. The dominant view, the view most widely held in the West, is that faster growth rather than improved distribution of the fruits of the growth is the answer to many problems, including the problem of world hunger.

I have already expressed skepticism about the effectiveness of accelerated growth of food production as a general solution to problems of hunger, malnutrition, and starvation. In pushing this solution, relentlessly and with little qualification, Western ideas have been less than helpful. Indeed, they have often been harmful in that they have diverted attention away from more important issues. Specifically, a corollary of the emphasis on growth is Western hostility to government interventions to improve either the distribution of income or the distribution of food alone—that is, to increase the entitlements of the hungry directly through food-rationing schemes and similar programs. Yet we know that the public distribution of food, even in exceedingly poor countries, can have an enormous impact on reducing hunger, as the experiences of food rationing in Sri Lanka, Egypt, China, Cuba, and the state of Kerala in India demonstrates.[39] Indeed, had Ethiopia established a nationwide food-rationing system, as it was advised to do in 1982,[40] many of the current horrors occurring in that country almost certainly could have been avoided (see Chapter 6).

Joined with the ideology of free markets is that of private enterprise. The paradigm in Western thought, when it comes to the agricultural sector, is the family farm, although in practice Western thought has been able to accommodate itself to a wide variety of tenure arrangements: tenant cultivation, large mechanized farms, foreign-owned plantations and small peasant holdings. All of these, to some extent at least, are acceptable, but what is not generally acceptable in Western eyes, whether liberal or conservative, is communal, cooperative, or collective tenure systems.

Yet nearly one-third of the world's population lives in countries where collective agriculture in one form or another is the characteristic mode of production. These countries include not only the Soviet Union and much of Eastern Europe but also several Third World countries, such as China, North Korea, Mongolia, and Cuba. The record of the latter group of countries in regards to the reduction of hunger compares very favorably with other Third World countries where individual, noncommunal tenure systems predominate. The key example, because of its immense size, is China. The broad facts about China's experience are no longer in dispute. Thus, it is known that the attempt in 1958 (the beginning of the Great Leap Forward) to form very large communes and apply communist principles of production and distribution was an utter failure; this undoubtedly helped to precipitate the disastrous famine from 1959 to 1961.[41] After the Great Leap Forward, however, the communes were successfully reorganized: Adequate production incentives were created,[42] and mechanisms to ensure a highly equitable distribution of food grains were installed. In 1986, thanks in part to a new set of reforms introduced after 1978, probably less than 3 percent of China's population suffers from chronic undernutrition.[43] The contrast with, for example, India, Pakistan, and Bangladesh, or with other large and poor countries in South Asia, could hardly be more vivid.

It is not coincidental that countries with well-developed communal tenure systems have tended to perform better than average. In fact, there are good reasons to believe that communal tenure systems have an advantage (1) in ensuring that labor is fully employed, (2) in achieving a more equal distribution of income, (3) in sustaining a high rate of capital accumulation, (4) in providing a framework for industrializing the countryside, and (5) in promoting grass-roots participation in the organization and delivery at the local level of a wide range of social services, including educational, family planning, and health facilities.[44] This does not imply that communal tenure systems can flourish under all conditions—far from it—but it is a mistake for us in the West to regard them as anathema rather than as one possible way to reduce hunger and rural poverty.

All of us, of course, are a product of our own societies: our historical memory, our cultural heritage, and our individual educational background. Western society, and particularly North American society, is very different from the societies of most Third World countries. Whereas Americans have enjoyed an open frontier and cultivated individualism, self-reliance, and competition, most of the Third World has experienced colonialism, restricted social and economic mobility, and few opportunities for material betterment. Capitalism was liberating in Europe and North America; in the rest of the world it was imperialistic and enslaving, or at least was perceived by the indigenous people to be so. Collective action thus became not only acceptable in many parts of the Third World, but during the struggles for national independence it often was regarded as essential. Similarly, once independence was achieved, a reaction against the economic system of the former colonial masters was common. The colonial governments preached the virtues of the market, of free enterprise, and of nonintervention by public authorities. The newly independent governments, in contrast, viewed the state as an engine of growth and development and feared that free trade, uninhibited competition with Western enterprises, and the unrestricted operation of market forces would result in a neocolonialism that was little better than the old colonialism. The newly independent countries, although seldom socialist or communist in orientation, tended to reject a full-blooded capitalist solution. Instead, they became receptive to ideas and ideologies that included a place for government ownership of some of the means of production, for intervention in market processes, and for some cooperative and collective institutions.

Transfer of Technology

Ideas alone, however, do not change the world; technology also is a powerful force. Indeed, it is a peculiarly Western conceit that there are technological solutions to political and social problems. If there is an ideological conflict with the Soviet Union, the solution is to send a man to the moon. If there is a threat to world peace, the solution is to invent more-accurate and more-destructive armaments. If the population is thought to be growing too rapidly, the solution is to produce a better contraceptive. And if the problem is hunger, the solution is to discover higher-yielding varieties of wheat and rice. This overweening faith in the power of science has put the technician, the engineer, and the scientist in the place once occupied by the Creator himself.

Alas, technological change cannot obviate the need for social and institutional change. Partly because of the absence of adequate change, the importing of Western agricultural technology into inegalitarian and socially divided Third World countries often has accentuated inequality and occasionally has further impoverished the weakest sections of the rural population. For example, the introduction of mechanical farming methods in Arsi province, Ethiopia, under a Swedish aid program resulted in the eviction of more than 5,000 tenant households between 1967 and 1975.[45] The introduction of mechanized wells and pumps in Niger and Mali, under a French scheme, and at a time when agricultural policies were causing pasturage to shrink, led to overgrazing by livestock and contributed to the ecological collapse of the Sahel in the early 1970s and with it the destruction of the Tuareg people.[46]

Even the Green Revolution has proved to be less green than was once hoped; certainly it has not made revolution of a different hue less likely.[47] Perhaps the most avidly promoted Western (or U.S.) agricultural technology in the Third World is large multipurpose dams. In fact, the very first loan ever made by the World Bank to a Third World country—to China in 1948—was for a dam. There is no sign that the World Bank or any other aid agency has lost its enthusiasm for large-scale water management projects. There are plenty of signs, however, that large dams have produced very low economic returns, have damaged forestry and fisheries, have caused widespread salination of the soil, and have inflicted much hardship on ordinary men and women.[48] This transfer of technology from the Tennessee Valley to other river basins in the world—be they in Maghreb, the Nile Valley, the Middle East, or the Indo-Pakistan subcontinent—has done remarkably little to alleviate global hunger.

Western aid, Western projects, and Western technology embodied in aid-financed projects are part of the problem of hunger, not part of the solution. Even the World Bank has begun to accept that the economic mess in which much of sub-Saharan Africa finds itself results in part from the policies of foreign-aid donors. "In many African countries," according to the bank, "the pattern of development spending has become increasingly determined by the aggregation of aid programs."[49] Yet the donors, sadly, have placed little emphasis on agriculture, rural development, or programs designed to raise the living standards of the poor. On the contrary, as the World Bank says, "financing big infrastructure projects has represented a large part of past donor programs."[50]

Yet these big projects with their advanced technology have produced neither growth nor an equitable distribution of income; they have produced a disaster. Again, in the words of a World Bank publication, "the heart of Africa's economic crisis is the low rate of return on its capital investment. Much of this failure comes from investment programs that have been extensively financed from external sources."[51] Thus it is that the continent that has relied most heavily on Western aid and technology is also the continent where famine is widespread and malnutrition is increasing at an alarming rate. Improvement in Africa requires much more than a shift from infrastructure projects to rural development. Indeed, case studies of agricultural projects and policies in seven countries—three in East Africa (Kenya, Tanzania, and the Sudan) and four in West Africa (Ghana, Niger, Nigeria, and Senegal)—show clearly that irrigation projects and settlement schemes usually have failed to meet their production goals, and that, in general, policies and projects have tended to increase inequality and have had little impact on reducing rural poverty and hunger.[52]

Possibly the most spectacular current attempt to apply advanced technology to rural development is the scheme of the Food and Agriculture Organization (FAO) of the United Nations to eradicate the tsetse fly over 7 million square kilometers of land in Africa from the Sahel to Botswana and Mozambique.[53] The intention is to eradicate trypanosomiasis from the region and thereby permit the land to be cleared of forest and converted to grazing for 120 million head of cattle. The 1.5 million tons of low-grade beef that could be produced each year presumably would be exported to Europe and North America. The project, however, is woefully misguided and certain to fail. First, dangerous chemical pesticides are used. Many of these are banned in the West because they are a threat to humans, wild animals, and fish. Second, these dangerous chemicals are applied through aerial spraying. The dosage is hard to control, and the area intended to be sprayed often is hard to identify from the air and consequently the chemicals are frequently dumped in the wrong place. Third, such crude methods of applying the chemicals mean that it is unlikely that the project will succeed in eradicating the tsetse fly.

Moreover, fourth, if the tsetse fly were eradicated and its habitat transformed into pastures for cattle, it probably would produce little economic benefit in the short run and considerable harm in the long run. The reason for this is that the tsetse fly occupies much marginal land on the fringe of the desert and semiarid areas of Africa. If the tree and bush cover of these lands is removed to permit cattle ranching, the likely effect will be increased soil erosion, a further spreading of the desert, impoverishment of the local population, and famine of the type now common in the Sahel.

THE NATURE OF THE STATE

Part of the reason for the meager success of imported technology has to do with the technology transferred, but another important part has to do with the nature of the state in the Third World. I take it for granted that the state is not a neutral institution, that governments reflect particular class and group interests and that government policies are designed, on balance, to promote the interests of those who control the state. Sophisticated analysts often argue that the state is "relatively autonomous" of the dominant economic class,[54] and even the unsophisticated have pointed out that when threatened from abroad the state may adopt a nationalist rather than a class orientation. Still others note that in the period immediately following independence, political leaders who partici-pated in the freedom movement have seemed to enjoy more latitude for action than politicians do in more ordinary times.[55] Although all of these points are well taken, for most purposes we will not go far wrong in assuming that the state acts on behalf of the dominant economic interests in society.

What are the dominant economic interests? In some parts of the Third World, including parts of Asia, political power has accrued to those who control the productive sectors of the economy—namely, large landowners and indus-trialists. In the Philippines, for instance, these are the plantation owners and the industrialists; in India, the industrialists and large wheat farmers in the north; in Pakistan, again, the industrialists. In most of Latin America these same groups are well entrenched, the class structure is well defined, and the political system (but not necessarily an individual government) is relatively stable—until, of course, it is overthrown by a revolution, as in Cuba or Nicaragua. In Mexico, power is concentrated in the hands of the industrialists and the large landowners in the irrigated regions of the north; in Guatemala, power is shared between those who own large coffee plantations and the cattle and cotton growers along the Pacific coast; in Colombia, power traditionally alternates be-tween the manufacturing center in Medellin and the upper classes of Bogota. In some Third World countries, the class hierarchy is in flux as various groups struggle against one another to fill the power vacuum created by the departing colonialists, whereas in other cases, notably in Africa, military and bureaucratic elites have taken power.

There is a link between the class structure of the state and government eco-nomic policy. In a majority of countries, public policy—be it investment alloca-tion, monetary and tax policies, exchange-rate and foreign-trade policies, or social programs—is biased toward the urban areas,[56] toward industry, toward large farmers, toward upper-income groups—in short, toward everyone ex-cept the poor and the hungry. The Western powers—through such practices as economic aid programs, diplomatic initiatives, and military assistance—tend strongly to support the very governments whose policies are responsible for perpetuating poverty and hunger in their countries and to oppose reformist, radical, and revolutionary regimes that hold out hope of a better life to the poor.

Thus in Chile, the West opposed the Allende government but supports the Pinochet dictatorship; in Nicaragua, it installed and then supported the Somoza dictatorship and now alleges the Sandinista government is undemocratic; in China, it supported Chiang Kai-shek and refused even to recognize the People's Republic; in Vietnam, it supported reaction and tried to bomb Ho Chi Minh's government back to the Stone Age. And so it goes, on and on, seemingly with-out end, in Guatemala and El Salvador,[57] in Morocco and the Sudan, in Pakistan and in the Philippines. In far too many cases in which the state oppresses the impoverished and the malnourished, the status quo is strengthened by the ac-tive intervention of the West.

SUMMARY

Hunger exists in spite of encouraging global improvements in economic growth rates, and in spite of a sustained increase in world output of agricultural products since 1960. As hunger is not caused primarily by inadequate production of food, it cannot be cured, except in the very long run, merely by increasing the production of food. Thus a commodity-oriented analysis of hunger will not take us very far. Instead, we need to focus on people and on the factors that determine the amount of food they consume.

The fundamental cause of hunger is the poverty of specific groups of people, not a general shortage of food. In simple terms, what distinguishes the poor from the rest of the world's people is that they do not have sufficient purchasing power or effective demand to enable them to acquire enough to eat. The problem is the relationship of particular groups of people to food, not food itself.

Relationships that establish food entitlements are governed by a society's laws, customs, and conventions, and by the domestic and international economic policies that grow from them. This approach to the analysis of world hunger naturally directs attention to the distribution of income and wealth and to institutional arrangements concerned with property rights that govern access to productive assets.

The incidence of poverty among certain groups, above all in the rural areas, has failed to decline significantly even where growth in per capita production has occurred. Hunger persists despite greater average prosperity. The persistence of inequality, poverty, and hunger is caused not so much by the absence of growth as by the characteristics of the growth that has occurred— rising landlessness; greater reliance on casual, nonpermanent employment; increased unemployment; reduction in the asset base of the rural poor; stagnation in or reduction in the real daily wage rate; a fall in yearly household income; and political, economic, and social discrimination. When these economic and social conditions prevail, growth in total economic output may actually increase rather than reduce poverty and hunger.

Important international linkages are also at work. Much has been written about patterns of international trade, direct investments by transnational corporations and other flows of private capital, concessionary loans and grants (including food aid), international stockpiles of grains and commodity price stabilization schemes, and others. In this chapter I have examined the contribution of Western ideas and ideology, Western technology, and the nature of the Third World state to the continuation of pockets of hunger in the world today.

The dominant capitalist ideology of free enterprise, free trade, and free movement of capital has shaped the international order and has been recommended whenever possible to Third World countries. However, Western society, and particularly North American society, is very different from societies of most Third World countries. Whereas capitalism for Americans meant individualism, self-reliance, and competition, for most of the Third World it meant colonialism, restricted social and economic mobility, and few opportunities for material betterment. It is no surprise that such countries have been susceptible to ideas and ideologies that included a place for government ownership of some of the means of production, for intervention in market processes, and for some cooperative and collective institutions. What is needed is a pragmatic view of all these institutions and practices. Where individualism, self-reliance, and competition can contribute to a reduction of hunger and poverty, let them prevail. Where they cannot, let them be tempered. And if temperance entails government intervention and the fostering of cooperative enterprises, let their possibilities be explored devoid of ideological dogmatism.

Technology, as well as ideas, changes the world. But technology cannot obviate the need for social and institutional change that is prevalently needed in most Third World countries if poverty and hunger are to be reduced significantly. Capital-intensive farming, Green Revolutions, massive water-management projects—none have contributed to an equitable distribution of income or to an appreciable reduction in global hunger. Appropriate technology is situation-specific and hardly ever succeeds as a direct plant from a Western country.

Finally, we turn to the Third World state. Part of the reason for lack of success with imported technology, and also for the maintenance of social and political institutions inimical to the reduction of poverty and hunger, may be laid to the dominant interests that control Third World states. States controlled by large landowners and industrialists infrequently develop economic policies that help reduce hunger. Investment allocation, monetary and tax policies, exchange-rate and foreign-trade policies, or social programs, all have been biased toward urban areas, toward industry, toward large farms, toward upper-income groups—toward everyone except the poor and the hungry. Sadly, Western powers, through such activities as economic-aid programs, diplomatic initiatives, and military assistance, tend strongly to support the very governments whose policies are responsible for perpetuating poverty and hunger.

Thus it is that in the international sphere, ideas, technology, and political power often reinforce local social structures within the Third World. These structures generate a distribution of income that makes it impossible for large numbers of poor people to acquire food, whether through purchase or self-provisioning, almost regardless of the total amount of food available. At present, in regard to world hunger, the West more often leans in the wrong direction than in the right, biased toward landlords and their allies rather than toward the peasantry and other ordinary working people. We can do relatively little directly to eliminate world hunger, but it would help if the Western governments would cease to provide massive amounts of military assistance. Such a withdrawal of military aid would give the poor in the Third World a little more room for maneuver to advance their own cause.

NOTES

1. See World Bank, *World Development Report 1984,* Annex: World Development Indicators, Tables 2 and 19. "Low-income economies" are defined as those with a gross national product (GNP) per capita of less than $410 in 1982 and the "middle-income economies" as those with more than $410 (rising to $6,840 in Trinidad and Tobago).

2. World Bank, *Toward Sustained Development in Sub-Saharan Africa,* Table 1.1, p. 10. The rate of growth of GNP per capita during 1960-1982 was negative in eight of the twenty-three countries—Chad, Somalia, Niger, Guinea-Bissau, Zaire, Uganda, Madagascar, and Ghana (Ibid., p. 57).

3. According to the Food and Agriculture Organization (FAO), in 1980 calorie supply in Eastern Europe and the Soviet Union was 132.8 percent of requirements, and in the United States it was 138.6 percent. (UN, FAO, *Socioeconomic Indicators Relating to the Agricultural Sector and Rural Development,* Table 27, pp. 84-86.)

4. Frances Moore Lappé and Joseph Collins, *Food First: Beyond the Myth of Scarcity.* It should be stressed, however, that the authors of this book advocate much more than merely giving priority to food production in the Third World.

5. Per capita calorie supply in India was 87.3 percent of requirements in 1967-1970 and 86.2 percent in 1980 (UN, FAO, *Socioeconomic Indicators*).

6. Pranab K. Bardhan, *The Political Economy of Development in India,* p. 11.

7. In the low-income economies of sub-Saharan Africa, the per capita rates of growth between 1970 and 1982 were as follows: GDP, −1.0 percent; investment, −0.2 percent; exports, −5.3 percent; manufacturing, −2.3 percent; agriculture, −2.1 percent; food, −1.8 percent. (World Bank, *Toward Sustained Development in Sub-Saharan Africa,* Table 1.1, p. 10.)

Much of the objection to cash crop production for export may arise not from the fact that it reduces the availability of food, but that it is sometimes closely associated with particularly inequitable land ownership patterns—for example, large plantations or extensive ranches and farms owned by multinational corporations. The resulting poverty and hunger is a consequence of the distribution of assets, not of the composition of output.

8. According to UN, FAO, *Socioeconomic Indicators,* during the period from 1971 to 1980, in 73 of 161 countries, per capita food production either fell or failed to rise. These countries varied in size from St. Lucia (with a population of 100,000) to Japan (118 million) and accounted for about 16 percent of the total population of the world. Excluding the rich countries (Hong Kong, Israel, Japan, Saudi Arabia, Belgium, Iceland, Poland, and Portugal), only 12 percent of the world's population lived in poor countries characterized by falling per capita food production.

9. Shlomo Reutlinger and Marcello Selowsky, *Malnutrition and Poverty: Magnitude and Policy Options,* Chapter 2.

10. UN, FAO, *The Fourth World Food Survey,* p. 53. More recently the FAO has estimated the number of rural poor in 1980 as 69.3 million. This may be regarded as an approximation of the number of malnourished in the countryside, as poverty is defined with reference to minimum dietary requirements. (See UN, FAO, *Development Strategies for the Rural Poor,* Table 26, p. 84.)

11. See Thomas T. Poleman, "Quantifying the Nutrition Situation in Developing Countries."

12. Amartya Sen, *Poverty and Famines: An Essay On Entitlement and Deprivation.*
13. Ibid., p. 112. The quotation refers specifically to the Ethiopian famine of 1972-1974.
14. See, for example, International Labour Organization (ILO), *Poverty and Land-lessness in Rural Asia*; and Keith Griffin, *International Inequality and National Poverty.*
15. Michael Lipton, "Conditions of Poverty Groups and Impact on Indian Economic Development and Cultural Change: The Role of Labour," p. 475. Emphasis in the original.
16. Azizur Rahman Khan and Eddy Lee, eds., *Poverty in Rural Asia,* p. 17.
17. M. Riad El-Ghonemy, *Economic Growth, Income Distribution, and Rural Poverty in the Middle East,* Table 11, p. 32. Also see Samir Radwan, *Agrarian Reform and Rural Poverty: Egypt, 1952-1975,* Table 4.3, p. 46.
18. Radwan, *Agrarian Reform,* Table 2.3, p. 23. Real wages in rural Egypt did not exceed the peak of 1966 until 1975, after which they continued to rise rapidly. The increase almost certainly is due to (1) migration abroad to Libya and the Gulf and (2) migration to construction activities in booming urban areas, the boom itself having been fueled by overseas remittances. (See Alan Richards, *Egypt's Agricultural Development, 1800-1980: Technical and Social Change,* Chapter 6.)
19. Keith Griffin, *Land Concentration and Rural Poverty,* p. 75.
20. In India, the proportion of agricultural laborers in the male rural labor force rose from 15.7 percent in 1961 to 25.2 percent in 1971. (Michael Lipton, *Why Poor People Stay Poor,* p. 488.)
21. For evidence from Kerala, West Bengal, the Punjab, and Bihar in India, see Khan and Lee, *Poverty in Rural Asia.*
22. Ibid., p. 10.
23. Lipton, *Why Poor People Stay Poor,* p. 483. Pranab K. Bardhan has shown that "average daily earnings in agricultural operations by men belonging to agricultural labor households . . . declined by 12 percent" between 1964/65 and 1974/75 for the whole of rural India. (Bardhan, *Land, Labor and Rural Poverty: Essays in Development Economics,* p. 189. Emphasis in the original.)
24. On Bangladesh and Nepal, see Khan and Lee, *Poverty in Rural Asia;* on the Philippines, see ILO, *Poverty and Landlessness in Rural Asia.*
25. Bardhan, *Land, Labor and Rural Poverty,* Table 14.1, p. 190.
26. See Keith Griffin, *The Political Economy of Agrarian Change: An Essay on the Green Revolution,* Chapter 2, and Griffin, *Land Concentration and Rural Poverty,* Chapter 5.
27. See Griffin, *The Political Economy of Agrarian Change,* Chapter 2.
28. See B. H. Farmer, ed., *Green Revolution? Technology and Change in Rice-Growing of Areas of Tamil Nadu and Sri Lanka,* Chapter 26.
29. See John W. Mellor, "Food Price Policy and Income Redistribution in Low-Income Countries," and Keith Griffin and Jeffrey James, *The Transition to Egalitarian Development,* Chapters 2 and 3.
30. For a more complete list of possibilities see Bardhan, *Land, Labor and Rural Poverty,* pp. 188-189.
31. Ibid., pp. 192-195. Ashwani Saith has shown that in India as a whole for 1960/61 to 1970/71, "the proportion of the rural population living in poverty was increasing over this decade at an alarming rate of approximately 1.5 percentage points a year" (Saith, "Production, Prices, and Poverty in Rural India," p. 201). Finally, in a study of thirteen

states in India, from 1959/60 to 1970/71, Dominique van de Walle found that in five of them (Maharashtra, West Bengal, Assam, Andhra Pradesh, and Punjab/Haryana) there was a significantly positive relationship between agricultural output and poverty—i.e., the higher was agricultural output, the higher was the number of persons in rural areas living in poverty. In three states (Gujarat, Karnataka, and Uttar Pradesh) the relationship was significantly inverse, and in the remaining five states the relationship was insignificant. (Van de Walle, "Population Growth and Poverty: Another Look at the Indian Time Series Data.")

32. Sen, *Poverty and Famines.*

33. For a theoretical explanation see Keith Griffin, *International Inequality and National Poverty,* Chapter 8.

34. William Shawcross, *The Quality of Mercy: Cambodia, Holocaust and Modern Conscience.*

35. Amartya Sen, *Resources, Values and Development,* p. 519.

36. See Griffin, *International Inequality and National Poverty,* Chapter 3.

37. Ibid., Chapter 2.

38. Note that the free movement of labor internationally is not part of Western capitalist ideology. See ibid., Chapter 4.

39. See, for example, Griffin and James, *The Transition to Egalitarian Development;* Harold Alderman and Joachim von Braun, *The Effects of the Egyptian Food Ration and Subsidy System on Income Distribution and Consumption;* P. S. George, *Public Distribution of Foodgrains in Kerala: Income Distribution Implications and Effectiveness;* and James D. Gavan and Indrani Sri Chandrasekera, *The Impact of Public Foodgrain Distribution on Food Consumption and Welfare in Sri Lanka.*

40. This was one of the recommendations of an economic mission to Ethiopia led by the author. The report is entitled "Socialism from the Grass Roots: Accumulation, Employment and Equity in Ethiopia." The government has not released the study to the public.

41. The impact of the famine on the Chinese people may be seen in the following figures:

	Birth rate	*Death rate*	*Natural growth rate*
	(persons per thousand population)		
1958	29.22	11.98	17.24
1959	24.78	14.59	10.19
1960	20.86	25.43	− 4.57
1961	18.02	14.24	3.78
1962	37.01	10.02	26.99

Source: States Statistical Bureau, Statistical Yearbook of China 1983, Hong Kong, Economic Information and Agency, 1983, p. 105.

42. See Keith Griffin, "Efficiency, Equality and Accumulation in Rural China: Notes on the Chinese System of Incentives."

43. Keith Griffin, ed., *Institutional Reform and Economic Development in the Chinese Countryside,* Chapter 1.

44. Keith Griffin, "Communal Land Tenure Systems and Their Role in Rural Development," in Sanjaya Lall and Frances Stewart, eds., *Theory and Reality in Develop-*

ment: Essays in Honor of Paul Streeten.

45. Oxfam, *Behind the Weather: Lessons to Be Learned: Drought and Famine in Ethiopia,* pp. 4-5.

46. Thurston Clarke, *The Last Caravan.*

47. Griffin, *The Political Economy of Agrarian Change.*

48. See, for example, Edward Goldsmith and Nicholas Hildyard, *The Social and Environmental Effects of Large Dams.* Also see the Special Report in *Ecologist* 14, no. 5/6, 1984.

49. World Bank, *Toward Sustained Development in Sub-Saharan Africa,* p. 4.

50. Ibid., p. 5.

51. Ibid., p. 41.

52. Judith Heyer, Pepe Roberts, and Gavin Williams, eds., *Rural Development in Tropical Africa.*

53. See Marcus Linear, "The Tsetse War."

54. Nicos Poulantzas, *Political Power and Social Classes.*

55. Bardhan, *The Political Economy of Development in India,* Chapter 5.

56. Lipton, *Why Poor People Stay Poor.*

57. See, for example, Raymond Bonner, *Weakness and Deceit: U.S. Policy and El Salvador.*

Comments on Chapter 2 and Author's Response

Alain De Janvry

Let me restate what I think are the two major theses that Keith Griffin has been advancing over the years. First, hunger is not primarily caused by inadequate production and cannot be eliminated merely by increasing production. Rather, the fundamental cause of hunger is poverty, and the way to eliminate hunger is to combat poverty. His second thesis is that poverty is created not so much by the absence of growth as by the characteristics, the styles, of growth itself. Of course, I agree with these propositions, but I do qualify each of them.

In terms of the first thesis I would say that increasing food production is not *sufficient* to decrease hunger. The experience of the Green Revolution confirms this. Still, to decrease hunger, production increases generally are *necessary*. And in some ways there is an interesting contrast here with John Mellor's contribution (Chapter 3), which basically looks at the necessary conditions to combat hunger, namely, an increase in food production. When Keith Griffin focuses on the sufficient conditions for creating food entitlements and eliminating poverty, he advocates creating effective demand for food being produced in increasing quantities.

Without restoring the scientist or the engineer to the position occupied by the Creator, I think we must be careful not to put forward an antiproduction bias, especially at Utah State University, where people's interest in the issue of international development and hunger basically comes from a technological orientation and the expectation that, in some way, they, with their technologies, are able to do something about hunger.

There are basically four situations in which production increase is necessary in order to decrease world hunger today. First, in the short run, who produces is an important determinant of entitlements. And to increase the food security of small farmers requires improving the productivity of their labor; it requires stabilizing the production systems in which they are engaged. Yet little research has been done on how to improve the use of modern science in the production systems of small farms.

Second, in the short run as well, in countries such as India hunger cannot be eliminated and the bulk of the population brought to a point at or above the poverty line without a substantial increase in production if we also want to avoid creating major inflationary pressures that in some ways negate efforts to achieve fairer income distribution for poor people. Still, as Keith Griffin argues, India has achieved food self-sufficiency at the national level with food stocks rising to an unprecedented level, but 45 percent of the population still is not nourished at appropriate levels.

Third, also in the short run, there are many areas of the world, as Griffin has mentioned, where food production per capita has been falling. In these areas, particularly in Africa and the lower-income countries, the elimination of hunger occurs when food production increases.

Fourth, it seems that in the long run we do face a rather precarious balance between supply and demand. Look how the annual growth rates of world food production have been behaving over the last thirty years. In 1950 the rate was 3.1 percent annually; in the 1960s it averaged 2.6 percent; in the 1970s it averaged 2.2 percent. Rates of growth in world food production are coming uncomfortably close to the current rate of population growth. Future food increases obviously will have to come from yield increases and not from increases in the area cultivated. Mellor gives some figures on this in Chapter 3. Yet, if we look at how yield increases have been behaving over time, we may note a marked slowdown in our ability to continually increase yields. For example, the annual rate of increase in wheat yields during the 1960s was 3.1 percent, on the average, worldwide. In the 1970s it was down to 1.7 percent. We now wonder if the potential for increased yields that the Green Revolution offered India in the 1960s has to a large extent been exhausted and no new Green Revolution of a similar magnitude is on the horizon for quite a few years to come.

The precarious balance between supply and demand has, in essence, been insured during the last twenty years by reliance on food imports from the United States and the European Economic Community. The bulk of the per capita food increases in the Third World come from the increase in imports and not from the increase in domestic production. For the United States to maintain the balance between supply and demand in the year 2000, its domestic production will have to increase between 30 and 40 percent. Such increases may not be possible given strains on U.S. production systems, such as soil erosion, pollution of aquifers, and so forth. More important, we may ask whether we will view with satisfaction a world food balance in the year 2000 that is increasingly dependent on food supplies originating in one single area of the world, the United States. Also, on a world scale, a major decline has taken place in food aid, which collapsed from 50 million tons a year in 1965 to 3.8 million tons in 1982.

So production is necessary, if not sufficient, to provide adequate food entitlements and to eliminate poverty. We must not be satisfied with the types of production we currently have. The issue of technological change and food research in future years will remain important.

Let me turn now to Griffin's second thesis. I agree that basically poverty is created by growth. As I remember, in *Underdevelopment in Spanish America,* Griffin says that underdevelopment was not discovered, it was actually created by those who colonized South America. Yet it seems to me that what is important here is to identify what the structural conditions are under which growth is going to be equitable or inequitable. At this juncture, we do have a number of success stories that we should learn from—Taiwan, South Korea, mainland

China—that have had a very substantial increase in food production, on average about 17 percent per year during the last five years. So the key question that we should address as development economists is what new development strategies might we pursue in place of former strategies that in some ways have run their course. Import substitution, one such old strategy, has created both inefficiencies in production and strong inequities in the distribution of income. During the 1970s through the early 1980s the promotion of exports as a strategy has also run its course, because access to the international market for Third World exports of industrial products has become quite limited.

In addition to these issues, as we explore new strategies we need to think beyond the issue of debt. Many countries are experiencing a serious debt crisis, which means that the nature of their policy is dominated by stabilization preoccupations—how to stabilize the economies at acceptable rates of inflation, how to mobilize foreign exchange to meet debt-service obligations. We need to think beyond this, considering how these economies are going to reorganize and what kind of structural changes have to be embedded in the process of stabilizing the economy so that, beyond debt, we consider how to engineer economic processes that will both stabilize economic growth and insure more equitable income distribution.

Here, it seems, there are basically three or four important issues. One is the question of the distribution of assets. The Taiwanese and South Korean growth patterns, for example, rose out of the exceptional concern for growth and equity that originated in very forceful and extensive land reforms that distributed assets very evenly throughout the population. Consistent with that experience is a proposition—namely, redistribution with growth—that some at the World Bank have advanced. They advocate that savings that originate in growth should be channeled as investments in the informal sector in rural development programs, where presumably the margin of productivity of investment can be high because so little investment actually has occurred in those sectors.

Second, consider the question of labor markets. In part, growth becomes equitable once surplus labor has been eliminated and when productivity gains eventuate in formal wage gains. And when we look at those countries where growth and equity have been occurring hand in hand, what we see are situations where productivity gains have been transformed into wage gains because the labor market is tight, surplus labor is low, and increasing employment is reflected in rising real wages.

Third, investment choices are problematic in economies that basically are led by the production of luxury goods or export goods. The wages that are paid do not create the markets for the products in the key sectors of growth of the economy. Bananas, for example, never find an effective demand in the wages paid to workers on a plantation. By contrast, when you produce wage goods, wages and rising wages create the market for the products that are produced. And as productivity gains on the side of production are translated into wage gains, they have to be translated into wage gains on the side of consumption to insure the effective demand for the products that are thus produced. Here, it seems, is where in essence export-led models have come to an end, where the international market economy is not engaging in terms of the capacity of re-creating economic growth based on exports. Countries have to look much more at their domestic markets, at the production of wage goods and the pro duction of wage foods, in order to cater to a demand that has to originate in wages and in peasant incomes.

Fourth, when we examine the nature of poverty, we see that often poverty is associated with the incapacity of peasants to move their assets to the booming sectors, or to the sectors that eventually take advantage of a rapidly increasing effective demand. Peasants cannot mobilize the credit to move into a booming sector—for example, irrigated sorghum in Mexico. They are trapped into corn production, a sector in which prices have been undermined by very cheap im-ports born of overvalued exchange rates. Or consider Chile, where the boom-ing sector has been fruits, with very remarkable growth since 1973. But peas-ants there are not able to capitalize fruit production, which requires a very demanding investment. They are stuck in the production of crops like wheat; given an overvalued exchange rate, domestic wheat has been underpriced by cheap imports that have bankrupted domestic producers.

This is an important issue: Large segments of the rural population are trapped in lagging sectors, unable to shift their assets to the booming sectors. Hence, the need arises to either increase the productivity of labor in the lagging sectors to make them more competitive or to help peasants shift their re-sources. That has been done, for instance, in Ivory Coast, where peasant's assets have been shifted to the more booming sectors of economic activity, including the export sector.

In conclusion, I would say that food production does remain a problem. Hence, appropriate technology, if properly directed, is an important element in a solution to the problem of world hunger. Further, I suggest that the defini-tion of equitable development strategies is a key area for work by social scien-tists who are preoccupied with issues of hunger.

Cheryl Christensen

I agree with the broad outlines of Griffin's and de Janvry's arguments, particu-larly on two points: first, that production, although probably a necessary condi-tion for eliminating hunger, is certainly not a sufficient one; and second, that the system of entitlements, and even more fundamentally, the structure of asset distribution and income distribution within and among countries, is probably the single most important cause of hunger.

However, let me elaborate on the notion that production is necessary, even if not sufficient. I do that by addressing the region of the world that all of the conference participants have acknowledged to be an exception to some generalizations concerning food security and that is the one I know best—sub-Saharan Africa.

Irrespective of the difficulties of eliminating hunger when production is increasing, those difficulties are even more intensive when production is stagnant or declining. This is true on the physical level; it is true on the social level; it is true on the economic level. The experience of sub-Saharan Africa illustrates some of the costs of failing to achieve production growth capable of keeping up with population growth.

Sub-Saharan Africa is a region where food production per capita has declined fairly steadily over the last fifteen years. The results of that have been threefold. First, and probably most important, the long-term decline in production, coupled with inadequate performance economically that might otherwise have been capable of generating the purchasing power to make up the difference on international markets, has eliminated virtually all slack in dealing with disruptions to the production system. In areas where rain-fed agriculture predominates, where political instability abounds, where human-made as well as natural crises have been occurring, the elimination of that slack makes some of the factors identified as causes of hunger even more operative. When supplies are fixed, particularly in parts of the world where it is difficult logistically to move large quantities of grain in periods of disruption, the political and economic factors that have been identified as operating in normal circumstances become even more significant. The discussion of Ethiopia (Griffin, Chapter 6) illustrates some of those interactions.

Second, many of the questions related to the distribution of income and wealth when agricultural production is growing apply equally, or perhaps more intensely, when agricultural production is not growing. The distribution of assets and income in countries and across countries not only structures what happens as a result of production, it structures the way in which conflicts over potential production are resolved.

In sub-Saharan Africa, several features tend to support this observation. One has to do with the impact in many of the countries of a long-term production decline in making weak economies more dependent, not only on commercial imports of food but increasingly on concessional imports of food—food aid. When food production has not grown sufficiently rapidly to keep up with population, and when it cannot be a vehicle for ensuring food security for large portions of the population, we find poverty and hunger in rural areas. In a country with limited foreign exchange and a food-aid system that requires a long lead time, and when there are difficult delivery processes, it becomes much more difficult to guarantee food security for the rural poor than it would be if rural food production were experiencing even moderate growth.

One study of food security in Africa came to the conclusion that guaranteed food security in many of Africa's poorer rural areas depends primarily on being able to have enough production in local areas with adequate storage to enable villages and families to see through variations in food production associated with weather. When the supply line for food security and for responding to food emergencies is a long one, complicated by both bureaucratic and logistical delays, the impact tends to fall hardest on the most vulnerable groups in the society.

Let me just give an illustration of what that may mean in practical terms. There have been, as is well known, severe food shortages in Ethiopia, severe food shortages in the Sudan, and a drought that could have led to equally severe shortages in Kenya. In Kenya, however, the government had adequate foreign exchange to be able to respond quickly to food emergencies. It was able to import commercially a half million tons of grain; it was able to limit the situation, which could have led to starvation, to one that simply led to severe hunger. The absence of those same resources in the Sudan made it much more difficult to respond. If either the Sudan, Ethiopia, or Kenya had a more robust system of production and storage in rural areas, that in itself might have been able to relieve a lot of the pressure on imports.

The third point I make is that asset and income distribution issues are not really separate from production issues. In essence, I am repeating many earlier points made by Keith Griffin, so I do not claim any novelty for this. In many areas the question of the design of the production system, and particularly the marketing system, is a critical component in determining whether increased food production eliminates hunger and whether it goes on to lead to economic growth.

Here I take issue with Griffin's sanguine comments (Chapter 9, on China) about collective systems on a large scale—collective agriculture—at least as it has been manifest in Africa. In the African setting, one of the major reasons for investing in state farms or collective systems of agriculture was, in point of fact, to give the state greater control over marketing, thus making it easier to procure food at relatively low prices on a relatively secure basis to feed urban populations. The consensus now is that those experiments have not been successful. The alternative to a collective system is a production and marketing system that is much more broadly based and that enables a variety of functions on small- and medium-sized farms to be handled efficiently. It is very crucial that such a system have access to roads and marketing facilities in such measure that rural families have the capacity to generate income above subsistence production. In much of sub-Saharan Africa, the failure to develop those systems, particularly broad-based marketing systems, has as much to do with the failure to achieve broad-based growth in food production as do some of the other issues relating to asset distribution.

My points of agreement with Griffin are probably more fundamental than my points of disagreement. But I do underscore the point that whatever the difficulties of equitable distribution are in periods of growing productivity, they are for the most disadvantaged people even more severe in periods when that growth does not occur. I remind us of the differences in the global environment between the current situation, when we have surplus production, and the era of the so-called world food crisis a decade ago, when global supplies were tight. Recently we have been able to mobilize large resources for African food emergencies, and although we had problems in delivering those resources, particularly in making them reach the people that most need them, the supplies have been available.

In the early 1970s, food aid tended to become acyclical and to become less available at precisely the time when production shortfalls occurred in developing countries, when global prices were higher, and when the foreign exchange earnings in poorer countries were weaker. Under those kinds of circumstances the international response to emergencies, as well as the domestic response to poverty, was less hopeful than that response is in the current environment.

Finally, I make just one comment on the role of the state, particularly regarding African countries. This is now a very significant topic of debate. It is frequently argued that the role of the state in African economies is too pervasive and that the state does intervene on the set of organized issues, primarily centering around policies that work to the disadvantage of the poor and hungry. I think, by and large, that is the case. However, the African setting is interesting because, as a result of international economic pressures, attempts are under way to engage in policy reform. At issue is whether reversing past policies without changing the political conditions that gave rise to some of those policies, or without developing the capacity to effectively implement policies, is in the long run a successful approach to policy reform. I think that in Africa we are seeing a fairly large-scale experiment in policy reform without political and social change, the results of which are not in, but that bear watching.

In conclusion, then, I agree with most of what Griffin argues. However, sub-Saharan Africa is something of an exception. [It is probably the exception that proves the rule because the difficulties that are encountered when production is inadequate are at least as severe or more so when production is adequate.]

Keith B. Griffin

Not so long ago it was widely believed that growth would suffice to eliminate poverty and hunger: If average incomes rose, some of the benefits were bound to trickle down to the poor. Alas, the evidence of the last forty years has shown this to be wishful thinking. And relatively few now believe in this fairy tale. A more recent version of the theory/tale is that although aggregate growth of income per capita may not suffice to eliminate hunger, growth in the food and agricultural sector will do the trick. This I have called the trickle-down modified hypothesis, or TDM for short. Many still believe in it; Alain de Janvry, Cheryl Christensen, and I do not.

Christensen and de Janvry, however, believe that increased food production is a necessary condition for reducing hunger even though increased production by itself will not solve the problem. This, evidently, is a reasonable point of view and in sub-Saharan Africa, the area of concern to Christensen, it is indisputably a correct point of view. Nonetheless, it makes me uneasy to formulate the problem in this way because it seems to imply (or may be interpreted by some readers to imply) that we should first increase food production (to satisfy a necessary condition) and then concentrate on ensuring that the increased food supply reaches the hungry and malnourished.

I do not believe that the sequence "produce first and distribute later" is possible in most societies for other than a short period. The reason for this is that in a market economy those who produce the additional food will receive most of the income generated by that additional output. Hence, unless the poor produce the food, they will not have the purchasing power to enable them to acquire more sustenance. In the short run, and in periods of emergency, the link between output and income can be broken by, for example, food-rationing schemes, but in the longer run the link between the two is almost certain to be reestablished. This, it seems to me, is one of the lessons political economy teaches us.

Alain de Janvry and Cheryl Christensen understand this perfectly well. Thus, de Janvry emphasizes the structural conditions that determine how the fruits of growth are distributed and Christensen states explicitly that the structure of assets and the distribution of income are the fundamental determinants of the incidence of hunger. I could not agree more. The important thing is not what is produced, or even how much is produced, but who produces and on what terms. This is far more important than, say, the rate of growth of the population. It is therefore surprising, as much as I agree with de Janvry, to find what appears to be a Malthusian fear lurking in the background of his analysis.

Broadly speaking, there are, I think, two institutional arrangements that can combine an equitable distribution of income among the rural population with sustained growth of agricultural production—a small, well-organized peasant farming system or an equally well organized communal or cooperative system. Neither is easy to establish or maintain, but either one may be made to work quite satisfactorily.

A small peasant system, as may be found in Taiwan and South Korea, requires a radical distribution of land ownership (to ensure that income from property is evenly distributed) combined with a tight labor market (to ensure that increases in labor productivity are translated into higher real wages). In addition, it requires an efficient marketing system and a reasonably well functioning rural credit and capital market. Finally, it requires a state with a pronounced peasant bias that is prepared to allocate substantial resources to areas such as irrigation, electrification, rural roads, basic health services, and primary and secondary education. It is a tall order, and in most Third World countries such a system could not be constructed except in the aftermath of a political and social revolution. I do not share de Janvry's optimism that grass-roots movements in Latin America can help to bring about the changes that are needed, nor do I share Christensen's hope that external economic pressures can force the existing regimes in Africa to introduce reforms that favor the peasantry.

A communal tenure system, as found in China, is equally demanding. Indeed, historically it has required a communist revolution. Most analysts in noncommunist countries, including Christensen and de Janvry, are at best skeptical of cooperative or collective institutions, but I believe this skepticism is based either on ignorance or on a misunderstanding of the contribution communal tenure systems can make to rural development.

Communal tenure systems have no particular advantage in the sphere of agricultural production. In most Third World countries, there are no significant economies of scale in cultivation and hence there are few if any gains to be reaped in collective field preparation, sowing, weeding, and harvesting. The benefits of cooperation arise elsewhere—for example, in processing agricultural output and marketing, in purchasing and distributing material inputs, in mobilizing resources for rural investment including seasonally unemployed labor, in diversifying the rural economy by channeling investment into nonagricultural rural industries, in providing essential social services, and in guaranteeing an equitable distribution of income.

Christensen rightly emphasizes the importance of adequate food storage at the village level to enable localities to cope with fluctuations in output associated with variations in climatic conditions. Most poor peasant households are unable to accumulate food stocks equivalent to more than six months' consumption. Most villages have no publicly owned or controlled stockpiles of food. As a result, food security at the local level is tenuous, and when a crisis occurs the poor often are forced to rely either on charity or on credit supplied by small merchants and middlemen. Under a communal tenure system, however, it is customary for the commune or cooperative or collective to build up its own stockpiles of food and to distribute this food to those in need through some form of a rationing system. The rationing system need not be permanent, and in any case a household's entitlement is likely to be strictly limited, but the existence of a local storage and distribution system can put a safety net under those at risk of starving. Particularly in parts of Africa where per capita food supplies now are precarious even at the best of times, strong rural cooperative institutions could, in principle, play an important role in containing future disasters.

One of the points de Janvry makes is that the poor in rural areas often are trapped in lagging sectors because of their inability to shift into activities that happen to be experiencing a relatively rapid growth of demand. This may be because the poor lack the required skills and have no access to training institutions; or because they lack information and have no access to extension services and technical assistance; or because they lack the capital necessary for the initial investment and have only restricted access to credit markets. A subsistence peasant farmer, for example, cannot readily switch from maize cultivation to, say, beef production or fruit-tree farming unless there are well-developed rural institutions capable of giving assistance.

Here again, communal institutions can play an important role. They can supply credit; they can provide technical knowledge; they can undertake to train their members in new skills; they can help to acquire the necessary raw materials for new activities; and they can assist with marketing. Moreover, the commune or cooperative itself can invest in promising new activities—particularly in small-scale industries and workshops or in other enterprises in which there are economies of scale—and thereby spread risks among all households while at the same time diversifying the base of the local economy. Finally, by retaining part of the revenue surplus generated by collectively owned and managed enterprises, a communal institution can amass savings for further investment in the same or alternative activities. In this way, savings, investment, and growth in the rural areas can become institutionalized and the benefits of growth can be widely shared. The same results may, of course, be achieved in other ways. My claim is merely that a communal tenure system is one way to reduce poverty, inequality, and hunger. This is a modest claim but one that nevertheless remains controversial.

At the end of the day, the fate of the peasantry depends on the nature of the state. Cheryl Christensen mentions that in Africa collective systems of agriculture (and state farms, too) have been used not to promote rural development but to extract food from the rural population at low cost for the benefit of the urban population. It is regrettable that what she says is true, and her point is equally valid in many countries outside the African continent. Far too often the squeeze on the peasantry formerly exerted by large landlords now is exerted by the state. It is important to recognize, however, that the squeeze on the peasantry is independent of the tenure regime. It can, and in fact does, exist in countries with small peasant farming systems, in countries with communal tenure systems, and in other countries where inegalitarian systems prevail. Whether the rural poor are squeezed depends on the macropolitics and class composition of the state, not on rural institutions. If the state is peasant-biased, the poor will gain; if it is landlord-biased or urban-biased, they will not. It is as simple as that.

3

John W. Mellor

Opportunities in the International Economy for Meeting the Food Requirements of the Developing Countries

Most of the human suffering arising from food insecurity is in the developing countries of the world; there the relative availability of food also plays a major role in determining the pace and pattern of economic development. The world's developed countries provide the major source of food exports to developing countries; they possess much of the technological capacity needed to stimulate economic growth in the developing countries. How well the developing and developed countries can cooperate in the mutually important processes of food supply and economic development will have a profound effect on the type of world in which we live.

My purpose in this chapter is to stress the need for increased food, capital, and technological exchanges between developing and developed countries. My thrust is to demonstrate how relations among these countries should be, rather than how they presently are. Such a normative orientation helps focus attention on the fact that present world food problems can—and should—be solved by a judicious mixture of intergovernmental cooperation and communication.

I begin by identifying the character of the food security needs currently facing the Third World. I then stress the need to accelerate current rates of food production growth throughout the developing world. Increased food production not only raises the total amount of foodstuffs, it also helps boost poor people's access to food. Through the direct and indirect multiplier effects of technological change, increased food production growth raises both the purchasing power and the employment opportunities of the poor. I then analyze the policy steps that need to be taken in developed countries to support this strategy of agricultural growth in the Third World. The high-income countries can do much here through the provision of food and technical assistance and the liberalization of trade restrictions. I conclude that a key element in meeting the food needs of the world lies in intelligently stimulating the political and

47

economic contacts between the developing and the developed countries of the world.

FOOD SECURITY CHALLENGES IN THE WORLD

Two problems are at the crux of the world's food security: chronic food insecurity in most developing countries and widespread fluctuations in annual food production in many developed and developing countries. The first is a long-term problem of aggregate food supply in developing countries, a problem that requires increasing current rates of food production growth throughout the Third World. The second problem is more a short-term one that draws attention to the need for smoothing out the substantial short-run fluctuations in annual food production that have a particularly negative impact on the poor.

The pressing nature of these two problems is easily demonstrated. With respect to the first problem, in recent years aggregate food production in the developing world has just barely kept pace with the rate of population growth. Between 1961 and 1980, food production in the Third World increased at an average rate of 2.6 percent a year (Table 3.1). This was only slightly faster than the average annual population growth rate of 2.4 percent. Thus, on a per capita basis, food production in the Third World as a whole increased by only 0.2 percent. However, this aggregate figure covers sharply different rates of food production growth in various regions of the developing world. For example, while per capita food production in Asia increased by a strong 0.5 percent per year, in sub-Saharan Africa it fell by a shocking 1.2 percent. In both of these areas, as well as throughout the Third World, accelerated rates of food production growth are needed to meet the pressing food needs of the poor.

Table 3.1   Population and Major Food Crop Production in the Developing World, 1961–1980

Country group	Average Annual Population Growth Rate, 1961–1980 (percent)	Average Annual Major Food Crop Production Growth Rate,[a] 1961–1980 (percent)
Developing countries[b]	2.4	2.6
Asia (including China)	2.3	2.8
North Africa and Middle East	2.7	2.5
Sub-Saharan Africa	2.8	1.6
Latin America	2.7	2.8

[a]Includes cereals, roots and tubers, pulses, groundnuts, bananas, and plantains. Rice is in terms of milled form.

[b]Includes a total of 105 Asian, African, Middle Eastern, and Latin American countries.

Source: Leonardo A. Paulino, *Food in the Third World: Past Trends and Projections to 2000* (Washington, D.C.: International Food Policy Research Institute, 1986).

With respect to the problem of fluctuations, in recent years the growth of world food production has been accompanied by a steadily increasing degree of production variability. Between the periods 1960/61 to 1970/71 and 1971/72 to 1982/83, the coefficient of variation of total world cereal production increased from 2.8 percent to 3.4 percent.[1] This represented a net increase in production variability of 21 percent (Table 3.2). The major source of this increase in production variability has been in increases in yield covariances among crops and among regions.

Given the importance of the new seed/fertilizer technologies in Third World agriculture, it is tempting to suggest that the introduction of these technologies is inherently related to the observed increase in yield variances. Yet it would be quite premature to draw such conclusions. On the one hand, increased yield covariances may be caused by the spread of varieties with common parentages over wide geographical areas. Now that this problem is recognized, breeders need to give greater emphasis to making full use of different seed and plant varieties to reduce variability. On the other hand, increased yield variances may also be caused by the erratic supply of essential components of the new agricultural technology—fertilizer, irrigation, and electric power. The solution to this problem is, of course, to continue improving the public institutions for providing these inputs and to eliminate any short-term fluctuations in their availability. In any event, it is clear that we need to know far more about the technological and the policy means for dealing with the whole problem of increased production variability. In the meantime, efforts to deal with this variability problem should *not* involve avoiding the use of the very seed/fertilizer technologies that have provided such a stimulus for Third World cereal production.

In recent years the steady growth in world food production has also been accompanied by a rising degree of price variability. Although international grain prices were relatively stable in the 1950s and 1960s, since 1971 they have become highly variable. The coefficient of variation for export prices was more than eight times as high in the 1970s as it was in the 1960s (Table 3.3). For rice, the coefficient of variation for export prices more than doubled between the two decades. The most important factor in increased price variability is the withdrawal of the United States from providing world price stability as a by-product of its domestic farm income support programs.

It is important to realize that the brunt of such fluctuations in price and production fall mainly upon those who can least afford them—the poor. For example, research in India[2] indicates that the poor spend between 60 to 80 percent of their increments to income on food; and that the bottom 20 percent in the income distribution make nine times the adjustments in food expenditures as do the top 5 percent on the distribution to a given decline in supply. Thus, as food supplies decline and prices rise, the poor must bear the brunt of the burden. The poor may suffer either through a reduction in their purchasing power from higher prices or through a reduction in their employment opportunities.

Table 3.2   Changes in the Mean and Variability of World Cereal Production[a]

	Average Production			Coefficient of Variation of Production		
	1960/61 –1970/71	1971/72 –1982/83	% Change	1960/61 –1970/71	1971/72 –1982/83	% Change
	(metric tons)			(percent)		
Wheat	253,454	352,982	39.3	5.46	4.83	−11.5
Maize	210,074	317,303	51.0	3.29	4.41	34.0
Rice	119,971	155,031	29.2	3.97	3.80	− 4.3
Barley	95,283	150,997	58.5	4.81	7.50	55.9
Millet	19,758	21,370	8.2	7.91	7.66	− 3.2
Sorghum	40,233	53,386	32.7	5.22	5.70	9.2
Oats	49,035	47,600	− 2.9	11.30	5.35	−52.6
Other cereals	41,404	35,321	−14.9	4.57	9.31	103.7
Total cereals	829,215	1,133,902	36.7	2.78	3.37	21.2

[a]Does not include People's Republic of China.

Source: Peter Hazell, "Sources of Increased Variability in the World Cereal Production Since the 1960s," *Journal of Agricultural Economics* 36, no. 2 (May 1984), Table 3.

As food prices rise, the wealthier classes try to maintain their food consumption by reducing their consumption of those very labor-intensive goods and services that provide employment for the poor. A decline in food production therefore not only reduces the food supplies available to the poor, but may also reduce their ability to procure those supplies at higher prices.[3]

FOOD NEEDS AND THE DEVELOPING WORLD

In order to ease the burden on the poor, it is necessary to accelerate current rates of food production growth throughout the Third World. This is because of the tremendous world need for food, if the poor are to prosper, as well as the critical role that the food production sector must assume in any equitable pattern of economic growth.

In some developing countries the initial benefits of a faster rate of food production growth may well tend to benefit the surplus-producing peasant cultivator and not the poorest rural people. However, the record is clear from time series data in India that increased food production and declining food prices are the dominant variables determining the incidence of rural poverty.[4] Concurrently, it is only through cost decreasing technological change that these two variables work to reduce the indigence of rural poverty. Increased food production growth tends to benefit the rural poor mainly through the creation of new employment opportunities.

In most Third World countries food production growth requires more attention to crop yields. Throughout the world, even in Africa, the rate of growth of the cropped area has declined sharply in recent years. This indicates that an ever-increasing proportion of the food needed to feed the world must come from increased yields per unit of land.

In the past two decades, increased crop yields have, in fact, become the main source of food production growth in the developing world. Between 1961 and 1980 output per hectare of major food crops in the developing world rose by 1.9 percent annually and accounted for more than 70 percent of total food production growth (Table 3.4). During this period increases in the harvested area averaged only 0.7 percent a year and contributed the other 30 percent of total production growth in the Third World.

Increases in yields require prolonged and continuous technological change in agriculture. Depending on the situation, improvements in agricultural technology (such as the use of high-yield seeds, fertilizers, and pesticides) produce yields two to four times higher than those achieved by traditional means. For example, the adoption of new technology in India increased average cereal yields 29 percent between the periods 1954/55 to 1964/65 and 1967/68 to 1977/78. As this point is often neglected, the role of the state in promoting such yield increases needs to be emphasized. In general, the new seed/fertilizer inputs commonly associated with the Green Revolution cannot succeed without considerable state intervention in agriculture. The state needs to come in and establish those types of rural institutions and services that the private sector will not undertake. Most developing countries would have to wait a very long time for the private sector to build efficient agricultural research and technical education systems, or even irrigation and fertilizer distribution systems,in the countryside. All of this focuses attention on the need for a high level of public investment in the basic building blocks of agricultural development: irrigation, input facilities, rural roads, and especially agricultural research systems.

The historic examples of Taiwan, Japan, and the Punjab of India illustrate quite graphically the benefits of a high rate of public investment in agriculture. In India, for example, about 20 percent of the central government budget was devoted to agriculture in the early 1960s.[5] A good deal of this investment focused on the Indian state of the Punjab, an area that already had good water supplies and soil fertility. When the new high-yield seed/fertilizer inputs ap-

Table 3.3   Variability in Export Prices for Wheat and Rice in Real Terms: 1950–1979

	Wheat		Rice	
	Standard Deviation	Coefficient of Variation	Standard Deviation	Coefficient of Variation
1950–1959	26.0	11.2	59.0	11.4
1960–1969	7.0	3.6	89.0	17.5
1970–1979	56.0	30.0	187.6	39.0

Source: Alberto Valdes, "A Note on Variability in International Grain Prices," paper prepared for IFPRI Workshop on Food and Agricultural Price Policy (Washington, D.C.: International Food Policy Research Institute, 1984), Table 1.

Table 3.4   Average Annual Growth Rates of Production, Area Harvested, and Output Per Hectare for Major Food Crops[a] in Developing Countries, 1961–1980

Country Group	Production[b]	Area Harvested	Output per Hectare
		(percent)	
Developing countries	2.6	0.7	1.9
Asia (including China)	2.8	0.4	2.4
North Africa/Middle East	2.5	1.1	1.4
Sub-Saharan Africa	1.6	1.5	0.1
Latin America	2.8	1.5	1.3

[a]Includes cereals, roots and tubers, pulses and groundnuts. Rice is in terms of milled form.

[b]Annual growth rates of production may differ slightly from those shown in Table 3.1 because the data here exclude the outputs of bananas and plantains, for which estimates on the area harvested are not available.

Source: Leonardo A. Paulino, *Food in the Third World: Past Trends and Projections to 2000* (Washington, D.C.: International Food Policy Research Institute, 1986).

peared, this investment enabled the Punjab to achieve a remarkable 8 percent annual increase in major food grain production between 1960/61 and 1978/79.[6]

Of course, the level of public investment is not the only factor determining agricultural success in the developing world. Certainly such factors as the character of land distribution, the quality of human capital stock, and other socioeconomic factors also play a leading role. But the public investment in agriculture is clearly an important factor, if for no other reason than that the common pattern in many developing countries is to underinvest in the rural sector. For example, in Africa, a continent where per capita food production is now declining, governments have typically spent very little on agriculture. During the period 1978-1980 the median annual expenditure on agriculture in fifteen African countries was only 7.4 percent of the total government budget (Table 3.5).

During this same time period, foreign donors have generally paid less attention to African agriculture than have national governments. As a result, most African countries today suffer from a poorly developed rural infrastructure, little research on food crops, and poorly developed input delivery systems. In the early 1960s, famine-prone Asia represented life for the poor without a Green Revolution; now Africa has taken over that role with terrible consequences for its poor.

In many developing countries the low level of government investment in agriculture is a reflection of the low priority assigned to the agricultural sector. In these countries, agriculture is commonly viewed as a "backward" sector, capable of only providing surpluses—especially taxes—to finance industrial and urban development. In these countries, agriculture is taxed by fixing low prices for its products and by overvaluing national currencies. In some situations the level of such taxation on food and export crops has been so high as to seriously impair production. In Africa, for example, the rate of taxation on export crops has varied between 40 and 45 percent in recent years.[7] Similarly, in the past, high effective rates of taxation on food crops in Africa have encouraged producers to actively avoid selling their produce to state marketing outlets. In more recent years, however, relative food prices have been rising in Africa, but this has had little effect so far on overall rates of food production growth. That is because of the poor state of public support for technological change in the smallholder farming sector. In Africa the combination of high taxation, a deterioration of the terms of trade against agricultural exports, and a lack of public investment in agriculture have helped create a severe foreign exchange constraint.[8]

If food production is to rise significantly in the Third World, the leaderships of many developing countries must adopt—and the donor community must encourage them to adopt—a more enlightened view of agriculture. Leaders of several Asian countries have already made the type of conscious policy shifts needed to encourage agriculture production, but this is the case in only a minority of African countries. Throughout Africa, investment, pricing, and exchange rate policies must be revised with a view to encouraging agricultural production, not penalizing it. Such policy reappraisals should be guided by a recognition of the three important roles that agriculture can play in the overall development process.

First, food and agriculture can help relieve the important wage goods constraint involved in development. As noted above, the marginal propensity of the poor to spend on food is quite high, typically 0.6 to 0.8. Thus, if development leads to a rapid growth in the employment (and income) of low-income

Table 3.5 Percentage of Central Government Expenditures to Agriculture in Selected African Countries, 1978–1980

	1978	1979	1980	Average All Years
Ghana	12.2	10.4	12.2	11.6
Rwanda	10.3	12.7	—	11.5
Madagascar	11.5	11.4	10.2	11.0
Sudan	9.0	11.3	9.4	9.9
Botswana	10.5	9.2	9.7	9.8
Somalia	12.6	10.6	5.6	9.6
Kenya	8.5	8.4	8.3	8.4
Tanzania	9.3	7.0	—	8.2
Niger	7.1	8.9	6.8	7.6
Liberia	9.0	2.7	3.1	4.9
Cameroon	4.1	4.3	4.2	4.2
Sierra Leone	4.2	4.1	—	4.2
Upper Volta[a]	4.2	3.9	—	4.1
Ivory Coast	2.9	—	3.4	3.2
Nigeria	2.6	1.4	2.5	2.2

[a]Upper Volta is now Burkina Faso.

Source: International Monetary Fund, *Government Finance Statistics Yearbook,* Vol. 5 (Washington, D.C.: IMF, 1982), p. 43.

people, the demand for food will rise concomitantly. If more food is not forth-coming, food prices will rise, the real cost of labor will increase, and invest-ment will swing to more capital-intensive processes.[9] Thus, any strategy of de-velopment that entails more employment for the poor will also require the wage goods—particularly food—to support such economic growth.

Second, food and agriculture have important employment and growth link-ages with the rest of the economy. As the dynamics of these linkage effects are often missed, it is useful to emphasize them here. Technological change in agriculture raises the incomes of landowning farmers, who spend a large pro-portion of their new income on a wide range of nonagricultural goods and ser-vices. In Asia, for example, farmers typically spend 40 percent of their incre-ments to income on locally produced nonagricultural goods and services.[10] The small enterprises that produce such goods tend to be far more labor-intensive than any fertilizer factory or steel mill. They thus provide the rural poor with a whole spectrum of new nonagricultural employment oppor-tunities. This increases the effective purchasing power of the poor at the same time that it provides for new rounds of growth in the economy at large. As the poor begin to work regularly, they demand more and higher-valued foodstuffs. This helps to stimulate the demand for foodstuffs and to strengthen the need for more widespread technological change in agriculture.

Third, a focus on food and agriculture in development helps produce the export goods needed to fuel the growth process. To succeed, any development strategy requires the importation of large quantities of capital-intensive goods—for example, fertilizer and pesticides for agriculture, and steel and pet-rochemicals for industry. In most developing countries such imports must be paid for by increased exports. An agricultural strategy of development, which stresses the increased production of primary and consumer goods, is able to contribute to those export needs. In the early stages of development, a focus on agriculture helps produce those agricultural commodities that are needed to earn foreign exchange. Although it has sometimes been alleged that in-creased export crop production interferes with domestic food production, re-cent empirical evidence suggests that this is not so. In general, those countries that have been doing well in export crop production have also been successful at expanding domestic food production.[11]

Similarly, in the middle stages of development, an agricultural strategy en-courages the production of those labor-intensive consumer goods—such as clothing and textiles—in which developing countries possess a distinct com-parative advantage. Over time, firms specializing in the production of these consumer goods acquire the experience and efficiency needed to compete on the world market. Taiwan is a good example of a country that has used rapidly growing domestic demand to establish the type of labor-intensive industries that eventually came to compete so successfully on the world market.

The relationship between food production growth and employment growth is highly complementary and must be a major focus of policy. In Asia, with the Green Revolution under way, the focus needs to be on seeing that capital allocations are efficient in order to keep employment growth commensurate with the improved agricultural record. Several Asian countries are deficient in this respect. In Africa, the initial effort must be more production-oriented, simply to get the now-stagnant agricultural sector moving.

FOOD NEEDS, DEVELOPMENT ASSISTANCE, AND THE THIRD WORLD

In the past, efforts by the developed world to assist agricultural development in the Third World have drawn fire from a number of critics, including such people as field practitioners, journalists, and academics. Whatever their perspectives, these critics have usually shared the belief that development assistance to the Third World encourages the neglect of agriculture and places more resources in the hands of the ruling class at the expense of the rural poor. For example, writing on the topic of food aid, T. W. Schultz declared that "aid in kind . . . has the effect of increasing the capacity of the government that receives such aid to continue discriminating against its own agriculture."[12] A more extreme version of this view is contained in the writings of Frances Moore Lappé, who believes that all development assistance "actually increases hunger and repression by reinforcing the power of national and international elites who usurp the resources rightfully belonging to the hungry."[13]

Despite these attacks, development assistance remains a major source of foreign exchange and capital in many developing countries. In some of the developed countries, food aid receives substantial political support from domestic farm groups, who are anxious to dispose of commodity surpluses abroad. In other high-income countries, capital- and technical-assistance programs are justified on moral and humanitarian grounds. In all of these countries, development assistance receives the intellectual support of many thoughtful people, who, although acknowledging the validity of some of the preceding criticisms, still believe that such assistance can make a valuable contribution to equitable growth in the Third World.

Food aid can play two important roles in facilitating Third World economic growth. First, food aid can help developing countries overcome the temporary food demand-supply imbalances that accompany the development process. In these countries the surge in demand for food that occurs in the middle stages of development frequently outstrips the production capabilities of domestic agriculture. Second, food aid can be an important instrument of income transfer from rich people in developed countries to poor people in developing countries. Because the poor spend the bulk of additional income on food, it does little good to raise their incomes without providing added food. Food aid can thus back up national programs for benefiting the poor. It may do so through food-for-work and food-subsidy programs.

The developed world has its most immediate role to play in supplying commercial and food-aid imports to the Third World. Between 1961-1965 and 1973-1977, net food imports by the developing world increased nearly fivefold, from 5 million to 23 million tons per year (Table 3.6). Linear projections of per capita production and consumption dynamics in the Third World suggest that the level of such food imports will reach 80 million tons by the year 2000. The factors underlying such a dramatic rise in food imports to the developing world may be easily summarized. In the initial stages of development, people are generally quite poor. They wish to consume more food, yet are unable to do so because of low income. In these early stages, poverty causes high death rates and hence leads to only modest rates of population growth. The result is a 3 percent or less growth rate in the effective demand for food, which can generally be met through traditional processes of growth.

As development occurs, the population growth rate increases. But, even more important, income begins to grow rapidly, and a high proportion of that income is spent on food. These factors together increase the growth rate of demand for food to 4 percent or more annually. Such a rate of growth in food demand exceeds all but the most rapid rates of food production growth. For this reason, most countries in the high-growth, medium-income stage find it necessary to rely upon food imports to meet a significant portion of their rising

Table 3.6   Net Imports and Growth Rates for Imports and Exports, Food Staples, in Developing Countries, 1961–1965, 1973–1977, and Projections [a] of Net Imports to 2000

Country Group	Net Imports (million tons) 1961–65	1973–77	2000[a]	Annual Growth Rate (percent) 1961–65 to 1969–73 Exports	Imports
Developing Countries[b]	5.3	23.0	80.3	2.1	5.4
By Region					
Asia[b]	6.3	10.9	−17.9	2.5	3.5
North Africa/Middle East	3.6	10.6	57.3	−2.0	7.3
Sub-Saharan Africa	−0.9	2.9	35.5	−4.6	7.1
Latin America	−3.7	−1.4	5.4	3.6	6.9
By GNP Per Capita Growth Rate					
Less than 1.0%	1.6	8.0	39.5	−5.1	7.7
1.0% to 2.9%	2.8	−1.1	−48.5	1.8	3.3
3.0% to 4.9%	1.7	4.0	24.1	4.8	5.5
5.0% and Over	4.7	12.1	65.2	2.9	6.6

[a] The projections are based on differences between extrapolations of 1961–1977 country trend production and the aggregate projections of demand for food, animal feed, and other uses; projections of demand for animal feed were assumed to follow the country growth rates of meat consumption, i.e., no change in feeding efficiency. A basis for such adaptation is being pursued at the International Food Policy Research Institute, but the results are not yet available.

[b] Excluding the People's Republic of China.

Source: Calculated by Leonardo A. Paulino and others at the International Food Policy Research Institute, Washington, D.C.

demand for food. In the later stages of development, of course, population growth rates decline and growth in income begins to have less effect on the demand for food. Meeting demand growth then becomes more manageable, because by then food production growth rates have become institutionalized at relatively high levels.

Consistent with this analysis is the observation that rates of growth in food imports in the developing world seem to vary positively with the rate of per capita income increase. For example, according to the data in Table 3.6, developing countries with the highest rate of GNP per capita growth experienced a 6.6 percent annual rate of growth in food imports, as they more than doubled their level of imports during the period of this study.

The only exceptions to this finding are the slowest-growth countries (less than 1 percent GNP per capita increase). On the whole, the high level of food imports by these countries reflects the impact of food-aid and assistance programs. Between 1976 and 1978 these slowest-growth countries received about 35 percent of their total cereal imports from food aid. Many of these countries are located in sub-Saharan Africa, an area that has been beset by chronic food production shortfalls. The importance of food aid to these very poor African countries serves to highlight the importance of this particular policy instrument.

In previous years, much attention has been focused on the alleged disincentive effects of food aid on domestic agriculture in the Third World. Yet more recent empirical studies suggest that the negative impact of food aid on local agriculture has been overemphasized. For instance, Simon J. Maxwell and Hans W. Singer, in their review of twenty-one studies on the impact of food aid, found only seven cases reporting "significant" disincentive effects on either prices or production. On this basis, they conclude that any disincentive effect of food aid on local agriculture "can be and has been avoided by an appropriate mix of policy tools."[14]

Food aid must not be allowed to adversely affect local agriculture because increased domestic production still represents the best long-term solution to the food problems of the Third World. This is so more because of the role of agricultural growth in increasing rural employment than in providing the food itself. As noted above, progress toward this long-term solution will require much assistance by the high-income countries of the world. Most important, it will demand that these countries extend the technical and financial assistance needed to support an agricultural-oriented strategy of development in the Third World.

From a technical standpoint, scientists of all kinds—social, biological, and physical—need to lend their services to the Third World. Economists need to help developing country governments create the proper incentives to encourage technological change in agriculture, and political scientists and anthropologists need to analyze the socioeconomic impact of such change on different rural groups. Agronomists, plant breeders, and the like also must lend their services to the agricultural research systems in the developing world. These specialists need to contribute to building the type of educational and research facilities in the Third World that will enable these countries to educate their own agricultural experts. In the process of building indigenous facilities, it is important to note that the current revolution in the biological sciences makes going it alone quite inefficient. Over the next few decades the returns to close international collaboration in science will be quite high.

From a financial standpoint, more support is required to underwrite the costly infrastructure improvements—especially road and water improvements —needed to increase food production in the developing world. One recent estimate puts the capital costs of producing enough food to feed the Third World by the year 1990 at $98 billion.[15] Increased levels of development assistance from the high-income countries of the world would be of immense help in meeting this need.

The industrialized countries also need to take certain steps to help the developing countries to help themselves. They need, for instance, to liberalize the international trade environment in such a way so as to encourage labor-intensive exports by the Third World. A number of developing countries, particularly those in Asia, possess a significant comparative advantage in the exportation of clothing, textiles, and other inexpensive consumer goods. In many cases, the sale of such goods on the world market can help pay for the capital and technological imports that are needed to support the whole development process. Finally, international institutions such as the International Monetary Fund (IMF) need to revise their institutional structures for financing food trade to the developing countries of the world.

CONCLUSION

The key to meeting the world's food needs lies in stimulating the political and economic contacts between developing and developed countries. These countries need to cooperate in order to achieve the central goal of accelerating food production in the Third World. Expanded food production provides the means for eliminating the most extreme cases of hunger and malnutrition in the world. It also helps to provide the wage goods and the income multiplier effects needed to stimulate further economic growth. Because such economic growth is labor-intensive, it is also equity-oriented in the sense of providing more income and employment for low-income people. It is important to recognize that although a rural-based, employment-oriented development strategy has its limitations, from both a growth and an equity standpoint it is far superior to either the capital-intensive or the import-substitution strategy of growth.

Such a pattern of development requires an active partnership between the developing and the developed world. The developing world must recognize the positive role that agriculture can play in its development. It must attempt to stimulate agricultural output by revising investment, pricing, and exchange-rate policies. The developed world, in turn, must seek to encourage such policy reappraisals by making available the resources necessary to support an agricultural strategy of development in the Third World. The developed world must also be prepared to provide the food imports (and food aid) that, surprisingly, accompany the process of agricultural growth in the developing world. From the dynamics of such a partnership, the world could conceivably evolve into a place where adequate food is not just a right of all people but an accomplished fact.

NOTES

I appreciate the assistance of several colleagues at the International Food Policy Research Institute and particularly Richard H. Adams, Jr., for his substantial work on this chapter.

1. Peter Hazell, "Sources of Increased Variability in the World Cereal Production Since the 1960s."

2. John W. Mellor, "Food Price Policy and Income Redistribution in Low-Income Countries."

3. John W. Mellor and G. Desai, eds., *Agricultural Change and Rural Poverty.*

4. Ibid.

5. Uma Lele, "Terms of Trade, Agricultural Growth and Rural Poverty in Africa."

6. Y. K. Alagh and P. S. Sharma, "Growth of Crop Production: 1960/61 to 1978/79— Is It Decelerating?"

7. World Bank, *Accelerated Development in Sub-Saharan Africa: An Agenda for Action,* p. 55.

8. Lele, "Terms of Trade, Agricultural Growth and Rural Poverty in Africa."

9. John W. Mellor, *The New Economics of Growth: A Strategy for India and the Developing World.*

10. Peter Hazell and Ailsa Roell, *Rural Growth Linkages: Household Expenditure Patterns in Malaysia and Nigeria.*

11. Lele, "Terms of Trade, Agricultural Growth and Rural Poverty in Africa."

12. Theodore W. Schultz, "Effects of the International Donor Community on Farm People."

13. Frances Moore Lappé, Joseph Collins, and David Kinley, *Aid as Obstacle: Twenty Questions About Our Foreign Aid and the Hungry,* p. 121.

14. Simon J. Maxwell and Hans W. Singer, "Food Aid to Developing Countries: A Survey," p. 231.

15. Peter Oram, Juan Zapata, George Alibaruho, and Shyamai Roy, *Investment and Input Requirements for Accelerating Food Production in Low-Income Countries by 1990,* p. 15.

Comments on Chapter 3

F. Tomasson Jannuzi

My comments are inspired both by John Mellor's paper and by related discussions among the participants in the conference. It is evident that we have areas of convergence and divergence of emphasis and perception as we reflect on issues that have bearing on how food security can be assured for the people on this planet. I propose now to outline these areas of convergence and divergence, as I see them.

First, we can agree easily with the proposition that sustained increases in food production are necessary to contribute to food security on a global basis. However, some of us do not believe that sustained increases in aggregate food production, even when achieved, are sufficient to guarantee food security for people—particularly in agrarian regions of the world where the benefits of increased production tend to be concentrated in the hands of the *few* who have land (and other economic assets), rather than the *many* who have either insecure rights in land or no land and who find it difficult to find employment outside of agriculture.

Second, we can agree with John Mellor that food production increases must be derived increasingly from more intensive use of already cropped land, and that regionally, specific application of improved technology will be necessary to ensure increased yields per unit of land. However, some of us do not see more intensive use of land and the application of appropriate technology as being antithetical to agrarian reforms, especially land reforms that have the effect of redistributing rights in land. Agrarian reforms, when implemented, can actually facilitate the attainment of goals that John Mellor has emphasized during our discussions: namely, the more intensive use of land and the wider distribution of new technology in agriculture among landholders—even those having small holdings.

Third, we can agree that there must be a continuing policy commitment in lesser-developed countries to public investment in agriculture. The examples of Taiwan, Japan, and the Punjab (in India) confirm the benefits of such investment in agriculture. However, not all of us would attribute these food production "success stories" to a high rate of public investment alone. We would want to emphasize also the role of land reform and socioeconomic change in the cases of Taiwan and Japan. And, in the case of the Punjab, we would want to emphasize the benefits conferred by an historic land system in which ownership of land, investment in production, and labor on the land were united in family agriculture. Moreover, in this latter case, we would want to take note of the importance of investment in the agriculture of the Punjab by both the

60

Moguls and the British prior to Indian independence and the subsequent notable successes in agricultural production.

Fourth, we are united in supporting the call for the "rich nations" of the world to continue to extend financial and technical assistance to developing countries, particularly assistance designed to support strategies of development that emphasize the importance of agriculture. However, when we talk of sending specialists of all kinds to assist developing countries, some of us, although accepting the importance of agronomists, plant breeders, and the like, would extend the list of needed persons to emphasize the importance of anthropologists, economists, and political scientists—especially when those persons have language and area skills that are relevant to the peculiar needs of particular countries and regions. Some of us also would give primacy to local definition of need, rather than to definitions imposed by outsiders, whatever their qualifications.

Finally, we agree with the proposition that there is a continuing need to associate the attainment of food security with investments in "human capital"— that is, investments in educational institutions in developing countries that contribute to the dissemination of scientific knowledge and new technology to agriculturists and others. However, some of us would express concern about the quality and relevance of existing institutions in developing countries (including, for example, some "agricultural universities" established over the last twenty-five years in lesser-developed countries with the assistance of "land grant" universities in the United States) and would emphasize the importance of strengthening and making relevant those institutions for agricultural education before building new ones patterned after the old.

Michael F. Lofchie

Discussing John Mellor's presentation is a daunting task because he has been teaching all of us a great deal about the political economy of agricultural development for a long time. The most useful response, therefore, may simply be to draw attention to Mellor's most urgent theme—namely, the stark differences in the production and availability of food between Africa and other developing areas. For virtually all of the developing world, food production has either kept pace with population increase or exceeded it for the past twenty years or more. Sub-Saharan Africa is a tragic exception. Here, food production per capita has fallen by more than 1 percent per year over a period of twenty years or more. As a result, Africa's problems are of an entirely different order of magnitude than those of other Third World countries. Whereas other developing areas have serious problems of food security or nutritional balance, Africa has famines on an unutterably tragic scale. Indeed, were it not for the high visibility of famine in Africa during the past several years, the issue of food security in the Third World would not be nearly so pressing.

As Mellor also points out, increases in food production for the developing world will, in all likelihood, need to come about as a result of increasing yields, because these regions have for all practical purposes exhausted the possibilities of increasing their food production by expanding the land under cultivation. Past performance in generating increased production per hectare suggests that Africa's future is infinitely bleaker than that of other Third World regions. Other developing regions have done reasonably well in generating increased yields, but Africa's performance has been abysmal. Virtually all of its meager increase in food production has come from increases in the area harvested. The implication is horrific. As a result of a variety of factors—including population growth, urban expansion, environmental degradation, and political turbulence that has effectively isolated important producing regions—Africa may now be entering a phase of decreasing land availability. At the very least, it appears that the gap between the continent's rate of population increase, now crudely estimated at between 3 and 3.5 percent per year, and land availability will grow wider rather than narrower in the foreseeable future.

There is no magical recipe for producing increased yields. As Mellor points out, they come about only as a result of heavy investment in the agricultural sector: in physical infrastructure, in increased procurement and distribution of vital inputs such as fertilizers and pesticides, in crop research, and in education and extension services. Here too, Africa's record is extremely poor. The data in Table 3.5 indicate that in the late 1980s the median national expenditure on agriculture for fifteen African countries was only about 7.4 percent of the government budget. Significantly, Africa's most populous country, Nigeria, appears at the very bottom of this scale. And the national budgets of the continent's most populated countries, including Ethiopia, the Sudan, Angola, and Mozambique, are under such stress because of civil wars that agricultural expenditures have become wholly subordinated to expenditures on military equipment and personnel. Were these countries included, the median figure for agricultural investment in Africa would undoubtedly be still lower.

The international donor community is unlikely to be of great assistance in developing the agricultural sector. The vast majority of Africa's donors have become convinced that the continent's agricultural woes are the result of inappropriate government policies. Certain of the major donors are in the throes of the neoclassical economic revolution and this has led to a profound and all-pervasive belief that market-based policy reform will provide the basis for Africa's future agricultural growth. Current donor community wisdom holds that the continent's difficulty lies in the African governments' ubiquitous tendency to suppress producer prices, to overvalue exchange rates, to tolerate gross levels of mismanagement and corruption in agricultural parastatals, and to engage in forms of industrial development that sap the agricultural sector of vitally needed investment capital and production inputs.

There is a great deal to be said for these views. Indeed, it is extremely unlikely that African agriculture will begin to recover unless there are far-reaching reforms in all of these areas. The problem, of course, lies in the fallacy of opposites. The fact that Africa's agricultural decline has been brought about to a large degree by an excess of government intervention does not necessarily sustain the conclusion that the magic of the free marketplace will provide an adequate solution. Reform of Africa's agricultural policies is a necessary precondition for agrarian recovery. It is not sufficient. The countries that have fostered productive and successful agricultural systems feature a substantial degree of government involvement in their agricultural sectors. The governments of North America and the countries of the European Economic Community, for example, are deeply involved in the determination of agricultural prices and in the formulation of economically desirable production targets. The critical question for Africa, then, is not how to remove the state as an actor in the agricultural sector, but how to formulate a policy framework that combines government intervention with the forces of the market.

On this point, I am not as optimistic as Mellor, who appears to feel that once the appropriate policy reforms have been identified, the changes necessary to accelerate agricultural growth will take place. The most important feature of the majority of governments in independent sub-Saharan Africa has to do with existing political realities. Here, I am referring to the point made in the exceptionally important article in this volume by Cheryl Christensen (Chapter 4)—namely, that African nations appear to lack a coalition for policy reform. The existing policy framework is reflective of a particular configuration of political interests. For want of a better term, some analysts have used the concept of "urban bias" to describe this configuration. The point is that African governments have not pursued inappropriate agricultural policies out of a simple lack of awareness of what the best policies might be but, rather, out of a need to respond to powerful forces in their societies. It has yet to be demonstrated that the political forces that have driven Africa's agricultural policies in the past are now prepared to accept fundamental policy reform.

Part 2
Africa's Food Crisis

Cheryl Christensen

Food Security in Sub-Saharan Africa

Sub-Saharan Africa faces serious economic and agricultural problems. What some scholars have characterized as an economic malaise was punctuated in 1983-1985 by severe food emergencies. The drought that began in southern Africa in 1983 affected more than twenty countries by 1985, in several cases leading to large-scale starvation. Although these food emergencies were often triggered by "short-term" factors like drought or conflict, Africa's food emergencies are not a set of anomalies, but the very logical consequence of structural economic and agricultural problems.[1] A sustained decline in per capita food production and a corresponding decline in per capita food availability have severely reduced the "slack" available for coping with both physical and economic shocks in an environment in which both types of shocks have become more prevalent. The precarious economic and agricultural situation makes increased food and agricultural production imperative.

The nature and magnitude of the international economic and political factors that have affected the crisis in sub-Saharan Africa are discussed in Chapter 5, which also documents the impact these external factors have had on food and agricultural performance. This chapter focuses on the role internal factors (primarily food and agricultural policies) have played in shaping domestic agricultural performance and in creating strengths (or weaknesses) that have affected the countries' abilities to respond to an often inhospitable international economic environment.

In many countries, the recognized need for economic and agricultural change led to commitments to major policy reforms. An admittedly cursory examination of some recent attempts at policy change demonstrates that such changes are being articulated, and increasingly implemented, in countries with strikingly different political experiences. The success or failure of policy reform will have a major impact on the economic and agricultural performance of countries across sub-Saharan Africa. Yet, although the likely economic impacts of policy reforms have been extensively debated, far less attention has

67

been paid to the requirements of successfully implementing these policies in sub-Saharan Africa.[2] The implementation process is a critical determinant of the outcome of the policy reform process. Successfully implementing such policy changes under current African conditions will depend not only on the technical soundness of the policies themselves, but also on political factors, such as the nature of the regime, the distributional coalitions that support (and oppose) policy reforms, and the strategies used to handle both the opponents and beneficiaries of change.

AFRICA'S ECONOMIC AND FOOD PROBLEMS

Agricultural Production and "Natural Shocks"

Inadequate domestic food production has seriously weakened Africa's capacity for coping with both short-term food emergencies and the longer-term nutritional needs of its population. Per capita food production has fallen steadily since 1970 (Figure 4.1). As a result, the per capita production in most countries is substantially below what it was fifteen years ago. Grain imports by sub-Saharan African countries have increased at an average annual rate of 14 percent from 1966 to 1984, reaching a record of 10.7 million tons in 1984. Food aid accounted for a significant portion of this growth, increasing from about 100,000 tons in 1966 to 4 million tons in 1984 (Figure 4.2). Despite the rapid

Figure 4.1   Index of Per Capita Food Production in Sub-Saharan Africa, 1960–1985

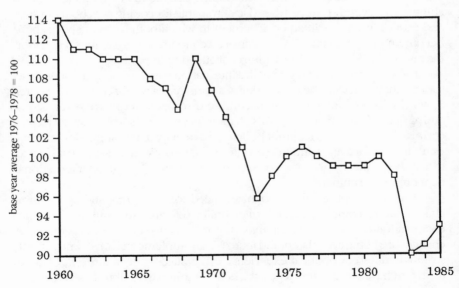

Source: Calculations made by Economic Research Service of the U.S. Department of Agriculture.

Figure 4.2 Sub-Saharan Africa Grain Imports, 1966–1985

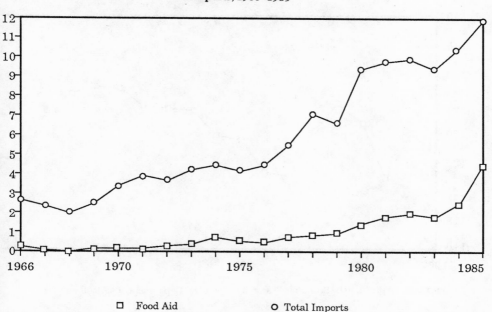

Source: Data provided by Economic Research Service, U.S. Department of Agriculture.

growth in both commercial and concessional imports, however, per capita cereal availability in 1980-1984 was lower than in 1966-1970 (Figure 4.3).

Even under the best of circumstances, assuming "average" production and equal distribution of food—which do not often occur in these countries—per capita calorie availability is now below the recommended levels for adequate nutrition in most countries of sub-Saharan Africa.[3] Recent analyses indicate that some 8.8 million tons of cereal imports would be required to bring per capita calorie levels up to recommended nutritional levels.[4] These figures do not imply that everyone is malnourished. The prevalence and location of under-nutrition depend on food distribution patterns, which generally reflect differences in purchasing power, location, and seasonality.[5] Most undernutrition occurs in rural areas, although recent economic pressures may have increased undernutrition among the urban poor. A chronic nutritional gap of this size does mean, however, that adequate nutrition could not be achieved by redistributing currently available supplies of food. Additional production, or imports, would be required.

The implications of sub-Saharan Africa's food production trends are stark. If the recent trends in per capita food production were to continue, sub-Saharan Africa's total grain imports would have to increase by 40 percent between 1984 and 1990 simply to hold per capita cereal availability at 1980-1984

Figure 4.3   Sub-Saharan Africa Per Capita Grains Situation, 1967–1985

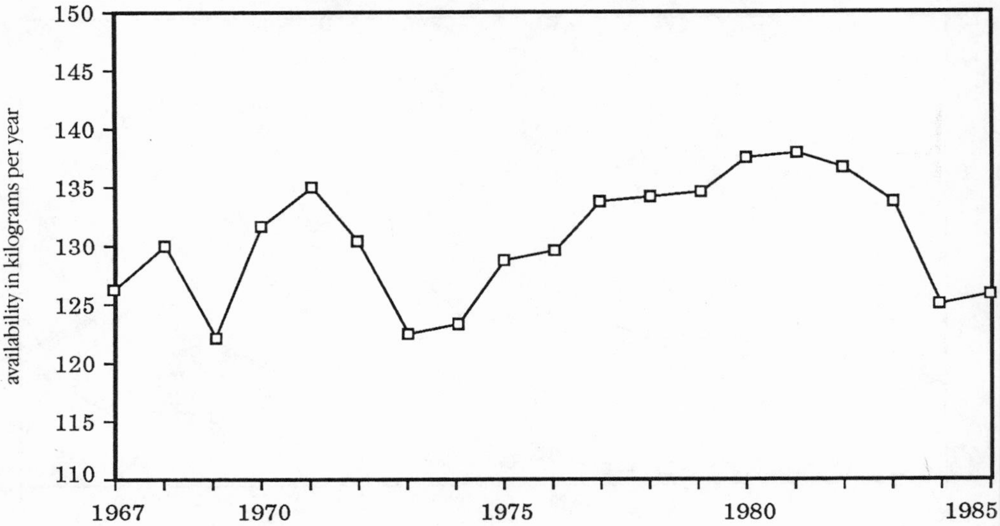

Source: Data provided by Economic Research Service, U.S. Department of Agriculture.

levels.[6] Sub-Saharan Africa would thus become far more dependent on imports —quite possibly on food aid—to fill its chronic food gap.

Government food production policies, and often more general agricultural policies, have contributed to the poor performance of food and agricultural production, although they are certainly not the only reason for faltering production.[7] The nature of these policies has been discussed extensively elsewhere.[8] Many governments have reduced farmers' incentives to produce food for the commercial domestic market, often by holding official producer prices low, creating institutions (parastatals) to control marketing channels, creating input delivery systems that misallocate scarce agricultural inputs, underinvesting in the agricultural sector, and pursuing inappropriate macroeconomic and trade policies.

One important, unintended, consequence of such policies and the attendant decline in per capita production has been to seriously weaken the ability of sub-Saharan African countries to deal with "natural shocks," such as drought, which frequently create sharp drops in production in systems where most agriculture is rain-fed. An analysis of eleven countries that have experienced recent food emergencies shows that production has been extremely variable. The probability of a serious shortfall in availability ranges between 0.11 and 0.38 (Table 4.1).[9] Countries' responses to such dramatic shortfalls were varied. In general, countries that were more self-reliant used trade to cover a greater portion of the shortfall, whereas countries that were already import-dependent (and facing serious foreign exchange constraints) changed import patterns less when domestic production declined.[10] Hence, availability declined sharply.

Inadequate aggregate production also exacerbates distributional in-equities, making severe deprivation (or starvation) more likely. This occurs for two main reasons. First, as aggregate supplies fall, and prices rise, the wealthier portion of the population will adjust its consumption relatively little. This forces a greater burden of adjustment on the poor. Analysis from the U.S. Department of Agriculture's Economic Research Service (USDA/ERS) indicates that if the upper 30 percent of the population were able to avoid adjusting con-sumption during a food emergency, a shortfall of only 5 percent in aggregate would translate into a 20 percent decline in already low availability in the lower 30 percent of the income distribution.[11]

Second, most rural food emergencies arise directly from production shortfalls. Although the urban areas in many African countries have "structural" food-aid requirements, which are regularly reflected in governments' request for food aid, most rural areas are not regular recipients of imported foodstuffs. It is often difficult to deliver food supplies to more remote rural areas. When production shortfalls occur, and exceed what can be handled through local storage, food emergencies that are difficult to detect and alleviate arise. Most rural populations have developed mechanisms for coping with production in-stability (including on-farm stocks of foodstuffs and substituting "famine foods" for more basic elements of their diet), but these mechanisms have often been weakened by the prolonged decline in aggregate production. The weaknesses

Table 4.1   Per Capita Growth Rates and Probabilities of Availability Shortfall: Analy-sis of Time Series Data, 1966–1984[a]

Country	Food Availability Growth Rate[b]	Probability of Availability Shortfall	
		0–5 Percent Below Trend	6 Percent or More Below Trend
	(1) Coefficient	(2)	(3)
		Percent	
Ethiopia	−0.65	0.0	33.4
Kenya	−0.13	11.2	33.4
Lesotho	0.31	5.6	38.9
Mali	−1.68	50.0	11.2
Mozambique	−2.72	27.8	22.3
Niger	0.23	11.2	27.8
Senegal	10.59	38.9	22.3
Somalia	1.52	33.4	27.8
Sudan	0.08	22.3	33.4
Zambia	−0.65	16.7	38.9
Zimbabwe	−0.78	33.4	11.2

[a]All cereals combined

[b]Regression coefficient of time trend

Source: Shahla Shapouri, Arthur J. Dommen, and Stacey Rosen, *Food Aid and the African Food Crisis,* FAER No. 221 (Washington, D.C.: U.S. Department of Agriculture, Economic Research Service, June 1986).

in these mechanisms become quite clear when drought persists beyond one year.[12] Food security for the rural population in many African countries will depend on general increases in food production, not on import-based systems of national food security.

If chronic production problems have weakened countries' abilities to cope with negative natural shocks, inappropriate policy implementation and weak administrative systems have also meant that most countries respond poorly to "positive" natural shocks (for example, surplus production in bumper years). Governments have frequently responded to food crises with dramatic increases in producer prices. High prices for foodstuffs in "informal" markets during shortages further encourage farmers to try to increase production.[13] Increased plantings, when coupled with good weather, have led to local "surpluses" that governments have been unable to procure and store. This pattern was apparent in 1985/86 throughout eastern and southern Africa, where good weather coincided with large increases in the planting of food crops affected by previous years' drought. The Sudan provides the most dramatic example. The land planted to sorghum and millet is estimated to have increased by more than 1 million acres, much of the increase occurring in the large mechanized sector where farmers brought large acres of previously uncultivated land into production. As a result, the 1985/86 crop is likely to exceed 5 million tons, almost four times the 1984/85 drought-damaged crop and 30 percent more than the previous record production in 1981.[14] Similarly, maize production in Kenya increased dramatically, as large plantings coincided with good weather. Production in 1985/86 is estimated to be 2.6 million tons, 53 percent above the previous drought-damaged crop. Pressure on storage facilities is already apparent, and Kenya is seeking to export the remaining quantities of imported (yellow) maize purchased during the food emergency. Zimbabwe and Somalia also have experienced significantly larger crops, with Zimbabwe planning to export limited quantities of its surplus white maize to South Africa.

Under such conditions, governments frequently have difficulty in supporting higher prices. Past surpluses have led to refusals to purchase from farmers once storage capacity is exceeded, delayed payments for purchases actually made, and attempts to reduce the price paid by imposing more exacting quality standards. As a result, farmers are not provided with consistent incentives to produce for the commercial market, and production that might offset future production shortfalls is exported at a loss, used in local "swap arrangements," or lost because of inadequate storage facilities and poor stock management.

Economic Development and International Shocks

These trends in food production coincide with a decade of economic problems for many of the sub-Saharan African countries. African economic and social conditions began to deteriorate in the 1970s. Although GNP grew moderately throughout the 1960s and even into the 1970s, from 1980 on growth in GDP for sub-Saharan Africa was negative. As a result, real per capita income is now lower than it was in 1970.[15]

International economic shocks are responsible for a significant portion of the downturn in sub-Saharan Africa's economic performance. These shocks created new, and in many cases very substantial, adjustment burdens, which frequently exacerbated domestic policy weaknesses at the same time that they made appropriate policy responses more imperative. The policies countries followed to cope with the initial oil shocks and the first global recession (1974/75) significantly affected their economic performance and their capability to cope with the more damaging second global recession (1980-1983).[16]

The 1974/75 recession was sharp but short in industrial countries, where GDP rose 6.1 percent in 1973, then slowed to 0.8 percent in 1974, and fell again to only 0.4 percent in 1975, then rose to 4.7 percent in 1976.[17] Developing countries in general entered the recession with higher growth rates than the industrialized countries and were less severely affected than the industrialized nations. GDP growth in developing countries was 7.4 percent in 1973, falling to 5.9 percent in 1974 and to 4 percent in 1975 before rebounding to 6.3 percent in 1976. Although the slowdown in growth hurt all non-oil-exporting developing countries, the impact was less severe for developing countries who were exporters of manufactured products and most serious for non-oil commodity exporters, including most countries in sub-Saharan Africa.

By contrast, the 1980-1983 recession was not as sharp in industrial countries, but it lasted longer. GDP growth was 3.3 percent in 1979, 1.3 percent in 1980, 1.3 percent in 1981, 0.5 percent in 1982, and 2.3 percent in 1983. Developing countries as a whole, however, were more severely affected than they were in the earlier recession. Their GDP growth was lower than that of the industrialized countries before the recession began. GDP growth was 2.5 percent in 1980, 2.4 percent in 1981, 1.9 percent in 1982, and 1 percent in 1983.

Low-income sub-Saharan Africa was affected more severely than other developing regions in both recessions. Its GDP growth rate in the 1973-1979 period was only 2.1 percent (less than the population growth rate). Weak performance during the first recession, in turn, made sub-Saharan Africa more vulnerable to the second recession, whose impact on developing countries in general was far more severe. The second recession had devastating results. Sub-Saharan Africa's GDP growth was lower than that for developing countries in general at the start of the recession, and it plummeted, falling from 1.3 percent in 1980 to 1.2 percent in 1981 to 0.5 percent in 1982, and to a catastrophic -0.1 percent in 1983.

Leaving aside the oil-exporting countries (whose prosperity rested almost exclusively on higher oil prices), developing countries that performed well economically did so for two basic reasons: They maintained or increased savings rates (often via open policies that facilitated adjustment); and they maintained or increased growth of exports, especially manufactured exports. Differences in export performance were associated with open domestic trade policies that permitted an effective adjustment.[18]

Low-income sub-Saharan Africa did not, in general, meet either of these two conditions. There was a general deterioration of public financing and a collapse of savings. Savings fell from 13.4 percent of GDP in 1970 to 7.5 percent in 1975. This figure was less than one-third the rate for all developing countries and contrasts especially sharply with low-income Asia, where savings were 24.3 percent of GDP. Despite an inflow of foreign capital, the rate of capital accumulation also fell. The pattern in the second recession was similar. Savings as a percent of GDP fell to 5.9 percent (1981) and was at about one-quarter of the level of savings in all developing countries, including low-income Asia. Sub-Saharan Africa's debt, which has increased from $9.5 billion in 1973 to $60.5 billion in 1984, became increasingly difficult to service. Per capita income declined every year after 1980 for low-income sub-Saharan Africa.

Trade performance was also poor. In part, this reflects the poor growth in primary product markets. World primary product exports grew only 0.9 percent between 1973 and 1979, compared with a 10.6 percent growth rate for manufactures. The decline in primary commodity prices over the last decade was not, however, a constant one. The period's two commodity cycles have been associated with periods of significant price increases, as well as rapid declines. During the first cycle (1972-1977), prices increased significantly, in both real and nominal terms. The decline in prices during the decrease phase was far less than the earlier increase and the recovery phase more than compensated for the decline, leaving both real and nominal prices above their 1972 levels. During the second cycle (1978-1984), however, there was less growth in both real and nominal prices during the increase phase, and the recovery phase inadequately compensated for falling prices during the decrease phase (Table 4.2). Sub-Saharan Africa's total terms of trade declined by 13 percent during the second commodity cycle.

However, low-income Africa did especially poorly within this admittedly weak niche. Production of agricultural export crops was held back by both adverse physical conditions and domestic policies. Hence, sub-Saharan Africa's export volume fell at an average rate of 1.3 percent between 1973 and 1980.

Table 4.2   Commodity Price Cycles (% Change in Commodity Prices)

	1972–74 Increase	1974–75 Decrease	1976–77 Recovery	
Nominal ($)		131	−26	+50
Real		54	−32	+36

	1978–79 Increase	1981–82 Decrease	1983–84 Recovery	
Nominal ($)		31	−28	+17
Real		2	−19	·+20

Source: IMF, *World Economic Outlook* (Washington, D.C.: IMF, April 1985).

Low-income sub-Saharan Africa therefore lost market shares to other regions of the developing world. In several instances, government responses to the positive shocks (price increases) weakened the capacity to cope with subsequent declines, as expenditures stimulated by the boom period continued to grow despite the downturn in commodity prices.

A few countries with relatively open economies and policies that supported an export orientation were able to do somewhat better, although they still faced serious economic problems. Although policies could not remove the very real limitations and uncertainty associated with the export of primary commodities, they did make it possible for selected countries to reap the benefits of the admittedly "short-lived" upturns in these markets. Hence Kenya, with supportive agricultural export policies and adequate marketing infrastructure has been able to take advantage of cyclical price increases for its major export commodities (coffee and tea). In contrast, Tanzania, with policies that discourage agricultural exports, and with declining quality and serious marketing problems tied to the operation of inefficient parastatals, has seen its export earnings plummet, even though it participates in the same commodity markets as Kenya. Increased export earnings fueled substantially greater growth in Kenya and provided an enhanced capability for dealing with the severe drought of 1984-1985.

In 1983, the impact of domestic and international shocks had generated strong domestic economic pressure and an international constituency for policy reforms, a matter we explore in detail later. The net effect of the past decade has been to leave African countries with fewer domestic resources for coping with international economic problems at the same time that the growing seriousness of those problems has increased the pressure on governments to produce economic improvements. Serious balance-of-payments problems and increased debt levels have led more countries into situations in which they must reschedule their debts. Agreement with the IMF is effectively a prerequisite for such reschedulings. In addition, both the World Bank and bilateral donors such as the United States have become increasingly involved in programs to support economic and agricultural policy reform.

THE POLICY REFORM AGENDA

In most of the countries of sub-Saharan Africa there is a general recognition that the situation that prevailed in agriculture for the last decade and characterized the economic environment for the last five or six years not only is unsustainable but must be changed. The Economic Commission for Africa's *Joint Economic Report on Africa* (1985) stresses the role of mistaken policies in decreasing agricultural output, fostering inefficient parastatal structures, and eroding incentives for private entrepreneurship. The OAU's (Organization of African Unity) July 1985 summit meeting similarly stressed the importance of agriculture and the need for policy changes to spur increases in economic growth. The World Bank's analyses of African agriculture have consistently stressed the need for policy reform, as has the "policy dialogue" of the U.S. Agency for International Development (Aid).[19] Although there is a growing consensus that changes must be made, there remain disputes about what form these changes should take.[20] The range of policy reforms being discussed includes changes in food and agricultural policies, changes in macroeconomic policies, and changes in institutions and structures.

Food and Agricultural Policy

Virtually all policy reform programs focus on the need to increase food and agricultural production. Policy changes, therefore, focus heavily on ways to create greater incentives to domestic agricultural production. The initial phases of the policy reform concentrated heavily on changes in agricultural price policy, primarily because the pervasive practice of holding down prices for officially marketed foodstuffs and key export crops was a major disincentive to increased production. Real prices for both foodstuffs and export commodities fell in many countries, turning the internal terms of trade against the rural sector. More favorable prices have been in many instances the necessary initial step in agricultural policy reform.

Although pricing policy has played, and continues to play, a key role in stimulating production, it is generally recognized that agricultural policy reform does not mean simply "getting prices right." Nonprice factors also affect producer incentives. These include the availability of desired consumer goods, as well the institutional support required to evoke a large supply response to improved prices, such as an effective marketing system, transportation, and financing. These institutional improvements must, in turn, be translated in practice into more timely reliable input supplies, the ability of a wide range of farmers to more effectively market agricultural products, and improved capability of governments and markets to deal more effectively with the variability of rain-fed agriculture. The latter issue is particularly important, for many of the failures in coping with natural shocks as well as policy implementation failures are traced to inadequate or inappropriate responses to production variability.

There is now abundant evidence that farmers respond quickly to increases in real producer prices for particular commodities. Analysis of cereal production in eleven low-income countries in sub-Saharan Africa, spanning a variety of institutional arrangements, demonstrates that price elasticities for major cereals are generally positive and significant (Table 4.3). In virtually all cases, however, weather remains the single most important factor affecting overall production levels. The interaction between price increases and weather is a powerful one. Food prices, official and unofficial, rose significantly in virtually all countries affected by drought in 1984/85. Higher prices, in combination with a return of "normal" weather, substantially increased staple cereal produc-

Table 4.3   Price Elasticities of Production and Marketed Surplus

Country and Crop	Of Production Short run	Of Production Long run	Of Area Short run	Of Area Long run
Production:				
Ethiopia				
Wheat	.53[a]	.72	.76[a]	1.26
Corn	.47[a]	.67	.38[a]	.38
Millet and Sorghum	.28	.35	.28	.51
Teff	.28	.28	.11	.37
Barley	.19	.31	−.03	—
Kenya				
Wheat	.46[a]	1.12	.29[a]	1.07
Corn	.40[a]	1.05	.17[a]	.66[a]
Millet	.39[a]	.63	.35	.68
Sorghum	.07	.07	−.02	—
Lesotho				
Corn	−.25	−.25	.16[a]	.16
Sorghum	.13	.15	.15	.15
Mali				
Corn	−.04	—	.07	.13
Rice	.34[a]	.34	.23[a]	.23
Millet and Sorghum	.35[a]	.35	.20[a]	.20
Niger				
Millet	.14[a]	.21	.09	.14
Sorghum	.11	.17	.29[a]	.88
Senegal				
Rice	.32	.32	.46[a]	.46
Millet	.11	.14	.40[a]	.40
Somalia				
Corn	.10[a]	.13	.08	.16
Sorghum	.03	.04	.14[a]	.14
Sudan				
Wheat	.34[a]	1.17	.28[a]	1.17
Corn	.31[a]	.94	.23	.30
Sorghum	.22[a]	.33	.33[a]	.34
Zambia				
Corn	.61[a]	.71	.31[a]	.57
Millet and Sorghum	.21[a]	.33	.06	.21
Zimbabwe				
Wheat	.34[a]	.92	.40[a]	1.30
Corn	.36[a]	.36	.92[a]	1.09
Sorghum	.43[a]	.49	.21[a]	.36
Marketed Surplus:				
Kenya				
Corn	1.13	n.a.	n.a.	n.a.
Zambia				
Corn	1.69	n.a.	n.a.	n.a.
Zimbabwe				
Corn	1.42	n.a.	n.a.	n.a.

— = Negligible or not significant
n.a. = Not applicable
[a] = Significant at 90 percent level

Source: Estimates calculated by the Economic Research Service of the United States Department of Agriculture.

tion in virtually all countries.

Marketed cereal production is even more price responsive. In countries where adequate marketing infrastructure exists, the price elasticity of marketed cereal production is three to four times that of total production (Table 4.3). Even in countries with poorer marketing infrastructure, marketed production is responsive to price increases. Officially marketed cereal production in Tanzania declined steadily, in response to both inadequate official prices and the negative impact of parastatal marketing practices. Over the past two years, however, official producer prices for maize have more than doubled in nominal terms and have increased 48 percent in real terms. Officially marketed production increased, albeit moderately, in 1985 for the first time in six years.

The impact of pricing policy in stimulating a general increase in overall agricultural production is much more difficult to determine. In general, increases depend on either drawing additional resources into agriculture or increasing productivity. Although some African countries face increasingly serious constraints on quality arable land, in most countries labor constraints which inhibit land clearing and the ability to perform critical peak-period activities such as planting, weeding, and harvesting, are more significant medium-term production constraints. In some countries—particularly where a combination of increasing agricultural prices and deteriorating urban conditions is able to reverse rural-urban resources—additional labor may flow into the agricultural sector. There is some evidence that this has begun to occur in Nigeria. In other instances, removing other constraints to land preparation may stimulate significant increases in cultivated acreage, as occurred in Sudan's mechanized sector in 1986 when higher food prices and the availability of fuel permitted an additional 2 million acres to be brought into production.

Sustained increases in productivity come primarily from technological changes flowing from agricultural research. Improved pricing policies can make a medium-term contribution to increasing productivity in cases in which known technologies are not being fully utilized because they were not profitable at previous price levels. In most instances, however, realizing these medium-term gains depends critically on the availability of key inputs (such as fertilizer) or investment in rehabilitating deteriorating production facilities (e.g., replanting stands of permanent cash crops). Given the absence of "new" technologies for much of African agriculture, investment in longer-term research will be critical to sustained gains in the agricultural sector.

Food policy is broader than agricultural policy as it also focuses on consumption and nutritional issues.[21] A major concern in policy reform dialogue has been the reduction or elimination of consumer subsidies, which have frequently (but not always) reflected an urban bias. Key elements of the discussion have focused on the need to reduce consumer subsidies (which have frequently served as the basis for derived agricultural pricing) in the process-ending systems that were frequently unable to provide guaranteed supplies of low-cost food. The initial steps on removing consumer subsidies frequently took the form of increasing official consumer prices, as has been the case in many East African countries since 1980. In most cases, however, such subsidies have been embedded in marketing systems that provided for heavy control by government parastatals, and reducing the impact of such systems has been an important component of policy reform (as in Guinea, Madagascar, and Mali). Increasingly, the issue is not one of setting prices that reduce subsidies, but of revamping the institutional structures within which government intervention in pricing occurs.

The Macroeconomic Policy Agenda

The second policy reform agenda focuses on macroeconomic policies, which are important not only for their impact on agriculture, but for their wider economic impact. These policy prescriptions generally follow the lines of the "neoliberal" model discussed by Alain de Janvry in Chapter 10 and broadly conform to IMF conditionality requirements.[22] The macroeconomic policy dialogue to date has emphasized the need for changes in the exchange rate, generally to end the overvaluation of African currencies.

Real effective exchange rates in sub-Saharan Africa appreciated significantly in the 1970s and early 1980s, both in higher-income countries (such as Nigeria) and in the lowest-income countries (Figure 4.4). Other developing regions did not experience the same appreciation and, in most instances, moved to correct initial appreciations much earlier. Hence, the adjustments necessary in sub-Saharan Africa are large, both in relation to present currency levels and in relation to the adjustment requirements in other parts of the developing world.

The agricultural sector has a large stake in the outcome of exchange-rate adjustments. Devaluation will, in principle, impact agriculture in two ways. First, devaluation will stimulate export crop production. Because most commodities are traded on hard currency denominated markets, the impact on domestic production depends critically on how much of the impact of devaluation is passed back to producers and how quickly they can respond to shifts in relative prices. Second, devalution will raise the price of imported food, which (if the price rise is passed on to farmers and consumers) should also stimulate domestic food production.

As de Janvry's analysis (Chapter 10) of Latin America demonstrates, however, devaluation does not have a uniform impact on the agricultural sector, or on producers with different resource endowments and production practices. Far less analysis has been done on the differential impacts of devaluation within the agricultural sector in sub-Saharan Africa. Preliminary analyses suggest, however, that the exchange-rate changes may powerfully affect the profitability of alternative export crops. In Sudan, for example, cotton has traditionally been a major source of foreign exchange, produced mostly on large irrigated schemes.[23] Cotton production on the irrigated schemes depends heavily on im-

Figure 4.4   Real Effective Exchange Rate Indexes in Developing Countries, 1971–1984

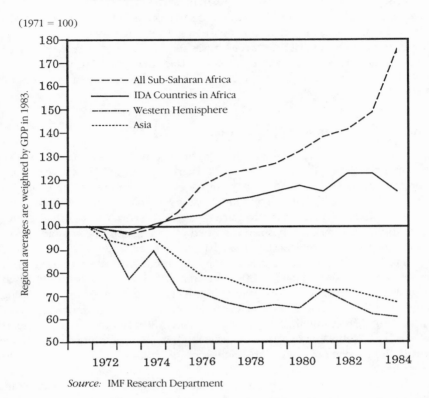

(1971 = 100)

Source: IMF Research Department

ported inputs—particularly fuel, but also fertilizer and pesticides. If Sudan devaluated its currency fully, and if the effects of the devaluation were passed through to the agricultural sector, crops produced under rain-fed conditions (including sorghum, groundnuts, and gum arabic) could provide a higher net foreign exchange earning than could the irrigated sector cotton.[24]

The experience with devaluation pass-throughs has varied substantially. In Kenya, where export commodities are not heavily taxed and prices reflect world markets, the effects of devaluation have been passed through to farmers, permitting significant income gains for coffee and tea producers in 1985/86. In the case of Sudan, the full cost of fuel and inputs for cotton production was not passed on to the irrigated schemes, significantly increasing subsidies to these schemes and complicating efforts to introduce new scheme management systems.[25] In Uganda, which devalued massively between 1980 and 1983, the effects of devaluation were poorly transmitted to the agricultural sector. Prices to coffee farmers increased, but by far less than the devaluation. Changes in the mechanics of taxing coffee exports, coupled with the use of a dual exchange-rate system as a means of generating government revenue, significantly increased the taxation of coffee producers. By 1982/83 the government was obtaining 33 percent of its recurrent revenue from coffee, compared with 3.7 percent prior to devaluation.[26]

The impact of broad macroeconomic factors and exchange rates on agricultural policy may be seen clearly in the experiences of Nigeria, which has consistently resisted devaluation. Government pricing policy shifted dramatically in favor of agriculture from the mid-1970s through the early 1980s, as the government eliminated its taxation of agricultural export crops and provided floor prices for basic cereals that were generally above the world market prices (calculated at the official exchange rate). In the 1960s, the average tax burden on cocoa, palm kernals, groundnuts, and cotton ranged between 15 and 30 percent. However, agricultural export taxation was phased out following the oil boom (1973/74) and the restructuring of marketing boards (1977).

By 1982/83, producer prices for traditional export crops were near (for cocoa) or above (for rubber, palm kernel, palm oil, groundnuts, cotton) the world market price at the official exchange rate. Financial subsidies to producers were substantial, ranging from 16 percent of the producer price for cocoa to a high of 78 percent of the producer price for palm kernel. The government's "floor price" for domestically produced food crops was also above world market prices, calculated at the official exchange rate. However, until recent trade restrictions flowing from severe foreign exchange constraints, producer prices were under pressure from imports, made cheaper by the overvalued naira.

As a result of the offsetting influence of macroeconomic policies, higher prices and financial subsidies did not adequately compensate producers. Producer prices, if calculated at the black-market rate would have been substantially lower. The exchange-rate overvaluation, coupled with the impact of increased oil revenue, created powerful disincentives for production, a situation common in other oil-producing countries suffering from "Dutch disease"[27] (see glossary). Between 1973 and 1983, expenditures from oil revenues—particularly on construction—drew workers from the agricultural sector and raised the wages of those remaining in rural areas. Increased oil earnings stimulated an appreciation of the naira, which was reinforced by the government policy of not devaluating to counter high domestic inflation rates. The exchange rate appreciated by 80 percent in real terms between 1973 and 1980 and increased another 34 percent between 1980 and 1984. The cost of production, therefore, rose substantially, while the overvalued exchange rate made production less lucrative, for food crops facing competition from "cheap" imports as well as for export crops. Only the severe foreign exchange constraints in 1984-1986, which triggered import bans on a wide range of foodstuffs (including corn and rice), changed the incentives for domestic food production.

Nigeria's reluctance to adjust its exchange rate is, however, not indicative of the pattern in many sub-Saharan African countries. Over the past five years there has been fairly significant change both in nominal and real exchange rates. There are a number of countries where the change in the last three years has involved a real exchange-rate adjustment of more than 20 percent. This includes some countries that have recently undertaken wider policy changes (such as Ghana, Uganda, Zaire, Ivory Coast, and Benin) and also countries (such as Kenya, Botswana, Togo, Mali, and Burkina Faso) that are near the 20 percent level.

The Institutional/Structural Policy Agenda

The institutional policy reform agenda has focused heavily on the state's role in the economy in general as well as the inefficiency and cost of the institutions created to support this role (parastatals). The state plays a larger role in the economy in sub-Saharan African than in any other developing region. There are a variety of historical reasons for this. In most instances, however, countries lacked the trained personnel to manage state involvement. In addition, these organizations created abundant opportunities for "rents," which constitute a major drain on government finances.

Consensus on the need for institutional changes has emerged more slowly than in some other areas (e.g., the need to examine agricultural pricing policies). Nevertheless, a variety of countries, generally in the context of financial stabilization programs, have begun to address the need to reduce public consumption, limit (or reduce) government employment, and eliminate or rationalize public sector enterprises. Public sector consumption in low-income sub-Saharan Africa declined in real terms by 1.5 percent a year between 1981-1984, compared with a real increase of almost 5 percent per annum between 1975-1980. Some of this decline reflects reductions in government employment. The remainder reflects declines in maintenance, equipment purchases, and a deterioration in public services.

Reducing government employment, and eliminating or reforming inefficient parastatals, is increasingly becoming a pragmatic requirement for countries facing severe, sustained, economic hardships. Major efforts to reduce or restructure public sector involvement are under way in Ghana, Senegal, Mali, and Zaire. Guinea, in a sweeping change of policy, has undertaken a thoroughgoing program to reduce government involvement in the economy, including the privatization of the banking industry and rice marketing. Madagascar has privatized the rice trade, and in 1986 Kenya permitted private traders to purchase and market cereals on a limited basis. In other countries (including Rwanda, Mali, Somalia, and Togo), governments abandoned their policies of guaranteeing public sector employment for secondary-school and university graduates and are reducing the portion of the budget spent for salaries.

In most instances, these programs are in their initial phases, and there is relatively little upon which to base an evaluation of their results. Because they frequently imply increasing economic hardship for previously privileged urban groups, however, their implementation entails real political risks in addition to the economic uncertainty inherent in moving toward a less controlled environment.

THE POLITICAL ECONOMY OF POLICY IMPLEMENTATION

Economic factors may force changes in policy, but politics drives elite perceptions of the acceptability of economic advice and shapes the path to adjustment. The importance of political structures and strategies in determining the success or failure of attempts to implement policy change is tacitly recognized if not extensively analyzed. In a review of its standby arrangements and Extended Fund Facilities, the IMF concluded that "political constraints" or "weak administrative systems" (or both) accounted for 60 percent of the breaches of credit ceilings.[28] Pointing to the importance of such political factors does not, however, "explain" the implementation outcomes. As Stephen Haggard correctly notes, "Economists explain success and failure in meeting plan targets by calling on such institutional and political factors as 'capacity' and 'will.' These are, of course, things to be explained, not an explanation."[29]

Robert Bates's initial work found that government revenue needs, some level of commitment to import-substituting industrialization as a development strategy, and the perceived requisites of political support strategies explained much of the attractiveness of flawed economic policies.[30] If his conclusions are broadly correct, then the required policy changes are those that demand the reduction or elimination of rents to favored groups, including government officials, urban residents, civil servants and politically influential larger farmers (see Table 4.4). This raises two important questions: Can these policies be implemented effectively within the current political/economic environment? Would such policies be maintained, in the event that economic conditions improved and/or the role of external agencies declined?

Bates's work gives no indication of the conditions under which policy changes might occur or the requisites of successfully implementing them. To move toward a better understanding of the distributional coalitions that might form in support of policy reform involves modifying and elaborating his framework in several ways.[31] First, it is necessary to differentiate among regimes and identify the regime characteristics that influence the implementation of policy change. Second, in order to characterize the distributional coalitions behind alternative agricultural policies, it is necessary to differentiate among groups within general categories, such as "government" or the "industrial sector," as well as to take into account the interaction between economic and social (e.g., ethnic, religious) identities in generating politically salient interests. Finally, attention must be paid to the strategies used to implement specific policies.

There is a significant literature—much of it reflecting Latin American experience—that suggests that major policy reforms, along the neoliberal lines

Table 4.4   Agriculture Policy Coalitions and Benefits

Policy	Beneficiary	Political Expectations	Uses	Secondary Benefits
Marketing boards (parastatals)	Government	Generate and control domestic revenue	Diversion of "stabilization" funds to other purposes (e.g., loans to finance development)	Industry (often with heavy state involvement) Labor aristocracy
		Provide low cost urban food supply	Marketing controls	Urban consumers
		Expanded control of foreign exchange earnings	Support consumption and investment priorities	Urban consumers and industrial sector
		Creation of employment and patronage	Increased administrative intervention in markets	Administrative bureaucrats
Export commodity prices below world market	Government	Expanded domestic and foreign exchange earnings	Export taxes, marketing monopolies	Urban consumers and industrial sector
			Administrative bureaucracies (via employment and "rents")	
Low food prices	Government	Political stability	Food subsidies	Urban consumers
			Overvalued exchange rates	Urban consumers
			Licensing arrangements	Private traders and administrative officials (via "rents")
Intervention in input markets	Government	Increased production under government control	Subsidies on fertilizer, credit, and machinery	State farms; larger farmers; administrative bureaucrats (via "rents")
			Import preferences for selected inputs (e.g., machinery)	Larger farmers, imports
		Political support/patronage	Selective access to subsidized inputs	Larger, politically salient farmers

described by de Janvry, are adopted and successfully implemented by authoritarian regimes. In part, this is explained by the fact that such regimes are often based on domestic political coalitions (large landholders, the military, selected portions of the industrial sector) whose economic interests are served by these policies. Chapter 10 in this volume analyzes the coalition of domestic interests underlying neoliberal economic programs and the gains they derive from adopting and implementing them, the relationships between authoritarian governments, and the willingness and capability to support such programs.

In addition, the argument goes, authoritarian regimes are frequently more capable of controlling opposition to such policies as they are implemented. Implementation requires eliminating at least some of the benefits enjoyed by distributional coalitions. Doing so, it is frequently argued, is far more difficult in competitive political regimes than in authoritarian ones. In his analysis of Latin America, Thomas Skidmore argues that democratic regimes permit the formation of alliances in which each element thinks it can best protect its fortunes if stabilization is scrapped.[32] As a result, democratic regimes (at least in Latin America) have been unable to carry out successful stabilization programs. On the other hand, several authoritarian regimes (for example, the post-1964 military regime in Brazil and the post-1973 regime in Chile) have been able to implement neoliberal policies.

The admittedly short experience with economic policy reform in Africa suggests a more complex relationship between regime type and policy implementation. One major difference is that these policy changes occurred primarily in the context of IMF or World Bank lending programs and, as such, have been intimately tied to the deteriorating external financial positions of these countries. Even in Nigeria, which has recently adopted a stringent package of economic policy changes without coming to agreement with the IMF, the reforms were adopted with a view toward managing the nation's extremely difficult debt situation and coming to terms with major commercial lenders. Thus, in most instances, the domestic coalition behind policy reform is relatively weak. In some cases, reforms that "rationalize" financial structures may pose a direct threat to the ruling elite themselves.

In addition, although many African governments are authoritarian, they frequently have less capability for political and societal control than do stronger authoritarian states in Latin America or Asia. Political power is frequently maintained by incorporating broader social, ethnic, or professional groups (often via representatives rather than by the broad-based provision of benefits) into networks of state patronage.[33] Government resources (economic, political, and symbolic) are frequently spent in attempts to consolidate viable networks of support. Where stable networks emerge, the resource requirements for sustaining them may be relatively limited, though crucial. In instances in which networks fluctuate significantly, the costs of seeking stable bases of support can be high.

Policy changes can threaten such regimes in two ways. They may unravel the carefully crafted networks that support the regime, generally by threatening the resources used to maintain the loyalty of key groups and their ability to deliver benefits to their more localized supporters. Policy reform may also create a more effective opposition to the regime, generally by creating hardships that are then used to forge a common political interest among previously divergent (or conflicting) groups. The rash of strikes faced by Nimeiry's regime in the Sudan, and his attempts to fragment his opposition, were major factors behind the regime's repeated failures to successfully implement economic adjustment programs.

Beyond all this, partly as a response to flawed economic policies and partly as a result of the worsening economic crisis, unofficial structures and procedures have become more central to the operation of the economy in many sub-Saharan African countries. There is now abundant evidence that in many countries formal economic institutions (for example, "official" markets, established prices and exchange rates, border control) are relatively weak, particularly in countries that have undergone severe economic decline (such as, Guinea, Zaire, Tanzania, Ghana) or prolonged political conflict (Mozambique, Uganda, Angola). In turn, informal institutions have frequently become major features of economic life; the most important of these include parallel and "black" markets for goods (food, inputs, energy) and currency and the rise in unrecorded trade (smuggling). The operation of these informal institutions has de facto limited the state's capacity to control the economy.

The role of informal economic institutions makes it far more difficult to accurately assess both the technical and social impact of proposed policy changes. In many countries, food commodities have not been regularly available at the "official" price, and urban consumers have been required to make substantial purchases at much higher parallel market prices. Depending upon the quantity of food available, upon official prices, and upon the differential between these prices and those on the parallel market, official price increases in the context of a reform in cereal marketing can have the effect of actually lowering effective consumer prices. This appears to have been the case in Mali, and perhaps more recently in Guinea. In such instances, broad-based urban resistance to price and marketing reforms can be substantially less than anticipated. On the other hand, when supplies are limited and markets do not operate competitively, prices may soar, triggering widespread protest, as occurred in the Sudan during the final days of the Numeri regime.

Similarly, the effects of currency devaluation on urban consumers are difficult to judge when there is a wide differential between official and parallel market rates. Where access to currency at the official rate is limited, most urban consumers may pay prices that reflect the unofficial exchange rate, with the differential constituting rent to those with privileged access to foreign exchange. Currency reforms that effectively eliminate the differential may therefore not initially stimulate broad-based political opposition, as appears to have occurred in Zambia and Zaire. On the other hand, when devaluations create new opportunities for rents and do not successfully close the gap between official and unofficial markets, as occurred in Uganda in the early 1980s and the Sudan in the mid-1980s, broad-based effects were felt.

The operation of unofficial economic structures can also complicate the task of assessing the economic consequences of specific reforms. In some instances, they may provoke serious disagreement about the technical efficiency of policy instruments themselves. For example, some argue that the existence of unofficial markets for food means that producers have already been responding to "market-determined" prices and that there is little, if any, latitude for increased production through price changes.[34] In other instances it is argued that devaluation will have limited effectiveness in dampening the demand for imported goods or inducing shifts in the consumption of traded and domestically produced and consumed commodities as both producers and consumers have already made many of these adjustments.

The domestic motivation for undertaking reforms similar to those discussed in the policy dialogue, to the extent that it exists, is thus likely to emerge from economic failure, rather than from the growth of a politically effective coalition that is able to embrace and implement such reforms. The distributional coalitions associated both with flawed economic policies and those that might form in support of policy reform are different from those that have commonly characterized Latin American "models." Import substitution in Latin America (for example, in Argentina and Brazil) was carried out under a populist coalition of national business, labor, and the state, with each component of the coalition sharing an opposition to landed agro-export elites.[35] Sub-Saharan Africa, in general, has lacked both the strong national business component of the coalition and the landed agro-elites that stood in opposition to it.

Indigenous economic elites were weak at the times of independence, were generally oriented toward small-scale production or trading, and were sometimes ethnically distinct from the emerging political elite (such as the Asians in East Africa or the Lebanese in West Africa). Import-substituting industrial strategies did not emerge because of the power of an influential indigenous private sector capable of entering into an alliance with the state, but as a reflection of national development aspirations, frequently as defined and implemented by the state. Parastatal operations, frequently more bureaucratic than entrepreneurial in character, dominated import substitution in more statist economies. In more open economies, manufacturers with strong foreign connections were generally more influential than national business interests. The "crisis" of import substitution in sub-Saharan Africa, therefore, was more directly a "state" and "institutional" crisis.

Moreover, most African countries lacked an indigenous, landed elite in rural areas. For the most part, with the exception of colonially based dualism in "settler" countries like Kenya, Zambia, and Zimbabwe, the agricultural sector lacked the inequality that characterized much of Latin America. Large landholders, with the capabilities and interests to form part of a conservative coalition opposing import substitution (or favoring more neoliberal policies), were not present. Although portions of the agricultural sector may well benefit from policy reform, they have not organized to create or support such measures politically.

If economic failure, rather than strong domestic interests, is the motivation for considering policy reform, then effective support for continued policy reform will need to emerge from the process of implementation itself. On the other hand, opposition to reforms will frequently come from some of the most mobilizable groups, including not only potentially volatile urban groups, but from elements of the state whose access to employment and rents will be jeopardized. In this domestic environment the effectiveness of the strategy for implementing policy changes becomes a critical issue.

Policies may impact a wide range of actors, not only those initially identified as immediately impacted by their content. Conflicting goals, and varying perceptions of benefits, mean that "who gets what" will be determined by the strategies, resources, and power positions of the actors involved (or those who perceive themselves to be involved). In systems characterized by clientelism or informal patronage networks, the network of involved actors may not be immediately apparent, and their strategies for exercising power in closed networks may be difficult to ascertain.

Successful implementation generally requires a strategy for obtaining compliance. In policies for which implementation occurs at diverse sites (as, for example, marketing reform), the government must obtain the support of local political elites (which may include local traditional elites), the compliance of implementing agencies (again including lower-level, local representatives), as well as the compliance of intended beneficiaries. This frequently means turning the opposition of those who might be harmed by policies into acceptance and keeping those who are excluded (but may want benefits) from subverting the intent of the policy. Eliciting this compliance may involve much bargaining, conflict, and accommodation. If the overall goals of the policy are to be achieved, *the resources traded to acquire compliance must not jeopardize the impact of the policy itself.*

In addition, implementation must assure an adequate level of continued responsiveness and be able to maintain interest and provide adequate feedback; at the same time, it must retain enough control over resource allocation and program direction to assure that the distribution of benefits is consistent with the intentions of the policy being implemented. Politically successful compliance strategies thus involve striking a delicate balance between open communication and private negotiation, as well as a good understanding of the environment within which compromises and conflicts occur.

Except in rare instances, the politics of implementation is likely to be invisible to external advocates of policy reform. What can be observed—the selected consequences of policy changes—may well be inadequate evidence upon which to judge the medium- to long-run viability of reform packages in complex political environments. This is particularly true when observations are made at an aggregate level. Bearing this in mind, I will attempt to characterize selected experiences with policy changes and what the limited evidence derived from such experiences suggests about the capacity to initiate and sustain agricultural and economic policy reform.

POLICY DIALOGUE: IMPLEMENTATION EXPERIENCES

Between 1983 and 1986, several countries have undertaken economic adjustment programs with heavy emphasis on agricultural policy changes. The experience with these is, of course, short. Nevertheless, it is possible to define some commonly encountered constraints to implementing policy changes and, in a tentative way, to suggest the relative strengths and weaknesses of some of the alternative strategies used to implement reform.

Ghana's adjustment program clearly emerged from deep and prolonged economic crises accompanied by political instability. The major components of the policy reform package included the adoption of a flexible exchange-rate strategy (accompanied by a large devaluation); incentives, focused mainly on price increases, to stimulate agricultural production; the gradual removal of price and distribution controls; successive increases in public sector wages (primarily to restore some of the sharp declines in real wages experienced before the program was initiated), accompanied by budgetary policies to increase domestic resources and control public expenditure; and flexible interest-rate policies aimed at achieving positive real interest rates by mid-1986.

The program, undertaken in the aftermath of a change in regime, has been judged by the World Bank and the IMF as reasonably successful in achieving its initial stabilization objectives. Nevertheless, there have been, and continue to be, serious constraints to implementation. These include severe foreign exchange constraints, the cumulative effect of the country's prolonged economic and social decline, and continuing weaknesses in the policy framework conditioning the country's response to recovery.

In the judgment of the World Bank, the most binding implementation constraint was the lack of foreign exchange. The World Bank argues that unless the country is able to expand its capacity to import, the ability to implement the program will be seriously compromised. Ghana's imports in 1984 were only half the 1970 level in constant dollars. In the context of an economically open policy adjustment process, additional foreign exchange is a critical resource for implementation. The need for foreign exchange spans sectors and reflects both economic and political requirements. Claims and requirements come because:

• Farmers need inputs and implements to increase both food and cocoa production;

- Industry needs raw materials and spare parts to produce the consumer goods that give farmers an incentive to increase their marketed surplus;

- Infrastructure needs major rehabilitation;

- In order to build support for policy implementation, the government must show some tangible progress in supplying essential goods and services.

For a variety of reasons, the policy adjustment process itself cannot generate additional foreign exchange quickly enough to meet these requirements. The World Bank, therefore, sees a critical role for increased external assistance in order to permit effective implementation. The emphasis has been on supplying fast-dispersing aid on highly concessional terms to loosen the foreign exchange constraint. This approach to implementing policy reform makes external donors a critical component of the policy reform coalition. It does not, however, provide effective control over the ultimate distribution of the imports stimulated by "fast-dispersing" external assistance. Whether these resources ultimately contribute to implementing policy change (as they may be doing in Ghana) or provide windfalls for selected segments of society (as they did in Uganda) depends heavily on the regime's commitment to the overall reform package.

Ghana's success in implementing policy change was uneven. Implementation began during a severe drought, which reduced the output of both basic staples and cocoa and significantly increased the political difficulty of maintaining reforms. Thus there was little improvement in aggregate growth and a significant increase in domestic inflation during 1983. By 1984, the interaction of good weather and very high parallel market prices for food significantly increased food production, which in turn stimulated agricultural sector growth, reduced the level of inflation, and stimulated a 7.6 percent increase in real GDP. In 1985, the country's real GDP was expected to grow by 5 percent—reversing the preadjustment declines in real per capita GDP.

Although food production increased significantly, cocoa marketing did not. The reasons for this illustrate both the difficulties in implementing macroeconomic and price reforms in the context of a rigidly controlled economy and the structural constraints to economic adjustment characteristic of many African economies. Despite massive (2,000 percent) devaluations of the cedi between 1983 and 1985, the currency remains overvalued, resulting in a flourishing parallel market and continued, costly, quantitative trade restrictions. Although cocoa prices were raised significantly during 1983, and again in 1984, price increases did not reflect the full impact of devaluation. In the context of rapid inflation (driven by sharp rises in parallel market food prices), real producer prices for cocoa fell.

Hence, farmers responded to high food prices with large plantings, whereas cocoa production lagged significantly. Even with another substantial price increase in 1984/85, the effects of inflation and the parallel currency market left incentives to officially market cocoa weak. World Bank analysis found that despite price increases, real producer prices were only 43 percent of their 1970/71 level in 1984/85. At the official currency rate, this was only 43 percent of the f.o.b. price; at the parallel market price it was 11 percent (providing a substantial incentive to continue the practice of smuggling cocoa). In the face of severe foreign exchange constraints and a flourishing parallel market for currency, the government continued its tight import-licensing system. The persistence of this system both contributed to delay in obtaining import licenses and generated substantial "rents" to importers.

Domestic financial constraints also hampered implementation. Government departments and public corporations—facing tight budget constraints—lacked funds to finance imports or pay import duties. Restrictions on public sector lending were coupled by banks' reluctance to finance imports by increasing either overdrafts or lending limits by the margins required, as they regarded many potential customers as uncreditworthy. Hence, private sector access to credit did not increase rapidly enough to cover the rising cost of imports associated with devaluation. The lending problems were complicated by the fact that, despite adjustments, real interest rates were still negative in 1985.

The combination of these factors means that there is still likely to be a premium on political/administrative connections via patronage networks. This, in turn, makes it more likely that decisions taken to "balance" interests and build compliance will undermine the goals of the adjustment process.

It has proved similarly difficult to implement major price reforms in an administered price system. Official price adjustments (as the cocoa case illustrates) have rarely kept pace with changing economic conditions. As a result, administered prices still distort incentives from production toward trading. There has been some liberalization of price controls. However, the government seems unwilling to widely disseminate information on its intentions for fear of a political backlash. In this climate, partial adjustments trigger uncertainty and opportunity for speculation and rents.

Madagascar's experience with rice market liberalization graphically illustrates these difficulties as well as the problems inherent in implementing policy reform at multiple sites.[36] Madagascar's macroeconomic policy performance is regarded as reasonably good, measured both in terms of its compliance with IMF standby agreements (it met the targets of five successful standbys) and its progress in reducing inflation and currency overvaluation. Again, however, although Madagascar's real effective exchange rate has fallen significantly (after appreciating by more than 20 percent between 1980 and 1983), the adjustments have not been enough to eliminate the thriving parallel market. Agricultural policy reform was a major component of the policy adjustment process. Producer prices were raised (about 20 percent) for coffee, cottonseed, and black pepper—all export crops. Nevertheless, except for cotton, real producer prices are still lower than they were for 1980.

The case of rice—the staple food crop—is significantly different. In May 1983, the government, in a major shift, liberalized rice marketing and pricing. There was to be free competition between the public and private sectors in marketing, except in two traditional surplus regions. The price increases in 1984 were moderate, in part because import levels remained high and a ceiling price remained in effect. In 1985, however, rice prices soared during the traditional high-price season (October-January) after price ceilings were removed in June 1985. They were double the previous high prices and four times the world market price. These rapid price increases, in turn, triggered sharp criticism of the price and marketing policy reform.

There is substantial, although not conclusive, evidence that the implementation of the reforms contributed to these dramatic price increases. First, import levels (limited by an IMF agreement) were lower than previous years' imports. Despite this, virtually all rice was imported and distributed during the first half of the year (the traditional low-price period), prior to a midyear election. Imports were then curtailed, and the price ceiling removed, shifting many consumers who traditionally relied on public distribution to the private market. Second, the government did not clearly communicate to market participants and local officials the significance of removing price controls. Some traders apparently believed that the traditional "differential" system of markups between official and parallel markets was still in effect. Local officials, in turn, frequently continued to enforce "price ceilings." The result was likely to have been a slowing of supplies flowing onto the open market.

Third, elaborate licensing procedures for traders limited market entry, especially for small traders and millers, and discouraged traders from holding stocks by requiring their declaration upon licensing. Finally, the ability of local officials to circumvent the reforms (via harassment of traders and illegal roadblocks) was significantly underestimated. Implementation difficulties, then, are likely to have both impeded the ability of new institutional structures to operate and to have increased opportunities for windfall profits while significantly increasing the financial hardships experienced by low-income consumers.

Both Zambia and Zaire have recently begun to experiment with different implementation procedures that may reduce the complications associated with piecemeal economic reforms in the context of a heavily administered system. Both countries are primarily mineral exporters and, as such, have experienced especially sharp declines in terms of trade and export earnings. Again, increasingly acute financial problems seem to have stimulated policy reform measures.

Zambia undertook a significant adjustment program in 1983. The program was far-reaching. The government decontrolled most wholesale and consumer prices and significantly reduced budgetary subsidies on basic foodstuffs and fertilizers. The currency was significantly devalued (20 percent) in January 1983, and by July the government had moved to a flexible exchange-rate system, with steady devaluations, leading to a real depreciation of 26 percent by the end of 1984.

This devaluation was sufficient to restore profitability in the mining sector and allow for an increase in agricultural prices, but it was not enough to eliminate the parallel currency market. A weak market for copper and structural constraints limited the growth of foreign exchange earnings. Hence, as in Ghana, a substantial unsatisfied demand for foreign exchange, plus the continued operation of an inefficient import allocation scheme, adversely affected economic performance and capacity utilization while generating significant opportunities for "rents."

By 1985, the economic situation had deteriorated further. The government's budgetary expenditures doubled, in part reflecting a retroactive 18 percent general wage increase to unionized workers in April 1985. Although the increases were less than the unions had initially sought, their adoption reflected the political power of unions in Zambia, especially in the mining sector. In addition, financial reforms were not strictly implemented during the period in which there was no agreement with the IMF.

The increasingly severe economic situation, coupled with severe debt problems, led to more fundamental changes by the end of 1985. The government established and implemented an auction system for foreign exchange. Auctions occur weekly, and the exchange rate is determined by the marginal bid that exhausts the available supply of foreign exchange. Although some transactions are not included in the auction (including payments for oil imports, mining company imports, government and party imports, and debt-service payments), the auction-determined foreign exchange rate is used in conducting these transactions. Under the auction system, the currency has depreciated rapidly and the parallel market has virtually disappeared. Similarly, an auction system established for treasury bills led to a steady rise in interest rates (from 9.5 percent to 20 percent), moving toward positive real interest rates.

Price adjustments were passed quickly through the system—including the parastatal system. This led, among other things, to significant increases in bread prices (100 percent) and rising prices for domestically produced sugar (49 percent) and maize meal (50 percent). Producer prices for maize doubled, and the floor prices of other commodities were significantly increased.

Zaire's policy reforms and progress toward implementing them were similarly the products of increasing economic adversity. Zaire's performance under structural adjustment programs was poor in the late 1970s and early 1980s, frequently reflecting required characteristics.[37] However, in the face of serious economic problems, Zaire adopted a series of policy changes in 1983 that have been implemented in ways that have permitted the country to meet the associated IMF standby conditions. Specific policy measures implemented since 1983 include a sharply reduced government budget deficit and improved management of public sector accounts and expenditures; a total restructuring of the foreign exchange system; liberalization of import regulations; the establishment of a domestic money market; and the elimination and/or restructuring of many parastatals—including all agricultural parastatals.

As in Zambia's case, drastic revisions of the foreign exchange system were necessary to eliminate the operation of the parallel market. In 1983, Zaire devalued massively (500 percent), which brought official rates in line with the thriving parallel market. Currency values have subsequently been determined by supply and demand in an increasingly active interbank market, replacing the government's previous practice of setting the interbank rate. Because the official exchange rate continually reflects supply and demand, foreign exchange has increasingly become available through legal channels for essential spare parts and manufacturing inputs as well as for some consumer goods. The revised foreign exchange system has also drawn trade in key commodities such as diamonds and gold back into official channels and has increased the cash flow of the country's large copper-exporting parastatal, Gecamines. This exchange-rate change, coupled with tax reform, made the operation a contributor to, rather than a drain on, the government budget in 1985.

Similarly, the removal of government controls on interest rates was coupled with the creation of a domestic money market, which again reflects supply and demand for credit. In 1984 the government began selling new issues of short-term treasury bills at attractive interest rates, moving toward longer maturities (180 days) as confidence and experience increased.

As in other countries adopting macroeconomic adjustments, the initial response was high inflation (100 percent) and a decrease in domestic liquidity. However, by 1985 inflation had dropped substantially and new investment was beginning to be undertaken. Again, however, agricultural sector reform has been more complicated. The decontrol of producer prices and the abolition of parastatal marketing provided a limited incentive to increased production. Some crop prices have doubled or tripled since 1983, but increases in the price of consumer goods, fertilizer, and gasoline mean that real prices have grown little or have actually declined. Rural supplies of consumer goods remain inadequate, even for such basics as soap, matches, salt, and kerosene.

In addition, despite the official decontrol of agriculture, some local officials continue to create, and enforce, production and marketing controls. Some reports indicated that local officials require the production of specified crops and fine those who fail to comply. Controls on producer and retail prices were similarly dismantled, although firms remain subject to a posterioric review to ensure compliance with legal profit margins, which in some instances results in de facto local price controls.

In both Zambia and Zaire, the softness of world mineral markets has meant that structural reforms have not generated the desired (or expected) increases in foreign exchange. Hence, as in the cases discussed earlier, foreign exchange shortages are a constraint to policy implementation, and continued flows of external assistance and debt rescheduling remain critical to the implementation process.

CONCLUSIONS

The admittedly tenuous evidence available suggests several points. First, as Merilee Grindle noted in her earlier work, implementation requires resources and frequently fails when policy or program announcements are not backed by effective resource mobilization.[38] This is certainly the case for policy reform in sub-Saharan Africa. In the short term, these resources include substantial quantities of foreign exchange that cannot be immediately generated by policy changes. The role of foreign donors and institutions in providing these resources makes them an integral part of the implementation process.

Second, implementation strategies that rest on frequent government decisions about future adjustments are difficult to effectively implement. Although the initial decisions may be appropriate in timing and magnitude, subsequent adjustments frequently are not. Mobilizing political support for repeated changes is difficult, which in some cases lead to (intentional) ambiguity about the intended magnitude and scope of policy changes. Similarly, in the process of routinely coming to decisions, bargains must frequently be struck that weaken key program features.

Third, such failures frequently mean that informal markets and arrangements continue. The operation of such markets, in turn, complicates (and sometimes frustrates) the implementation of policy reforms. The persistence of sizable "rents" similarly provides multiple opportunities for the economically nonproductive use of both external assistance and domestic resources.

Fourth, implementation that appears initially to be "single site" is frequently "multiple site" and hence much more complex.[39] Announcing the abolition of centrally imposed price controls, for example, does not ensure that such controls will in fact be eliminated at all the sites where they were previously enforced. This is especially true where local enforcement generated substantial rents to government representatives. Similarly, decontrolling marketing may not ensure that barriers to the movement of goals are eliminated— especially where such practices are an important source of revenue for local officials or those able to effectively coerce farmers, merchants, or citizens into complying with their demands.

Fifth, the "demand management" aspects of policy reform have by and large worked better than the supply response portions. Although this may be viable in the short term, it is an unsustainable medium- to long-term situation. Effectively increasing production and productivity will depend heavily on the ability to remove structural constraints to increased agricultural production and marketing that, in turn, requires both substantial investment and effective management of the resources. How effectively current policy reforms are integrated with longer-term development strategies is therefore an initial issue.

Sixth, although the distributional effects of the programs have not been extensively studied, it is very likely that they impose costs on key urban groups as well as on state officials in both rural and urban areas. There is evidence that real wages (primarily in urban areas) have declined substantially in some cases

(Madagascar, Zaire, Ghana), leading to substantial declines in living standards. The fact that such declines were occurring before policy reform may soften initial opposition, whether through resignation or an inability to effectively mobilize opposition. However, continued decline without tangible evidence of improvement will almost certainly undermine, and discredit, reforms.

Finally, despite some instances in which political disorder followed attempts to accept structural adjustment (such as Uganda and the Sudan), even very harsh, demand-management programs have not triggered the political consequences foreseen by many.

NOTES

1. For an overview of these problems and their implications, see Cheryl Christensen et al., *Food Problems and Prospects in Sub-Saharan Africa.*
2. For a general discussion of implementation in Third World contexts, focusing heavily on project implementation, see Merilee S. Grindle, *Politics and Policy Implementation in the Third World.*
3. For recent figures, see UN, FAO, *State of Food and Agriculture, 1984,* pp. 179-180.
4. U.S., Department of Agriculture, Economic Research Service, *Food Needs and Availabilities, 1985: Update.*
5. For a summary of the literature on these factors, see Shahla Shapouri, Arthur J. Dommen, and Stacey Rosen, *Food Aid and the African Food Crisis.*
6. Peter Riley and Margaret Missiaen, "An Analysis of Rising Grain Imports in Sub-Saharan Africa: The Outlook for Wheat and Rice," p. 29.
7. In many countries, prevalent drought contributed to the downturn, especially where drought extended beyond a single year. See Shapouri, Dommen, and Rosen, *Food Aid.* In addition, external factors—such as worsening terms of trade and rising debt service—were major contributors, as Michael Lofchie notes in Chapter 5.
8. See, for example, Cheryl Christensen and Lawrence Witucki, "State Policies and Food Scarcity in Sub-Saharan Africa," in F. LaMond Tullis and W. Ladd Hollist, eds., *Food, the State and International Political Economy.* The classic statement on the weaknesses of domestic agricultural policies remains the World Bank's *Accelerated Development in Sub-Saharan Africa.*
9. Shapouri, Dommen, and Rosen, *Food Aid,* p. 11.
10. Ibid., p. 44.
11. Ibid., p. 12.
12. Ibid.
13. This has been a periodic response in many sub-Saharan African countries. Robert Bates's analysis for Kenya details some of the factors involved. See Robert Bates, "The Maize Crisis of 1979/80: A Case Study."
14. U.S. Department of Agriculture, Economic Research Service, *World Agriculture: Outlook and Situation Report.* See also Mary Burfisher, "Food Production Recovers from Drought," p. 4.
15. International Monetary Fund (IMF), *World Economic Outlook, April 1985.*

16. Bella Balassa, *Adjustments to External Shocks in Developing Countries.* For a similar analysis of African countries, see Balassa, "Policy Responses to External Shocks in Sub-Saharan African Countries," pp. 75-105.

17. The discussion follows that presented in IMF, *World Economic Outlook, April 1985.*

18. Ibid.; See also Balassa, *Adjustments to External Shocks.* The World Bank's analyses of African agriculture have consistently stressed the need for policy reform, as has AID's "policy dialogue." See note 20.

19. The basic elements of AID's policy dialogue are reflected in U.S., Agency for International Development, *Blueprint for Development: The Strategic Plan of Action of the Agency for International Development and Pricing, Subsidies and Related Policies in Food and Agriculture.*

20. For a contrasting view of the solution, see Timothy M. Shaw, *Towards a Political Economy for Africa: The Dialectics of Dependence.*

21. C. Peter Timmer, Walter P. Falcon, and Scott R. Pearson, *Food Policy Analysis.*

22. For a range of papers discussing conditionality, see John Williamson, ed., *IMF Conditionality.* For a discussion of these points, with an emphasis on their relation to agriculture, see Bela Mukhoti, *The International Monetary Fund and Low-Income Countries.*

23. Brian D'Silva, *Sudan: Policy Reforms and Prospects for Agricultural Recovery After the Drought.*

24. Ibid.

25. Ibid.

26. P. S. Mulema, *Reflections on Uganda's Economic Performance.*

27. For a discussion of Dutch disease, see G. Nankani, "Development Problems of Mineral Exporting Countries," and Sweder van Wijnbergen, "Dutch Disease: A Disease After All?"

28. Tony Killick, ed., *The Quest for Economic Stabilization: The IMF and The Third World,* p. 261.

29. Stephen Haggard, "The Politics of Adjustment: Lessons from the IMF's Extended Fund Facility," p. 508.

30. Robert H. Bates, *Markets and States in Tropical Africa.*

31. Grindle, *Politics and Policy Implementation.*

32. Thomas Skidmore, "The Politics of Stabilization in Postwar Latin America."

33. For a discussion of society-state relations and the differences between African patterns and Latin American corporatism, see Thomas M. Callaghy, *The State-Society Struggle: Zaire in Comparative Perspective.*

34. John C. DeWilde, *Agriculture, Marketing, and Pricing in Sub-Saharan Africa.*

35. For a discussion of the coalition behind import substitution, as well as export-led growth strategies, see John Gerard Ruggie, ed., *The Antinomies of Interdependence.*

36. The discussion on Madagascar draws on Elliot Berg, "Report to the Mission on Madagascar January 19-February 6, 1986," unpublished report.

37. Haggard, "The Politics of Adjustment."

38. Grindle, *Politics and Policy Implementation.*

39. Ibid.

Michael F. Lofchie

The External Determinants of Africa's Agrarian Crisis

Africa's agrarian crisis is well known.[1] The continent is increasingly unable to feed its people. Domestic food production in many countries is now woefully inadequate. The gap between production levels and national needs throughout the continent has greatly increased, requiring massive grain imports. And in certain of the most seriously affected countries, such as Ethiopia, the Sudan, Mozambique, and Chad, even extraordinary efforts to provide food assistance have not prevented starvation. Refugee camps and starving children symbolize a continent-wide agrarian malaise. As television documentaries portray a human tragedy of unutterable anguish, World Bank reports provide cold statistical confirmation of the underlying problem: a pattern of economic deterioration of ever-deepening proportions. Basic to this deterioration, and to the pandemic food shortage it has created, is Africa's seemingly irreversible agricultural decline, particularly in the food-producing sector.

Although Africa is primarily an agricultural continent, most countries suffered a precipitous decline in per capita food production during the 1970s. A major study by the U.S. Department of Agriculture found that of twenty-five sub-Saharan countries it surveyed in 1981, seventeen had suffered declines in per capita food production from the early 1960s to the late 1970s.[2] Seven of these countries had registered declines in per capita food production of 25 percent or more (Mali, Senegal, Burkina Fasso, Guinea, Angola, Ethiopia, and Uganda). With an average annual population growth rate of approximately 3.5 percent (the highest for any of the world's continents), Africa managed to increase its annual food production only about 1.5 to 2 percent during the 1970s and early 1980s. Overall, per capita food production dropped between 15 and 20 percent during this period. Africa is the only region where per capita food production has fallen during the past two decades. By contrast, per capita food production in Asia and Latin America increased approximately 10 percent during the same period.

An enduring, visible symptom of declining per capita food production is the skyrocketing demand for food imports. By the early 1980s Africa's annual grain imports had rapidly approached 10 million tons, an amount roughly equal to the needs of its entire urban population.[3] If current production trends continue, this figure could easily double by 1990.[4] Even under the most optimistic scenario—stabilization of present levels of per capita food production—annual food imports would grow to almost 12 million tons by 1990 because of population increases. Even this level of imported food would do little to alleviate the caloric and nutritional deficiencies that may already affect as many as 80 to 100 million people, approximately 20 percent of the continent's population. If per capita food production continues to decline, demand for food imports could easily soar to virtually incalculable heights. Food imports could approach 20 million tons per year by 1990. If a heightened demand does occur, it is unclear whether funds to import the food will be available. Many countries can barely afford current levels of food imports even when these include a large proportion of food aid.

Export-oriented agriculture has also stagnated, resulting in foreign exchange shortages for most African countries. As most African countries depend upon export agriculture to generate the earnings necessary not only for food purchases but to acquire other vital imports—including medical and educational supplies, petroleum products, transportation equipment, and consumer goods—the stagnant trend in agricultural exports is at least as alarming as that for food production.

Stagnation in export performance thus contributes directly to the inadequate industrial performance of many African countries. As much of Africa's industrial sector is built on the principle of import substitution, it depends almost entirely on the foreign exchange earning capacity of other economic spheres, particularly agriculture, to finance the import of critically important inputs: capital goods, raw materials, and spare parts. For this reason, the extremely low rates of capacity utilization that now characterize many of Africa's industries are directly attributable to the disappointing performance of export agriculture. In some of the most seriously affected countries, the rate of capacity utilization in industry has dropped to 25 percent or less, thereby contributing to high rates of urban unemployment. Thus, because of the poor performance of export agriculture, many African governments face a cruel political choice: whether to allocate foreign exchange reserves for additional food imports to avert starvation in the countryside, or to expend them for industrial inputs to avoid higher rates of urban unemployment.

Since there is little evidence of improvement in the performance of the export agricultural sector, this choice will continue to confront political leaders. A World Bank study completed in the early 1980s suggests that the aggregate volume of agricultural exports at the end of the 1970s was approximately equal to that of the early 1960s, noting that "a modest rate of increase of 1.9

percent a year in the 1960s was offset by an equal decrease in the 1970s."[5] Although Africa's volume of agricultural exports may have begun to increase slightly in the early 1980s, this has not been adequate to offset a declining share of world trade in certain key commodities such as coffee, tea, cotton, bananas, and oilseeds. Today, it appears unlikely that Africa will be able to recapture its former share of the world market for these commodities, for there is no evidence of an upward trend in production levels. As a result, the sub-Saharan countries seem destined to confront a continuing and severe foreign exchange crisis. Consequently, the availability of financial resources both for food imports and for the industrial sector remains uncertain.

Africa's cities already seem wholly unable to provide economic opportunity for displaced members of peasant society who migrate to urban centers in a desperate quest for livelihood. With the absolute decline of industrial activity in many countries, rates of unemployment of 40 percent or more are common, and this figure excludes the "underemployed." Even the better-off African countries already confront a situation in which the number of individuals leaving school annually far exceeds the creation of new jobs; and, in countries where the foreign exchange constraint has brought about a closure of much of the industrial sector, annual job creation is a negative number. Those new economic opportunities that are created tend to be limited to the informal economic sector. For vast numbers of new urban dwellers the only realistically available opportunities are in beggary, crime, or prostitution. In addition to stimulating an increase in urban degradation and crime, the inexorable deterioration of Africa's agricultural base has produced a steadily widening gap between the poor and the well-to-do.

These broad social trends clearly indicate that food deficits, once considered the momentary and localized outcome of episodic events such as droughts or civil wars, have now become a permanent and widespread feature of the African landscape. This enduring character of the agrarian crisis has already begun to affect the way in which Africa's donor nations view their food-aid programs. Food-relief efforts once viewed as short-term humanitarian responses to specific and temporary situations increasingly are considered a long-term programmatic necessity originating in the fundamental, structural decline of Africa's agricultural economies.

This change of attitude has ominous implications. Increasingly, donor policymakers consider Africa's food deficits to be the product of African policy mistakes, poor management, and inadequate political leadership. As this perspective grows, the donors' patience with costly and administratively burdensome food relief efforts will be exhausted and the amount of food available on concessional terms will decrease accordingly. As there is virtually no possibility that most African countries will be able to maintain food imports out of their own financial resources, the already intolerable levels of human starvation may yet increase dramatically.

Food deficits are only the most visible symptom of Africa's agrarian decline. Political and social instability, factors that are both the cause and effect of agricultural deterioration, abound throughout Africa. One of the most tragic indications of the continent's overall malaise is the high incidence of refugees. Although the people of sub-Saharan Africa constitute only about 10 percent of the world's population, about 25 percent of the world's refugees, approximately 2.5 million persons, reside there. This figure includes only those refugees who cross international boundaries, ignoring the many who remain within their own countries. High infant mortality rates further confirm the continent's economic decline. Infant mortality is now double that of other developing regions. Among children who survive, evidence mounts that food deficits are taking an additional toll, measured in terms of declining height- or weight-to-age ratios.[6]

If the serious decline in the quality of such vital public services as education and health is included as part of the broader outcome of agrarian crisis, even Africa's middle and upper classes have been affected by poor agricultural performance. In those countries where the crisis is particularly severe, public services exist in name only. Political repression can also be partly understood as the outcome of poor economic performance. Political leaders intent on maintaining their status and perquisites amid diminishing resources and growing popular discontent sometimes have turned to authoritarian methods to retain power.

Public sector corruption in Africa may also be rooted in the continent's agrarian malaise. Civil servants, whose real incomes have been severely eroded by the inflation that has accompanied agricultural stagnation, have sometimes turned to corruption to maintain purchasing power. This is most apparent in such societies as Ghana, Tanzania, and Uganda, where inflation has been so severe that a civil servant's monthly salary is often barely adequate to finance food purchases, let alone other basic requirements. In these cases, corruption has become the only alternative to white-collar destitution. Corruption inevitably fuels political demoralization by fostering the growth of cynicism and disillusionment toward government among the majority of citizens. This, in turn, makes it all the more difficult for even well-intentioned governmental reform efforts to succeed. Under these conditions, it is difficult to foresee any future other than convulsive political instability. Poverty, striking inequality, corruption, and social demoralization in Africa seem destined to evoke political demonstrations, food riots, more military coups, and anomic violence.

Almost no hope exists that these bleak trends can be reversed. For almost every indicator points to a further worsening of the current situation. During the past decade, for example, Africa has become one of the world's major debtor regions, a status that, in itself, casts serious doubt on the prospects of economic recovery. Debt servicing now represents still another burdensome claim on dwindling foreign exchange reserves. As late as 1974, the total outstanding debt for Africa's low-income countries was only about $7.5 billion and the debt-service ratio (debt service as a percentage of export earnings) was only slightly more that 7 percent. In just one decade, the total foreign debt of these countries nearly quadrupled to more than $27 billion, and the debt-service ratio increased more than four times to over 31 percent.[7] The total debt burden of Africa's low-income countries is now equal to approximately six years of export earnings, and the service ratio on this debt is now rapidly approaching 50 percent and beyond. More than a dozen African countries have already had to reschedule their debts, and many others have fallen far behind in their payments on foreign trade accounts. Debt servicing now competes with food and industrial imports for its share of hard-currency reserves.

Another portentous trend is the virtual stoppage of foreign private investment. Africa's economic crisis has had a chilling effect on foreign private capital, which has ceased to flow to the continent in any significant amounts. Although foreign donors have continued to provide public assistance, Africa today may well have become a net exporter of capital. For, if the expatriation of capital by political and entrepreneurial elites interested in securing their resources by relocating them abroad is added to other sources of capital outflow, including debt repayment, the total could well exceed the net amount of capital entering the continent. Contemporary Africa exhibits all the symptoms of a continent rapidly depleting its capital base. Consequently, many economists predict an even bleaker future for the 1990s. The Economic Commission for Africa (ECA), for example, has forecast a nightmarish scenario. In a report entitled "ECA and Africa's Development 1983-2008," the ECA portrays a continent-wide fall in life chances to below the minimal level of human subsistence:

> At the national level, the socioeconomic conditions would be characterized by a degradation of the very essence of human dignity. The rural population, which would have to survive on intolerable toil, will face an almost disastrous situation of land scarcity whereby whole families would have to subsist on a mere hectare of land. . . . The conditions in the urban centers would also worsen with more shanty towns, more congested roads, more beggars and more delinquents.[8]

As urban unemployment would reach levels that are today considered unimaginable, it is not unlikely that social violence could destroy what remains of the social and political fabric.

In 1972, Colin Turnbull published an account of an African people who had endured nearly three generations of extreme deprivation. His book, *The Mountain People,* generated much attention when first published because of its chilling description of the effects of prolonged starvation on a once relatively prosperous and socially unified community.[9] Turnbull's description of the IK people of northeastern Uganda portrays a community in which the pursuit of food had assumed a morality of its own, replacing previous social values. The IK had developed an ethic of individual survival at any cost. This ethic became so all-pervasive that it not only replaced any sense of overall social cohesion but it also corroded the bonds of loyalty between parents and children.

Turnbull's book today enjoys a small revival among social scientists concerned with the societal effects of extended periods of food deprivation. Although his imagery, which includes the utter disappearance of familial bonds, seems too harsh to be plausible, severe and seemingly permanent food deficits in some African countries or regions nevertheless provoke great apprehension. Traces of the amoral individualism of the IK may already be seen in situations where food assistance is treated as a source of elite corruption or as a vehicle for the manipulation of political support.

The causes of Africa's contemporary food crisis are complex and deeply rooted. Scholars commonly divide them into internal and external factors. Those who emphasize internal explanations of agricultural decline point to the poor economic practices of African governments. They argue that improved economic performance is attainable for those governments prepared to dramatically alter their policies. Scholars who emphasize external factors tend to decry the adverse features of the international environment, noting economic factors that are beyond the jurisdiction of African governments. It is regrettable that these schools of thought often have been posed as adversarial interpretations. In truth, the continent's agrarian malaise is the product of both sets of causes. Each perspective provides insights as to why effective remedies have proven so elusive. It is impossible to understand the agricultural predicament of any single African country without reference to the interplay between domestic agricultural policies and the character of the international economic system.

My purpose is to call attention to some of the external factors that contribute to Africa's difficulties. The colonial period left African countries with economic systems that, in the vast majority of cases, were heavily dependent upon the export of primary agricultural commodities, and this dependence is at the heart of contemporary Africa's economic difficulties. This dependence is responsible for the historical neglect of the food-producing sector and, therefore, for the growing crisis of food deficits. It is the major reason why Africa's terms of trade vis-à-vis industrial and commercial exporters have declined. Falling price levels for primary agricultural products in world markets, given Africa's export dependence, further exacerbate Africa's already chronic balance-of-payments deficits, its inability to finance the development of an industrial sector, and the rapid deterioration of its public services.

THE EXPORT BIAS AND FOOD DEFICITS

From its colonial era, Africa inherited an acute dependence upon agricultural exports. In country after country, these exports accounted for an overwhelming share of foreign exchange earnings, an extremely high percentage of gross domestic product, and a large portion of government revenue. In the three countries of East Africa, for example, agricultural exports accounted for be-

tween one-half and three-fourths of total export earnings, a condition that prevailed throughout western Africa as well.[10] For most countries, export agriculture also employed the largest single segment of the wage-labor force. Through
the remittances of family members engaged as migratory workers on export
plantations, export agriculture also provided an indispensable source of financial support for peasant families engaged in subsistence production.

This overemphasis on the export sector can be directly related to Africa's
current food crisis. Colonial governments vigorously promoted agricultural exports, but neglected food production. Consequently, by the eve of independence in the early 1960s, numerous African countries had already become net
food importers. They exhibited a weakness that would, within a decade, manifest itself as the severe Sahelian famine of the early 1970s and the equally critical food shortages in Ethiopia and Tanzania in 1974.

For a variety of reasons, the food imports of the 1960s did not appear to be
a matter of compelling concern. Because import levels were relatively low, and
because abundant supplies could be obtained on a concessional basis through
donor-nation foreign-assistance programs, grain imports were not a serious
drain on foreign exchange reserves. They thereby "imposed little financial
hardship."[11] The cost of food imports in the 1950s was offset by buoyant markets
for Africa's agricultural exports, markets stimulated by the worldwide commodities boom following the Korean War. This boom greatly augmented the
foreign exchange reserves of most African countries, which, in any event, then
confronted few potentially burdensome claims on their hard-currency reserves. Debt-servicing obligations or energy costs, for example, were not yet
heavy. Consequently, initial food deficits could be managed without serious
episodes of famine or starvation; most observers did not treat food imports as
an early warning sign of future crisis.[12]

Out of the colonial bias favoring export agriculture emerged a marked discrepancy between the pattern of production characteristic of export-oriented
agriculture and that which prevailed in the production of food staples for
domestic consumption. This discrepancy is sometimes referred to as agrarian
dualism. Roger Leys early defined the concept:

> [Dualism] is characterized by:—(a) an *export enclave* in turn characterized by
> the production of a few raw materials for export and processing in the fac-
> tories of the developed countries. The expansion of this enclave is primarily
> determined by the growth of effective demand for these (mainly agricultural)
> raw materials in the developed countries.
> (b) a *hinterland* in which the majority of the population lives and works in the
> traditional agrarian economy. The main contribution of this hinterland to the
> export enclave is a flow of cheap, unskilled migrant labor.[13]

The concept of agrarian dualism calls attention to the relatively advanced
character of export production, its capital intensiveness and systematic use of
advanced agricultural techniques, and to the striking differences between

these features and the relatively undeveloped patterns of production that prevail in the cultivation of food crops.

Dualism characterized colonial policy. Colonial governments expected their colonies, insofar as possible, to be financially self-sufficient and to provide at least limited markets for the home country's manufactured goods. To meet these expectations the colonies had to develop a capacity to earn hard currency on world markets. This required the development of a profitable export sector, stimulating policies designed to meet the needs of export-oriented farmers. To profitably produce Africa's key export crops—coffee, tea, cotton, sisal, oil palms, and cocoa—fairly large farms or plantations were established, and where it was economically attractive and feasible to introduce technologically advanced practices, these too were officially supported. Under the careful nurturing of attentive colonial administrators, the production of exportable commodities was boosted by intensive research on the applicability of high-yielding seed varieties and other innovative methods of crop husbandry and by the use of chemical fertilizers and pesticides.

Typically, the land devoted to export crops was privately held either by individuals or corporations and could thus be used as collateral for loans to finance the acquisition of costly inputs. Almost always when export agriculture and food crop production competed for arable land, colonial governments devised ways to displace food producers to more distant regions. Export agriculture also benefited from a whole array of vitally necessary "soft" services such as market research and credit assistance. Colonial governments commonly supported export-oriented infrastructural development, including transportation facilities needed by agricultural exporters. Usually, these supports were provided on a subsidized basis; tax revenues used to finance them came from other economic sectors, including small-scale agricultural producers.

Food production, by comparison, enjoyed few of these supports. Small-scale peasant farmers produced food on communally held land that could not be used as collateral for development loans. Technologically, peasant farms were virtually prefeudal. Peasants used the hand-held hoe; animal-drawn cultivation was rare. Food producers received almost none of the agro-scientific inputs common to the exporting regions. High-yield seed varieties, chemical inputs, and irrigated cultivation were almost nonexistent, as was governmental assistance with demand prediction, price stabilization, and marketing. Other vital services such as agricultural extension and infrastructural development were generally perfunctory. For much of colonial Africa, a typical farm-to-market route for a food staple began with a bicycle path to a painfully distant roadside. From there foodstuffs were transported on a haphazard assortment of vehicles—buses, passenger cars, and animal-drawn carts—along the remainder of the route. Spoilage was high because infrastructure was poor and rudimentary practices such as pest control were seldom followed. For all these reasons the supply of food staples often fluctuated erratically from one season to the next.

Radical observers of rural development in Africa have suggested a direct link between the technologically advanced pattern of agricultural production for export and the backward character of the food-producing sector. Rodolfo Stavenhagen, for example, strongly argues that the backwardness of the peasant sector is not the product of benign neglect or misplaced overemphasis on export production. Rather, he contends that export production required the impoverishment of peasant food producers. For, in addition to all the other agro-scientific and infrastructural inputs that colonial governments made available, the export farms required one other indispensable condition to succeed economically—namely, an abundant and readily available supply of low-wage agricultural laborers.[14] To thrive, export plantations needed cheap, migratory labor during periods of peak labor demand such as planting and harvesting.

Only peasants could supply such labor. However, if the peasantry were virtually self-sufficient, able to provide for its material needs by producing and consuming its produce or by trading and bartering in exchange systems that did not require the painful social dislocations that accompany participation in a wage-labor force, there would have been no incentive for individual peasants to seek employment on the export farms. For this to occur, the living standards of the peasantry had to be deliberately lowered to the point that wage labor became the only alternative to starvation or utter destitution. An entire genre of African history documents the various policies that colonial governments used to compel formerly self-sufficient peasants to become agricultural workers. These included various systems of taxation such as the head tax and poll tax, the direct imposition of minimal labor requirements for adult males, and, in the Portuguese territories, outright forced labor. Less dramatically visible but equally consequential were rural policies that so deprived peasant society of vital governmental services, infrastructural supports, and agro-scientific inputs that peasant production faltered to a point at which wage labor became an imperative for survival.

In the long run, none of these methods was as effective as the introduction of governmentally regulated pricing systems for peasant-grown food crops. Price controls lowered peasant family incomes to the point at which survival depended upon some wage income. Price controls of food staples further benefited the export farmers. As food is a wage good, low food prices contributed directly to low wage costs on the export farms. The cumulative impact of all these policies was to alter fundamentally the very character of African peasant society. The notion of an independent African peasantry that survived by cultivating its own land and selling a portion of its produce became a misnomer. Rare, indeed, was the African rural family that did not survive, at least in part, on the basis of wage income, generally earned by seasonal migratory labor on the export farms.[15]

The suppression of peasant society set the stage for the food crisis that began within a decade of the end of formal colonial rule. This historical analysis has a direct bearing on the importance to be attached to drought as a cause of famine in Africa. Drought only complicated an already desperate situation; it was not a fundamental cause of the epidemic of famines that now afflicts African societies. In virtually all cases, droughts have occurred in societies whose food production was already far below the level of national self-sufficiency.[16] Throughout the 1960s, the continent's capacity to increase food production fell so far below the rate of population increase that major food deficits would have occurred even if rainfall had continued unchanged.[17]

Like other natural calamities, the effect of drought is mediated and shaped by intervening political, social, and economic arrangements. These can either mitigate or accentuate natural disasters. The effect of African droughts, when they occur, is to disrupt catastrophically peasant systems of food production already undermined by several generations of colonial policies that maximized agricultural exports at the expense of the food-producing sector.[18]

EXPORT AGRICULTURE: IS THERE A THEORETICAL DEFENSE?

The most uncompromising defense of the colonial governments' concentration on the development of export sectors has been advanced by economic historians who consider these exports essentially cost-free vis-à-vis other sectors of agricultural production. In their theory, generally termed "vent-for-surplus," the development of export agriculture should not be blamed for the decline of the food-producing sector because it largely employed hitherto unused land and labor.[19] Vent-for-surplus theorists argue that the labor needs of export-oriented farmers were not an important factor in undermining African food production. In their view, the labor needs of export farms could be met out of peasant leisure time or worker migration from more distant regions.

Vent-for-surplus theory originates with Adam Smith. It differs from other theories of international trade in that it does not assume full existing utilization of the factors of production: land, labor, and capital. Rather, at least land and labor are assumed to be significantly underutilized. Therefore, these unused factors may be called into production without affecting the existing allocation of resources.

Hla Myint, the major contemporary exponent of vent-for-surplus, defended this position in his classic 1958 article:

> ... the rapid expansion in the export production of the underdeveloped countries in the nineteenth century cannot be satisfactorily explained without postulating that these countries started off with a considerable amount of surplus productive capacity consisting both of unused natural resources and under-employed labor ... the surplus productive capacity provided these countries with virtually 'costless' means of acquiring imports which did not require a withdrawal of resources from domestic production but merely a fuller employment for their semi-idle labour.[20]

In 1976, J. S. Hogendorn applied the vent-for-surplus model to West Africa, analyzing the history of five export commodities.²¹ Although experiences varied within the West African region and from one crop to another, Hogendorn concluded that "the vent-for-surplus model often has similarities with African experience and results in some excellent insights into that experience."²² His basic criticism was that the vent-for-surplus model did not give sufficient credit to the dynamism of African entrepreneurs.

Critics of the vent-for-surplus theory have called attention to a variety of shortcomings: its failure to emphasize the critical role played by colonial governments in nurturing the export sector by providing research and development services, as well as their inattention to the profound impact export development had in restructuring indigenous systems of production and trade.²³ For W. M. Freund and R. W. Shenton, for example, the colonial emphasis on export development is directly related to today's economic crises.²⁴ In their view, Hogendorn and Myint ignore a whole range of factors that demonstrate the considerable costs to West African society involved in the creation of its export sectors, paying no attention whatsoever to the slave trade and its disruptive effects or to the disruption of already existing intraregional patterns of trade and commerce.

Freund and Shenton argue convincingly that the development of West Africa's major export crops did not simply energize unused factors of production. Rather, it contributed to a wholesale restructuring of production and social organization in West African society. They contend that the "costs of this [reorganization] have only become fully apparent as the import-export economies of West Africa have stagnated under the weight of mounting international debts, worsening terms of trade, and declining living standards."²⁵ Even Myint acknowledges that vent-for-surplus theory would not be well adapted to societies in which the development of mines or plantations had already taken away surplus land or labor and that, in such cases, export production might entail "not merely a reduction in the subsistence output but also much heavier social costs in the form of the disruption of the tribal societies."²⁶ The error in the vent-for-surplus approach may well have been its failure to recognize just how ubiquitous such enclave development was and, therefore, how deeply its development depended upon the suppression of domestically oriented agricultural production. Carl Eicher and Doyle Baker, for example, note that "the model assumes away the food problem."²⁷

A somewhat more cautious defense of specialization for export is provided by another classical economic doctrine: comparative advantage. According to this theory, countries can maximize their economic growth by specializing in the production and export of commodities that they produce most efficiently, given available capital and labor inputs. This theory strongly asserts that every country should seek to produce goods that will yield the highest possible value on world markets, trading these for goods that it needs but cannot produce so efficiently.²⁸ Although the theory of comparative advantage was originated nearly 200 years ago, in the writings of David Ricardo, it has changed little and remains today a powerful argument for free trade and the benefits of specialization for export. Ricardo believed that international trade worked to the benefit of all nations involved and, indeed, that the poorer nations of the world would be particularly well advised to follow this strategy. By concentrating on the production of a small number of exportable commodities, they would use scarce resources optimally and would thereby gain the greatest possible level of wealth and material welfare for their people.

Comparative advantage theorists acknowledge that specialization for export may result in less food production for local consumption but insist that this is not an economic problem. If economic resources—land, labor, and capital—can produce two or three times the monetary value in exportable commodities than it would yield in food crops, then it makes sense to grow export crops and purchase food items. The difference between the value of the exports and the cost of food imports could be used to purchase additional commodities. Agricultural economists who have examined Africa from this perspective tend to see considerable benefits from the emergence and development of export-oriented economies. Agricultural exports have enabled African countries to be active in international trade and, thereby, to avail themselves of a range of commodities that would otherwise not be available. William O. Jones succinctly states,

> The great African production of coffee, cocoa, tea, peanuts, palm oil and cotton occurred because these crops could be sold; that is, because consumers in Europe, North America, and elsewhere manifested an economic demand for these commodities, and because a marketing system was developed to communicate the character and magnitude of this demand to African farmers. As a consequence, African producers were able to enjoy more nonfarm goods, such as textiles and utensils, than they had before. By the simple expedient of reducing their non-agricultural efforts and increasing their agricultural production, their activities became more specialized. Incomes increased because of greater ability to buy the production of others. Europeans, on their part, not only obtained more of the products of the tropics, but also enjoyed expanding markets for the products they themselves produced.[29]

Jones's analysis suggests, at least hypothetically, that however poor African countries were at the end of the colonial period, they were better off as a result of the export emphasis than they would have been without it.

The doctrine of comparative advantage has attracted a number of contemporary adherents. It is, for example, the operative idea in the World Bank's famous report entitled *Accelerated Development in Sub-Saharan Africa.*[30] It is also the driving conceptual force behind the strategies of many of Africa's donor organizations, especially those that provide funding for large-scale export-oriented agricultural projects. Comparative advantage also has strong currency in the academic community.[31] The widespread support for this idea is not surprising, for there is an entire range of goods and services that small agricultural countries cannot possibly produce for themselves and that must be obtained on the world market. These include petroleum and its derivatives, medical equipment and most medications, capital goods for industry and certain industrial raw materials, and large-scale industrial products such as jet planes or railroad locomotives. The country that diverts its resources away from the production of exports toward the production of goods for its domestic use reduces its ability to pursue a number of invaluable social and economic activities.

Nevertheless, there is an emerging consensus that specialization for export has been harmful to Africa because it has failed to promote diversified and balanced economic development. A powerful statement of this position has been put forward by Hollis Chenery, formerly vice-president for development policy at the World Bank. He posits a major distinction between trade theory and growth theory, insisting that the doctrine of comparative advantage is one of trade maximization and that it has little bearing on the promotion of overall economic development. Chenery notes that "classical analysis [comparative advantage] focuses on long-run tendencies and equilibrium conditions, while modern theories of growth are concerned with the interaction among producing and consuming units in a dynamic system."[32] Chenery's analysis makes it clear, contrary to the expectations of those who felt that the development of agricultural exports would have spillover benefits for other sectors of the national economic system, that the export enclaves of agricultural countries have flourished with virtually no such additional stimulative effects.

This is of utmost importance. Growth theory concerns itself with promoting the development of many sectors of a national economy, not simply the export sector. If growth theory does deal with the need to promote foreign trade, this is a somewhat secondary consideration. For it primarily addresses the effects that exports may have in stimulating secondary areas of development. For this reason, "growth theory either ignores comparative advantage and the possibilities of trade completely, or considers mainly the dynamic aspects, such as the stimulus that an increase in exports provides to the development of related sectors, or the function of imports as a carrier of new products and advanced technology."[33] For economic planners who make investment decisions to promote overall national development, growth theory suggests a pattern of resource allocation different from that implied by comparative advantage theory. It is doubtful that, in promoting export agriculture, colonial administrators in Africa were operating on any explicit theory of long-term growth, much less a Ricardian notion of comparative advantage. But the principle of comparative advantage has been invoked to defend the export-oriented economic system they installed. Chenery's analysis provides compelling theoretical illumination of one of the system's major shortcomings—namely, its failure to promote broad-based development outside the narrow sphere of agricultural exports.

The reasons for this failure are not fully clarified by Chenery. However, analysis of the activities of multinational corporations in international commodity trade provides some insight. African societies were not the major economic beneficiaries of the development of specialized export sectors. Rather, the profits from export agriculture were principally absorbed by the large multinational commodities corporations that dominated international trade in agricultural products. In their book *Agribusiness in Africa,* Barbara Dinham and Colin Hines have shown that the profitability of export agriculture does not occur at the level of initial production, but rather from the host of secondary transactions that occur after the crop has become the property of an international trading firm.[34] Following this argument, the financial rewards from the production of coffee, tea, cocoa, and sugar do not accrue as much to the plantation areas where these crops are grown as they do to the large corporations that process, trade, transport, market, and distribute them.[35] Comparative advantage theory glaringly ignores the distortion to international trade introduced by multinational corporations.

The extreme weakness of African producer countries vis-à-vis others in the international marketplace contributes to Africa's current crisis. Those who hoped that export specialization would promote economic development failed to anticipate the market conditions that would pose a fundamental constraint on the presumed benefits of agricultural exports. Early developers of Africa's export sectors assumed that tropical agricultural products would remain scarce, high-demand goods available only from a small number of suppliers, whereas food and other commodities produced in the temperate zones would be abundantly available. Many expected that product scarcity would not only allow producers to influence price but also to control the terms of their participation in the international economic system.

INTERNATIONAL MARKET CONDITIONS

The workings of the international marketplace in 1987 contradict this expectation. For the production of tropical export crops is now enormously competitive; new suppliers regularly enter the already overcrowded market, sometimes responding to minute and temporary upward shifts in commodities' prices. Coffee, cotton, and sugar, thus oversupplied, sell at prices at or barely above the cost of production. Kenya, Uganda, Tanzania, Ethiopia, and Ivory Coast not only compete with one another for a share of the international coffee market, they also compete with Brazil, Colombia, and Peru. Cotton exporters such as the Sudan and Egypt compete against one another and other major cotton producers such as the United States. Far from generating enough revenue to finance a wide range of imported goods, the export earnings of any number of African countries now seem barely adequate to finance such vital necessities as food, medical goods, and energy.

The most likely prospect for the foreseeable future is a steady, if gradual, worsening of the situation. World demand for most of Africa's products is expected to grow only slightly between now and the end of this century, and, as oversupply will remain a chronic problem, price levels are not likely to increase. If Africa is to recover economically, world demand for such pivotally important commodities as coffee, cocoa, tea, sugar, and cotton would have to improve substantially over the next decade. But, according to one World Bank study, the demand for these products will increase by only between 2 and 3 percent per year during this period. For three of these crops (coffee, cotton, and sugar) the rate of increase in international demand may well be under 2 percent.[36]

Only one of Africa's present agricultural exports, palm oil, is expected to enjoy a 5 percent increase in demand. But it is ironic that, with the deterioration of Nigerian agriculture, Africa's share of world trade in palm oil may actually *decrease*. The outlook for Africa may well be bleaker than even these figures indicate, as much of the growth in world demand will probably be captured by countries outside Africa. Nations that have a strong industrial base can do much to intensify their agricultural production. As a result, such newly industrializing countries as China, India, Brazil, and Argentina are far better equipped to succeed in a competitive international marketplace than the far less industrialized countries of sub-Saharan Africa.

Additional factors militate against the possibility of an economic turnaround triggered by improved performance of the export sector. Africa's agricultural exports confront increasing competition not only from producer countries just entering the international market, but from synthetic substitutes manufactured in the industrial world. For example, cotton has had to compete with polyester and Dacron; coffee and tea with soft drinks; sugar with artificial sweeteners; and natural rubber with manufactured substitutes.

The long-term economic predicament of Africa's agricultural exporters is worsened by the low demand for their products. Unlike industrial exporters that can often boost export revenues by lowering prices to stimulate demand, the exporters of agricultural commodities do not enjoy this option. Western consumers do not increase their usage of such products as coffee, tea, or cocoa when the price falls. On the other hand, any noticeable increase in the price level of one of these commodities is met almost instantly by decreased consumption. In some cases—including sugar, cocoa, cotton, and rubber—the price effects of synthetic alternatives and intense international competition have been disastrous. Chronically depressed economic conditions in Ghana, Liberia, and the Sudan provide compelling evidence of the disastrous impact of weakened world demand in countries that had become particularly dependent upon one of these products. Thus, contrary to the early imagery that portrayed Africa's primary commodities as having every possibility of high profitability, the real economic world of tropical agricultural exports is one in which innumerable producers generate a horrific supply glut on world markets and have almost no leverage whatsoever over the prices they can obtain for their products.

NEO-PROTECTIONISM IN THE INDUSTRIAL WORLD

Failing dramatic growth in world demand for primary agricultural commodities, Africa's best prospect for generating increased revenues from its exports is to develop agricultural processing industries. However, the current
structure of the international economic system militates against the development of export processing. Shamsher Singh has observed that "exports of processed products face escalating tariffs and other barriers in the industrial countries."[37] Although Africa's losses from neo-protectionism are not nearly as great
as those of many Latin American countries, they are considerable. In its 1985
World Development Report, the World Bank estimated that protectionism in the
industrial world cost sugar-exporting countries approximately $270 million
annually between 1979 and 1981. This figure rose to more than $420 million by
1983.[38]

Protectionism has consequences that go far beyond its directly measurable
monetary costs. By reducing the value of the continent's existing set of exports,
it adds to overall balance-of-payments difficulties and thus impedes Africa's capacity to acquire externally produced agricultural inputs. Even more important, protectionism sends a strongly negative signal to those countries prepared
to consider ways of improving the performance of their export sectors. And,
because protectionism also reduces the prospects of secondary or tertiary industrial development (industries to service export industries), it is directly related to the continent's dwindling appeal for foreign private investors. Most
important, however, protectionism dooms African countries to an economic
future as primary commodity exporters, a status that, in today's international
system, insures that they will suffer indefinitely from the worst possible terms
of trade.

THE TERMS OF TRADE

No inventory of external economic factors that have adversely affected the performance of Africa's agricultural sector would be complete without reference
to the terms of trade, perhaps the most commonly cited of any of the outside
economic forces that impinge upon the continent. Among many observers, it is
virtually an article of faith that Africa has suffered severely from declining terms
of trade and that this factor, almost alone, can help explain the crippling foreign
exchange constraint that now figures so prominently as a cause of the overall
economic crisis. For those who believe this proposition, it is axiomatic that the
real price levels of Africa's agricultural exports have declined substantially relative to the price levels of industrial goods and other processed commodities
that Africa must obtain through the world trading system. As Africa's imports
include the capital goods, raw materials, and spare parts for its own industrial
sector, the falling rate of capacity utilization can be attributed directly to the

declining purchasing power of its agricultural exports.

As compelling as these "terms-of-trade arguments" appear, we need to consider them cautiously, for the evidence is by no means unambiguous and the precise relationship between the terms of trade and Africa's current agricultural crisis is not altogether clear. World Bank studies illustrate just how contradictory terms-of-trade statistics can be. In its three recent books on Africa, the World Bank's economists have taken three different positions on this issue. The authors of the World Bank report entitled *Accelerated Development in Sub-Saharan Africa*, for example, doubt that declining terms of trade can be blamed for the present crisis. They argue, instead, that "the main cause of rising current account deficits and shortages of foreign exchange in the 1970s was *not the terms of trade*, but the slow growth of exports."[39] They argue that for the majority of African countries—mineral-exporting countries being the principal exception—the terms of trade were actually favorable for the entire period from 1960 to 1979.

A follow-up study by the World Bank, more equivocal on this point, entertains the proposition that the deterioration of the international trading environment has been partly responsible for the economic predicament of African countries: "Developments since 1980 warrant a greater degree of concern about the external economic circumstances confronting African countries. Over the past few years, the externally determined foreign exchange situation has become a major constraint on almost all African countries. Falling export prices . . . have undermined attempts by governments to improve their balance of payments."[40] This study presents evidence of the extent to which efforts by the governments of Sudan, Senegal, and Kenya to augment export earnings through policy reforms designed to increase export volumes have been undermined by falling world prices for their products. Sudan, for example, was able to expand its exports of cotton by about 50 percent in 1981 and 1982, but because of a drop in the world market price for that product, its foreign exchange earnings from cotton did not increase at all during that period. And, because some of the inputs necessary to increase production had to be obtained abroad, its net foreign exchange position may actually have been worsened by policies that were successful in promoting exports. Moreover, this report anticipates that price levels for the agricultural commodities that African countries export will continue to decline for the next twenty years. Despite its concern with the terms of trade, the report nevertheless stresses the policy mismanagement of African governments.

A 1984 World Bank study of Africa notes a severe decline in the terms of trade since 1980. The authors of *Toward Sustained Development in Sub-Saharan Africa* report that, between 1980 and 1982, the terms of trade for Africa's low-income countries declined by approximately 15 percent and that the continent's middle-income, oil-importing countries suffered a terms-of-trade loss of over 11 percent.[41] According to this study, the prices of nonoil primary commodities fell by 27 percent, perhaps accounting for a 2.5 percent fall in GDP.

The World Bank's *World Development Report 1984* presents an analysis of changing terms of trade for Africa for the period 1965 to 1983 that is generally consistent with this recent study. Its figures suggest that, between 1965 and 1980, Africa's low-income countries suffered a slight drop of about 1.6 percent in their terms of trade, but that in 1981 and 1982 there was an abrupt decline of approximately 11 percent.[42] The 1984 report leaves little doubt that when the effects of declining terms of trade are combined with rapidly rising interest rates on foreign debt and other, more diffuse consequences of the world recession, they provide a major explanation for independent Africa's current economic malaise.

Drawing conclusions from this welter of contradictory evidence is a daunting task. The statistical evidence on terms of trade allows different conclusions. Overall, the World Bank's studies of Africa's trade prospects clearly show that the majority of Africa's principal agricultural exports peaked at very high price levels in the mid-1950s during the post-Korean War commodities boom, but declined abruptly to a very low level in the early 1960s. The price levels of these commodities fluctuated over the next twenty years, reaching but one momentary, high peak in the late 1970s.[43] Thus, the base period 1960 to 1979 is one in which commodity prices began at very low levels but ended at an all-time high, thereby indicating a sharp upward trend. If the base period chosen had been 1955 to 1982, the terms of trade calculations would have begun at a moment of very high prices and ended at a moment of the lowest prices in thirty years, thereby indicating a precipitous downward trend or sharply falling terms of trade. Thus the report *Accelerated Development in Sub-Saharan Africa* is vulnerable to the criticism that it selected an arbitrary base period to reveal improving or stable terms of trade.

The evidence presented here suggests unambiguously that the terms of trade began to shift dramatically against Africa toward the end of the 1970s. The price levels of its agricultural (and mineral) exports either stagnated or dropped; the price levels of critical imports, especially petroleum products, rose precipitously. During the period of high rates of international inflation, the price increases of industrial commodities and energy far outpaced those for primary agricultural exports. Because of global inflation, interest rates also increased dramatically. In all these respects, then, African countries suffered a discernible adverse impact from trends in the international economic system. These trends weakened Africa's economic base by lowering its foreign exchange reserves and thereby deprived low-income countries of capital that was vitally needed for investment in agriculture and other sectors. Moreover, the foreign exchange constraint, originating in poor terms of trade, has made it impossible for many African countries to purchase food on world markets at moments of acute crisis in their own food production systems.

Preoccupation with declining terms of trade should not obscure another aspect of this issue that is of equal, if not greater, importance—namely, the extreme fluctuation, often over short periods of time, in the price levels that African countries have received for their primary commodities. The World Bank's

study of Africa's trade prospects shows that the price levels of such commodities as coffee, tea, cocoa, and rubber can vary unpredictably and dramatically from one year to the next, even within the context of fairly identifiable
long-term trends.[44] The consequences of such fluctuation can be onerous. The
effect of a price shift of only a few dollars can add or subtract millions of dollars
from the export earnings of a country that ships hundreds of thousands of tons
of a particular commodity.

At the very least, such fluctuation confounds long-term planning by making
it impossible to predict foreign exchange reserves. Countries that plan the introduction of new projects, anticipating foreign exchange earnings on the basis
of low price averages, run the risk of allowing much of their hard currency to
rest unproductively in European banks. Countries that plan more venture-
somely, expecting high average prices, risk having to borrow hard currency, at
increasingly high interest rates, to cover foreign exchange shortfalls during
low-price years.

CONCLUSION

Independent Africa's colonial heritage—a pronounced overemphasis on the
production of exportable agricultural commodities—serves it poorly. The
prosperity of export-oriented farms has long depended upon pricing policies
that compelled peasants to become migratory agricultural workers and that ultimately reduced the productivity of smallholder food producers by lowering
their incentives. Pricing policies were not the sole means by which colonial
policy harmed the food-producing sector. The systematic denial of infrastructural supports and other critical inputs also hurt food producers.

Organizing to export agricultural commodities has left Africa vulnerable
to adverse trends in the international economy. As the price levels for agricultural commodities have fallen or stagnated, African nations have found it increasingly difficult to generate the foreign exchange earnings necessary to finance food purchases, let alone other necessities such as medical supplies,
energy, and industrial goods. As import costs have risen, African nations have
experienced declines in educational- and medical-system quality and in capacity utilization in the industrial sector. Export agriculture likely cannot provide
a viable basis for economic recovery. World demand for primary agricultural
products is not growing fast enough to affect price levels discernibly. Nor do
African nations generally have the option of increasing their foreign exchange
earnings by the establishment of processing industries; neo-protectionism in
the industrial world effectively discourages this strategy.

Despite hopes voiced by vent-for-surplus and comparative advantage advocates, little benefit has spilled over from export agriculture to other sectors.
Aside from transportation, storage, and the minimal processing capacities used
to prepare a commodity for shipment, export agriculture has done little to

stimulate secondary industrial growth. Its disappointing performance in world markets, moreover, has sorely handicapped efforts to industrialize through import substitution. These industries depended upon agricultural exports to finance imported capital goods, raw materials, and spare parts. This was not to be, however. The import-substitution industrialization strategy would appear to be a casualty of the collapse of agricultural commodity export prices.

The international donor community has not distinguished itself either, because it has failed to develop policies and programs that can effectively arrest the process of long-term structural decline. During the 1960s, the majority of Africa's donors wholeheartedly adopted a large-scale project approach. Convinced that the solution to Africa's agricultural problems lay in the introduction of capital-intensive, highly technological, Western systems of cultivation, donor nations spent hundreds of millions of dollars on demonstration farms. The failure rate of these farms has been extraordinarily high; the African countryside is littered with the debris of abandoned projects. But, before they were abandoned, many of these projects may have contributed to the continent's agrarian malaise. They not only became a heavy burden on the financial and managerial capacity of African governments, but, in some cases, they produced food products that competed with peasant-grown foods and thereby lowered the price levels of peasant-grown foods even further.

Many of Africa's largest donors are now convinced that the reasons for the economic crisis are internal and that the solution requires the adoption of a free-market approach that will stimulate the production of agricultural commodities for export. Not only does this approach fail to recognize how Africa's export orientation has contributed to the present crisis, but it also fails to acknowledge the realities of today's international economy. The world market for tropical agricultural goods has a decidedly zero-sum quality: One country's gain can only be purchased by another country's loss. Moreover, one country's success in increasing its export sales can only result in a decline in future price. Kenya, for example, has begun to face this problem with respect to tea exports. Its ability to generate an export boom by expanding the production of high quality teas has already begun to affect its foreign exchange earnings by weakening tea prices on the London exchange. Other countries that are also major exporters of a particular commodity could well anticipate the same experience.

African countries, nevertheless, cannot withdraw from the world economy by shifting agricultural production to domestically consumable products. Foreign exchange is indispensable. Aside from Nigeria, no independent African country has any prospect of becoming self-sufficient in important industrial goods and energy. Internal markets are too small for these countries to entertain economic isolation. Even the harshest critics of the global trading system acknowledge that trade is the quickest means for small nations to industrialize and to improve health, education, transportation, and other services. In a very real sense, the only course of action that would be worse than continuing to produce agricultural goods for glutted international markets would be to withdraw completely from the international economy. The depth and complexity of Africa's current crisis and the extent to which remedies exceed the policy jurisdiction of African nations are reflected in this paradox.

It is hoped that at least partial solutions to some of Africa's problems are available. Despite generations of neglect, Africa's smallholder farmers continue to demonstrate enormous social resiliency, market responsiveness, and productive capacity. Moreover, private voluntary organizations have demonstrated the capacity to work effectively with these farmers and to generate recovery projects that succeed at the grass roots level. These are the building blocks for economic recovery. However, unless there are wholesale changes at the level of the international economic system, the energies and potential inherent in these groups will not prevail.

NOTES

1. In this chapter, unless otherwise indicated, "Africa" refers to sub-Saharan Africa only and does not include the North African countries.

2. U.S. Department of Agriculture (USDA), *Food Problems and Prospects in Sub-Saharan Africa: The Decade of The 1980s,* p. 3.

3. World Bank, *Toward Sustained Development in Sub-Saharan Africa: A Joint Program of Action,* p. 10.

4. USDA, *Food Problems and Prospects in Sub-Saharan Africa,* pp. 7-8.

5. World Bank, *Accelerated Development in Sub-Saharan Africa: An Agenda for Action,* p. 46.

6. World Bank, *Toward Sustained Development,* p. 9.

7. World Bank, *Coping with External Debt in the 1980s,* pp. 6-7.

8. As quoted in World Bank, *Sub-Saharan Africa: Progress Report on Development Prospects and Programs,* p. ii.

9. Colin M. Turnbull, *The Mountain People.*

10. Yoeri Kyesimira, *Agricultural Export Development,* pp. 7-9.

11. USDA, *Food Problems and Prospects in Sub-Saharan Africa,* p. 4.

12. The obvious exception is René Dumont's classic work, *False Start in Africa.* This book was originally published in its French version in 1966.

13. See Roger Leys, *Dualism and Rural Development in East Africa,* "Introduction," p. 7.

14. This theoretical position is central to Rodolfo Stavenhagen's classic work, *Social Classes in Agrarian Societies.* See especially Chapter 6, "Agrarian Changes and the Dynamics of Class in Black Africa," pp. 72-93.

15. Writing of this process in Kenya, Colin Leys has suggested that within a single generation, more than 50 percent of the able-bodied males in the two largest tribes had become wage-dependant agricultural workers. See his *Underdevelopment in Kenya: The Political Economy of Neo-Colonialism, 1964-1971,* p. 31.

16. For precisely this point with respect to the Sahel famine of the 1970s, see Richard W. Franke and Barbara H. Chasin, *Seeds of Famine: Ecological Destruction and*

the Development Dilemma in the West African Sahel. For an extraordinarily fine treatment of the Ethiopian famine of this period, see Jack Shepherd, *The Politics of Starvation.*

17. UN, Economic Commission for Africa, *Survey of Economic Conditions in Africa.* See especially Chapter 4, "Agriculture." See also Alan Rake, "Collapse of African Agriculture," pp. 17-19.

18. Small wonder that one radical observer has gone so far as to suggest that Western capitalist nations welcome African droughts as a final phase in the dispossession of the African peasantry. Claude Meillassoux has suggested that droughts serve to sweep the countryside free of peasant producers, thereby paving the way for large-scale capital investment. See his article "Development or Exploitation: Is the Sahel Famine Good Business?"

19. A useful summary and discussion of vent-for-surplus theory appears in Carl K. Eicher and Doyle C. Baker, *Research on Agricultural Development in Sub-Saharan Africa: A Critical Survey,* pp. 31-33. See also I. Livingstone and H. W. Ord, *Agricultural Economics for Tropical Africa,* pp. 71-72, and 179-183.

20. H. Myint, "The 'Classical Theory' of International Trade and the Underdeveloped Countries," p. 333. See also his article "The Gains from International Trade and the Backward Countries."

21. J. S. Hogendorn, "The Vent-for-Surplus Model and African Cash Agriculture to 1914." See also his article "Economic Initiative and African Cash Farming: Pre-Colonial Origins and Early Colonial Development," in Peter Duignan and Lewis Gann, eds., *Colonialism in Africa, 1870-1960,* Vol. 4. of *The Economics of Colonialism,* pp. 283-328.

22. Hogendorn, "The Vent-for-Surplus Model," p. 328.

23. For an extended critique of vent-for-surplus theory as it applies to the economic behavior of peasant families, see Barbara Ingham, *Tropical Exports and Economic Development,* especially Chapter 6, "Concluding Remarks," pp. 88-96.

24. W. M. Freund and R. W. Shenton, "'Vent-for-Surplus' Theory and the Economic History of West Africa."

25. Ibid., p. 195.

26. Myint, "The 'Classical Theory' of International Trade and the Underdeveloped Countries," p. 327.

27. Eicher and Baker, *Research on Agricultural Development in Sub-Saharan Africa,* p. 32.

28. The author is indebted to Rhys Payne, Department of Political Science, UCLA, for making available his manuscript entitled "Economic Development and Comparative Advantage."

29. William O. Jones, *Marketing Staple Food Crops in Tropical Africa,* p. 233.

30. World Bank, *Accelerated Development in Sub-Saharan Africa.*

31. See, for example, Subrata Ghatak and Ken Ingersent, *Agriculture and Economic Development,* especially Chapter 10, "Agriculture and International Trade," pp. 279-307.

32. Hollis Chenery, *Structural Change and Development Policy,* p. 273.

33. Ibid., p. 275.

34. Barbara Dinham and Colin Hines, *Agribusiness in Africa.* See especially pp. 33-35. See also Mohamed S. Halfani and Jonathon Barker, "Agribusiness and Agrarian Change," in Jonathon Barker, ed., *The Politics of Agriculture in Tropical Africa,* pp. 35-63.

35. In an important case study whose academic reputation has been limited by a somewhat polemical tone, Robert Fitch and Mary Oppenheimer show that the profits

from Ghana's cocoa trade following World War II were critically important in helping to capitalize Britain's postwar economic recovery. See *Ghana: End of an Illusion,* especially pp. 40-52.

36. Shamsher Singh, *Sub-Saharan Agriculture: Synthesis and Trade Prospects,* Table C, p. 8.

37. Ibid., p. 11. See also Douglas R. Nelson, *The Political Structure of the New Protectionism.*

38. World Bank, *World Development Report 1985,* pp. 40-41.

39. World Bank, *Accelerated Development in Sub-Saharan Africa,* p. 19.

40. World Bank, *Sub-Saharan Africa,* p. 3.

41. World Bank, *Toward Sustained Development,* p. 12.

42. World Bank, *World Development Report 1984,* p. 24.

43. Singh, *Sub-Saharan Agriculture,* Chart 1, p. 21.

44. Ibid., pp. 21-24 and 39.

Keith B. Griffin

6

The Economic Crisis in Ethiopia

On the eve of its revolution in 1974, the economy of Ethiopia was perhaps the most backward in the world. Life was short. Indeed, life expectancy at birth—37.5 years for males and 40.6 years for females—was the lowest in the world. This short life expectancy was accompanied by a high infant mortality rate (178 per 1,000 live births) and a high maternal death rate (20 per 1,000 births). Ethiopia had the least favorable ratio of doctors to population (one physician per 75,320 people) and the lowest rate of calorie consumption per capita (1,754) of any country on earth.

About 85 percent of the population lived in rural areas, yet 90 percent of the rural people lived in shelters that offered minimal protection against the weather. Additionally, the shelters were shared with domestic animals and posed many safety and health hazards, especially for children. In the country as a whole, only 6 percent of the population had access to safe water, and most people had to work and live without the assistance of mechanical or electrical power. (Energy consumption per capita was only about 20 kilograms of coal equivalent.) The economy had to rely largely on manpower and womanpower, supplemented by animal power, and in consequence the productivity of labor was very low.

The population as a whole was both ignorant and extremely poor. Prior to the revolution, about 52 percent of the urban population were illiterate. In rural areas the rate of illiteracy was 91.5 percent. Of all the nations in the world, only Bhutan and Mali suffered from a comparable degree of lack of education. Similarly, annual income per capita, at roughly $115, was as low as could be found anywhere.[1]

This is the inheritance of underdevelopment. It would of course be unrealistic to expect that the poverty of centuries could be eradicated in a few years, but it would be reasonable to hope that a decade after the revolution some progress would have been made in increasing the appallingly low standard of living of the mass of the population. Alas, such progress has not occurred.

The economy of Ethiopia has been in crisis for a long time. In particular, the value of agricultural output per capita has been falling at least since 1960, and given that the overwhelming majority of the people live in rural areas, this implies that living standards of most people have been declining for a quarter of a century. The decline has not been steady: Living standards have tended to fluctuate with the harvests, which in turn are strongly influenced by the timing and amount of rainfall, but the trend has been clearly downward. As a result of the negative trend the likelihood of a famine increases with each downswing of the cycle, and each famine now tends to be worse than its immediate predecessor. Thus the current famines are worse than those of 1972-1974,[2] which resulted in the overthrow of Emperor Haile Selassie,[3] and those in turn were worse than the famine of 1965-1966.

An alarming feature of Ethiopia's economy is that the rate of deterioration has accelerated since 1970 and the economy today teeters on the verge of collapse. For example, between 1960 and 1970 the value of agricultural output per capita declined 0.2 percent a year on average, but between 1970 and 1982 the rate of decline accelerated to 1.1 percent a year. Similarly, investment per capita actually increased 3.3 percent a year during the first period and then declined 1.3 percent a year during the second (See Table 6.1). Although the dividing line between the two periods does not coincide with the date of the downfall of the emperor, it seems clear that economic performance under the revolutionary regime has been even worse than under the ancient regime.

The most obvious immediate cause of the acute suffering currently being endured by the people of Ethiopia is the drought. The rains were particularly bad in 1984-1985 and the 1984 harvests are estimated to have been between 25 and 40 percent below normal.[4] A second cause is the depressed world economy and the poor trading environment that now confronts the country. This is reflected in a plummeting in the country's terms of trade, a decline in exports per capita, a contraction of the country's capacity to import, and a pronounced

Table 6.1 Ethiopia: Indicators of Crisis, 1960–1982

| | (annual percentage rate of growth) | |
	1960–70	1970–82
Population[a]	2.4	2.0
Value of agricultural output per capita	−0.2	−1.1
Volume of agricultural output per capita	0.6	−0.5
Volume of food output per capita	0.5	−0.3
Exports per capita	1.3	−0.7
Imports per capita	3.8	−1.8
External terms of trade	n.a.	−4.9
Gross domestic investment per capita	3.3	−1.3

[a]The projected rate of population growth between 1980 and 2000 is 3.1 percent per annum.

Source: World Bank, *Toward Sustained Development in Sub-Saharan Africa* (Washington, D.C., 1984), Statistical Annex.

decline in imports per capita. (See the export, import, and terms-of-trade lines of Table 6.1.)

Third, there are the civil wars. The separatist movement in Eritrea goes back to 1961, but the violence of the conflict intensified greatly after 1975 when the Dergue (the Provisional Military Administrative Council) decided to seek a military solution to the problem.[5] In addition, there have been rebellions by several other non-Amhara groups, including the Somalis in the south, the Tigreans in the north, and the Oromos, largely from Wollega in the west. In each case the Dergue has chosen to respond to these nationalist movements by using force rather than persuasion and negotiation.[6] The cost, in terms of resources and human life, has been high.

Finally, the economic policies of the government must bear much blame for what has happened. Investment has been stagnant; national savings have been allowed to decline; foreign aid has increased substantially since 1974, but most of it has been used for military purposes. As a result, national product per capita is lower today than at the time of the revolution. What little investment there has been has been concentrated on large-scale, capital-intensive industry in the three largest cities. Peasant agriculture has been utterly ignored; only the state farms have received significant resources, and these have been wasted on huge, highly mechanized, and inefficient operations. It is ironic that a government that came to power because of the incompetence of the previous regime in coping with famine was itself unprepared when famine struck. The army, civil servants, and the population in the larger urban centers had access to rationed food, but the majority of people did not, and hence when food became scarce and prices rose dramatically in 1984, millions of inhabitants in the rural areas suddenly were threatened with starvation.[7]

THE SOCIAL REVOLUTION OF 1974

Unlike the situation in other countries in Africa where radical change has occurred, in Ethiopia in 1974 the revolution was directed not against a colonial power[8] but against an indigenous ruling class and imperial dynasty that had existed since the middle of the nineteenth century. The revolution was led from above by a bureaucratic and military elite. Indeed, it may be regarded as a revolution from within the state itself, but its underlying cause was a prolonged agrarian crisis that drove an increasing proportion of the peasantry into destitution and, ultimately, mass starvation.

Destruction of the Feudal Order

The revolution was directed against an order that can best be described as feudal. Landownership and claims to land based on political office were highly concentrated; most, by far, of peasant households were subjected to an onerous extraction of rent, to compulsory labor, and to tribute in the form of cattle and honey. The main beneficiaries of this system were the Amhara monarchy, the nobility, the Coptic church, and those whose services to the imperial regime were rewarded by grants of land, particularly in the conquered region of the Oromo people to the south of Shoa.

Ethiopia before the revolution was a true empire. The country was highly stratified along linguistic, religious, and ethnic lines. At the top was an Amharic-speaking, Christian elite from the central highlands. Below them were Muslim and other religious groups and numerous ethnic and tribal nationalities speaking more than eighty languages. Stratification was accompanied by fragmentation. The difficult mountainous terrain in the central highlands and the semideserts surrounding them led to regional heterogeneity, and the exiguous communication system led to the acute isolation of most of the population.

The destruction of this feudal and imperial order was the first achievement of the revolution of 1974. The creation of a new order, however, has been painful and, so far, unsuccessful. Despite the fact that military expenditure accounted in 1982 for over half of total government expenditure and more than 6 percent of gross domestic product, civil disturbances, armed conflict, and separatist movements have continued and have possibly gained in force.

Redistribution in Favor of the Peasantry

A second achievement of the revolution was a redistribution of income in favor of the peasantry. The chief instrument for achieving this redistribution was the land reform of 1975. Under the reform, tenancy was abolished, the titles and rights of the former landlords were extinguished, and the land was nationalized. Peasant associations were formed and given responsibility for redistributing land to households, establishing service cooperatives, collecting agricultural taxes, introducing improved technology, and generally mobilizing the rural population for development.

It is not possible to calculate accurately the extent to which the reform improved the standard of living of the mass of the rural people, but it is evident that the improvement must have been considerable. Indeed, it is possible that incomes of the beneficiaries increased by as much as half within a year. Given that the incomes of the peasantry had been falling prior to the revolution, this constituted a dramatic reversal of fortunes. Unfortunately, however, the rate of growth of agricultural output remained alarmingly low; in fact, during the five years after the revolution, and long before the current drought began, agricultural output per capita continued to fall approximately 0.8 percent per annum.

Mass Literacy Campaign

The third achievement of the revolution was the National Literacy Campaign. Launched in July 1979 with the objective of reducing the rate of illiteracy from roughly 87 percent of those aged ten or older to zero within eight years, the campaign was able to mobilize thousands of students, teachers, and educated youths, first to increase literacy in the urban areas and then to do the same in rural areas. By the end of 1982 the literacy rate in the nation as a whole was thought to have risen to about 45 percent.

A STRATEGY FOR ECONOMIC PROGRESS

These, then, were the achievements of the revolution by 1982, when I was invited by the government to advise on economic policy. Still, the economic problems of the country were extremely serious and the government faced a formidable challenge. Unemployment in the urban areas was about 20 percent and rising, and among youngsters leaving school it was higher still and rising faster. Real incomes of wage earners had fallen by about a third since 1975 and those of salaried workers by even more. A person receiving the minimum wage could no longer provide a family with its minimum food requirements even if the whole of his income was spent on food. In the rural areas, living standards were even lower. Real incomes were falling, and the gains of the land reform were fast eroding. Sadly, a majority of the people in Ethiopia were poorer in 1982 than they had been in 1974.

Gross domestic product per capita had risen only fractionally if at all. The economy had been based on war for most of the previous six years, and a rising proportion of a stagnant income had been allocated to military expenditure. Government administration and other items of public consumption also had increased their share of the domestic product. In contrast, the gross fixed investment ratio remained low and constant while the share of private consumption in domestic product remained high at around 80 percent. Food production per capita had declined by about 5 percent.

Some of the essential facts about the economy are contained in Table 6.2. Private and public consumption in 1980/81 accounted for over 95 percent of gross domestic product, thereby leaving domestic savings at less than 5 percent. Consumption was at an extraordinarily high level and underlined a serious problem of domestic resource mobilization. Ethiopia had also become increasingly dependent on foreign aid: The negative foreign resource balance rose from 2.37 percent of GDP in 1974/75 to 5.6 percent in 1980/81. Despite the greater abundance of foreign capital, average incomes failed to rise.

The reasons are not hard to find. Between 1974 and 1981 the share of foreign aid in GDP rose by 2.73 percentage points. At the same time the domestic savings ratio fell 2.46 percentage points, and the proportion of public consumption (including military expenditure) in GDP rose 2.89 percentage points. These changes not only are of equal magnitude, they are intimately related; that is, we might conclude that most of the inflow of foreign resources went directly into increased public consumption. Alternatively, domestic re-

Table 6.2   Expenditure and Savings Ratios

	(percentages of GDP at market prices)	
	1974–75	1980–81
Private consumption	79.99	79.66
Public consumption	12.75	15.64
Fixed investment	10.13	10.40
Foreign resource balance	−2.87	−5.60
Domestic savings	7.26	4.80

Source: Government of Ethiopia, Central Statistical Office.

sources were diverted from savings to public consumption, and foreign resources made up for the shortfall in domestic savings so that investment could remain unchanged. Essentially, these are two ways of saying the same thing. Either way, the key point is that the mobilization of domestic resources for investment and growth was seriously neglected and in consequence a catastrophe was inevitable. Only the timing of the catastrophe was uncertain.

An alternative vision of economic development within a socialist framework—the political constraints under which the government could entertain any advice—evidently was urgently required. That is what we attempted to supply in a report prepared for the Ethiopian government.[9] In that report we argued for attention to labor-intensive grass roots development that would be quite compatible with the ruling elite's socialist sentiments.

Accumulation and Cooperation

The point of departure was agriculture, the foundation of the economy, the largest sector of production and the source of livelihood for the greater portion of the population. Unfortunately, agriculture was by far the weakest sector of the economy, and major efforts were required to reverse the decline. Incomes and the productivity of labor in the countryside were extremely low, and hence both the marketable surplus and the internal rate of savings in agriculture were insufficient to finance either its own expansion or the development of the rest of the economy.

The main resource available was the seasonally surplus labor force. Our strategy for rural development was based on mobilizing this force for a series of capital construction projects that would (1) bring more land under cultivation; (2) raise yields in existing land through land improvement projects and other activities; (3) increase the cropping ratio through, for example, small irrigation works; (4) increase the productivity of labor by improving the quantity and quality of farm implements; (5) lead to the development of a local construction industry based on locally available materials; and (6) encourage the establishment of small workshops and factories to process agricultural products, produce simple consumer goods used locally, and provide inputs for further agricultural development. The initial investments would be financed not by lower consumption of the peasantry but by greater work and less seasonally idle time. Once output per capita began to rise, part of it could be siphoned off as savings to finance further investment.

This process of labor investment followed by savings investment would have to be carefully organized. It is here that cooperation could play a vital role. Any form of viable cooperation should be encouraged, be it service cooperatives or producers' cooperatives. The thrust of the cooperative movement, however, should not be collective production, as the government envisaged, but collective accumulation. That is, the cooperatives should be regarded as institutions to promote investment, first, by organizing labor for capital construction projects and, second, by amassing accumulation funds out of the revenue surpluses of cooperative-owned undertakings. At best, collective agricultural production should be a secondary objective of cooperatives, surely one that is subordinate to the imperative of accelerated accumulation.

In addition, great care should be taken to ensure that cooperation is in the material interest of the peasantry. It is important that two dangers in particular should be avoided. First, force should never be used to establish cooperatives. Ultimately, it will only lead to resistance, not accumulation. Second, the incomes generated by cooperatives should not be appropriated by the state in the form of higher taxes or compulsory deliveries of grain at fixed low prices. Despite warnings, however, the government has committed both errors[10] and thereby nullified the purpose of the policy, which was to encourage local initiative, local effort, and local savings for investment in projects of direct benefit to the people making the sacrifices. The whole purpose of the strategy was to promote grass-roots development, building on the peasant associations. These purposes were never realized, and the 1985 disaster is in large part the result.

Infrastructure and Social Services

Our advice to the government was that the state should concentrate whatever resources it could devote to rural development on two things: providing economic and social infrastructure and improving the performance of the state farms.

Ethiopia has systematically, over a long time period, underinvested in rural infrastructure—roads, power, irrigation, storage, and processing facilities—and in the health, education, and training of the rural population. One consequence of this is that the return on investment in other activities—in agriculture, industry, and commerce—is low because their efficiency is greatly hampered by the lack of complementary services, facilities, and skills. Investment in rural infrastructure, primary education, basic health services, potable water supplies, and training not only are necessary in themselves, they also are a precondition for profitable investment in agriculture, rural industry, and urban manufacturing. Unless the fragmentation and disarticulation of the economy can be overcome, the national market will forever remain small and the return on capital will remain low. Hence the importance of state investment in infrastructure.

Aside from physical infrastructure, the state also will have to provide basic social services. A good start was made immediately following the 1974 revolution, particularly with the literacy campaign and the provision of primary education, but progress was interrupted by the famine and civil war that soon followed. Still, improvement had occurred, in education and in other areas as well. The peasant associations and urban kebeles still exist, and they have demonstrated their ability to organize and run campaigns in their localities. They should be encouraged to expand their activities to include health, nutrition, family planning, and the care of children.

There are two great advantages to a mass approach to the provision of basic social services. First, such an approach is essential in providing a floor to poverty and preventing large numbers of people from suffering economic catastrophe every time there is a fluctuation in the harvest. The central government cannot be solely responsible for the eradication of illiteracy, for universal primary education, widespread preventive health measures, and maternal and child care. Yet these are the services every community must have if poverty is to be contained and every family is to enjoy minimum economic security.

Second, local involvement in administering the social services can lead to local involvement in financing them. This would relieve the central government of part of the financial burden and at the same time provide an incentive to the mass organizations to mobilize local resources for their continuation and expansion. Just as cooperation can lead to capital accumulation in the rural areas, so too can mass organization play an important role in limiting economic hardship and guaranteeing minimum standards of public welfare.

Food Rationing

The most important piece of social infrastructure needed in Ethiopia is an efficient food-rationing system. Given the precarious nature of food supplies, the government cannot escape the responsibility of ensuring that the entire population receives a guaranteed minimum amount of grain at prices the poor can afford.

Ethiopia in 1982 was in the fortunate position of having in place most of the instruments necessary to operate an effective rationing system. It would not have been difficult to cover the entire country, as was recommended, by distributing rationed food supplies through the kebeles in urban areas (as already happened in the larger towns) and through the peasant associations in rural areas. The tragedy of mass starvation could and should have been avoided.

Rationed supplies of grain could have been obtained from a number of sources: directly from the state farms, through open-market purchases by the Agricultural Marketing Corporation, and by making agricultural taxes payable in grain. Some help might have been forthcoming from the United Nations World Food Program and the European Economic Community, particularly in building up the stocks necessary to launch a nationwide program.

The principles to be applied in distributing rationed goods should be considered carefully. First, the entire population should be entitled to purchase a specified quantity through the mass organizations to which they belong. In this way a minimum would be guaranteed to everyone. However, second, the rationing system should in practice discriminate in favor of the poor by choosing the kinds of goods and, more important, the quality of goods that normally are purchased predominantly by low-income groups. In Ethiopia this implies a concentration on inferior cereals such as sorghum, maize, and black teff.

Third, the number of goods to be rationed should be as few as possible consistent with the government's ultimate objectives and with its actual ability to ensure that the rationed quantities are in fact delivered to the outlets and are available when people come to purchase them. Fourth, price controls should be applied to the rationed supplies, but the prices of unrationed supplies should be allowed to rise on the open market to soak up excess demand. The controlled prices of grains should be set in such a way that a person employed on a minimum wage could cover a household's minimum needs for food.

State Farms

From the perspective of the central government, one of the disadvantages of a grass-roots strategy of development is that local resources will be mobilized and retained locally and not be made available to urban areas. An obvious worry is that the supply of food in urban areas will not be sufficient to feed the urban population. In principle, and in the long run, this should not be a problem in Ethiopia because less than one person in five lives in the cities. If agricultural output can be raised significantly the huge rural population should be able to feed the small urban population with ease. At a time when food production per capita is low and falling, however, the government is right to be concerned about the size of the marketable surplus of food.

It is in this context that state farms assume importance. In Ethiopia, state farms are few in number and account for less than 5 percent of the land area and agricultural output. The average size of farm, however, is very large, often several thousand hectares. Moreover, the state farms absorb about 90 percent of all investment in agriculture. They have been treated by the government as an insurance policy against severe food shortages in the cities and virtually the whole of the output from state grain-producing farms is available to the Agricultural Marketing Corporation to supply the army, government institutions such as hospitals, and the public food distribution system in the larger urban centers.

Unfortunately, the insurance policy has proved to be very expensive. The state farms are both technically and economically inefficient and consequently the great majority operate at a loss. That is, they make a negative contribution to the resources available for accumulation and growth. Given that the absence of growth is the cause of the country's economic crisis, this is a pity.

The farms suffer from a great many difficulties, including (1) very high overhead costs; (2) an excessive degree of mechanization; (3) poor capital equipment, high machine operating costs, inadequate maintenance, and consequently low-capacity utilization; (4) shortages of labor; (5) undesirable labor recruitment practices and wage payment systems; (6) poor choice of location partly resulting from excessively rapid expansion; (7) an overcentralized management structure; and (8) an apparent disregard of financial considerations when making decisions. Until these difficulties are overcome and the state farms are reorganized and made profitable, further expansion of their activities can only aggravate the country's problems. The best that can be said of them so far is that they have supplied some food to the urban areas and thereby made a small but costly contribution to the government's program of industrialization.

Industrialization

The future of industrial development in Ethiopia should be profoundly affected by the structural changes that have occurred and hopefully will continue to occur in the agricultural sector. There has been a radical change in the distribution of landed assets and this has led to a more equal distribution of income in rural areas. This, in turn, can be expected to lead to a change in the pattern of demand and potentially to the creation of a much larger national market for manufactured goods consumed by the rural population. I say "potentially" because whether these opportunities in fact materialize depends on whether agricultural incomes begin to grow and on whether an integrated national market can be created through government investment in infrastructure.

Assuming the necessary conditions are fulfilled, growth and structural change in agriculture have enormous implications for the composition of industrial output, the location of industrial activities, and the choice of technology. Indeed, industrial and agricultural development should be seen as closely linked, the one supporting the other. Specifically, industry should serve agriculture by (1) processing agricultural commodities such as coffee, meat and leather products, and vegetables and fruit; (2) producing improved agricultural implements and modern inputs such as fertilizer for accelerated rural development; (3) supplying the rural sector with simple consumer goods at prices that can be afforded; and by (4) developing a large, widely dispersed, and efficient construction-goods industry that can provide the physical foundation for rapid capital accumulation.

This last point is especially important. Regardless of the development strategy one follows, a major part of total investment, usually well over half, will be expenditure on construction. Therefore, a country that has a large, well-organized, and efficient construction industry has the physical capacity to undertake a large investment program based on domestic resources alone. Foreign resources then become unnecessary for sustained accumulation, although they may be welcomed on other grounds. In Ethiopia, the construction industry should be dispersed throughout the country, partly to overcome the fragmentation of the economy and partly to support the grass-roots strategy of development that is being advocated.

An industrialization strategy based on agro-industries and rural development creates many opportunities to reduce the regional concentration of manufacturing activities. New undertakings can be located near their sources of supply of raw materials or near the rural markets they will serve. The advantages are that transport costs (which are high in Ethiopia) can be minimized, industrial capital can be widely spread in efficient small-scale units, and regional inequalities in the distribution of income and industrial employment can be reduced.

This approach to industrialization, however, is based on choosing labor-intensive technologies and spreading capital thinly. Present practice in Ethiopia is the opposite. The technology selected tends to be capital-intensive, the scale of operation tends to be large, and the factories tend to be located in or near the three existing centers of manufacturing activity. The disadvantages of present industrialization practice are, first, the country's dependence on foreign exchange and foreign aid has been increased rather than reduced; second, unemployment in the cities has not been reduced nor have incomes in the countryside increased; and third, regional income differentials have been exacerbated, thereby aggravating regional conflicts and resentments.

THE HORRENDOUS CONSEQUENCES OF WRONG PRIORITIES

For Ethiopia, the vision of grass roots development within a socialist framework has failed to materialize. The most charitable explanation is that famine struck before the government had time to reorient its policies. The most uncharitable explanation is that the government's priorities were unforgivably bad and greatly aggravated the effects of drought. At the top of the list of bad priorities was the decision to allocate a high proportion of the country's resources to the armed forces. Ethiopia now has the largest army in black Africa. This army absorbs human resources and finances that are desperately needed for development. Next was the decision to spend approximately $275 million in September 1984 on celebrations connected with the tenth anniversary of the revolution. The desire of the government to consolidate its power evidently was regarded as a more important use of funds than purchases abroad of grain for starving peasants.

Then there was the decision, again taken in 1984, to concentrate administrative talent not in combating the famine but in organizing the Workers Party, the single political party allowed in the country. The task of organizing the new party not only diverted attention from the economic emergency, it actually made the work of famine relief more difficult. As one reporter put it, where once Ethiopian officials of the government's Relief and Rehabilitation Commission "made immediate and on the whole pragmatic decisions, there is now the local party official to be considered. Often it seems that no decision is taken for fear of its being, in the party's eyes, the wrong one. Political priorities have come to supercede humanitarian ones."[11]

Finally, there was the decision to seek a military solution to the country's political problems and to prosecute the civil wars with utter ruthlessness. The result was to disrupt production in the northern parts of the country and thus to make the effects of the drought worse than they might otherwise have been. The government repeatedly rejected offers of a cease-fire to enable the starving in Eritrea and Tigre to be given relief. They also rejected proposals that vehicles carrying emergency supplies to areas controlled by guerrillas be given safe-conduct passes. And they rejected two offers from the assistant secretary-general of the United Nations in charge of famine relief operations in Ethiopia that food should be distributed independently by the Red Cross and the UN in areas outside government control.[12]

The government claimed that its relief program could reach the hungry wherever in the country they might be found, that the guerrillas did not occupy permanently any territory but were little more than roving bandits, and hence that special measures to feed the starving in Eritrea and Tigre were unnecessary. It subsequently became known, however, that the Relief and Rehabilitation Commission, in an internal report, estimated that only 22 percent of the population of Tigre was receiving famine relief.[13] These people were concentrated around the provincial capital of Mekele and were supplied by air; the remaining 78 percent of the province's population was ignored. A similar situation probably prevails in Eritrea.

The circumstantial evidence thus suggests that famine in Ethiopia is being used as an instrument of war. A large number of people in the country, perhaps the majority by now, oppose Amhara domination in general and the present regime in particular. The country, undoubtedly, is in danger of falling apart, and if this happens the claims of the Dergue to national leadership will vanish. The government uncompromisingly has responded to these threats by attempting to starve its opponents into submission.

Whether deliberate or not, the extent of starvation is horrific. Approximately 500,000 people are believed to have died in the first part of 1985, and the United Nations estimates that another 8.5 million people in Ethiopia are at risk from starvation.[14] In addition, well over a million Ethiopians have fled the civil wars and the drought and have sought refuge in neighboring countries. Accurate figures are difficult to obtain, but it seems there are between 500,000 and 700,000 Ethiopian refugees in the Sudan, 700,000 in Somalia, and 15,000 in Djibouti.[15] In total, between one-quarter and one-third of the entire population has been forced to take desperate measures to avoid dying because of insufficient food.

The options open to starving people and to the authorities are limited. First, people can stay in their villages, live off their reserves as long as possible, and when the reserves are exhausted hope that emergency supplies will be brought to the village. This is by far the best way to handle relief. It avoids dislocation of the population and enables agricultural activities to commence again as soon as the rains return.[16] If the relief is distributed as food-for-work, the population can be mobilized to undertake small-scale investment projects that should raise average incomes in the future.

Second, the hungry can leave their villages and move to feeding centers in the provincial capitals and other large towns. Because of the poor transport facilities and poor security in much of the affected countryside, this appears to be the way most relief is provided in Ethiopia. However, the disadvantages of doing this are obvious. Not only must food be provided, but also housing and sanitation facilities. While people are in the feeding centers, they are unemployed and bored and are likely to become demoralized because of having to live on charity. In any case, being away from their farms, they are unable to resume cultivation even when climatic conditions improve. As a result, the relief operation is likely to last longer and be more costly than under the first option.

Third, if relief is not available in someone's own province, and on terms that are tolerable, the person can emigrate to a neighboring country and become a refugee. As we have seen, mass distress migrations from Ethiopia have become common, and the burden that has fallen on the Sudan and Somalia is enormous; indeed, it is practically unendurable. From the point of view of the migrant, too, the cost of emigration is high. All of the disadvantages associated with migration to internal feeding centers apply here also, and in addition there are the problems that arise from moving to a strange land and living among people who speak a different language and who probably do not welcome large numbers of foreigners competing for limited resources. If someone must suffer and starve, it is better to do so at home than as an alien abroad.

Lastly, the government can organize resettlement programs in other parts of the country where land is thought to be more abundant, more fertile, or less subject to drought. The Ethiopian government does, in fact, have an ambitious scheme to move 1.5 million people from the northern provinces of Tigre, Wollo, and Gondar to the southwestern provinces of Kaffa, Illubabor, and Wollega, and already about 70,000 people have been moved.[17] Such programs inevitably are very costly. Transportation must be provided not only to move food to the hungry but also to move the hungry to the areas of settlement, and if transport vehicles are in short supply, as they are in Ethiopia, this means that the feeding centers in the north will be inadequately supplied.

Once the settlers have been moved, they will have to be supported, often for several years, until they are able to produce enough for subsistence. The land will have to be cleared, houses constructed, sources of safe water identified, road communications established, and a commercial and trading network created. It is most unlikely that Ethiopia has the resources to undertake a resettlement program of the size envisaged. Indeed, the government seems to have realized this, but instead of abandoning the program it has abandoned the settlers. Each settler household is allocated two hectares. Thereafter, "the assistance provided is minimal. . . . Essentially, it is the same relief assistance that is being provided presently at relief shelters."[18] Unlike the relief centers in the north, however, resettlement in the south is intended to be permanent. The settlers are, in effect, being dumped. They are being transferred from the highlands to the lowlands, where they are expected to learn a new type of farming, to cope with new diseases, to build new communities, and, presumably, to learn the language and customs of the surrounding peoples, all with minimal assistance.

The government claims the resettlement program is voluntary, but there is much evidence that suggests the contrary. There are reports, for example, that in the north the government withholds grain from relief centers for weeks on end but provides two cooked meals a day at resettlement transit camps half a mile away; that the government deliberately withholds trucks to move grain in order to starve those in relief centers into volunteering for resettlement; and, when these tactics fail, families are split up and the men are ordered at gunpoint into trucks and airplanes for the journey south.[19] The economic justification for the resettlement program is slight, and there is no moral justification for the tactics employed by the government. The explanation must be essentially political—namely, an attempt by the government to use the famine as an opportunity to weaken and scatter those in the north who oppose the regime and support the opposition.

What lessons does this sorry tale hold for us in the West? First, famines often are not short-term economic phenomena but the outcome of long-term political factors. Second, a political solution in Ethiopia must take into account the claims of Eritrea and Tigre in the north, the Oromos in the west, and the Somalis in the Ogaden. Third, the involvement of the superpowers and the peninsular Arabs in the Horn of Africa has exacerbated conflict and made it more difficult to reach a political settlement.[20] Fourth, the response of the United States, Britain, and the European community to the famine in Ethiopia was tragically slow,[21] presumably for political reasons, and humanitarian aid commensurate with requirements did not begin to flow until the compassion of the general public was roused by the sight on its television screens of mass death by starvation.

We have also learned, fifth, that even emergency food aid cannot be politically neutral in a country racked by civil wars, that aid inevitably strengthens the recipient government relative to its opponents, and that in a world of sovereign nation-states the international community has few effective means of feeding people if they are in open rebellion against their government. Finally, perhaps the most painful lesson of all, it has become clear that unless care is taken, the long-term effect of emergency aid may be to perpetuate the very conditions that made aid necessary. This is not an argument for being less than generous in times of crisis, but it is a warning that in trying to do good some harm is done as well. With luck and skill and perseverance, we can hope the gains will exceed the losses. As T. S. Eliot said so well,

There is only the fight to recover what has been lost
And found and lost again and again: and now, under conditions
That seem unpropitious. But perhaps neither gain nor loss.
For us, there is only the trying.

NOTES

1. Data on Ethiopia should be treated with caution. Agricultural statistics in particular are not very accurate, and, as agriculture accounts for about half the GDP, the figures for national income and output are subject to considerable error. Ethiopia was the only major country in the world that had never had a population census when its first census was conducted in 1982; the results have not been released. Thus, neither the size of the population nor its rate of growth are known with certainty, but it is assumed there were 33 million people in 1982 increasing at a rate of 2.5-3.3 percent a year. The level and rate of growth of output per capita is little more than a guess, given our ignorance of both the numerator and the denominator.

2. For an analysis of the famines of the 1970s, see Amartya Sen, *Poverty and Famines: An Essay on Entitlement and Deprivation,* Chapter 7.

3. For a description of the emperor and his court in their final days, see Ryszard Kapuscinski, *The Emperor: Downfall of an Autocrat.*

4. The Food and Agriculture Organization (FAO) estimates the 1984 harvests were 25-30 percent below normal; the government of Ethiopia estimates they were 40 percent below normal. See UN, FAO, Relief and Rehabilitation Commission, *Early Warning System Meher (Main) Crop Season Synoptic Report, 1984 Crop Season.*

5. For a concise statement of both sides of the Eritrean issue, see Minority Rights Group, *Eritrea and Tigray.*

6. The best book on the recent political history of Ethiopia is Fred Halliday and Maxine Molyneux, *The Ethiopian Revolution.*

7. The UN Food and Agriculture Organization, in an October 1984 report to the Relief and Rehabilitation Commission, made provisional estimates of gross production of carbohydrate food items—grains, pulses, enset, root crops, etc.—as follows (in thousand metric tons)

1980/81	7,113
1981/81	6,610
1982/83	8,249
1983/84	6,667
1984/85	5,280-5,610
1985/86	7,410

The projection for 1985/86 is based on an assumption of "normal" rains in that year.

8. Ethiopia was colonized by the Italians only briefly. On 3 October 1935, Italy invaded the country and captured Addis Ababa on 5 May 1936, but the Italians in turn were driven out by the British in 1941. See Anthony Mockler, *Haile Selassie's War.*

9. The report to the Ethiopian government that advanced the alternative vision—unfortunately never published—is entitled "Socialism From the Grass Roots: Accumulation, Employment and Equity in Ethiopia."

10. See, for example, Paul Vallely's report "How Mengistu Hammers the Peasants."

11. Paul Vallely, "Fear, Ethiopia's New Disease."

12. Michael Prest and Paul Vallely, "Drive to Resettle Refugees."

13. Paul Vallely, "Ethiopians Admit Tigre Crisis," p. 9.

14. In December 1984 the Ethiopian government estimated that 7.75 million people required emergency relief. Since then independent observers have revised this estimate upwards. The Ethiopian government, in January 1985, raised the estimate to 7.9 million people. (See UN, FAO, Relief and Rehabilitation Commission, *Review of the Current Drought Situation in Ethiopia* and *Early Warning System.*)

15. The estimate of 700,000 Ethiopian refugees in the Sudan comes from the *Guardian,* 25 February 1985. All other estimates were supplied to me by Rights and Justice, London. It is curious that there are between 15,000 and 120,000 Sundanese refugees in Ethiopia who have fled from the civil war in the southern Sudan.

16. The United Nations estimates that even if "normal" rainfall occurs, production would be 10 percent below "normal" because of the dislocation of the population and the death of many ploughing oxen.

17. UN, FAO, Relief and Rehabilitation Commission, *Review of the Current Drought Situation in Ethiopia,* p. 24.

18. Ibid., p. 21.

19. See, for example, Paul Vallely, "Lack of Lorries Hinders Ethiopia Relief Work," p. 9 and Vallely, "How Mengistu Hammers the Peasants," p. 16.

20. The United States supported the Ethiopia of Haile Selassie but switched its support to Somalia after the 1974 revolution. The Soviet Union, which formerly supported Somalia, then began to support Ethiopia. The conservative Arab states have supported the Eritreans, despite the socialist orientation of the separatists. The Sudan, presumably with the backing of the United States, has provided at least indirect support to the Tigreans and Eritreans; it is alleged that, in retaliation, Ethiopia provides some support to the rebels in the southern Sudan.

21. The Relief and Rehabilitation Commission first requested aid in December 1982. The response to this and subsequent appeals was negligible until a final appeal was launched on 7 August 1984. By this time it was evident that the 1984 harvest would be poor and starvation inevitable and massive.

Part 3
Food and Agriculture in Asia

7

F. Tomasson Jannuzi

Toward Food Security in South Asia

In this chapter I cite South Asia's age-old race between food production and population growth, outline successive strategies of rural development in the region (following the emergence in 1947 of India and Pakistan as "new states") to ensure sustained increases in food production, and discuss some of the shortcomings of those strategies. I suggest that the various strategies have emphasized the need to address food security for growing populations by ensuring increases in aggregate food production. I suggest further that the emphasis on the aggregate output of food has given primacy to development strategies that focus on the introduction of new technology and the elimination of physical constraints (such as lack of water) to production increases. Although such strategies may be said to address the important question "How can we grow more food?" they reflect a limited perception of what is needed in South Asia to provide food security to millions of people who remain hungry and malnourished even when food production increases are sustained.

Following a discussion of the environment for agricultural innovation in the Permanent Settlement Region of India and Bangladesh, I suggest that there are additional relevant questions to be asked if rural development strategies are to be evolved that meet both production and distribution goals in South Asia (and particularly in the eastern region of the subcontinent). The most important of these questions is "Who is producing on whose land for whose benefit?" I emphasize that such a question reflects a different definition of what constitutes rural economic development leading to food security for the greatest number of people. Such a question grows out of the work of scholars whose contributions are generally neglected by people who equate food security with the attainment of aggregate production goals. I conclude by stating that there is a need to appreciate the continuing relevance of the intellectual tradition that asks the question "Development for whom and for what?" This tradition is represented in the work of Vera Anstey, Malcolm Darling, Harold Mann, Daniel

Thorner, Wolf Ladejinsky, and Walter Neale—all of whom would be uncomfortable with an approach to food security in South Asia that emphasizes aggregate production increases while neglecting the issue of distributive justice.

THE REGIONAL NEED FOR INCREASED FOOD PRODUCTION

The race between food production and population growth is age-old in South Asia. Food production had failed to keep pace with population growth for many years in the region before Pakistan and India gained independence from Great Britain in 1947. The new states were created in the midst of a post-World War II food crisis, and the partition did nothing to alleviate that crisis. Transforming traditional agriculture and ensuring sustained increases in food production were self-evident needs for both states in the postindependence period. Thus, the stated long-term goals of both India and Pakistan clearly included providing food security—the prospect of self-sufficiency for each country in food grains—for their people.

It was easier, of course, to articulate the general need for productivity increases in basic foodstuffs than to design, implement, and sustain appropriate rural development programs. In India, for example, two good monsoons at the end of the First Five-Year Plan contributed not only to agricultural production increases but also to the impression that productivity increases in agriculture could be achieved with a minimum of effort and investment. The subsequent neglect of appropriate emphasis on agriculture was, to some degree, a derivative of the misinterpretation of the nature of the success achieved in the First Plan period. And, before the end of the Second Five-Year Plan, it had become evident that food production was still lagging in relation to population growth.

That there might be a continuing crisis in food production in South Asia (and particularly in India) seemed evident to specialists of the Ford Foundation as early as 1959.[1] They recommended major new investments in agriculture for the Third Plan, but the Planning Commission was not then prepared to accord as high a priority to investments in agriculture as the Ford report suggested.[2] The food crisis deepened in the 1960s. By 1964, India was importing grain at the rate of approximately 8 million metric tons per annum. In 1966 and 1967 famine conditions prevailed in many districts of Bihar. Pressure mounted on the government to find effective means of achieving rapid increases in food production.

INTERNATIONAL APPROACHES TO THE REGIONAL NEED

To an unusual degree, it had already been fashionable in the subcontinent to look for answers to development problems in the experience of others. Although Mahatma Gandhi had projected a particular vision of idealized village communities in which people would act in concert to address common needs, Nehru looked beyond Indian tradition and outside of the subcontinent for inspiration and advice on how best to modernize traditional agriculture.

The Indian subcontinent soon became the adopted home of scores of specialists, mostly from the United States, in rural development. Each had his or her own perception of how food security would be ensured for the region's growing population. Yet, although particular projects and rural development strategies varied over time, imbedded in the various approaches were values and assumptions associated with mainstream neoclassical economics as taught in Western institutions of higher education. It is not surprising, then, that the diverse approaches to rural development in the subcontinent (such as pilot projects, community development programs, intensive agricultural district programs, the creation of agricultural universities patterned after land grant institutions in the United States, and, finally, the new strategy in agriculture associated, somewhat misleadingly, with the phrase "Green Revolution") had a common focus and therefore asked the same question—"How can we ensure more rapid increases in food production in the aggregate?"

It seemed axiomatic at the time that any strategy effecting rapid increases in aggregate food production would ensure benefits to the mass of the people. Existing inequalities in the distribution of land and the quasi-feudal nature of the rural economy in some regions of the subcontinent were not generally perceived to be impediments to the process by which food, when produced, would in fact be distributed. Besides, the food production issues seemed to be paramount and to require concerted action, orchestrated by public and private sector institutions. If, subsequently, there were to be distribution problems, these would be addressed automatically through the "market" after productivity increases had been achieved.

This way of thinking about the subcontinent's food problems did not focus on the socioeconomic environments of the region. Neither did it focus on historical institutions that defined those environments and would affect the process by which productivity goals and food distribution needs would be addressed. In short, the whole issue of food security was defined—mainly by outsiders—in a fashion that abstracted from the actual conditions affecting people's relationships to the land in the subcontinent. This, in itself, should not be surprising. Those who helped to shape rural development strategies in the subcontinent were, for the most part, devoid of prior experience in the region. They were specialists in agronomic research and extension services who had been trained in other environments. Through no fault of their own they were not "language and area scholars" in the field of South Asian studies. Such a "tribe" did not then exist.

With few exceptions they were not inclined even to question whether local institutions (including historical land and tenure systems) might impede or facilitate the realization of their goals. As they looked for ideas and answers to India's food security and rural development needs, they drew inevitably on their own training and experience—training and experience derived else-where under different historical and institutional conditions. It is no wonder then that their collective definition of modernity in agriculture—and how to achieve it—would be rooted in the theory and practice of U.S. agriculture.

It is in the context of this external focus on "modernity in agriculture" that successive rural development strategies have been promoted in India and Pakistan. Analyses, policies, and programs have generally been abstracted from socioeconomic conditions in the region that affect both food production and food distribution. In practice, this has meant that rural development programs contained implicit assumptions about local environments, including, for example, assumptions that indigenous farmers would be rational, profit maxi-mizers when extension agents properly exposed them to new ideas and tech-nology and appropriately supplied them with new inputs at prices ensuring favorable returns on investments. Moreover, when a favorable socioeconomic environment—including the existence of a fully developed "free market econ-omy"—could not be assumed, steps were sometimes taken to introduce new ideas in districts, areas, and states (for example, the Punjab) where actual condi-tions were perceived to be favorable because agricultural production increases had already been achieved.[3]

When qualified successes in production-oriented rural development pro-grams were achieved, extravagant claims sometimes followed. "The impact of the new seed production levels is a result of their prairie-fire like spread wher-ever conditions are suited to their use. . . . The principal constraint on the spread of the new seeds is water."[4] At the time, the only limitations on the "prairie-fire like spread" of the new technology that seemed to be recognized were those linked to the nonavailability of adequate amounts of water and other physical inputs. Indeed, for some time the availability of these essential physical inputs was the only internationally recognized "local condition" that seemed critical to the success or failure of that production-oriented rural de-velopment strategy. In this fashion it became an international cliché—and an accepted axiom of rural development—that "local conditions" could be de-fined in purely technical, agronomic terms. Local conditions, by this measure, had nothing to do with the socioeconomic environment that would in some regions of South Asia and elsewhere inhibit people's abilities to behave as profit-maximizing farmers.

THE NEW STRATEGY OF AGRICULTURAL DEVELOPMENT

In India, years of trial and error culminated in a "New Strategy of Agricultural Development," outlined in the government's Fourth Five-Year Plan. Again, the approach was production-oriented. The critical new element was the availabil-ity of high-yielding varieties of seeds (wheat) to go along with a package of com-plementary inputs, including fertilizer and water.

The new strategy was developed and acclaimed internationally before being introduced in the subcontinent. Its initial reputation was fostered by the Rockefeller and Ford foundations (and notably in India by Rockefeller's Ralph Cummings). But the path to its adoption in India as a national program was initially uncertain. According to C. Subramaniam, who supported the new strategy from his position in the Indian cabinet as minister for food and agriculture and community development from 1964 to 1967, some Indian scientists were skeptical about the need to import high-yielding varieties of wheat from far-off Mexico. They pointed out that Indian scientists had themselves been evolving new varieties and should continue to do so.[5] Others in India were cynical about the dissemination of the new varieties, suggesting that the new seeds were likely to be successful in demonstration plots, but not within the framework of traditional agriculture in the subcontinent. Similarly, there were indigenous economists who worried about the cost of introducing seed varieties so dependent on large quantities of fertilizer—especially given the likelihood that the strategy would require the importation of fertilizer with scarce foreign exchange. Others pointed out that, with the failure to implement meaningful land reforms in much of India, it seemed likely that farmers with large holdings would have greater access to the new seeds and other inputs than would small and less powerful farmers. Consequently, there would be widening income inequalities in the countryside, and rural tensions would be a concomitant of the introduction of the new strategy. Meanwhile, the communist group in Parliament had its own perspective and line. It associated the new strategy with increasing dependence on the United States and expressed the fear that (with the need to import large quantities of fertilizer) the country would be increasingly vulnerable to U.S. exploitation.[6]

Subramaniam pressed for the adoption of the new strategy, especially at a time when India was importing annually more than 10 million metric tons of food grains. He argued that it would be better to import fertilizer from the West, in an attempt to become self-sufficient in the production of basic foodstuffs, than to remain dependent on food imports from the United States.[7] In due course, the internal climate turned in favor of the new strategy and steps were taken to implement it. The era of the Green Revolution began.

"Green Revolution" became the internationally accepted and somewhat misleading term used to describe the process by which high-yielding varieties of cereals (supported by intensive use of chemical fertilizers in controlled quantities, insecticides, pesticides, and regulated water supplies) would be disseminated in many regions of the subcontinent in the 1970s. The rapid spread of the effects of this package of inputs in some regions (notably in west Pakistan, the Punjab, Haryana, and western Uttar Pradesh) created enormous expectations for continuing aggregate production increases (especially of wheat). It became increasingly fashionable to refer to the "prairie-fire like spread" of the new technology and to express the belief that the only constraint on the spread of the new seeds was a physical one, the assured and controlled availability of water.[8]

Later, Green Revolution successes were expressed in qualified terms:

"Wheat has . . . been the crop that has benefited most from the new technology. . . . Aggregate rice production has . . . told a very different story: indeed, while wheat production was nearly trebling rice production rose only by some 16 per cent."[9] It is clear that there were some physical constraints to the spread of the new technology. The spread was less rapid in areas prone to waterlogging and deep flooding and in nonirrigated areas prone to drought. Moreover, as B. H. Farmer has emphasized, the deep-flooding areas are the principal rice-growing areas of the subcontinent (and constitute 80 percent of the rice-growing area in India alone).[10] Thus, the Green Revolution became a *qualified* success story.

But, even if the new technology would not spread as rapidly as a prairie fire, there was comfort in the impression that the only constraints on its dissemination could be discussed in technocratic, physical terms. If water was a primary constraint, dams could be constructed, channels deepened, and tube wells dug. These were engineering problems—easy to conceptualize and address in physical terms. Moreover, such problems could be examined in a fashion that need not take into account the socioeconomic conditions (associated, for example, with the evolution of historical land systems and the hierarchy of rights in land) in some regions that would limit people's access to water, even after irrigation systems were in place.

The pendulum swung gradually from enthusiasm for the productivity effects of the new technology to qualification concerning the strategy's appropriateness in some regions and, finally, to concern that the technology would be associated with widening income inequality. Could there be rapid growth plus equity? Even if a production-oriented rural development strategy seemed to be consistent with the interests of those who ruled Pakistan, could such a strategy be reconciled with the long-term Indian commitment to distributive justice?

The debate continued in 1985 in Rajiv Gandhi's India, though in muted tones. But, there is now an international consensus that peasant cultivators with secure rights in land (classified appropriately enough in the West as land-owners) "have gained relative to tenants and laborers from the adoption of the higher yielding grain varieties."[11] Although it can be argued that marginal farmers with insecure rights in land, and tenants, sharecroppers, and wage laborers, have often received *some* benefits from increases in aggregate production, there is also evidence of a widening absolute gap in the income distribution between landowners and those having insecure rights in land or no land at all. This generalization is especially pertinent for those classified as tenants, sharecroppers, and landless agricultural laborers in the eastern region of the subcontinent—a zone currently inhabited by more than 250 million people in India and Bangladesh.

There is no need here for a final judgment on the effects of the new technology in agriculture. The new technology's productivity effects have been important, if regionally differentiated in South Asia and elsewhere in the world.

The rudiments of the approach are neither inherently good nor bad. But what must increasingly be understood is that the technology, when introduced in regions of great inequality, will have spread effects that are limited and are distributed in a fashion that reflects and reinforces existing inequalities. One such region of inequality—the Permanent Settlement Region—lies within South Asia and overlaps the boundaries of the contemporary states of India and Bangladesh.

THE HISTORICAL ENVIRONMENT FOR AGRICULTURAL INNOVATION IN THE PERMANENT SETTLEMENT REGION

The Permanent Settlement Region embraces the territory of the Indian states of Bihar, West Bengal, and parts of Orissa, and virtually all the territory of Bangladesh. It is defined by history rather than geography or other natural features. The Permanent Settlement was introduced by the British in 1793. It established the principle that the revenue demand from the region's agricultural lands would be fixed in perpetuity. This was seen as a means of encouraging the area's landlords (*zamindars*) to satisfy the East India Company's revenue needs (and later those of the British government of India), while at the same time giving those landlords an incentive to increase the land's productivity in ways ensuring increased returns to them.

Whatever the intent of those who introduced the Permanent Settlement, we know that the final arrangement was with zamindars who had served in the region as agents of Mogul power in the collection of tribute from subservient peoples. As such, they could be classified appropriately as "revenue-farmers," already divorced from agricultural operations. The British did not change them, by means of the Permanent Settlement, into enterprising landlords of the British sort. Instead, the zamindars continued to use their authority to collect "rent" from their "tenants," the actual cultivators. The zamindars also had unqualified authority to make their own terms with those cultivators—the rights to land of such cultivators having been entirely ignored by the Permanent Settlement.[12]

Over time, then, the actual tillers in the region were compelled to continue sharing their produce with an essentially parasitic group[13] of noncultivating landlords (whose only specified responsibility was to transfer a fixed amount of "land revenue" to the British authority). As this system evolved in the nineteenth century, little was done in the region to prevent zamindars from demanding increasingly higher income shares from the tillers of the soil. Moreover, the actual cultivators (whether classified nominally as tenants or as sharecroppers) could be evicted at will by the zamindars from the lands they tilled. Tillers enjoyed no security of tenure on the land, even though the British made attempts toward the end of that century to confer some de jure rights to peasant cultivators.

At the time of independence and partition in the mid-twentieth century, the Permanent Settlement Region had a more intricate and hierarchical system of land rights than any other region of the subcontinent. The Permanent Settlement and its evolving system of rights had been designed, after all, to perpetuate the rights and prerogatives of a landholding elite whose primary function was to act in behalf of established authority in the collection of land revenue. Given this overriding goal of state policy, it was inevitable that the rights of rent receivers would remain paramount. The residual effect of the system was "a pervasive dichotomy in the region between rent-receivers and the actual tillers of the soil."[14]

The new states of India and Pakistan now replaced the British raj at the apex of the Permanent Settlement Region's agrarian hierarchy. Below the state were the noncultivating landlords (still classified technically as intermediaries of the state in the collection of rent from tenants). These landlords could themselves be differentiated; among them were zamindars, tenure-holders, and under-tenure-holders—all having rent-collecting powers over those below them in the agrarian hierarchy. Below the landlords were the "occupancy *raiyats*" (rent-paying holders of land having occupancy rights to that land). Still lower in the hierarchy were nonoccupancy raiyats (rent-paying holders of land not having occupancy rights to land in their temporary possession). Below these were under-raiyats (rent-paying holders of land in their temporary possession under a raiyat). Finally, at the base of this agrarian hierarchy were sharecroppers (*bataidars* in Bihar and *bargadars* in West Bengal and Bangladesh, who by custom took in land temporarily on oral agreements and were required to give up at least 50 percent of their produce to the superior landholders) and landless wage laborers having no rights in land.

It should be noted that this brief description of the complex hierarchy of interests in land in the Permanent Settlement Region at independence is only representative of the actual stratification of interests in land at the time. There were many unusual, complex relationships that existed according to custom. The hierarchy of relationships was further complicated by many agrarian people having multiple interests and roles—functioning simultaneously, for example, as a landlord (rent collector) over a portion of a holding and as a raiyat (rent payer) over another portion. Others in the hierarchy might exist as under-raiyats or sharecroppers in one growing season and as landless wage laborers in the next.

The predominant characteristics of this system of land rights may be summarized as follows: First, landlords (zamindars, tenure-holders, and under-tenure-holders) acted as intermediaries of the state in collecting rent but were generally divorced from all agricultural operations. However described, they could not be classified as cultivators. In the general case, they were absentee holders of land who neither labored on the land nor assumed any of the risks of production. Though they had some "responsibility" for the well-being of those below them in the agrarian hierarchy (and were known, on occasion, to remit payment of rent in time of local famine), their most noteworthy attribute was a capacity to exercise absolute authority over those below them having inferior rights in land. Second, the actual cultivators (however classified in a de jure sense), those who labored directly on the land and assumed the full risks of production, remained insecure in their rights to land and were subservient to a differentiated array of more powerful people.

In the 1950s and 1960s India and Pakistan passed, in the guise of "agrarian reform," extensive legislation affecting the Permanent Settlement Region. It was politically fashionable at the time to argue that the Permanent Settlement had served the interests of large numbers of noncultivating, absentee landlords whose only function was to act as intermediaries between the cultivators and the state. It was said that these landlords had contributed to the impoverishment of the actual tillers of the soil. If this view were accepted, then it followed that the whole system of intermediary interests had to be abolished so as to provide an end to the exploitation of the peasantry by various kinds of intermediaries, among them the zamindars. Thus, "zamindari abolition" became a widely enunciated goal in the region; and the terms "zamindari abolition" and "agrarian reform" were used interchangeably to allude to the need to transform the traditional agrarian structure as a means of providing the basis for continuing economic progress within an environment favoring the mass of the people.

As is widely known, the rhetoric of reform was more extravagant than the reforms themselves. Although this holds generally for the subcontinent as a whole, more striking is the degree to which the agrarian reforms initiated in the Permanent Settlement Region included provisions designed to preserve the traditional landlord rights and prerogatives. A casual reading would suggest that the various statutes enacted (mainly in the 1950s and 1960s) had the effect of repealing the Permanent Settlement of 1793. The legislation seemed to dismantle the whole system of revenue-farming. In a qualified sense, this was so. The enacted reforms did abolish the right of rent receivers to act in behalf of the state in the collection of land revenue.[15] This had the effect in the region of placing the state in a direct de jure relationship with rent-paying holders of land. But this had little to do with transforming the traditional agrarian structure or removing zamindars.

Landlords' intermediary rights were abolished, but landlords were not abolished. They persisted in their traditional relationships to those below them in the agrarian hierarchy. Only their names changed. For example, zamindars became raiyats in Bihar (peasant cultivators with permanent rights to their lands). In Bangladesh, the erstwhile zamindars and tenure-holders became *maliks* (landholding tenants of the state).

Clearly, this was land reform by "definitional obfuscation."[16] Moreover, the landlords' acquisition of the new titles was frequently associated with the "legal eviction" of cultivators who could not prove that they had enjoyed an occupancy right (roughly equivalent to ownership) to the land in their possession.

For example, loopholes in the laws made it possible for landlords to claim as their own any lands that they cultivated personally. But, personal cultivation was defined to include lands cultivated also by "servants" (who in many instances were at least the equivalent of bonded laborers) or "hired labor" with their stock. Such a broad definition of possession enabled the landlords to claim lands that they had never cultivated—so long as those who were indeed the actual tillers did not possess the means (monetary or documentary) of establishing their rights to the same land. In this fashion, some of the erstwhile landlords retained all of the lands they had held prior to abolition, excepting only such lands for which a peasant cultivator had incontrovertible, documentary evidence in support of a claim.[17]

In short, following the enactment of agrarian reform legislation the landholding elites in the Permanent Settlement Region continued to maintain their superior rights in land and the prerogatives of power derived mainly from its control. With appropriate qualification, this generalization may be made even in 1987 for the Permanent Settlement Region. With exceptions, the actual tillers in the region have not had their status enhanced. Many till the same lands they (or their parents) had worked before reforms were initiated—now in diminished status as personal servants or hired laborers of their former landlords. Thus, even after agrarian reforms, the traditional hierarchy of interests in land in the Permanent Settlement Region looks very much as it did in the nineteenth century.

The situation is even worse for some. The case can be made that the reforms often left the weaker section of the peasantry even more vulnerable to those having secure rights in land. In Bangladesh, for example, the agrarian reforms have actually denied sharecroppers (bargadars) such limited protection as had been in effect under provisions of the Bengal Tenancy Act of 1885. Earlier, it had been possible, in a legal sense at least, for bargadars to secure a permanent right to the lands they tilled. The reforms of independent Pakistan (fully accepted by contemporary Bangladesh) now specify that sharecroppers are *not* to be classified as tenants (holding land under another person and paying rent to that person within the terms of a contractual understanding). Instead, persons in Bangladesh holding land under another person (e.g., a former landlord who is now a malik) are classified as bargadars and the share of the produce payable by such bargadars is not considered to be "rent." This is surely definitional obfuscation, not land reform; legally, rent-paying tenants no longer exist in Bangladesh, but sharecropping bargadars do. By ceasing to be "tenants," sharecroppers therefore are further diminished in status and no longer have even the de jure possibility (a right enjoyed 100 years ago) of acquiring permanent rights to the lands they till. Meanwhile, the former rent receivers, now maliks, till their lands by subletting them to others; they continue to realize the usufruct of the land while relying mainly on sharecroppers to assume the risks and responsibilities associated with crop production.[18]

THE CURRENT ENVIRONMENT FOR AGRICULTURAL INNOVATION IN THE PERMANENT SETTLEMENT REGION

In 1986 the Permanent Settlement Region's agrarian structure continues to condition and to qualify the environment in which successive strategies of rural development have been used to promote the "transformation of traditional agriculture." The agrarian structure is an environmental variable that critically affects both the process by which new technology is disseminated and the distribution of that technology's final product. It is a variable that people wishing to promote food security in the region should not ignore. To ignore the agrarian structure is to ignore the relationship between those who till the land and the landlords who exercise authority over them.

The actual tillers of the soil in the Permanent Settlement Region are those who till their own small holdings (for example, raiyats or maliks with de jure rights to the land they till) and those who till the land of others (for example, tenants or sharecroppers, whether classified as bataidars or bargadars). Landless day laborers are not included here as tillers because, although they do labor on the land, they do not have, generally, "rights in land"—even such tenuous and periodic rights as may be secured within the context of oral leases between themselves and others who enjoy "superior" land rights.

In general, these are intelligent, hard-working people. They work from dawn to dusk in several seasons annually to prepare the soil, to nurture crops, and to harvest them. They understand the environment in which they live and work. They know of the capricious interventions of nature and stoically accept them. They know and understand the rules that govern their interactions with others in the agrarian hierarchy. They know before whom they must be subservient, but they are rational decision makers as they face the struggle for survival on the land.

They have dignity. They are not without pride, especially when they have some land in their cultivating possession. They place high value on security in a world that is for them noteworthy for its insecurity. Indeed they might be called "security maximizers." They generally shun schemes by which they could become "profit maximizers," because such schemes are generally laden with risk and uncertainty. Living as they do at the margin of subsistence (almost by definition not having the assets, especially land, necessary to secure government-subsidized or other loans at nonusurious rates), it is not surprising that they do not want to take unnecessary chances, especially if the chances involve additional costs for hybrid seeds, or other modern inputs, costs that must be borne mainly by them within the context of a rural credit system still dominated by moneylenders.

They crave land. For them land is not merely a "factor of production." Land confers status and enhanced dignity—even power in relation to those who do not have it. The conditions under which they till the soil are rooted in tradition, which means that the actual tillers do not have the freedom to innovate on such lands as they may till for others. What they produce and how they produce it is a matter not of their choice but rather of the decisions of those who "own land" and dictate the terms of tenancy or sharecropping. These tillers of the soil are responsive mainly to the dictates of the powerful (those having economic assets, and especially secure rights in land), not to "price signals" in a market economy that has yet to evolve.

The landowners enjoy a "permanent occupancy right" to the lands in their possession. In a de jure sense they are often classified as "personal cultivators." This can be misleading[19] if we assume that landowners till the land themselves. Legally, a landowner can enjoy the classification of "personal cultivator" even as an absentee landlord who tills with sharecroppers or with servants or hired labor. By custom, also, it is unlikely in the general case that landowners will either till their own lands or employ family labor to do so. If they can, they will live at some distance from their landholdings—possibly in a town or city.[20] In this event the landowner will also be separated from the day-to-day supervision or management of the holding.

In the Permanent Settlement Region, landowners are likely to be as risk averse and as security minded as those who labor for them.[21] There is evidence that they will avoid investing in all of the new inputs associated with the new technology in agriculture, although they may on occasion provide some new technology in agriculture to their tillers in the form of seed.[22] After all, landowners derive income from their lands even if they eschew all investment in the production process. By custom, they receive at least 50 percent of a final crop no matter what they do. In addition, as demand for land in the region has grown, the terms of tenancy or sharecropping have become more severe. I have encountered arrangements in which the landowner expects to receive 50 percent of the rice seedlings at the time of transplanting and 50 percent of the final crop. There are even extreme arrangements in which the person "taking land in" for personal cultivation from a landowner must agree to give the landowner the equivalent of 50 percent of the anticipated crop in cash in advance. Such arrangements certainly minimize a landowner's risks of production. The deal may be even sweeter for the landowner who has also functioned as the facilitating moneylender in the process.

Although there is some evidence from field studies that landowners are seeing advantage in ending sharecropping arrangements altogether—in effect, deciding to till their lands by employing landless wage laborers for daily rates of pay (either in cash or in kind), it is uncertain whether this is a meaningful trend that will in time end the region's historic dichotomy between landownership and direct involvement in agricultural operations. In the meantime, it can be said in 1987 that the landowners of the Permanent Settlement Region look more like the revenue-farmers (zamindars) of old than the profit-maximizing cultivators who are imbedded in the logic and economic theory of the Green Revolution.

CONFLICTING DEFINITIONS OF DEVELOPMENT

However we assess the history of successive rural development initiatives in the subcontinent over the last several decades, there have been common elements in the process by which the initiatives were introduced and gained acceptance. Generally, the initiatives gained currency and credibility outside of the South Asia region, were introduced in the region with the advice and counsel of foreign experts, and became in due course part of the conventional wisdom of the international political economy—fit for dissemination on a global basis.

Many of the initiatives were derived from favorable, perhaps even wishful, interpretations of development success stories in the United States. Success stories have a momentum of their own. They become more convincing as they are retold in progressively less qualified terms. Complex issues become simple. Hard to resolve questions are given easy answers. Achievements are magnified. Failures are not much discussed or long remembered. The benefits of development are proclaimed, some of the costs ignored. An example is the issue of farm mechanization. In the conventional wisdom of the international political economy, "mechanization" can be made virtually a proxy for "modernity in agriculture." The very word conjures up the popular image of a giant combine marching across an endless expanse of prairie—one man in the air-conditioned cab, a vivid portrait of the application of technology to agriculture and of a particular definition of success (productivity measured in terms of output per unit of labor).

But, the word "mechanization" may also conjure up equally vivid, but less favorable, images of economic progress in the United States. Consider the following from Lester Brown:

> Perhaps the most striking illustration of farm mechanization without regard to social consequences is the mechanization of cotton picking in the United States. Mechanical cotton picking spread very rapidly during the years following World War II, until virtually all cotton was being harvested mechanically. The principal reason that blacks had been brought from Africa to the United States—to pick cotton—suddenly vanished. Employment on farms on the Mississippi delta declined nearly 90 percent over the two-decade span from 1940 to 1960. For hundreds of thousands of blacks there was no alternative to migration to the urban areas of the North—Cleveland, Watts, Newark, Detroit, Harlem, and Chicago. Culturally, socially, and vocationally, they were unprepared for urban living. Confined to their black ghettoes and unable to find work, they became alienated, bitter and resentful.[23]

It seems evident to me that the image of mechanization that has gained international currency (notwithstanding persistent, periodic concern about "appropriate" technology) is the former one, not the latter. The hidden and not-so-hidden social costs of our agricultural revolution in the United States are mainly buried in the footnotes of history. The common elements in the development strategies tried out in South Asia, I believe, are as susceptible as the concept of mechanization to both favorable and unfavorable interpretations. It depends on the definition of success that we employ.

The definitional debate goes on. It is often polarized and imbedded in ideological preferences. One side tends to measure success in aggregate production terms; the other in terms that emphasize the need for mass participation or distributive justice. One side sees economic progress mainly as a derivative of profit-oriented commercial agriculture in which free market principles are venerated. The other side sees economic progress in some regions as requiring changes in traditional institutions affecting rights in land—changes to be fostered by government that remove socioeconomic constraints to the broadest possible distribution of the benefits of appropriate new technology in agriculture.

It is now time for a new approach to rural development in South Asia—an approach that does not vacillate between the poles of "growth" and "equity" and recognizes the need (particularly in difficult subregions, such as that defined by the Permanent Settlement) to address both goals at the same time. Growth and equity goals cannot be approached in sequence in the Permanent Settlement Region; you cannot have one without the other. This principle holds, I believe, for many other regions of the world.

NEW PRINCIPLES FROM AN OLD INTELLECTUAL TRADITION

There is a continuing need to foster sustained increases in food production in South Asia to meet the needs of a still-growing population. There will be considerably more than 1 billion people there within fifteen years. We must recognize that the issue of the region's food security would be even more complicated today if there had not been a sustained effort to ensure increases in the aggregate production of food over the last several decades. We must recognize also that the growth-oriented food production strategies that have been employed in South Asia have produced results that are regionally differentiated.

Production-oriented strategies of rural development have been fostered and sustained in South Asia by indigenous elites and are not to be attributed only to the advice of foreign donors. Foreign donors may have written the tunes, but indigenous elites sang the songs. Indigenous elites accepted production-oriented strategies of rural development because those who ruled did not have the political will[24] to implement reforms in the agrarian structure (particularly in the Permanent Settlement Region of South Asia). Both sides favored rural development strategies based on "easy options"—"projects that drew on donor expertise and promised a rapid rate of return."[25] Both sides have found it convenient *for different reasons* to measure economic progress in South Asia in terms of increases in aggregate food production.

By this standard, for many years—certainly from the 1950s through the early 1970s—"growth" and "development" could be perceived as synonymous even in a country (India) said to be committed to a socialist pattern of development. Radical slogans (e.g., "Banish Poverty") and proposals for reform (e.g., Indira Gandhi's Twenty-Point Program) were periodically enunciated, perhaps as a means of confirming that distributive and social justice remained legitimate concomitants of the economic growth process. But, throughout South Asia, and most emphatically in the Permanent Settlement Region, the verbalizations of those who ruled were seldom translated into purposeful programs designed to deliver *direct* benefits to millions of small farmers, tenants, sharecroppers, and landless laborers dependent on agricultural employment for subsistence.

Given the weight of mainly external ideas about rural development in South Asia and the well-documented propensities of the ruling elites of that region, it is all the more necessary today that we recognize the limitations of the success that has been achieved—in terms of both growth and distributive justice—in the Permanent Settlement Region especially. If there are to be better answers to rural development issues (including those of food production and distribution) than have been supplied to date, we must now consider questions that are different from and equally important as those that were posed in the past. The primary question cannot continue to be only "How can we ensure rapid increases in food production in the aggregate?" Our primary concern must also include the question *"Who is producing on whose land for whose benefit?"*

Such a question brings in its train a different definition of development and requires the integration of ideas in the intellectual tradition of Vera Anstey, Malcolm Darling, Harold Mann, Daniel Thorner, Wolf Ladejinsky, and Walter C. Neale. This tradition is rooted in participant observation methodologies of social science research, methodologies that do not find general favor with economists. It is a tradition that shows no embarrassment in soliciting information concerning rural development issues directly from peasants (even illiterate ones), and it is a tradition that values the attitudes and opinions of such persons.

It is a tradition that argues for regionally differentiated strategies of rural development—a tradition that recognizes that there are no rural development strategies applicable to whole countries (even geographically small ones like Bangladesh). It is a tradition, therefore, that need not use the nation-state as its arbitrary and exclusive unit of analysis of development problems. Accordingly, the tradition encourages analysis that links historical events (such as the Permanent Settlement of 1793) with contemporary issues (problems associated with the distribution of rights in land in Bangladesh, Bihar, and West Bengal). Its policy recommendations, therefore, need not be tied only to national politics and the geographic boundaries of states, even when appropriately cognizant of such politics and boundaries.

Above all, the tradition that I have identified is associated with an attempt to understand from the ground up how traditional institutions (especially those affecting the relationship of people to the land) condition and qualify the environment in which agricultural innovation and change is to be encouraged. It is a scholarly tradition that, in the Permanent Settlement Region, links the historical evolution of the zamindari system to contemporary development issues, recognizing in 1986 the persistence of an agrarian system in which ownership of land is divorced from family labor and personal investment. It is a tradition that long ago recognized that there are no technical, agronomic reasons why East India and Bangladesh should be economically "backward," especially given land and water resources that are superior to those in so-called progressive farming areas like the Punjab.

Finally, the tradition that I have identified is prone to ask the question "development for whom and for what?" Such a question becomes a means of redefining rural economic development *in a context*. From this perspective it becomes possible to recognize that, under the prevailing conditions in the Permanent Settlement Region, production and distribution problems are best addressed together within the framework of reforms that finally end the tradition of revenue-farming and unite ownership of land, labor on land, and investment in appropriate technology in one person. Whether such reforms were politically possible in the past or are now possible, it is amply apparent that the more than 250 million people who live in the Permanent Settlement Region have not been prime beneficiaries of either economic growth or distributive justice.

In these circumstances, if the international community and the indigenous elites continue to pursue rural development strategies in this region that focus mainly on aggregate production goals, we should anticipate that the spread of new technology in agriculture will be slow. Aggregate production increases will not be impressive and, when achieved, will be hard to sustain. And, to the extent that a production-oriented, growth strategy favors the few with secure rights in land rather than the many who lack such secure rights, growing income inequalities will be a persistently derived effect of such production successes as may be achieved. The final product may well be the economic polarization of the countryside and the political destabilization of the region.

The scholarly tradition that I have endorsed in these concluding paragraphs does not begin with answers developed in one historical, institutional, and cultural context, nor do I presume that those "answers" are everywhere applicable. It is a tradition that does not assume that the technology on Western shelves is part of a stock of knowledge that has universal significance and applicability, without adjustment and modification in local context to meet real needs defined indigenously. It is a tradition that begins with questions rather than with answers. Who is producing on whose land for whose benefit? What goals are imbedded in the definitions of development that we employ? To whom are those goals relevant? What would be some of the effects of achieving those goals, on local elites and on the majority of the people?

Such questions must precede any approach to food security in any region of the world. Otherwise the approaches we adopt will continue to be divorced from the context in which human beings live and work in developing countries and will be linked instead to external "truths" or ideological predilections that are only vaguely related to people's definitions of their own needs.

NOTES

1. India, Ministry of Food and Agriculture and Ministry of Community Development and Cooperation, *Report of India's Food Crisis and Steps to Meet It.*

2. No one person can be blamed for the diminished outlay on agriculture in the Second Plan. However, the distinguished Indian economist and statistician, P. C. Mahalanobis, was clearly among those favoring investments in industry over agriculture. When questioned in March 1957 concerning the place of agriculture in the Second Plan, Mahalanobis made plain in blunt terms that if economic growth was to be maximized in India, "we cannot waste our resources in agriculture; indeed, we must, for a generation or two, write off sections of the peasantry, especially the landless" (Mahalanobis/Jannuzi interview, Indian Statistical Institute, March 1957). Mahalanobis's view aside, documents of the government of India—e.g., *The Second Five Year Plan: A Draft Outline*—had emphasized that "the Indian economy could not proceed very far within the bounds of an essentially agrarian economy, and that, beyond a point, capital enrichment necessarily means industrialization."

3. Interpreters of the subsequent record were peculiarly unrestrained in making generalizations from the results of a program designed consciously to work within selected districts having a prior record of agricultural success—that is to say, *atypical* districts: "The implications of the IADP experience for policy decision makers concerned with agricultural development in India *and in other less developed countries* are summarized below. . . . *Most cultivators make economically rational decisions,* given the prevailing level of technology, economic opportunities, and social restraints, within the generally available system of communication" (emphasis added). Dorris D. Brown, *Agricultural Development in India's Districts,* p. 101.

4. Lester Brown, "The Green Revolution, Rural Employment and the Urban Crisis," p. 2.

5. C. Subramaniam, *The New Strategy in Indian Agriculture: The First Decade and After,* p. 23.

6. Ibid.

7. Ibid., p. 28.

8. Brown, "The Green Revolution," p. 2.

9. B. H. Farmer, *An Introduction to South Asia,* p. 181.

10. Ibid., p. 182.

11. Vernon W. Ruttan, "The Green Revolution: Seven Generalizations." Quote is on p. 18.

12. This section contains some simplification of a complex history. For elaboration, see my *Agrarian Crisis in India: The Case of Bihar.*

13. The late Vera Anstey of the London School of Economics was not given to strong language in discussing issues pertinent to the economic development of the subcontinent. Her strongest language was reserved for rent-receiving landlords whom she described as "mere Parasites, who batten on the product of the actual cultivators." Anstey, *The Economic Development of India,* p. 99.

14. F. Tomasson Jannuzi and James T. Peach, *The Agrarian Structure of Bangladesh: An Impediment to Development,* p. 9.

15. Thus, the whole spate of legislation can legitimately be classified as "revenue reform" rather than "agrarian reform" or "land reform"—terms often mistakenly applied to the process. This point has not always been appreciated by those who have evaluated the effects of the legislation. John Mellor, for example, has assumed that agrarian reform has actually been implemented. Thus, although admitting that the zamindars of the Permanent Settlement Region "did not play a major constructive role," he goes on to state that the "removal of the zamindars has improved the environment for innovation. But the opportunity thus presented has not been acted upon—a fact which indicates that a favorable land-tenure system is by no means a sufficient condition for technological change." Mellor et al., *Developing Rural India: Plan and Practice,* p. 54. Mellor has missed the point. He assumes a favorable land tenure system resulting from an agrarian reform that in fact was never implemented.

16. This is a phrase that I attribute to Daniel Thorner, but I have no recollection of the precise source.

17. See for example, Doreen Warriner's comments on this phenomenon in *Land Reform in Principle and Practice,* pp. 163-164.

18. Sample surveys conducted by me and my associate, James T. Peach, in the Bangladesh segment of the Permanent Settlement Region in 1977 and 1978 provide documentation for this generalization. Our surveys, which produced data endorsed by the government of Bangladesh, showed that tillers of the soil with inferior rights in land (roughly classified as bargadars, or tenants) generally could not count on those with superior rights in land (roughly classified here as owners of land) to provide any of the inputs associated with the agricultural production process. Only 1 percent of landowners provided any irrigation facilities; only 2 percent provided pesticides, and only 6 percent provided fertilizer. The most likely input to be provided by landowners to their tenants, or bargadars, was seed, but even that input was distributed to tenants by only 25 percent of landowners. We could not get reliable data on the actual amounts of the inputs supplied by landowners to those who took in land from them. It is our impression that our data may actually provide an exaggerated index of landowners' involvement in the supply of inputs. Jannuzi and Peach, *The Agrarian Structure of Bangladesh,* p. 112.

19. Confusion persists concerning the term "personal cultivator." Some still refer, mistakenly, to Bangladesh as a land of small peasant proprietors (who are said to be subsumed within the malik classification) who till their own lands. In fact, the malik of contemporary Bangladesh and the raiyat of contemporary Bihar may be landlords—indeed, even ex-zamindars or other intermediaries—who remain remote from all agricultural operations.

20. This holds especially in recent years for large landholders who feel uncertain about their personal security in the face of a less subservient peasantry.

21. On this general theme, the late Doreen Warriner, making reference only to the Bihar region of the Permanent Settlement, said that "Bihar may be an extreme case; but it is one which must be borne in mind when it is claimed that the ex-zamindars are becoming progressive capitalists, raising the level of agricultural production by investment." Warriner, *Land Reform in Principle and Practice,* p. 164. Having done field studies in both Bihar and Bangladesh, I would agree with Warriner, but would at the same time make Bangladesh, rather than Bihar, the "extreme case" within the region.

22. See, for example, Table E.7, "Source of Agricultural Inputs as Reported by Tenants," in Jannuzi and Peach, *The Agrarian Structure in Bangladesh,* p. 112.

23. Brown, "The Green Revolution," pp. 3-4.

24. See Ronald Herring's note on "political will" in *Land to the Tiller: The Political Economy of Agrarian Reform in South Asia,* p. 285.

25. I borrow this phrase and its definition from an article entitled "When Foreign Aid Fails" in the April 1985 edition of *Atlantic.* Although the author of the article, Jack Shepherd, was writing about Africa, much that he says is relevant to the theme of this chapter.

8

Ronald J. Herring

The Dependent Welfare State: Nutrition, Entitlements, and Exchange in Sri Lanka

Conventional wisdom suggests that a poor nation substantially raising its economic growth rate and simultaneously moving from a condition of food deficits in its dietary staple to near self-sufficiency constitutes success on the hunger and malnutrition front.[1] Although the reality is, of course, more complex, Sri Lanka (Ceylon until 1972) does present an interesting experience. This chapter, focusing on that experience, identifies the factors that mediate between economic growth and increased food production on the one hand and improved nutritional security for the bulk of the population on the other. Disjunctures occur because of the central importance of class structure, income distribution, international exchange position, and domestic entitlement policy.

Hunger and malnutrition are profoundly individual issues. Nevertheless, the individual biological experience is determined by interlocking supraindividual institutions and dynamics. At a proximate level, the individual's nutrition is affected by the access of the family to food (thus, by class position in market-dominated exchanges) and by decision rules within the family over consumption expenditures and allocation of produced or purchased food. At a second level, local institutions mediate between a family's economic status and nutrition within face-to-face communities—villages, tribes, kinship nets, neighborhoods, local religious communities. As in the family situation, collective resources of a community are influenced by operating rules in superior tiers of the system; nevertheless, at a given level of resources, priorities affecting hunger are made locally within long-standing institutional practices, a central problematic in the "moral economy" paradigm.[2] Institutions governing microlevel food entitlements operate within structures that translate food resource capabilities into a distribution of relative security and relative hardship.[3]

Of most interest to students of development policy is the third tier—the level of the nation-state. The state mediates nutrition conditions at both higher

158

(international systemic) and lower (local) levels. Despite the increasing recognition that global processes impinge on individual welfare regardless of artificial national boundaries, the nation-state matters crucially in several respects. Just as the family's food requirements are mediated—for all but those increasingly rare self-sufficient producers—by their exchange position vis-à-vis markets, so too are consumers in any but an autarkic nation affected by international exchange conditions. Whatever their wage rate in rupees, Sri Lankans cannot buy imported food without some rupee-dollar exchange. The exchange rate is a function of national political decisions on economic policy, of international trade dynamics over which no regime has real control, and of decisions by specific international actors about the level and terms of external flows. The nation-state's compliance behavior affects flows from higher levels of the system and thus the capacity of the domestic state to affect nutritional situations within the domestic society.

The nation-state's role in nutritional intervention may require real resources or merely political will. Funding nutritional programs for the poor requires real resources; redistributing assets to reduce the incidence of poverty (and thus hunger) requires "only" political will.[4] These are important distinctions because of the pervasiveness of arguments along the lines that "in poor societies malnutrition is inevitable." Sri Lanka has quite rightly been used in the policy literature to illustrate the capacity of even quite poor societies to ameliorate hunger and hunger-related maladies significantly through specific policy priorities.[5] Just as individual nutritional entitlements are mediated by community and nation-state entitlements, national capacity is, in a dependent political economy, determined in large part by capabilities, stresses, and entitlements generated by the international political economy.

There are several reasons. First, the capacity of the dependent state to alleviate hunger, assuming political dynamics producing the will to do so, is critically conditioned by exchange with the international system. This essay focuses on two such exchanges: the terms of trade and concessional resource flows. Obviously there are others, including the decisive historical residues of the literal restructuring of the island's economy and society under colonialism.[6] The plantation economy built under colonial rule provided the tax revenues that, under particular political conditions (competitive democratic patronage politics), provided the material support for a fairly extensive welfare system. The dependent character of that welfare system is demonstrated by its material *vulnerability* to a long-term serious decline in the international exchange position of Sri Lanka (from the mid-1950s to the mid-1970s). The contemporary form of the dependent welfare state is influenced by dependence on international financial flows from actors hostile to the welfare state itself.

Conceptualizing a hierarchy of arenas affecting individual hunger demarcates more clearly what political analysis seeks to explain and what public policy can affect. If household consumption rules favor liquor and tobacco over rice, or males over females, redistribution of income may make no difference in levels of hunger, but rice transfers and school lunch programs probably will. Likewise, *given* an exchange position in the international system, regimes have considerable freedom to arrange priorities in ways that alleviate, exacerbate, or ignore the hunger of particular strata. Some nations, like some families, cope with poverty better than others. Theoretically, this position constitutes an assumption of potential autonomy of the state—even in very dependent societies—vis-à-vis the international system and vis-à-vis domestic class structures.[7]

The following case study reinforces three widely held, yet still disputed, themes in the development literature. First, growth alone is not a sufficient condition for alleviating hunger. Indeed, some policies commonly perceived to be necessary for increasing growth rates (such as reducing social consumption in favor of investment) may easily offset the positive effects of higher aggregate income. Second, aggregate national food self-sufficiency, though it increases domestic capacity and reduces national vulnerability, is no guarantee that the aggregate level of malnutrition will fall. Mediating variables include class structure, income distribution, and national entitlement policy. Third, both growth prospects and entitlement capacities are driven by specific dimensions of the dependency situation; domestic politics matter, but must be conceptualized as a locus of international-external linkages.

DEVELOPMENT STRATEGY IN A DEPENDENT WELFARE STATE

Food and other welfare entitlements in Sri Lanka, when compared to entitlements in other poor societies, have been substantial and widespread. The elections of 1977 were something of a watershed in the positive theory, moral economy, and priorities of government. For over three decades prior to 1977, both conservative and populist regimes steadily expanded the state's economic role, driven by domestic political stresses and extensive democratic competition. Statist intervention was deemed necessary to protect volatile social groups from internationally induced shocks and simultaneously generated jobs, patronage, and discretionary resources to serve partisan regime interests.

Critics termed the ensemble of policies that evolved prior to 1977 a "closed economy." Yet events of the period 1970-1977 proved how open the system was, despite its extensive regulatory apparatus, as it was severely battered by adverse external economic conditions and proved incapable of adequate response. Elections in 1977 became in part a referendum on the interventionist "closed economy"; champions of liberalized "open economy" triumphed decisively.[8] The liberalization regime promised a profound shift in economic philosophy and priorities. Rather than being seen as the *solution* to deficient economic performance, government intervention came to be perceived as the cause.[9] Specifically, as the World Bank and the International Monetary Fund had long argued, the opportunity costs of resources allocated to social consumption—the entitlement programs—were seen as too high, producing a retarding effect on growth.

The logic connecting social welfare spending and average individual well-being in a physiological sense, given shortfalls in entitlements at the individual, family, and community level, is so straightforward that it is astonishing to find the issue disputed. The question of opportunity costs of entitlement spending in terms of investment and growth is, of course, a more complex question, but the payoffs of social spending in terms of the quality of human existence seem very clear. Among low-income Asian nations, Sri Lanka's pre-1977 priorities produced extraordinary results in terms of human welfare. Data reported in Table 8.1 for low-income subcontinental nations and for China, summarized in the Physical Quality of Life Index (PQLI),[10] support this claim. The control for income is crucial, as quality of life indicators are highly and positively correlated with national wealth; about two-thirds of the variance in PQLI scores can be explained by GNP per head alone.[11] All nations listed in Table 8.1 are poor nations by international standards, although China stands out as decidedly wealthier than the average South Asian nation. Despite well-known failings,[12] Sri Lanka's record in terms of life expectancy, literacy, and infant mortality is unsurpassed.

Although it seems self-evident that social-consumption expenditures compete with growth-inducing investment expenditures, the reality is more complex. No one knows precisely the contribution of a better-nourished, healthier, better-educated population to material growth, but that contribution must be significant.[13] More speculatively, consumption subsidies may buy legitimacy and social peace, reducing the economic dislocations of class warfare. Cer-

Table 8.1   Development and Growth: Indicators for South Asian Nations and China, Late 1970s

Nation	1977 GNP/ Capita (U.S. $)	Avg. Real Annual Growth Rates (GNP/capita) 1960–1977	Crude Death Rate (per 1,000)	Infant Mortality Rate (per 1,000)	Life Expectancy at Birth (years)	Literacy (%)	PQLI[a] Score
Afghanistan	190	0.2	23	205	40	12	17
Nepal	110	0.2	14	150	43	19	28
Bangladesh	90	−0.4	19	136	46	26	35
Pakistan	190	3.0	21	126	51	24	40
India	150	1.3	15	123	49	36	42
Sri Lanka	*200*	*2.0*	*7*	*37*	*65*	*85*	*82*
China	390	5.1	7	45	65	66	75

[a]Physical Quality of Life Index (unweighted additive index of fourth through sixth columns) (cf. Morris David Morris, *Measuring the Condition of the World's Poor: The Physical Quality of Life Index* (New York: Pergamon, 1979).

Sources: First and second columns: World Bank, *World Development Report 1979* (New York: Oxford University Press, 1979), Appendix Table 1, pp. 126–127; third through last columns: ODC, 1983, Appendix C3.

tainly the comparative growth rates of the nations presented in Table 8.1 do not suggest that social consumption expenditures depress aggregate growth rates. Sri Lanka did better than the South Asian mean for the period 1960-1977, despite decidedly welfarist priorities in spending, as illustrated in Table 8.2.

Despite some messiness in the comparability of the data, important conclusions flow from Table 8.2. Sri Lanka's spending on social security and welfare on the eve of the liberalization regime constituted a much higher priority than in any of the other societies of the subcontinental region. Indeed, Sri Lanka on this measure stood closer to norms of advanced industrial nations than to those of its neighbors; in 1977, the percentage of central government expenditures of this sort actually exceeded the percentage of similar expenditures by Great Britain (24.7 percent). Although Sri Lanka's percentage (25.8) was only half that of Sweden (47.8), it dwarfed that of India (2.3 percent). Of equal importance, Sri Lanka's priorities reflected clear preference for human welfare spending over military expenditures; Asian nations as a whole allocated 23.9 percent of central government spending to defense, compared to 2.2 percent in Sri Lanka.

Individual well-being is a composite reflection of (1) domestic parameters that may become variables (the class structure and income distribution, for example, although domestic structure reflects historical processes such as the colonial structure of the plantation economy); (2) parameters affecting aggregate capacity of regimes but beyond regime control in the short term (the international division of labor and terms-of-trade movements); and (3) external discretionary resource flows (grants, aid). Given this structural configuration, regimes have variable room for maneuvering; given capacity, political

Table 8.2   Government Priorities in Spending, 1976 (percentage of total central government expenditures)[a]

Nation	Defense	Social Security and Welfare		Education	Health
		1976	1977		
Nepal	7.2	0.7	0.6	12.2	6.7
Bangladesh	9.3	6.3	2.8	9.2	5.0
Pakistan	36.2	1.6	2.7	2.8	1.8
India	23.3	3.2	3.3	2.3	2.5
Sri Lanka	2.2	19.9	25.8	11.3	6.2
Asian Mean	23.9	n.a.	n.a.	9.4	3.3
Industrialized Nations	14.1	38.0	37.8	5.6	11.5

[a]Figures introduce some distortion in percentages because of differences in political structure; Sri Lanka is highly centralized in a fiscal sense, as the central government accounts for more than 95 percent of total public spending, whereas in federal systems such as India the central government accounts for between 60 and 70 percent of total spending. Recalculations reduce somewhat the defense percentage for India and Pakistan but do not change significantly indications of relative priorities on social security and welfare.

Source: International Monetary Fund, *Government Finance Statistics Yearbook*, vol. 13 (1984), pp. 46–47.

priorities become crucial in determining the relationship between national poverty and individual destitution. The evidence displayed in Tables 8.1 and 8.2 demonstrate concretely that priorities including basic human needs may significantly raise the average welfare of the population despite national poverty and extreme dependency, within limits *set by national capacities that are influenced by the international system.*

VULNERABILITY AND WELFARE POLICY

Historically, Sri Lanka has represented an archetypal case of extreme dependency. At independence, the nation imported about half its domestic food needs, paid for with foreign exchange earned by the export of plantation crops. Three primary commodities—tea, coconut, and rubber—accounted for 90 percent of export earnings. Government revenues were sensitive to changes in the level and value of plantation exports, linking capacity to dependency.[14] The welfare system, including, most centrally, subsidies to consumers of food grains, was thus tied to the international exchange position both directly through hard-currency earnings and indirectly through government revenues. This vulnerability left regimes of whatever ideological hue susceptible to shocks beyond their immediate control. As the terms of trade deteriorated after formal political independence in 1948, means of reducing vulnerability and intervening between external shocks and domestic discontent became central policy problems for regimes in a closely competitive and volatile political environment.

Few nations have experienced so long and serious a deterioration in terms of trade as did Sri Lanka from the 1950s to the mid-1970s. From 1950 to 1975, the export price index rose from 17 to 29 while the import price index rose from 8 to 49. The terms-of-trade index thus fell from 208 to 58 (Table 8.3). Concretely, although the *volume* of exports increased by more than 35 percent over that twenty-five-year period, the *purchasing power* of exports fell by nearly 70 percent. Imports did not decline proportionately (falling only from index 62 to index 52); part of the gap was met by borrowing hard currency or importing on credit. As a result, the debt-service ratio rose from negligible levels in the 1950s to more than 20 percent in 1975, creating an additional claim on hard-currency export earnings while aggravating mounting budget deficits.[15]

Structural dependency is a double-edged sword. Export concentration in primary commodities may, under specific conditions, improve national capacity to meet nutritional needs (as apologists for colonialism argue from the logic of comparative advantage). With buoyant export prices, a plantation economy provides a healthy, readily available, administratively simple revenue stream and generates the foreign exchange necessary to import food and other necessities. Indeed, the welfare system in Sri Lanka was built on precisely this base. Relief for the poor, free education (through university), and subsidized or free

Table 8.3   International Exchange Position, Sri Lanka 1950–1984 Index Numbers (1978=100)

	1950	1955	1960	1965	1970	1975	1980	1984
Import Volume	62	74	101	65	77	52	140	185
Import Price	8	9	9	11	16	49	152	415
Export Volume	79	91	92	111	107	107	99	127
Export Price	17	19	17	16	17	29	126	207
Terms of Trade[a]	208	203	185	142	106	58	72	50

[a]Terms-of-Trade Index $= \dfrac{\text{Export Price Index}}{\text{Import Price Index}} \times 100$

Source: Central Bank of Ceylon, *Economic and Social Statistics of Sri Lanka* 1984: 6.8, 6.9.

medical care were all introduced in the late colonial period. Subsidized rice and flour distribution and a ration system began in 1942, reflecting wartime pressures and continuing the long-standing concern for making rice available to the plantation work force at relatively low prices.[16] The colonial state also took an active role in increasing domestic rice production (and more proximately important, reducing the level of landlessness in the peasant sector) by planning and subsidizing "colonization schemes" on newly irrigated tracts in underpopulated areas.[17]

Public welfare schemes in political democracies become objects of partisan competition for votes and means of servicing electoral machines. Ceylon received universal franchise very early (1931), while still a colony. Though the autonomy of domestic politicians was limited, they could compete in patronage. The prosperous plantation economy supported such predictably popular programs as subsidized food and free farms, but as the terms of trade turned against Ceylon after independence, the economy's capacity to sustain those policies deteriorated. Food subsidies alone claimed about 20 percent of government expenditure.[18] This vulnerability became evident when imported rice prices increased during the Korean War. When the government in 1953 attempted to reduce rice subsidies, a well-established and strategically placed leftist opposition called for the "Great Hartal" (general strike) that paralyzed the nation.[19] The prime minister resigned; the finance minister (who later became president of Sri Lanka) lost his seat in the subsequent elections. "Rice politics" thus became central to regime perceptions of popular political tolerance thresholds.

Vulnerability of the domestic welfare state, given highly politicized electoral competition, produced pressure for import-substituting agricultural development and continued protection of consumers' food needs through an elaborate public distribution system for essential food items. The net food subsidy to consumers averaged something over 10 percent of government expenditures in the 1960s and peaked at 17 percent in 1975.[20] In a typical year in the 1960s, 30-35 percent of the country's calories and 25-30 percent of its protein moved through the public distribution system.[21] Extensive health and educational subsidies complemented the nutritional effects of a distribution of calories far more egalitarian than the Asian norm, enhancing national performance in caring for human needs.

The capacity of the state to fund welfare programs was eroded over time by the internal accumulation of public debt, expanding budget deficits and the external escalation of food and fuel prices that became severe in the 1973-1975 period.[22] Sri Lanka's economic crisis in the early 1970s was similar to that of comparably dependent nations in the period and was largely external in origin.[23] Unemployment was high, aggravated by reduced import capacity for intermediate goods; growth rates slowed, and austerity budgets reduced the coverage of the welfare net.[24]

Among the economic crises faced by the pre-1977 leftist United Front regime, food was especially urgent; reduced rations were purchased at higher cost. Suffering and deprivation in the 1973-1974 period were severe, although class differentiated.[25] To illustrate the linkage between international structural vulnerability and regime constraints, we need only note that although rice imports were cut 12.5 percent in 1973/1974, contributing to increased malnutrition, the rice import bill increased by 166 percent.[26] The precipitous rise in costs of petroleum-based products dislocated the economy further and added to unemployment.[27] Paddy production suffered from bad weather, fertilizer shortages, and the government's mandatory procurement policy at prices that did not keep up with inflation in costs of production—a policy strongly conditioned by the perceived political necessity of protecting mass welfare with low rice prices and the fiscal necessity of reducing producer subsidies.

Any regime presiding over these crises would be threatened with a crisis of legitimacy. Scarcity and discretionary authority predictably produce externalities in the form of corruption, victimization, and favoritism. The United Front government was widely perceived to be guilty of these and other abuses of power and eventually it unraveled internally.[28] But, more important, the policies that clearly produced hardship and facilitated corruption were perceived to be ineffectual: Hunger was widespread, unemployment reached 25 percent, economic growth slowed, and essential goods became increasingly scarce. Although the principles of the welfare state itself may not have been brought into question by the regime's incapacity in the face of severe external shocks, the incumbents associated with these crises predictably lost favor with the electorate.

THE LIBERALIZATION REGIME AND WELFARE POLICY

The elections in 1977 produced a new regime and a dramatic rejection of the policies that had evolved over the previous three decades. Those policies had emerged as ad hoc efforts to alleviate the constraints and shocks induced by structural dependence in the context of high levels of politicization, partisan competition, and patronage expectations. Social welfare coverage had been eroded by austerity budgets before the sweeping 1977 electoral victory of the United National Party (140 of 168 parliamentary seats). Whereas earlier bouts of austerity were reluctant responses to budgetary and foreign exchange pressures, the new regime further reduced subsidies on the theory that their opportunity cost in terms of competing developmental expenditures was too high. The core assumption was that the national economy had been shackled by excessive regulation, an excess of social consumption expenditure over investment, and "wasteful and complacent" public sector enterprises.[29] The Central Bank termed the new ensemble of policies "a sweeping departure from a tightly controlled, inward-looking, welfare-oriented economic strategy to a more liberalized, outward-looking and growth-oriented one."[30]

The new strategy's prospects would depend on powerful investment incentives to foreign and domestic capital,[31] a shift in the composition of public spending, and a liberalized international trade policy, all premised on export-led growth. Creating employment was a central objective, both through encouragement of domestic and foreign capital and through ambitious developmental public works such as the Accelerated Mahaweli Development Scheme, a plan for bringing new tracts of irrigated land under cultivation while substantially increasing hydroelectric generating potential. Fiscal logic suggests that the strategy was necessarily dependent on international support; if tax incentives were to be given to business and if the government were to increase infrastructural investment when budget deficits were already large and chronic, additional financial resources on a large scale would have to be found externally. Likewise, relaxing import controls would generate balance-of-payments pressures in the current account, aggravating a chronic planning problem.

The international development community did indeed rally to the regime's new strategy. Following a sharp devaluation of the rupee in November of 1977, the International Monetary Fund announced support for "the comprehensive program of economic reform . . . in support of which the present stand-by arrangement (of SDR 93 million) has been approved."[32] IMF approval is an important signal in international financial and development communities, and the regime pressed its case globally. The finance minister traveled widely, meeting investors and officials of aid-giving nations and agencies. Official loan commitments in 1978 more than doubled the 1977 level, despite a global attitude of "aid-weariness." These official loans carried a grant element of 64.8 percent.[33] The *net* flow from all lenders increased from $48 million in 1977 to $175.9 million in 1979.[34]

In his budget speech for 1981, the finance minister claimed that "due to the confidence placed by the international community in our new economic policies, we have been able to obtain a greater volume of foreign aid and foreign assistance *per capita* than perhaps any other third world country."[35] Significantly, more than a third of the assistance was in the form of outright grants, the balance was in long-term loans "at minimal interest." The minister acknowledged the direct connection to the new economic policy: "Without the courageous and imaginative steps we took . . . nothing would have moved, nothing would have happened."[36]

Increased international flows allowed the economy to cover unprecedented balance-of-trade deficits that resulted from import liberalization and deteriorating terms of trade. Outright grants and the substitution of long-term subsidized loans and IMF drawings for high-interest suppliers' credits and commercial loans forestalled debt-servicing problems. These flows facilitated a higher level of imports and, indirectly, exports (as the import component of intermediate goods is over 75 percent). Likewise, fiscal capabilities are directly influenced by levels and terms of international trade. Without external support, current account deficits would necessarily curtail the level of trade and thus present severe political and fiscal problems for the government. Table 8.4 summarizes the movement of key variables in priority shifts and international supports.

The shift in national economic policies was successful with respect to the regime's logic: Public consumption as a percentage of gross domestic expenditure fell from 11.5 percent in 1970 to 9.8 percent in 1976 to 6.1 percent in 1984, whereas gross domestic capital formation increased from 14.9 percent in 1976

Table 8.4   Welfare Spending Shifts, Debt, Deficits, and Aid after 1977

Year	Education, Health, and Welfare as Percentage of Government Expenditures	Balance of Trade (SDR[b] million)	Gross External Debt (Rs[c] billion)	Budget Deficit (Rs[c] billion)	Foreign Resources Utilized in Financing Budget[a] Deficit (Rs[c] billion)
1976	44.9	−61	5.0	3.6	1.3
1977	43.5	+58	10.0	3.1	1.8
1978	34.3	−138	14.6	7.2	4.5
1979	31.0	−325	15.8	8.8	4.2
1980	23.9	−718	22.3	16.8	6.7
1981	24.1	−689	29.2	14.9	8.2
1982	22.9	−903	34.6	20.1	8.8
1983	n.a.	−857	46.0	21.6	11.0
1984	n.a.	−446	53.7	16.5	12.3
1985[d]				21.5[d]	14.1[d]

[a]Gross figures, including grants, project loans, commodity loans, and unspecified "other" loans (Central Bank of Ceylon, *Annual Report*, 1984, Appendix Table 30.)

[b]SDR = Special Drawing Rights

[c]Rupees

[d]Approved estimated.

Sources: First column: International Monetary Fund, *Government Financial Statistics Yearbook*, vol. 2 (1984), p. 524; second through last columns: Central Bank of Ceylon, *Annual Report* (1984), Appendix Tables 24, 29, 37.

to 24.8 percent in 1984.[37] From 1970 to 1984, net receipts of international gifts and transfers increased from 0.8 percent of gross domestic expenditure to 6.8 percent. Although the connection between high rates of capital formation and high rates of growth is by no means automatic or simple, external flows clearly figured significantly in reducing the rate of unemployment and in generating economic expansion. Growth rates have indeed increased under the liberalization regime, leading to early claims for an "IMF success" story. Real GNP by official calculations grew at a rate of 8.2 percent in 1978, far surpassing performance of the troubled early part of the decade, but fell to 6.2 percent in 1979, 5.5 percent in 1980, 3.9 percent in 1981, 5 percent in 1982, 4.1 percent in 1983, and 5.4 percent in 1984 (Central Bank of Ceylon data). The rate of growth in real national income has been significantly less, however, because of deterioration in the terms of trade after 1978.

It is unclear whether the relatively high growth rates of the 1978-1984 period represent self-sustaining processes. International conditions in the early stages were quite unusual. Foreign inflows were large relative to the size of the economy and relative to historical experience. Moreover, the terms of trade, which had worked against the economy for decades (Table 8.3), experienced a 35 percent improvement in 1976, 31 percent in 1977. Tea prices rose by 80 percent. Improved trade conditions produced a rare surplus in the current account, as well as in budgetary resources (as taxes on international trade constituted 55 percent of revenue in 1978).[38] Subsequently, as the terms of trade deteriorated, budget deficits and current account deficits rose, highlighting the crucial contribution of external supports.

Under the liberalization regime, Sri Lanka became one of the most fiscally dependent nations in the world. Consolidated IMF data available for the period 1977-1982 show that Sri Lanka had the highest ratios of foreign financing to total governmental expenditure in Asia for the years 1978 (19.14 percent) and 1981 (17.06 percent) and the lowest ratio of government revenues to government expenditures in Asia in 1980, 1981, and 1982 (47.6, 53.3, and 49 percent respectively).[39] Few governments can spend twice the amount they raise in revenues for any length of time; the fragility of the domestic boom, and its external dependence, seemed clear long before the escalation of civil conflict (1983-1986) disrupted economic performance and clouded evaluation of policy outcomes.

External support for the liberalization regime was, of course, not to be open ended or unconditional. As budget deficits mounted, officials of the World Bank and IMF pressed for tighter fiscal discipline. Although the government responded in part by withdrawing some incentives to the business community (taxes on profits and income fell from 17.5 percent of revenues in 1976 to 9.8 percent in 1978 but bounced back to 17.4 percent in 1982), deeper cuts in welfare programs were inevitable. The finance minister in 1983 argued against cuts in mass-consumption subsidies urged by the IMF on the grounds that the nation's records in health, education, and welfare "are our pride and we cannot afford to throw them away."[40] But more than pride is at stake; domestic tolerance levels may be stretched too thin for the government to comply fully with persistent external pressures.

IMPORT-SUBSTITUTING AGRICULTURAL DEVELOPMENT

Given the vulnerability of the national economy and the volatility of "rice politics" (most dramatically in the Great Hartal of 1953, which prompted the resignation of the government), Sri Lankan regimes have naturally sought to assure stable food supplies at affordable prices. The long-term rice-rubber barter with the Chinese was an early solution. But with mounting evidence that the terms of trade could easily erode the nation's purchasing power internationally, a strategy of *domestic* production of rice to meet consumer demand seemed inevitable; this commitment paralleled the general strategy of import-substituting industrialization popular in the 1960s. In both cases, dependence on final products was replaced by dependence on sources of imported intermediate and capital goods and thus on stable sources of foreign exchange, including borrowing.

Food imports were a major part of the balance-of-payments difficulties (and associated external debt and financial dislocations) during the 1960s. As a result, strenuous efforts were made to increase the domestic production of rice, particularly under the United National Party regime of 1965-1970. The success of these efforts was dramatic, with paddy production tripling between 1952/53 and 1970/71, almost doubling the cereal self-sufficiency ratio.[41] The gains in paddy production came both from significant increases in area, largely through costly state-subsidized development of irrigated colonization schemes in the dry zone, and from increased yields obtained through extension of high-yielding varieties, heavily subsidized fertilizer and water distribution, provision of rural credit with a large de facto grant element, and price supports to encourage production.[42] Although these policies contributed significantly to reducing the food dependency of the national economy, their costs contributed directly and heavily to the fiscal crisis that the government faced in the following decade. By one estimate, subsidies to rice producers and rice consumers in the 1965-1970 period were equal to 36 percent of public sector capital expenditure and in some years exceeded 50 percent.[43]

Despite criticisms of the heavy public sector expenditures in Sri Lanka in the 1960s, the growth rate of the economy over this period was not noticeably low by the standards of poor Asian societies. Moreover, this growth rate was achieved while significantly increasing domestic food production capacity. The fiscal costs were indeed great and resultant debt burdens and budget deficits restricted policy choices for succeeding regimes. But it is reasonable to argue that this fiscal problem could have been managed had the purely conjunctural forces of the 1970s not been so unfavorable: Continuing decline in the terms of trade, dramatic worldwide jumps in the cost of food grains and petroleum-based products, and unfavorable weather conditions.[44]

Under the liberalization regime, heavy emphasis has been placed on further development of agricultural infrastructure, freeing up intermediate-good imports, allowing prices of agricultural products to rise, and abandoning compulsory procurement and marketing regulations. Although the weather remains a central determinant of production, substantial progress has been made, at least in the rice sector. Domestic production of rice in 1983 was more than double that of the low points of the mid-1970s (when unfavorable weather and shortages of imported inputs crippled production). More impressively, *yields* have continued to rise (although at considerable cost to the environment), from a low of 2271 kilograms per hectare in 1972/73 to 3591 kilograms per hectare in 1982/83 (see Table 8.5). These numbers become more significant when put in the context of rice imports. In the early 1970s, rice alone accounted for up to 20 percent of the total import bill; in 1983, rice imports were less than 2 percent of total import costs, and in 1984, less than 0.2 percent.[45]

Agricultural production and prices are notoriously unstable, yet the long-discussed goal of rice self-sufficiency can no longer be dismissed as political propaganda. Indeed, the Central Bank's *Review of the Economy* for 1983[46] explicitly recommends consideration of rice varieties that might be suitable for export and the substitution of rice flour for imported wheat flour.

Growth in agricultural production, however, even if concentrated in food, does not necessarily have any positive influence on food consumption by the most vulnerable sections of the population.[47] Increasing yields lowers the land size threshold of security for small landowning farmers, assuming costs of pro-

Table 8.5 Domestic Production and Yields of Paddy, 1970/71–1983

	Production (1,000 metric tons)	Yields (kg/hectare)
1970/71	1396	2367
1971/72	1312	2417
1972/73	1312	2299
1973/74	1602	2354
1974/75	1154	2271
1975/76	1252	2315
1976/77	1677	2520
1977/78	1890	2621
1978/79	1917	2748
1979/80	2133	2930
1980/81	2229	3260
1981/82	2156	3591
1982/83	2477	

Source: Sri Lanka, Department of Census and Statistics, Ministry of Plan Implementation, *Socio-Economic Indicators of Sri Lanka* (1983), Table 23.1; Central Bank of Ceylon, *Annual Report*, 1984, Appendix Table 10.

duction necessary for optimal yields do not escalate out of their financial reach. As yields rise, a family can be nutritionally secure on a smaller plot. This yield/security ratio is important in nations such as Sri Lanka in which a high percentage of the poor own some land and the size distribution of holdings is heavily loaded at the bottom end. Table 8.6 presents the data on holdings for the nonplantation sector in 1982.

Holdings outside the plantation sector are extremely small in Sri Lanka, even by South Asian standards. The average size of holding in what used to be called the "peasant sector" was 1.95 acres; more than three-fourths of all holdings (77.9 percent) were less than 3 acres, covering little more than one-third (37.8 percent) of the area cultivated. More than two-fifths (42.4 percent) of the holdings in this sector are less than 1 acre, averaging 0.37 acres each. More important, tiny as these holdings are, they are not all *owned* by the cultivating families; a significant portion of the gross produce (typically one-half) must be paid as ground rent. About 36 percent of the holdings are operated as tenancies by families owning no land at all or owning only home and garden sites.[48]

Even in the peasant sector, only a fraction of the population could thus be considered nutritionally secure. For most rural people, nutritional security is a function of the terms of trade between their households and sources of food: real income levels for laborers, value of subsidiary tradable food crops (onions, chili, beans, etc.) and nonfood crops (spices, etc.) for landholders. Aggregate growth in production is helpful to the rural majority in Sri Lanka so long as it increases the family's purchasing power at a faster clip than food prices rise. This is a serious problem because of the rising cost of production in modern energy-intensive agriculture and the rise in rupee costs of imported food (aggravated by both induced devaluations and unplanned deterioration of the rupee/SDR exchange rate. (See glossary.)

Outside the landowning agriculturalist sector, family food security is subject to similar considerations of class structure and income distribution. For the urban working class, the issue is levels of income (days of employment times the wage rate) relative to food prices. A similar dynamic affects the plantation proletariat. Though we know what has been happening to food prices since liberalization, wage and income trends are not precisely known. Data is collected mostly on the formal sector, ignoring a large and vulnerable section of the population, and annual days of employment per worker are not available. Though the empirical situation is by no means clear, it seems that incomes are lagging behind food costs for the weaker sectors of the economy. This would not be surprising, as there has been rapid inflation since the "opening up" of the economy, trade union power has diminished, and an unemployed pool of labor remains to be absorbed despite a fall in unemployment rates.

To be more precise than the preceding paragraph is possible but problematic. Data on inflation are unreliable; although the official Colombo consumer price index (CPI) is frequently used, it is easy to confirm with some on-the-street price comparisons that inflation is understated by the published

Table 8.6   Size Distribution of Agricultural Holdings, Smallholding Sector, 1982

Size (acres)	Percentage of Holdings	Percentage of Area	Average Size (acres) of Holding
less than 1	42.4	8.1	0.37
1–2	21.9	14.2	1.27
2–3	13.6	15.5	2.23
3–20	22.1	62.2	5.56
All	100	100	1.95

Source: Sri Lanka, Department of Census and Statistics, Ministry of Plan Implementation, *Census of Agriculture, 1982*, Preliminary Report.

numbers. Nevertheless, Table 8.7 gives some indication of the acceleration of food prices since liberalization. Food prices by the end of 1984 were more than triple prices in 1977. By the official calculations, the real wage rate index for workers in agriculture improved significantly over that period (from 76.3 to 96.3), whereas the real wage index for workers in industry and commerce declined significantly (93.7 to 77.7).[49] However, if we use David Sahn's calculations based on the alternative consumer price index (ACPI), we find *declining* real minimum wage rates in both agriculture and industry, although agriculture remains relatively better off. Sahn goes on to compute the real average daily wage rates in selected sectors, adjusted by the ACPI. This series begins only in 1979, but shows declining *average* wages in the paddy, coconut, tea, and construction industries.[50]

As the official CPI is obviously inaccurate, ought we not to compute real wages using the ACPI as Sanderantne,[51] Sahn, and others have done? Deflation by the ACPI yields seemingly anomalous results. Sahn's recalculations of consumption data show a *decline* in real expenditures for every income decile in Sri Lanka between the Consumer Finance Surveys of 1978/1979 and 1981/1982.[52] Given the increased level of economic activity over the period and the extensive visual evidence of a consumption binge by the island's wealthy since liberalization, this can be true at the upper end of the income pyramid *only* if the real benefits of growth are concentrated in a tiny stratum of the top decile of income receivers. This is entirely possible.[53]

The implications of deflating nominal income by the ACPI are dramatic: Real household consumption fell for most people on the island during the mid-period of the economic boom, and real national income has been growing at far lower rates than reported real GDP. In short, the implication is that the miracle of liberalization is overblown in both official and academic treatments of the period. Although a definitive empirical resolution on the real income front is not yet available, evidence for real weaknesses in consumption security for the poorest sectors seems indisputable. Given these market-induced weaknesses, policy toward entitlements and welfare spending becomes even more critical.

INCOME INEQUALITY AND FOOD POLICY AFTER LIBERALIZATION

Sri Lanka was celebrated as a "basic needs" success story in the mid-1970s, when the paradigm shift in the intellectual community began to stress equity over growth.[54] One strand of that celebration, in addition to outstanding PQLI performance, was the *reduction* of income inequality for the decade 1963-1973 as measured by the Consumer Finance Surveys.[55] The reality of that phenomenon has, however, been called into question, generating a serious empirical dispute.[56] The disagreement hinges on the validity and reliability of the data in the Consumer Finance Surveys conducted by the Central Bank in 1953, 1963, 1973, and 1978/79 and 1981/82. The numbers are problematic because of reporting biases at the upper end, particularly during the leftist United Front period (1970-1977) and because of disagreements in how income in kind should be evaluated (higher rice prices artificially raise the "income" of subsistence farmers).

Keeping in mind these caveats, provisional data from the 1981/82 Consumer Finance Survey indicate increased inequality between 1973 and 1981/82; indeed, the Gini coefficient (see glossary), which had fallen to 0.41 in 1973 and was precisely the same in 1978 as in 1963 (0.49), increased to 0.52, the highest level since the surveys began in 1953. Since property income increased after 1977, tax concessions were granted to capital, and indirect taxes were in-

Table 8.7   Food Prices and Wage Rates in Sri Lanka

Year	Index of Food Prices[a] (1952 = 100)	Real Wage Rate in Agriculture (official)	(Sahn[d])	Real Wage Rate in Industry/Commerce (official)	(Sahn[d])
1966	109.1	51.8[a]	—	74.3	—
1970	136.6	50.8	—	75.3	—
1975	204.3	60.8	—	86.8	—
1976	202.1	60.9	—	88.1	—
1977	203.1	76.3	—	93.7	—
1978	237.5	99.0	94.2	102.6	98.8
1979	263.3	116.0	103.4	105.2	93.5
1980	116.0	115.9	98.4	105.4	88.9
1981	339.6	98.3	79.3	96.2	77.8
1982	450.4	104.2	85.8	92.6	77.8
1983	506.3	100.4	78.2	82.5	64.2
1984	611[c]	(96.3)[b]	83.9	(77.7)[b]	56.4

[a]From Cost of Living Index Numbers, Colombo; wage rates from Central Bank of Ceylon, *Review of the Economy* (1983), Appendix Table 63.

[b]December 1984; Central Bank of Ceylon data.

[c]Central Bank of Ceylon, *Annual Report* (1984), Appendix Table 15.

[d] David E. Sahn, "Malnutrition and Food Consumption in Sri Lanka: An Analysis of Changes During the Past Decade" (Washington, D.C.: International Food Policy Research Institute, 1986), Table 11. Wages are deflated by Alternative Consumer Price Index and relate to workers in trades regulated by Wages Boards.

creased, income inequality after taxes and before subsidies has almost certainly increased.[57] Moreover, the real value of the most important consumer subsidies has been significantly eroded. Likewise the management of public sector enterprises has historically had a purposive redistributive impact,[58] now contrary to official policy.

Even if there has been a real and substantial increase in income inequality, there is obviously no necessary connection to increased hunger. After all, the pie (by some measures) has been expanding, although not so fast as is officially claimed. For the poor, rural and urban, food policy has traditionally set a floor under consumption, limiting the extent of severe hunger and physiological damage from malnutrition. That floor was critical in maintenance and improvement of Sri Lanka's PQLI record; it has come under increased pressure since the liberalization.

Food consumption policy has been central to both domestic politics narrowly conceived and to conflicts between Sri Lankan regimes and important international actors. The long-established policy of heavily subsidized food (at times gratis) for the population at large (over time limited somewhat by income criteria) was specifically targeted for criticism by international actors. A fundamental change in food policy was effected in June of 1978 when the general subsidy of food consumption was restricted to households earning less than 3,000 rupees per year. Approximately 7.72 million people—about half the population—claimed to be eligible. Further targeting accompanied a revision of the program from a ration provision to a food-stamp program limited to those with incomes less than 300 rupees ($12 in 1986) per month.

About half the population remains on the food-stamp rolls, despite international pressures to reduce the subsidy and domestic discussions of further coverage restrictions. The regime has undercut the effect of the subsidy in any event by refusing to revise the purchasing power by indexing either the income criterion or the stamp values to counter inflation. Moreover, despite the dynamics of economic change, which accelerated after 1977, new additions to the rolls have been forbidden.[59] Between the inception of the program and July 1981, the purchasing power of a typical family's food stamps had been cut in half.[60] Subsequent inflation has cut the benefits in real terms even further, and the prohibition on additions to the rolls has left some of the new poor without redress.

The value of food stamps is greatest to the poorest households. The bottom 20 percent of the income pyramid spend about three-fourths of their total income on food; in the poorest decile, food stamps account for 22 percent of food purchases; the range for the poorest half of the population is between 10 and 22 percent.[61] An evaluation by the Food and Nutrition Policy Planning Division of the Ministry of Plan Implementation found that the effect of policy changes has been a deterioration of the nutritional status of preschool children and an increase in the number of cases of serious malnutrition.[62] That study concluded that the food-stamp system, although cheaper, put more families at risk nutritionally than did the older ration system. An analysis of consumption data from the periodic Consumer Finance Surveys concluded that "there is no significant difference in the *average* nutritional situation between 1978/79 and 1981/82, but the calorie intake levels of the bottom 20 percent of the households have undergone serious deterioration."[63]

International pressure on the government to reduce welfare expenditures has been successful; food subsidies, which were roughly 14 percent of government spending in 1979 and 6 percent of GDP, declined to 7 percent of expenditures and 2 percent of GDP by 1981. Despite significant reduction in entitlement coverage under the food-subsidy program, the gross food-subsidy bill remains sensitive to exogenous shocks from higher international food prices (wheat, flour, and rice) and devaluation. As Table 8.8 illustrates, the share of food subsidies and transfers to households (into which food subsidies were incorporated after the food-stamp program replaced the ration system in 1979) in the total budget has declined. Moreover, because food *prices* have escalated so rapidly since liberalization (Table 8.7), rising expenditure levels do *not* indicate rising levels of food purchases for distribution. Taken together, these indicators suggest that either there is less need or that food needs now have lower priority; as the evidence suggests, certainly the latter is the case.

CONCLUSION: EXTERNAL FORCES AND DOMESTIC WELFARE

The form and viability of a dependent welfare state are externally conditioned. In Sri Lanka, social welfare policies and the potential to finance them evolved under unusual historical conditions: the development of a wealthy plantation export sector, early popular representative political forms, and the development of human and physical infrastructure to service the plantation economy.

Table 8.8   Food Subsidies and Transfers After Liberaliziation

Year	(1) Food Subsidy (Rs million)[a]	(2) Transfers to Households (Rs million)[a]	(1) and (2) as % of Budget
1977	1,424.1	322.8	19.8
1978	2,162.7	1,253.6	19.3
1979	2,321.0	727.5	15.0
1980	304.6	2,378.4	9.4
1981	309.8	2,572.7	9.8
1982	93.0	2,632.2	7.7
1983	81.0	2,579.6	6.4
1984	100.0[b]	3,358.4[b]	7.1[b]

[a]Millions of Rupees

[b]Approved Budget Estimates.

Source: Central Bank of Ceylon, *Review of the Economy* (1983), Appendix Table 93.

The development of the structure of the national political economy simultaneously opened important opportunities for social welfare development and left that potential vulnerable to external forces in the global economy.

The interaction of internal and external forces produced the tightly regulated, "closed" economy that characterized pre-1977 Sri Lanka. High levels of politicization, competition, and clientelism produced responses to vulnerability, driven by the domestic political necessity of protecting the mass public from further impoverishment from exogenous shocks. Development strategies from the mid-1950s to 1977 did not, however, alleviate the structural vulnerability of the economy. Unusually unfavorable external pressures of the early 1970s resulted in a genuine economic cul-de-sac of high unemployment, internal and external deficits, scarcities, slow growth, and austerity budgets. The realignment of domestic political forces, strongly influenced by the inability of governing elites to cope with external shocks, created conditions under which specific international actors obtained the power to redirect certain domestic priorities. Liberalization has—by positive theory, fiscal logic, and external pressure—been hard on social welfare priorities.

Nonetheless, despite cuts in the social wage, the contemporary configuration of Sri Lanka remains a dependent welfare state and thus continues to protect vulnerable populations to an extent unusual in South Asian nations. Effects of liberalization on the mass public have been ambivalent, although for the poorest people the effects have been clearly negative. Unemployment has been cut, in part because of economic expansion fueled by foreign aid and deficit spending, but income inequality has increased. To reduce inequalities of income and wealth contradicts the logic of accumulation on which the strategy depends. The regime resurrects as justification a logic that is essentially that of the Simon Kuznets "inverted U" hypothesis, contending that inequalities necessarily increase in the early stages of growth, then subside.[64]

Whether the new policies produce growth with equity, equity *after* growth, or indeed any growth at all is still dependent upon external factors. Implementing the liberalization policies was a necessary condition for the extraordinary international support the new regime has received; reciprocally, external support is a necessary condition for sustaining the policy changes. Budget deficits that would seem intolerable—26.1 percent of GDP in 1980, 22.1 percent in 1982—are sustained by high levels of concessional foreign assistance. Unprecedented current account deficits could not have been covered without significant hard-currency largesse. The large grant element in foreign assistance has enabled the regime to escape a debilitating debt-service burden. Still, by 1984, interest on the public debt—domestic and foreign—was the largest single expense in the budget, exceeding the categories of capital transfers, salaries, and subsidies and grants.[65]

International tolerance for Sri Lanka's fiscal indiscipline has been greater than for many dependent nations. Yet pressures for fiscal discipline continue to threaten social consumption spending of which nutritional programs are a major part. Welfare policy is determined by the vector sum of external pressures and internal constraints introduced by domestic political calculations. With the recent escalation of civil disorder in the nation,[66] the additional burden of military spending threatens to add significantly to the claims competing for discretionary funds. At 6.4 percent of the 1985 budget, the military still consumes a small share of the budget relative to military expenditures in the rest of Asia, but that share is almost three times the share of a decade ago (see Table 8.1) and continues to rise.

Although new competition for government spending complicates the political configuration, the decisive factors remain more constant than altered: The form and extent of growth are heavily conditioned by external forces over which any dependent regime has little control; the impact of growth on various sectors, classes, and individuals remains subject to crucial mediation by the state. Despite the reduction of aggregate, national vulnerability to food crises because of import-substituting agricultural development, the vulnerability of the weakest sectors of society in Sri lanka has increased. Exchange and entitlement conditions are less mediated by a national guarantee of a floor consumption level. Nutritional security of individuals—both rural and urban—is thus more subject to market dynamics, international and domestic, with the familiar mix of opportunities and risks associated with a market society.

NOTES

1. Compare Cheryl Christensen, "A Structural Approach," and D. Gale Johnson, "World Food Institutions: A 'Liberal' View."

2. James C. Scott, *The Moral Economy of the Peasant: Rebellion and Subsistence in Southeast Asia.*

3. See Amartya Sen, "Famines."

4. Herring, Ronald J. *Land to the Tiller: The Political Economy of Agrarian Reform in South Asia.*

5. See James Warner Bjorkman, "Health Policy and Politics in Sri Lanka: Developments in South Asian Welfare State;" Davidson R. Gwatkin, "Food Policy, Nutrition Planning and Survival: The Cases of Kerala and Sri Lanka;" Herring, "Economic Liberalization Policies in Sri Lanka: International Pressures, Constraints and Supports;" Paul Isenman, "Basic Needs: The Case of Sri Lanka;" G. H. Pieris, *Basic Needs and the Provision of Government Services in Sri Lanka: A Case Study of Kandy District*; and, Peter Richards and Wilbert Gooneratne, *Basic Needs, Poverty and Government Policies in Sri Lanka.*

6. Asoka Bandarage, *Colonialism in Sri Lanka: The Political Economy of the Kandyan Highlands, 1833-1886*; Gamani Corea, *The Instability of an Export Economy*; Satchi Ponnambalam, *Dependent Capitalism in Crisis: The Sri Lankan Economy, 1948-1980*; and, Herring, "The Janus-Faced State in a Dependent Society: Determinants of Shifts in Sri Lanka's Development Strategy."

7. Herring, Ronald J. "The Janus-Faced State in a Dependent Society: Determinants of Shifts in Sri Lanka's Development Strategy."

8. Herring, "Economic Liberalization Policies in Sri Lanka;" and, S. W. R. de A. Samarasinghe, "Sri Lanka in 1982: A Year of Elections."

9. P. A. S. Dahanayake, "Growth and Welfare: Some Reflections on the Effects of Recent Development Policy Reforms in Sri Lanka;" and, H. N. S. Karunatilake, "The Impact of Welfare Services in Sri Lanka on the Economy," and "The Public Sector in the National Economy."

10. For a discussion of alternative measures, see Norman Hicks and Paul Streeten, "Indicators of Development: The Search for a Basic Needs Yardstick." The inclusion and weighting of literacy is particularly problematic in the PQLI because of the different real advantages implied by different kinds of literacy in different economic and cultural contexts; with regard to Sri Lanka on this point, see Ann R. Mattis, "An Experience in Need-Oriented Development." On the inadequacy of traditional measures, and a defense of the PQLI, see Morris David Morris, *Measuring the Condition of the World's Poor: The Physical Quality of Life Index.* On the persistence of severe poverty in Sri Lanka despite the impressive aggregate indicators, see Marga Institute, "An Analytical Description of Poverty in Sri Lanka"; Paul Isenman, "Basic Needs: The Case of Sri Lanka"; E. L. H. Lee, "Rural Poverty in Sri Lanka, 1963-1972"; and G. H. Pieris, *Basic Needs and the Provision of Government Services in Sri Lanka: A Case Study of Kandy District.*

11. Bruce E. Moon and William J. Dixon, "Politics, the State, and Basic Human Needs: A Cross-National Study."

12. Marga Institute. "An Analytical Description of Poverty in Sri Lanka." See also endnote No. 25 below.

13. Rati Ram and Theodore W. Schultz, "Life Span, Health, Savings and Productivity."

14. Corea, *The Instability of an Export Economy,* and International Labour Office, *Matching Employment Opportunities and Expectations: A Programme of Action for Ceylon.*

15. Central Bank of Ceylon, *Annual Report.*

16. Corea, *The Instability of an Export Economy.*

17. Herring, *Land to the Tiller,* B. H. Farmer, *Pioneer Peasant Colonization in Ceylon: A Study in Asian Agrarian Problems.*

18. W. A. Wickremeratne, "The Emergence of Welfare Policy, 1931-1948," p. 488.

19. Sidney Wanasinghe, "The Hartal of August 1953;" W. Howard Wriggins, *Ceylon: Dilemmas of a New Nation,* pp. 75-76; and, Ponnambalam, *Dependent Capitalism in Crisis,* p. 25.

20. G. H. Pieris, *Basic Needs and the Provision of Government, pp.* 24-25.

21. Gwatkin, "Food Policy, Nutrition Planning and Survival," p. 249.

22. See ARTI, *Sri Lanka and the International Food Crisis.*

23. Nihal Kappagoda and Suzanne Paine, *The Balance of Payments Adjustment Process: The Experience of Sri Lanka,* pp.101-110, and R. A. Jayatissa, "Balance of Payments Adjustments to Exogenous Shocks During 1970-1981: The Case of Sri Lanka."

24. Amita Shastri, "Politics of Constitutional Development in South Asia in the Seventies: A Case Study of Sri Lanka," Chapters 6 and 7.

25. Lee, "Rural Poverty in Sri Lanka," documents deterioration of real wages in the estate sector as well as in urban areas. Godfrey Gunatilleke, "Participatory Development and Dependence: The Case of Sri Lanka," pp. 48-51, discusses the sources that led him to report widespread malnutrition in Sri Lanka in the mid-1970s. Nutrition data presented by James D. Gavan and Indrani Sri Chandrasekera in *The Impact of Public Food-grain Distribution on Food Consumption and Welfare in Sri Lanka,* Table 7, p. 22, indicate serious malnutrition effects, especially in the plantation sector. The available

nutrition data of a systematic sort relate to a period after the most severe stage of the food crisis. Isenman, "Basic Needs," p. 244, presents data and analysis to link an increase in mortality, particularly on the plantations, to the food crisis in 1974 (compare Marga Institute, "An Analytical Description of Poverty"). On Sri Lanka's international food situation, see ARTI, *Sri Lanka and the International Food Crisis.*

26. Bank of Ceylon, *Annual Report.*

27. N. Balakrishnan, "Industrial Policy and Development Since Independence," pp. 202-210.

28. Shastri, "Politics of Constitutional Development," Chapters 6 and 7.

29. Dahanayake, "Growth and Welfare," and Karunatilake, "The Impact of Welfare Services in Sri Lanka" and "The Public Sector in the National Economy."

30. Bank of Ceylon, *Annual Report,* p. 2.

31. Sri Lanka, "The New Tax Policy."

32. International Monetary Fund, *IMF Survey* 6:23 (1977).

33. World Bank, *Annual Report,* I:191.

34. Ibid., I:102.

35. Sri Lanka, Minister of Finance and Planning, "Budget Speech, 1981," p. 2.

36. Ibid.

37. Central Bank of Ceylon, *Annual Report 1984,* Appendix Table 5.

38. International Monetary Fund, *Government Finance Statistics Yearbook 1984.*

39. Ibid., p. 24.

40. Salamat Ali, "Off the Standby List," pp. 74-75.

41. James D. Gavan and Indrani Sri Chandrasekera, *The Impact of Public Food-grain Distribution on Food Consumption and Welfare in Sri Lanka,* and International Labour Office, *Matching Employment Opportunities and Expectations: A Programme of Action for Ceylon,* I:87-88.

42. International Labour Office, Ibid., II:Chapter 11, and Ponnambalam, *Dependent Capitalism in Crisis,* Chapter 4.

43. Gavan and Chandrasekera, *The Impact of Public Foodgrain Distribution on Food Consumption,* p. 48.

44. World Bank, *Annual Report,* p. 90.

45. Central Bank of Ceylon, *Annual Report,* 1984, Appendix, Table 21.

46. Central Bank of Ceylon, *Review of the Economy,* 1983, p. 28.

47. Christensen, *A Structural Approach,* and Herring, *Land to the Tiller,* Chapter 9.

48. See Herring, Ibid., Chapter 3.

49. Central Bank of Ceylon, *Review of the Economy,* 1983, Table 6.

50. David E. Sahn, "Malnutrition and Food Consumption in Sri Lanka: An Analysis of Changes During the Past Decade," Table 11.

51. Nimal Sanderantne, "The Effects of Policies on Real Income and Employment."

52. Sahn, "Malnutrition and Food Consumption," Table 10.

53. Macro-level data will not decisively resolve the issue. Gross domestic *expenditure* has been growing at even higher rates than gross domestic *product* of late, but of course expenditures include government as well as households. Although gross domestic capital formation has been rising as a percentage of GDP between the survey years (1978/79 to 1981/82), the domestic savings ratio actually fell (from about 14.5 percent to about 11.7 percent), suggesting increased consumption. However, government *dis*savings *could* account for the decline, leaving the household *aggregate savings/consumption ratio intact.*

54. Douglas Rimmer, "'Basic Needs' and the Origins of the Development Ethos."

55. Lal Jayawardena, "Sri Lanka."

56. E. L. H. Lee, "Rural Poverty in Sri Lanka, 1963-1972;" Dahanayake, "Growth and Welfare;" and, W. D. Lakshman, "Income and Wealth Distribution in Sri Lanka: An Examination of Evidence Pertaining to the Post-1960 Experience."

57. Compare Lakshman, Ibid., and S. W. R. de A. Samarasinghe, "Current Economic Policy: A Comment."

58. Lakshman, Ibid., p. 22.

59. Robert C. Oberst, "Foodstamps and Government Nutrition Policy: The Battle over Basic Needs in Sri Lanka."

60. Sri Lanka, Minister of Finance and Planning, "Budget Speech, 1981," Table 3.

61. Neville Edirisinghe, "Preliminary Report on the Food Stamp Scheme in Sri Lanka: Distribution of Benefits and Impact on Nutrition."

62. Sri Lanka, Minister of Finance and Planning, "Budget Speech, 1981," p. 30. See also Sahn, "An Analysis of the Nutritional Status of Pre-School Children in Sri Lanka, 1980-81," and "Malnutrition and Food Consumption in Sri Lanka: An Analysis of Changes During the Past Decade."

63. Edirisinghe, "Preliminary Report on the Food Stamp Scheme," p. 49.

64. Simon Kuznets, "Economic Growth and Income Inequality." See also Irma Adelman and Cynthia Taft Morris, *Economic Growth and Social Equity in Developing Countries,* 178ff.

65. People's Bank, *Economic Review,* 1983, 9:8 (1983):16.

66. See James Manor, ed., *Sri Lanka in Crisis and Change.*

9

Keith B. Griffin

The Chinese Economy After Mao

Chairman Mao died in September 1976, and with his death an era in Chinese and world history came to an end. Nearly a quarter of mankind was directly affected by Mao's politics, and in this sense he undoubtedly was the greatest revolutionary leader of this or any other century. He was also the architect of a distinctive strategy of socialist economic development. Yet within two or three years of his death, China embarked upon a major series of economic reforms that, if implemented in full, will profoundly alter the way the Chinese economy functions. Indeed the reforms currently under discussion, when combined with those that already have been introduced, are far more radical than anything previously considered, let alone implemented, in any other communist country. These reforms are the subject of this chapter.

But first let me put China into perspective. It is by far the world's largest underdeveloped country. The recent census revealed that there are over a thousand million Chinese living in the mainland. This is half again as large as India, the next most populous country, and it is nearly double the size of the other thirty-one lowest-income underdeveloped countries. In global terms, nearly a quarter of mankind lives in the People's Republic of China.

According to conventional measures of national income, China is also one of the poorest countries on earth, having an average income per capita comparable to that of India and Pakistan but significantly lower than that of Indonesia, Nigeria, or Brazil. As we shall see, however, there are indications that China has done much better than most other Third World countries in alleviating the worst forms of poverty.

China is, of course, a socialist country. All large enterprises belong to the state, agricultural land is collectively owned, private property in productive assets still is of relatively little significance, and the provision of many basic needs—including food, shelter, health, and education—is largely the responsibility of the state. Some of these features currently are being modified—and we shall want to consider whether these modifications signal an end to socialism in China—but it is evident that the Chinese economy is organized on principles very different from our own.

How well has this economy performed? Let us begin with growth and accumulation and focus on the period between 1970 and 1982.[1] During that period China's domestic product grew 5.6 percent a year. This exceeds by a considerable margin the rate of growth achieved in India and the other low-income countries and is about the same as the rate of growth of the middle-income countries.[2] What is true of aggregate output is true also of the two most important sectors—agriculture and industry. Chinese agriculture grew 2.8 percent a year, half a percentage point faster than the low-income economies as a whole and nearly as fast as the growth in middle-income countries. As a result, food production per capita in China was 24 percent higher at the end of the period than at the beginning, compared to 1 percent in India, minus 3 percent in the other low-income countries, and 11 percent in the middle-income countries.[3] In industry, China grew nearly twice as fast as India, more than twice as fast as the other low-income countries and 43 percent faster than the middle-income countries. Thus the growth performance in China compares very favorably with that of the rest of the Third World.

Reasons are not hard to find. First, China devotes a larger share of its domestic product to investment than do other underdeveloped countries. For example, in 1982 the investment rate was 28 percent in China, 25 percent in India, and 13 percent in the other low-income countries. Second, the rate of growth of investment in China is high; in fact it is much higher than in the other low-income countries and not much below the rate currently achieved in the middle-income countries.

Not only has production increased more rapidly in China than in most other Third World countries, but the population has increased significantly less rapidly. As a result, output per capita has tended to rise much faster in China than elsewhere. The recent census indicates that the rate of demographic expansion in China is about 1.5 percent a year and is projected to fall further. This compares favorably with population growth rates in India (2.3 percent), other low-income countries (2.6 percent), and the middle-income countries (2.4 percent). Indeed, combining the estimates of the rate of growth of domestic product and population, we see results in estimates of the rate of growth of output per capita between 1970 and 1982 of 4.2 percent a year in China, 1.3 percent in India, 0.8 percent in other low-income countries, and 3 percent in the middle-income countries. It is clear that China has done much better with its general economic performance than have most Third World countries.

Other indicators show that the benefits of rapid growth have been spread widely and have reached all sections of the population. For example, both the birth and death rates in China are much lower than in most other underdeveloped countries. The infant mortality rate, at 67 per 1,000, is well below that of India, less than 60 percent of that of the other low-income countries, and lower even than the infant mortality rate in the middle-income countries, where average incomes are five times higher than China's. Indeed, China enjoys a demographic profile more like that of a rich country than a poor one. Life expectancy is sixty-seven years compared to only fifty-five in India and even less in the majority of the other low-income countries. The adult literacy rate is nearly double that of the low-income countries and marginally higher than that of the middle-income countries.

Equally significant is the secondary-school enrollment ratio. In China, more than four out of ten children of secondary-school age are in school; in India, three out of ten; in the other low-income countries, two out of ten. These differences underline in the most vivid way possible the differences in development priorities between China and most of the Third World.

The purpose of presenting these statistics is to demonstrate that the motives behind the economic reforms in China cannot have been primarily economic or demographic; the motives must have been largely political. Economic growth rates were relatively high; average incomes were rising and were equitably distributed; population expansion was under control; and there was no danger of a Malthusian crisis. The reforms may or may not improve the long-run performance of the economy, but it is evident that they were not introduced in response to an economic crisis or in response to a failure of the Maoist strategy for economic development.[4]

REFORMS IN THE AGRICULTURAL SECTOR

Whatever the reasons were, radical changes have occurred, particularly in the countryside, and it is appropriate therefore to begin with the reforms in the rural areas, the place where 80 percent of the Chinese live.

I shall concentrate on the four most important reforms. First, the prices received by farmers have been raised sharply whereas the prices paid by farmers for industrial products have been held down. As a result, agriculture's terms of trade improved by at least 37 percent between 1978 and 1982. I say "at least" because this calculation does not take into account prices in the free market, which usually are higher than the official prices.[5]

Second, the policy of local grain self-sufficiency has been relaxed and producers now have greater freedom in deciding what to grow and how best to grow it. That is, both the output mix and the input mix are determined locally on the basis of profit calculations rather than centrally on the basis of administrative calculations. Regional comparative advantage is beginning to be exploited. Some effects may already be seen, notably in the reduction in the amount of land devoted to grains and an increase in the acreage allocated to industrial crops such as cotton and rapeseed.

Third, the private household economy has been liberalized. The private plot has been enlarged (from 5 percent to 15 percent of the collectively owned land), private nonagricultural or "sideline" activities have been encouraged, and most restraints on the free market have been removed. The result has been an enormous surge in private incomes in rural areas. Between 1978 and 1982 average private income rose nearly threefold, and the share of private income in total peasant income rose from 27 to 38 percent.

Finally, collective farming has been abandoned and instead the collectively owned land has been turned over, under contract, to individual peasant households. The production team, the smallest collective unit in each commune, no longer is responsible for cultivation: Its main task today is to allocate land among households and ensure that they comply with contractual agreements. The peasants no longer receive work points for cultivating the collective fields but instead receive whatever they produce from the land allocated to them after discharging their contractual obligations to their production teams. Thus, China has adopted a small peasant farming system (called the production responsibility system) under which the peasantry has been converted into tenant farmers paying fixed rents in kind. The commune system as we knew it for over twenty years has ceased to exist.

Two questions immediately arise: Have the reforms worked and were such radical changes necessary? That is, have the economic results of the reforms been positive and, if so, could the results have been achieved within the earlier economic and institutional framework?

There is no doubt that there has been an acceleration in the rate of growth of agricultural output. In terms of production, the short-run effects clearly have been positive. Moreover, the incomes of the rural population have increased even faster than output, thanks to the improvement in the agricultural terms of trade. This rise in average rural incomes, contrary to what was feared, has not been accompanied by a sharp rise in inequality in the distribution of income. Land and other productive resources have been evenly distributed, and the initial impact of the reforms, at least at the local level, has often resulted in less rather than more inequality. Thus far the reforms deserve high marks.

As time passes, however, a few problems may emerge. These problems are likely to center on the level of capital accumulation, the long-run rate of growth of production, and the distribution of income.

Capital Formation

Let us begin with capital formation. There are five sources of investment and savings in rural China: (1) investment undertaken by the state; (2) investment undertaken by the commune by organizing seasonally available labor on public works projects; (3) investment financed from the profits of collective enterprises owned by the commune or its production brigades; (4) investment financed by the production teams from their collective accumulation funds; and (5) private household savings and investment.

State Investment.   State rural capital formation in China as a whole seems to have declined slightly, possibly reflecting national policy decisions to reduce aggregate investment in order to raise consumption levels quickly. One of the major political objectives of the economic reforms was to "mobilize the enthusiasm of the people"; another was to restore the status and prestige of the Communist party. Both could be achieved, it was thought, by raising living standards more quickly and thereby showing that the party had not lost touch with the masses and was concerned about the well-being of the people, above all the rural people. In the short run the easiest way to improve the standard of living of the majority of the people was to reduce the high level of investment and channel these resources into consumption, and this was the strategy that was adopted.

It is unlikely, therefore, that the decline in total state investment, or of that part directed to the rural areas, will be reversed in the near future. The significance of this for the countryside should not be exaggerated, however, as state investment in rural areas before the reforms usually was little more than 10 percent of total state investment.

Commune Labor Investment.   Labor investment by communes and brigades was much more important. Indeed, China is known throughout the world for its success in mobilizing seasonally unemployed and other "surplus" labor for investment in rural areas. An enormous amount of work was undertaken (field terracing and leveling, irrigation and flood-control projects, tree planting, road and bridge building), and these projects changed the face of the Chinese countryside. Some of the work was of poor quality and required frequent repair and maintenance, and the return on investment often was long delayed and disappointingly meager. Nonetheless, much good was achieved.

Under the new reforms, however, the emphasis formerly placed on labor investment has been reduced. This form of investment has not disappeared entirely, but the new institutional arrangements built around small peasant farms have undermined the sense of solidarity and communal participation that used to be such a striking feature of the commune system and have weakened incentives for collective labor investment. It is sad that the decline in labor investment is likely to be felt most strongly in the poorer communes rather than in the rich.

Investments from Profits of Collective Enterprises.   The richer communes tended to rely relatively little on labor investment to achieve high rates of capital accumulation. The engine of growth in their case usually was the reinvested profits of commune- and brigade-run enterprises. Unfortunately for these communes the profits of collectively owned enterprises have been squeezed through a combination of higher wages, higher taxes, and higher raw material prices. To make matters worse, the proportion of profits retained by the enterprises for reinvestment has fallen. This is a deliberate act of policy and is one of the methods that has been used to increase consumption standards of the peasantry.

The joint effect nationally of a falling profit rate and a lower reinvestment ratio has been to reduce the rate of increase of fixed assets in commune- and brigade-run enterprises. Indeed, between 1978 and 1982 the rate of fixed asset formation declined precipitously—by about two-thirds.

Investments from Collective Accumulation Funds.   Increasingly, then, the burden of collective accumulation in the rural areas will fall upon the collective accumulation funds of the production teams. Here, too, however, there are worrying trends. Many teams have begun to sell their assets to individual households, and in most cases the money thus obtained has not been reinvested but has been held in the form of idle balances. As a result there has been a decline in the stock of collectively owned means of production.

In principle, it would be possible to adopt a strategy whereby teams sold off their draft animals and small items of collectively owned capital equipment and reinvested the proceeds in larger pieces of equipment in which economies of scale are important, generating new investment through the collective accumulation fund. Such a strategy would permit a change in the composition of collectively owned assets while ensuring that the stock of productive assets continued to increase. But alas, this has not been done. Assets are being liquidated and not replaced, and the rate of collective investment has been reduced.

Private Sector Investment.   This means that if investment is to be maintained at a high level, the private sector will have to shoulder more responsibility for rural savings and investment. Whether the private sector can shoulder this responsibility remains to be seen. So far all we know is that private savings have increased sharply—often to 25 percent of total household income. A high proportion of these savings are channelled to housing and the purchase of consumer durables, and only a relatively small proportion is used for investment in fixed productive assets. Moreover, the productive investment undertaken by households often consists of purchases of assets from the production teams. This transfer of ownership does not represent an increase in the stock of the means of production in the countryside, because what the household gains the team loses.

Of course, other corporate forms could emerge that are compatible with the new Chinese socialism—and we must not underestimate the inventiveness of the Chinese—but so far at least, private corporations or joint private-state corporations have not arisen in the rural areas. Thus the private sector remains restricted largely to the household economy, and private savings are amassed and largely invested by individual households.

On balance, then, it is likely that the overall rate of investment in rural areas will fall. State investment probably will decline slightly; labor investment will fall sharply but there may be an offsetting rise in the efficiency of such investment; investment financed from the profits of commune- and brigade-level enterprises is certain to fall, as will collective accumulation by production teams. Investment by households, on the other hand, surely will rise, and the productivity of that investment is likely to be high. My guess is that the rise in private investment and in the average productivity of investment will not fully compensate for the fall in various forms of collective investment. There is thus a danger that the long-run rates of capital formation and of agricultural growth may decline slightly.

Long-run Production Growth Rates

Much of the recent spectacular growth of output is caused by a once-for-all increase in efficiency. The benefits of an improved allocation of resources have not been exhausted, but it is virtually inevitable that the additional gains will diminish year by year and hence this source of growth is bound to be of declining importance in the longer run. Added to this is the danger that the new institutional arrangements will make it more difficult for farmers to exploit economies of scale where they exist. The old communes had weaknesses, but one of their strengths was the ability to take advantage of economies of scale. That strength may have been sacrificed in order to obtain what the reformers regard as the even greater advantages of a small peasant farming system.

Quite a separate issue is the maintenance of the existing stock of large, lumpy collective assets: such things as irrigation channels and drainage ditches, terraced fields, and antierosion works. There is a risk, to put it no stronger, that if the administrative structure of the commune is weakened, these valuable collective assets will fall into disrepair. If that happens, the long-run rate of growth will be adversely affected.[6] In summary, there is a danger—not a certainty but a danger—that the reforms may have the unanticipated and unwelcome effect of lowering the rate of growth of agricultural production. This could occur because of a combination of a lower investment ratio, diminishing gains from an improved allocation of resources, an inability fully to exploit economies of scale, and a deterioration in part of the collectively owned and constructed rural infrastructure.

Distribution of Income

Speculation about future trends in the distribution of income in rural areas is even more difficult than assessing future agricultural growth rates. In principle, inequality need not increase. To avoid it happening, however, a number of conditions will have to be fulfilled. For example, land must continue to be allocated equitably and reallocated periodically as households change in composition and size. Ideally, the "rent," or the amount paid to the team by each household, should reflect the true scarcity rent of the land allocated to that household. Failing this, subcontracting or subtenanting of land between households should be prohibited and all land not wanted or required by a household should be returned to the team for reallocation. When land is returned, the team should fully compensate the household for any immovable assets and any improvements made to the land. Comparable conditions would have to apply in the capital and labor markets.

In practice, the necessary conditions are not being applied in full, and there is a genuine likelihood that inequality will increase somewhat in the future. Land "rents" are well below true scarcity values, and consequently farming households receive large unearned incomes. This would not matter too much if land were reallocated fairly frequently, but in fact the period of a contract recently has been extended to fifteen years. More remarkable, land reclaimed by peasants from previously uncultivated areas is classified as "private land" and becomes virtually the property of the household that organized the reclamation. Similar phenomena have been observed in the capital market. For example, the sale or rental to households of tractors and other collectively owned assets have been at prices substantially below market clearing rates. This, of course, enables the lucky buyer to earn large quasi-rents with little exertion. In such cases inequality increases merely because of the way the reforms were introduced, not by intent. These are some of the possible consequences of the reforms.

Were the Reforms Necessary?

The debate centers on the institutional reform of the commune system and the reintroduction of a small peasant farming system. Three of the four major reforms could have been implemented without having to dismantle the communes—namely, the raising of farm prices, the exploitation of regional comparative advantage, and the liberalization of markets and the household economy. The issue is whether the large recent gains in output could have been achieved with these three policies alone within the framework of collective farming by production teams.

The official view is that the production teams were inefficient because they did not provide adequate material incentives to their members. Small peasant farms, in contrast, give an incentive to people to work longer hours than before, to work with greater intensity per hour, and also to work with greater intelligence, imagination, and creativity. This argument is persuasive, I believe, but only if we compare the present system with the previous one, warts and all. I am less persuaded that the production teams are inherently less efficient than small family farms.

Three points of criticism are made about the structure of incentives in the production teams. First, an excessive proportion of the income of the team was distributed "according to need" rather than "according to work". Consequently, everyone received enough to eat whether or not they made a full contribution to production. Second, the wage (or strictly speaking what the Chinese call "work points") differentials were very narrow, and hence there was little encouragement to work harder to obtain a higher income. Everyone was paid much the same regardless of the effort expended. Third, such differentials as existed were arbitrary and did not reflect the difficulty of the task, the skill required, or the worker's marginal product. The link between effort and reward was weak, not least because differentials often were based on such personal characteristics as sex, age, and political attitude.

Assuming all these points are valid, it nonetheless would have been possible in principle to modify and improve the incentive structure without altering more grain available for distribution "according to work"; work-point differentials could have been widened to stimulate greater effort; and the criteria by which work points were awarded could have been changed, possibly switching to a piece-rate from a time-rate payment system. No doubt some problems which work points were awarded could have been changed, possibly switching to a piece-rate from a time-rate payment system. No doubt some problems would have remained, but it is perhaps a pity that China did not experiment with alternative incentive schemes within the framework of the production team to see if it were possible to retain the advantages of the commune system while enjoying the growth of output achieved under the new household production system.

THE REFORM OF STATE INDUSTRIAL ENTERPRISES

The reforms in industry have followed those in agriculture with a lag of about five and a half years. The motives behind the reforms are several. A chief motive has been a desire to reverse the tendency for the rate of growth of industrial output to decline gradually over time, notwithstanding the fact that by world standards the present rate of growth continues to be impressive. In addition, the authorities are keen to introduce new technology, to raise the quality of industrial products, to expand the range of goods offered, and to improve the marketing and distribution system in order to eliminate both acute shortages of some products and unsaleable stockpiles of others. In the initial period the reforms have concentrated on increasing the autonomy of state enterprises and giving managers greater freedom and responsibility in decision making. In this respect the industrial reforms are analogous to the production responsibility system in agriculture.

It is not hard to understand why enterprise autonomy has been singled out for priority attention, as the situation before the reforms was one of almost total centralization and little discretion allowed to managers. Production targets were specified in the plan; material inputs were allocated by the state; labor, too, was allocated by the state, as was credit and foreign exchange. All profits were remitted to the government, where they formed a vast pool of financial resources available for allocation in accordance with plan priorities. Finally, all fixed investment by state enterprises was determined centrally, and the necessary funds were provided at virtually no cost. Enterprises thus were responsible for neither profits nor losses, and managers consequently had little incentive to use resources efficiently.

The reforms, introduced in 1984, still require most managers to meet a production quota, but once the quota is fulfilled managers are free to produce additional output and sell it where and how they wish at whatever price it will fetch, provided only that the price neither exceeds nor falls below the fixed state price by more than 20 percent. Managers also are given greater freedom in selecting workers and administrative staff, in designing (within specified limits) pay and bonus systems, in determining the internal organization of the enterprise, and in forming joint ventures or mergers with other enterprises. Finally, firms now are allowed to retain 70 percent of their depreciation funds and, in theory, 45 percent of their profits. This all sounds like common sense run riot.

There is, however, a difficulty. As the reform process has proceeded, the need to change the methods by which prices are determined has assumed growing importance. Decentralization and the relaxation of administrative controls and physical, quantitative planning imply that decisions increasingly will be taken in response to price signals. That being so, it is vital that the price signals received by managers reflect true scarcities, true costs. Otherwise resources will be misallocated and decentralization will lead to a decline in efficiency rather than to an increase. It matters little if, say, coal is underpriced and refined petroleum products are relatively overpriced when production, distribution, and investment decisions in these industries are based on nonprice criteria. But if prices are used to guide decisions, underpricing of coal will result in suboptimal levels of production and investment in mining and excess demand by users; the converse will, of course, occur in the petroleum industry.

The Chinese leadership, for understandable reasons, has been unwilling to reform the price system while other major changes are occurring. They fear that a general overhaul of relative prices could lead to inflation, as it probably will be easier to raise the prices of products experiencing excess demand than to lower the prices of products suffering from excess supply. They fear, too, that a radical change in relative prices may introduce considerable uncertainty into the economic system and make planning at the enterprise level exceedingly difficult. This, in turn, could result in a fall in industrial output and a decline in employment. Finally, the authorities recognize that a change in relative prices will alter the distribution of income, possibly in ways that cannot readily be foreseen, and they wish to avoid creating unjustified inequalities or undermining political support for the reform process as a whole.

Price reform thus is likely to occur gradually, on a step-by-step basis. Indeed, several changes have already been introduced, and in 1987 China has a multiple pricing system. Some output continues to be determined in accordance with planned quota targets and is sold at official fixed prices established by the state. Some output is produced under guided (or indicative) plans, and above-quota production is freely sold by the enterprise at any price within the range of plus or minus 20 percent of the official prices. Finally, some products, mostly consumer goods, are sold on totally free markets at whatever price is determined by the forces of supply and demand.

There is a debate in China today about what principles should be used in setting prices in the future. Several different strategies are possible and it will be fascinating to see what procedure ultimately is agreed upon. My expectation is that the Chinese will continue to be highly pragmatic and that decisions will be taken largely on a case-by-case or category-by-category basis.

One possibility would be to begin with the commodities China exports and imports and to adjust gradually the prices of these goods to a moving average of world prices. Next, the Chinese could tackle the nontraded commodities currently subject to official pricing regulations. Here it would be desirable, I think, to allow domestic demand and supply to operate and to adjust the official price gradually each year until a market clearing price is established. Thereafter, prices could reflect domestic market conditions without further official intervention.

No doubt some residual price controls or price ceilings will be necessary for state enterprises that enjoy a monopoly position. And some subsidies will continue to be necessary for some goods and services for reasons of social policy and an equitable distribution of income. Housing, medical services, and urban transport are cases in point.

We turn now to industrial products sold under a guided plan. The objectives should be (1) to continue to reduce compulsory quotas, (2) to abolish immediately the fixed official price when this is higher than the floating price, and (3) when the floating price is higher than the official price, to raise the latter in stages until the two coincide, thereafter allowing supply and demand to clear the market.

The price for food grains raises difficult problems because grain is the most important wage good and any change in grain prices will have widespread implications for living standards in both the cities and the countryside. The official retail price of grain in urban areas has remained roughly constant for the last decade, whereas the purchase price paid to peasant producers increased by about 26 percent between 1978 and 1982. As a result, a wide gap has emerged between the price paid by the state for grain and the price at which it is sold to consumers. This gap is filled by subsidies financed out of general state revenues. In 1982, these subsidies were equivalent to 7.5 percent of the national income. This represents an enormous sum, and, moreover, one that will continue to grow as grain production expands. It is clear that some adjustment is essential.

The adjustment process, however, is bound to be delicate and will have to occur over a number of years. What is required is (1) some combination of a lower compulsory production quota, (2) a reduction in the quantity of grain urban consumers can obtain through the rationing system, (3) a higher price of rationed grain, and (4) abolition of the price premium on above-quota grain deliveries to the state in favor of purchases at the free market price. The latter, in turn, should slowly be brought into line with world prices, as previously mentioned. These changes will raise the average cost of food grains to urban consumers and hence lower their standard of living. This, almost certainly, is undesirable, and it surely will be necessary to compensate workers for a higher cost of living through an appropriate increase in their nominal wages.

Finally, there are the commodities traded on free markets. The number of such commodities is few, probably no more than 10 percent of the total, and every opportunity should be taken to increase the volume of transactions on unregulated markets. Indeed, the presumption should be that all commodities are traded on open markets at prices determined by supply and demand unless the government has strong reasons to insist on regulated prices. Often, I believe, strong reasons will not be forthcoming, and if the reformers keep their nerve, it should be possible to combine greater autonomy of state industrial enterprises with widespread liberalization of prices. In fact, in my judgment, if price liberalization is not possible, greater autonomy may be undesirable. There may be no comfortable stopping place between, on the one hand, centralized planning and quantitative controls and, on the other, enterprise autonomy plus rational market prices. Either system can work reasonably well but a hybrid of the two is likely to fail.

CONCLUSION

Let us assume the reforms in industry and in agriculture are carried through to completion. What sort of economy will China have then? Will China still be a socialist state? Many observers in the West, both those who admire what is happening and those who deplore it, believe China is rapidly creating a capitalist economy. They cite as evidence the abandonment of collective farming, the enlargement of the private plot and the switch to a small peasant farming system with long-term security and rights that in some respects are similar to those normally associated with private property. They adduce, too, the reduced emphasis on central planning and quantitative controls, the reinstatement of profit as a management yardstick in the state industrial enterprises, and the intention to expand the role of prices and the market mechanism in allocating resources. Finally, a topic we have not touched upon, they mention the greater integration of China into the world economy and the tentative steps taken to encourage foreign investment in China.

Perhaps the answer depends on one's definition of socialism. If by socialism one means a society in which ownership and control of the instruments of production are in the hands of the community as a whole, then China most definitely is a socialist country. Agricultural land continues to be collectively owned, large-scale industry is almost entirely in the hands of the state, and most small and medium enterprises, in both rural and urban areas, are collectively owned. In the cities, almost all housing is owned and allocated by the government. By the criterion of ownership, then, China is clearly socialist.

Some people regard the defining characteristic of socialism to be central direction of the economy by the government. By this test, too, China remains a socialist country. Certainly, central planning will be less detailed than before and the instruments of planning will become increasingly refined, subtle, and indirect, but central guidance and direction will remain: There is no likelihood that anything approaching laissez-faire will be allowed to operate for long in China.

Finally, some people, particularly those who come from the social democratic tradition of Western Europe, judge a country by its social policies and the degree of equality in the distribution of income these help to produce. It is perhaps a little artificial to compare China to the welfare states of Northern and Western Europe, as the differences in levels of income are so large, but there is no doubt that the relative degree of equality in China is remarkable by any standard and is matched by very few countries in the world.

In the last analysis I am not much concerned about what label is put on China. Following Deng Xiao Ping, I am inclined to believe that it does not really matter whether the cat is white or black so long as it catches mice. Whatever the color, the Chinese economy after Mao is an unusual cat, and if I were a Chinese mouse I would reckon the chances of being caught were more than negligible.

NOTES

1. The best official data on the Chinese economy are provided by the People's Republic of China, State Statistical Bureau, *Statistical Yearbook of China,* published annually. The data cited, however, are taken from the World Bank's annual *World Development Report* in order to facilitate comparison with other Third World countries. The period selected for comparison, 1970-1982, is essentially arbitrary and conforms to the World Bank's presentation. Inclusion of the decade 1960-1970 would not alter the qualitative conclusions, whereas extension of the period beyond 1982, when the effects of the economic reforms became dramatic, would greatly favor China in comparison with the rest of the world, then suffering from the effects of widespread international recession.

2. Following the World Bank's classification, low-income countries are defined as those with a GNP per capita of less than $410 in 1982 and middle-income countries as those Third World economies with a GNP per capita of $410 or more.

3. Population growth rates in 1970-1982 were 1.4 percent per annum in China, 2.3 percent in India, 2.6 percent in the other low-income countries and 2.4 percent in the middle-income countries.

4. The reformers in the Chinese government, in this interpretation, were reacting to what they regarded as the excesses of the Great Leap Forward, the Cultural Revolu-

tion, and the period of the Gang of Four and, particularly in agriculture, were attempting to remodel the economy so that it conformed more to the pattern that prevailed in the early 1950s. An unkind critic could label this movement as literally reactionary, an attempt to return to an earlier golden age of socialist development.

5. It is difficult to obtain accurate estimates of the size of the free market. One indication of the rapid growth of such transactions is the fact that "retail sales by peasants to non-agricultural residents" rose from 31,100 million yuan in 1978 (of which 28,000 million yuan was food) to 110,800 million yuan in 1982 (of which 96,500 million yuan was food). Factors beyond simple exchange-rate calculations conspire to make dollar equivalents for these transactions not very meaningful. Nevertheless, the 1987 yuan/dollar exchange rate is 3.67:1.

6. Of course, irrigation companies could be formed to maintain and expand irrigation facilities, but the author is not aware of any such company. An easier solution would be to maintain a strong commune administrative structure for the management of collective assets such as irrigation systems, and this seems increasingly likely in many parts of China, although responsibility will probably fall to the township (or *xiang*, as communes are now called).

Part 4
Agricultural Development and Hunger in Latin America

Alain de Janvry 10

Latin American Agriculture from Import Substitution Industrialization to Debt Crisis

During the last fifteen years, and under a variety of circumstances, most Latin American countries have shifted from late policies of import-substitution industrialization (ISI) to neoliberal economic models (NL). In Chile (1973), Uruguay (1973), and Argentina (1976), this occurred in the form of military coups and imposition of authoritarian forms of government. In Peru, the transition from ISI to neoliberalism was initiated in 1975 under the military regime of Morales, but NL policies were pursued with equal intensity under the democratic presidency of Belaúnde. In debt-ridden countries, such as Mexico (1982) and Brazil (1982), the shift happened as a result of austerity policies imposed by the International Monetary Fund that forced both drastic devaluations of the exchange rate and elimination of most forms of public subsidies.

These neoliberal attempts were, of course, not new in the history of Latin America. Political instability during the period of ISI, which began systematically in the 1930s, can largely be associated with the alternating in power of the interests of protectionism and of free trade. Transitions to neoliberalism in the 1970s and 1980s were, however, strongly defended at the political level and had the time necessary to produce observable results. For instance, countries such as Chile offer laboratory-like situations to study the effects of liberalization and free trade on the economy and social welfare.

The historical path of neoliberalism, however, was not smooth; and the observed results were eventually far different from those prognosticated by theory for both internal and external reasons. It is particularly important to distinguish between three periods of neoliberalism in countries such as Chile and Argentina: first, a period when the model was being imposed through devalua-

An earlier draft of this chapter was circulated as Giannini Foundation Paper No. 774 (for reprint identification only). I am indebted to Luis Crouch for his contributions to this chapter.

tion, deregulation, and austerity policies; second, a period of neoliberalism with Dutch disease (see glossary) created by either oil (Mexico) or, more frequently, debt revenues; and third, a period of debt crises with a return to equilibrium exchange rates but with serious constraints on public expenditures and imported goods.

In this chapter, we concentrate on the economic and social effects of neoliberalism on the agricultural sector. The discourse of neoliberalism has emphasized the damage that ISI policies have wrought on agriculture and has justified many of the liberalization policies in terms of the presumed positive role they would have on agriculture and on its role in economic development. In a sense, the success of the policies of the ideologues of neoliberalism should be judged, at least partially, on the basis of their effect on agriculture, and this is what we propose to do here.

IMPORT-SUBSTITUTION INDUSTRIALIZATION AND NEOLIBERALISM: THE MODELS DEFINED

Since Latin America gained independence from colonial powers, its history has been one of oscillation between economic models whose drives can be explained in terms of the concepts of articulation and disarticulation. The two models differ in the geographical and social location of the market for final goods: (1) abroad or in the expenditure of profits and rents under social disarticulation, and (2) domestically in the expenditure of wages and peasant incomes (implicit wages) under social articulation. Under the first, growth is rooted in deepening inequality and cheap labor, which naturally leads to authoritarian forms of government; under the second, the balance between production and consumption implies a necessary balance between profit and wages that also provides the objective basis for participatory forms of government.[1]

The republican period of the first forty years of Latin American independence was one of protectionism and involution. The rise of domestic manufacturers was to satisfy a domestic demand originating in the rents of the oligarchic landowners' class and in the profits of a merchant class. Domestic demand did not originate in the expenditure of wages and peasant incomes. As a result, even in the period of inward-looking development, the model that became established was one of disarticulation.

With the victory of the liberals by the late nineteenth century, the export market became the dynamic source of effective demand. Many countries were able to grow rapidly by entering into the international division of labor. Argentina and Uruguay were exporting beef and corn; Peru, guano; Ecuador, cacao and bananas; and Central America, coffee. The growth path was determined by the booms and busts of the international commodity markets. But relocation of the market from inward to outward did not change the structural feature of social disarticulation. Growth was still based on the reproduction of cheap labor.

It was in the 1930s that the ISI model began to relocate the market for the key sectors of economic growth from abroad to the domestic economy, and, initially at least, it promoted a growth path based on social articulation. With the Great Depression, the collapse of the international market (having the capacity to import manufactured goods against the export of primary commodities) created serious foreign exchange shortages. The governments rationed foreign exchange in order to deal with balance-of-payment problems without having to devalue. In addition, tariffs were applied on many goods, again largely as balance-of-payment instruments. Deficits in the balance of payments implied a tendency for the Latin American economies to slow down severely as they were highly dependent on foreign trade. Domestic market opportunities for manufacturers, thus created, were then seized by domestic producers. The bases for these market opportunities had been created by the gains during the period of outward expansion and involved a demand for both wage and luxury goods. The ISI was, however, more than an historical opportunity. It eventually became a well-developed body of policies with clairvoyant theoretical thinkers such as Raúl Prebisch, Celso Furtado, and Albert O. Hirschman.[2]

As import substitution progressed, however, it underwent a double transformation. First, the combination of foreign exchange bottlenecks, calls on foreign capital and technology, domestic market saturation, and strong social inefficiencies (because of the permanence of strong rent-seeking behavior and hangovers from the semifeudal past) all led to an increasing relocation of effective demand for the key sectors of economic growth in the consumption of profits and rents. Late ISI thus was guided by the logic of disarticulation. Second, as ISI spread from consumer industries back toward heavy industry, inefficiencies became cumulative, the cost of final goods increased, and foreign exchange bottlenecks worsened. This was because of the need to import both capital goods and raw materials and because of the disincentive to agriculture caused by the transfer of rents through overvalued exchange rates and by tariffs on industrial inputs used by agriculture.

Import-Substitution Industrialization in Theory

What was the "theory" of ISI? It should first be evident that any theorizing on ISI would have to depart markedly from the neoclassical analysis of resource allocation and comparative advantage that is carried on in static terms. The ISI deals, by contrast, with dynamics in which disequilibria are to be optimally induced and managed to create structural transformations with growth. The theorists of ISI thus boldly stepped into the then-unchartered area of disequilibrium dynamic economic analysis. Unavailability of a consistent body of such theory implied the need to rely on a set of loosely coordinated principles that Hirschman organized under the guidelines of a "strategy of economic development."[3] This strategy was to be translated into policies according to the specific conditions of particular countries. Thus, the ISI is less an ideal doctrine than a body of pragmatic guiding principles.

The strategy of ISI aims at fulfilling two fundamental objectives.[4] One is to create new investment opportunities that will mobilize the abundant un-realized sources of growth. Here the role of policy is to serve as a catalyst for investment—that which Hirschman called a "premium mobile." The other is to use the investment of resources to induce institutional innovations so that the new structure will be a more productive and more self-sustaining (i.e., more complete and less dependent) engine of growth than the one inherited from the liberal period of outward growth and, before that, from the colonial past.

The instruments of ISI were to insure protectionism to selected branches of industry through tariffs or quantitative import restrictions. In addition, sub-sidies on imported inputs (capital goods) were granted through overvalued exchange rates, eventually managed through a system of multiple rates. In-come transfers to industry were to be principally borne by agriculture, which tended to be hurt on several counts. Agricultural importables were generally not protected and thus had to compete with imports cheapened through over-valuation of the exchange rate. Exportables were taxed because the overvalued exchange rate decreased the national currency equivalent of the foreign ex-change earned. Further subsidies to industry were given through price con-trols on food items as part of a package of cheap labor policies. Industrial in-puts (for agriculture) were made more expensive by the same set of policies. The result was a strong income squeeze on agriculture.

Negative rates of protection for agricultural products, however, were not totally a factor in determining internal prices. Marketing boards at times suc-ceeded in stabilizing prices at levels higher than international levels. Much of the price management was carried out via quantitative restrictions on imports. Not only was there limited protection to some crops in this sense, but farmers also had access to subsidized inputs, the most important of which was credit. Also, to the extent that exchange rates were overvalued, imports of unprotected agricultural inputs were inexpensive.

The ISI policies were designed on the basis of three fundamental struc-tural postulates. The first is that the impact of price distortions on physical vari-ables is secondary. Argentina's agriculture, for example, was thought not to be highly responsive to prices, with the result that higher prices create rents for the large producers whereas a price squeeze does not reduce supply signifi-cantly. Similarly, in industry, price distortions were expected to affect only mini-mally the substitution of capital for labor and of imported for domestic inputs. The structuralist world is, in other words, akin to the classical world of fixed agricultural coefficients in industry. The second important postulate is that economies of scale are important in determining average production costs. Consequently, this justifies protectionism as a transitory phase to establish in-fant industries until growth makes them competitive in the international economy. Finally, capital accumulation was seen to be the key source of growth, whereas sufficient concern was not given to productivity growth, use of investments at full capacity, and an expanding effective demand.

Regarding agriculture, the structuralist advocates of ISI held that structural change, not price incentives, was the key instrument to improve the production performance of agriculture. Land reform directed at remnants of semifeudal social relations thus became an important policy. Its design was under the Inter-American Commission for Agricultural Development's (CIDA) guidelines and its implementation motivated by the Punta del Este charter. The redistributive impact of land reform had as its economic purpose to increase the productivity of the land and to expand the domestic market for wage goods, thus potentially contributing to social articulation. However, although the antifeudal purpose of the reforms was highly successful, income distribution was not achieved, and social articulation remained a rhetorical issue in most countries.

In the political sphere, the structuralists believed that industrialization and the concomitant formation of an urban working class would create the social basis for democratic forms of government to emerge. Growth itself was thus looked upon as the principal instrument of the distribution of benefits and social change. Extrapolating to the political sphere the logic of Lewis's model,[5] growth would eventually absorb surplus labor and equalize the distribution of income, thus providing the objective basis for participatory forms of government.

These fundamental structuralist postulates proved, however, to be erroneous; and the doctrine elaborated on this basis ran into protracted difficulties. Prices did matter in the choice of activities, in the allocation of resources, and in the choice of techniques. In agriculture, in particular, unfavorable prices and distortions in favor of capital led to both stagnation of output and massive labor displacement. Economies of scale were, by no means, clearly established; and resistance to lowering tariffs has become the source of permanent inefficiencies leading to higher instead of lower distortions. Capital accumulation proved necessary but not sufficient to induce self-sustained growth.

The result was an increasing incapacity of ISI to maintain the momentum of growth in spite of growing disarticulation. Increasing costs, foreign exchange bottlenecks, market saturation, excessive capital intensity, excess capacity, disincentives to exports, substitution of imported for domestic inputs, and decreasing saving rates led to declining growth rates in industry and to agricultural stagnation. Politically, the transition to disarticulated growth and increasing regressivity in the distribution of income led to increased antagonisms between capital and labor as well as between factions of capital associated with wage goods and luxury on export goods production. The result was a shift away from democratic forms of government and toward authoritarian regimes. By the mid-1960s, ISI had run its course, and a new model had to be introduced to sustain growth and legitimize the social status quo. This was found in redefining social disarticulation toward export growth through a neoliberal, authoritarian model.

Objectives and Instruments of the Neoliberal-Authoritarian Model

The objectives and instruments of neoliberalism are best understood through the experiences of Chile, Uruguay, and Argentina, where the model was applied not under external pressures but as a fully rationalized economic and political program. The crisis of ISI opened the way to neoliberal-authoritarian (NA) programs in Chile (1973), Uruguay (1973), and Argentina (1976). These programs were designed to not only eliminate many of the "distortions" created by ISI but also to achieve a major restructuring of economic and political power away from the remnants of the "articulated" bourgeoisie and organized labor that had resisted the onslaught of "disarticulated" ISI. The objectives of NA were, consequently,

1. Reallocation of resources according to international comparative advantages. This would eliminate the inefficient industries created by ISI and reallocate resources toward internationally competitive sectors.
2. Control of inflation through limited expansion of the money supply and elimination of budget deficits, the latter by both curtailing social expenditures and raising taxes.
3. Elimination of the deficit in the balance of payments through international borrowing and devaluations.
4. Removal of state intervention from the setting of prices, privatization of as much economic activity as possible, and the termination of subsidies to both production and consumption.

The instruments to be used to reach these objectives were both economic and political. First, the economy was to be opened to the free movement of capital and products. International prices then would determine domestic prices, and free movement of interest rates would induce the entry and exit of capital and, consequently, determine the domestic money supply. Second, all subsidies received through negative interest rates would be eliminated, even in agriculture, and rising interest rates would reflect the true opportunity cost of capital. Finally, nominal wages would be controlled, and real wages would be expected to decline to reflect the opportunity cost of labor under conditions of abundant labor supply. In the political sphere, authoritarianism was to be used to enforce the consequent (and necessary) process of concentration in the distribution of income—on the one hand, the liquidation of the "inefficient" articulated domestic bourgeoisie created by ISI protectionism; on the other, the suppression of wage demands and the eventual need to sustain high rates of unemployment (hopefully only in a period of transition). By contrast to ISI, NA is thus not an ad hoc strategy of complex implementation but a fully coherent theoretical model of simple application, as it is noninterventionist in the economic sphere and dictatorial in politics.[6]

For agriculture, NA was expected to eliminate the negative effect of cheap food policies and negative effective rates of protection that monetarists had denounced as the prime cause of agricultural stagnation.[7] This would reallocate resources toward those sectors with international comparative advantages and would lead to increased imports of the commodities displaced by resource competition. Because agriculture was seen to be highly sensitive to price incentives, improved prices would enhance the adoption of new technologies and increase supply. With flexible prices in free markets, the gains from technological change would be passed on to consumers as falling prices. The interplay of technological change and free markets would launch agriculture onto a dynamic "technological treadmill" of falling costs and falling prices. The NA ideology thus advocated "consumer sovereignty" in identifying the ultimate beneficiaries of its policies.

The theory of NA was, however, too perfect; and implementation in a structural context different from that postulated by theory not only did not match expectations but led, instead, to economic and political crises of unprecedented magnitudes. At the macrolevel, performance failures were noted on three variables. The rate of unemployment remained excessively high, with little prospect of improvement even beyond a transition stage. In itself, unemployment did not matter, as authoritarian governments were not particularly concerned with legitimacy. More important, the real rate of interest reached unprecedented levels, commonly as high as 60 percent, and tended to remain there. Thus, capital inflows were massive, inducing large foreign debts. Simultaneously, productive investments were stifled. Finally, the rate of inflation remained higher than that of the dollar after devaluations (particularly in Argentina but also in Uruguay and Chile) so that there was a continued tendency to overvalue, especially after a monetary approach to balance-of-payments management was taken around 1978. Together with a reduction of tariffs, this resulted in the growth of imports of all types of consumption goods, which outsold large segments of domestic production of tradable goods, both in agriculture (especially when imports were subsidized by the United States or the EEC) and in industry created by ISI.

At the microlevel, severe rigidities in the allocation of resources reduced the potential gains from comparative advantages and trapped large segments of the population in lagging or declining sectors, creating extensive poverty. For limited sectors with strong international comparative advantages and privileged access to international capital (in the form of dollar-denominated loans), the NA model proved to be an important source of growth. For much of the balance of the economy, however, practice did not match theory, at least not soon enough to matter; and serious setbacks were the result.

The imbalances of continued overvaluation without compensatory protectionism on industry and of relying on a deepening of debt to maintain the balance of payments could not be sustained forever, particularly once falling oil prices severely limited international liquidity and access to international loans. The results were massive devaluations of the exchange rate and imposition of austerity programs to control inflation and reduce import needs. For agriculture, devaluations meant improved prices for tradables as well as higher prices for imported inputs. Austerity policies implied limited access to credit and high interest rates, creating difficulties to reactivate production in those sectors most dependent on credit. Neoliberalism thus entered into a third phase when it was applied for the sake of economic stabilization in debt-ridden economies.

In the following sections we analyze the economic and social impacts on Latin American agriculture of five alternative development strategies. We do this by choosing Latin American countries and time periods that provide archetype models of these strategies: Brazil (1907-1981) and Mexico (1909-1977) for late ISI; Chile (1974-1979), Uruguay (1973-1979), and Argentina (1976-1979) for the transition to NL; Mexico (1978-1982) for oil-exports-created Dutch disease under late ISI; Chile (1980-1982) for debt-created Dutch disease under NL; and Brazil and Chile (after 1982) for stabilization policies under debt crisis conditions.

AGRICULTURE UNDER LATE
IMPORT-SUBSTITUTION INDUSTRIALIZATION

The cases both of Brazil throughout the economic miracle (1967-1977) and until the debt crisis (1981) and of Mexico before the oil boom of 1978 are good illustrations of how agriculture fared under late ISI. The common features of the framework of agricultural development were (1) *industrial protectionism* resulting, for agriculture, in high-priced industrial inputs but, also, in an expanding domestic market through urbanization and industrial employment creation, particularly for nontradable goods; (2) overvalued *exchange rates* resulting in negative price effects for agricultural tradables; (3) *institutional rents* selectively distributed by the state to compensate certain productive and/or social sectors from unfavorable agricultural prices, principally under the form of subsidized credit, infrastructure investment, research, and extension; and (4) *social disarticulation* that distorts the structure of effective demand for agriculture toward luxury consumption goods—animal products in particular—and export goods.

The dominant feature of Brazilian agricultural growth during the economic miracle is the extraordinarily rapid growth in the production of export and industrial crops and stagnation in food crop production relative to population growth (Table 10.1). Between 1966 and 1977, the production of food crops, such as cereals, grew at the average annual rate of 5.8 percent, whereas that of black beans declined by 0.8 percent and that of root crops by 0.7 percent. By contrast, the production of export and industrial crops increased at the average annual rate of 23 percent, with soybeans growing at the rate of 38 percent. In spite of overvaluation of the exchange rate and protectionism on industrial inputs, which deteriorated the terms of trade for agriculture, profitability of investments in agriculture was selectively maintained by generous institutional rents, particularly in the form of subsidized credit.

The real value of annual agricultural credit increased sixfold between 1960 and 1972. In 1977, disbursed agricultural credit was equal in value to the total GDP of agriculture. This credit was principally allocated to export and industrial crops. Thus, in 1977, soybeans, coffee, sugar, and cotton received 50 percent of the Bank of Brazil's agricultural credit when they accounted for 44 percent of the gross value of crop output, whereas beans, cassava, and corn received 12 percent while accounting for 27 percent of the gross value of crop output. Credit was highly concentrated in the large farms, with 80 percent of the farms excluded from access to credit and 40 percent of the total credit received by the largest 1 percent of farms that are principally involved with production of export crops. With subsidized credit used to produce export crops, public subsidies—which were partially derived from increased foreign debt—ended up subsidizing foreign consumers from whom loans were being taken.

The bias against food crops in favor of export crops was reinforced in several ways—by price controls on food items, although such controls did not exist on export crops that faced rising international market prices and benefited from export promotion policies; by research priorities favoring technological advances in export crops; and by a greater level of price risk in food crops relative to export crops.[8] The result was that the rate of profit was lower in food crops than in export crops, and the variance of this rate was

Table 10.1   Brazil: Structure of Production by Crops

Crops	Share of gross value of crop output 1977	Average annual growth rate 1966–1977	Share of production in small farms 1975[a]	Share of production credit 1977
		(percent)		
Cereals	20.4	5.8		
Wheat	2.8	13.4	14.2	11
Rice	7.5	3.4	31.5	16
Corn	10.0	4.2	55.0	8
Root crops	13.6	−0.7		
Cassava	10.7	−0.8	68.3	1
Black beans	6.5	−0.8	76.6	3
Export crops	54.2	22.7		
Soybeans	17.3	37.6	12.5	20
Cocoa	4.2	3.2	3.7	1
Coffee	13.1	−4.8	4.6	13
Sugarcane	8.5	3.8	4.9	9
Cotton	5.3	−1.1	17.3	8
Oranges	3.5	12.1	28.7	11
Others	5.3	5.9		

[a]Small farms are defined here in terms of value of agricultural production equal to or less than two minimum wages.

Source: Gervasio Rezende, "Price of Food and the Rural Poor in Brazil, 1960–80" (Rio de Janeiro: Instituto de Planejamento Economico e Social, January 1985).

greater in the former than in the latter, making food crops a clearly inferior economic alternative to export crops. The only reasons why peasants remain in food crops are that shifting their resources to the production of export crops is an option generally unavailable to them and the opportunity cost of food production is given for them by employment conditions and wage levels.

From the standpoint of food dependency, total cereal production per capita did not have a growth rate significantly different from zero between 1967 and 1981 (Table 10.2). The share of cereal net imports in total availability (cereal dependency) remained trendless, with an average of 5.7 percent during the period 1967-1977. It is only with the rapid buildup of debt in the period 1978-1981 that it increased to 17 percent; however, it fell back to 11.3 percent in 1982/83 once the debt crisis occurred. Imports of selected staple foods increased, such as black beans, which were being displaced in production by soybeans, sugarcane, and wheat; however, the coverage of agricultural imports by agricultural exports remained trendless at 570 percent between 1967 and 1977. All in all, it may be said that agriculture under ISI performed modestly in terms of food security in an aggregate sense. Although ISI failed to increase food production per capita, it allowed it to increase via trade in a modest fashion without putting pressure on the balance of payments.

The social impact on rural welfare of these policies was, however, highly negative. The process of land concentration continued in large farms involved in the production of exports, industrial inputs, and luxury goods. Between 1967 and 1972, the number of small farms declined relative to large ones even though absolute numbers continued to rise. This relative decline in small farms was caused by favorable urban labor markets and by a virtual impossibility of access to land for small farmers under conditions of rising land prices and lack of access to credit.[9] With large farms principally producing the majority of beef, soybeans, wheat, sugar, cotton, cacao, and rubber, and small farms the majority of corn, beans, and cassava, changes in the land tenure pattern correspond to the relative growth performance of these two types of crops (Table 10.1). The poor performance of food crops is the symptom of the demise of peasants as producers of a marketed surplus under the force of a double resource competition: within agriculture between food and export crops with land being reallocated to export crops through land concentration; and between agriculture and the urban sector with labor being reallocated to the urban sector through migration. Only in specific sectors of small farms producing nontradables did the boom of Brazilian agriculture benefit the peasants. This was the case for family farms producing vegetables for the rapidly growing metropolises in the vicinity of Sao Paulo.

Capital-intensive production techniques on large farms in the southern states reduced labor requirements and increased the seasonality of labor needs. The result was a decline by 9 percent in the number of small farms between 1970 and 1975 in the south and large migratory flows toward the Amazon, where the number of farms increased by 29 percent. Thus, food produc-

Table 10.2 Brazil: Agricultural Growth and Food Security

	Whole period 1967–1983	Late Import Substitution Industrialization 1967–1981		Debt crisis 1982–1983	
	Average growth rate[a]	Average level[h]	Average growth rate[a]	Average level	Average growth rate[b]
All agriculture	3.9*	97	3.9*	131	3.1
Cereal					
Production (Q) (millions of metric tons)	3.0*	26	3.2*	32	−14.3
Exports (thousands of metric tons)	−10.2*	811	−17.8	735	24.2
Imports (thousands of metric tons)	6.8*	3,450	7.8	4,708	9.2
Dependency[c] %	7.5*	8.7	8.2	11.3	18.7
Production per capita (kilograms)	0.4	240	0.6	240	−17.6+
Availability per capita[d] (kilograms)	1.1*	264	1.5*	270	−14.8+
Agricultural exports (E$_A$) (millions of dollars)	14.2*	4,786	15.3*	8,092[e]	f
Agricultural imports (I$_A$) (millions of dollars)	15.8*	1,026	16.9*	1,798[e]	
E$_A$ = I$_A$/E^g %	−4.9*	50	−4.8*	31[e]	
E$_A$/I$_A$ %	−1.6	522	−1.6	450[e]	

Q = Production
E = Exports
I = Imports

[a]The symbol * indicates growth rates significantly different from zero.
[b]The symbol + indicates growth rates significantly different from rates in late Import Substitution Industrialization period.
[c]Dependency is measured by (1 − E)/(Q + I − E).
[d]Availability is measured by Q + I − E.
[e]1982 only.
[f]Blanks indicate no data available.
[g]E indicates total country exports.
[h]1974–1976 = 100

Source: UN, Food and Agriculture Organization, Production Yearbook and Trade Yearbook (Rome: UN Food and Agriculture Organization, various issues).

tion was increasingly removed from the most fertile areas of Brazil and pushed toward the frontier along with the displacement of small farmers. In southern agriculture, labor was increasingly proletarianized and seasonal. Between 1964 and 1975, participation of nonresident workers in the total agricultural labor force of Sao Paulo increased from 16 percent to 36 percent; and, even though rural wages were rising, the increasing instability of employment led to deteriorating incomes for the landless labor force.

Brazilian agriculture between 1967 and 1977 thus offers an example of the impact of large ISI policies in which unfavorable terms of trade for agriculture resulting from overvaluation of the exchange rate were more than compensated by institutional rents allocated to export products and large farmers. Agriculture thus became a dynamic complement to industry, growing at the exceptional average annual rate of 3.9 percent between 1967 and 1981. It helped Brazil generate foreign exchange and cover the cost of 48 percent of its imports, improve its energy supply through alcohol production, and avoid food shortages. However, it led to an increasing food dependency and a deepening structural dualism, and it rarely benefited small farmers. Late ISI gives us a first characterization of the fate of peasants in the duality between lagging (food) and booming (export crops and urban economy) sectors: Although peasants were unable to shift their land to booming-sector activities, large farmers did shift land into the booming sector; peasant labor was absorbed as wage labor in either export or urban sectors. Labor absorption in the rest of the economy thus mitigated the negative welfare effects on peasants of stagnant food production.

Mexican agricultural growth between 1969 and the oil boom of 1978 also offers a good example of the impact on agriculture of late ISI. Between 1959 and 1968, Mexican agriculture had grown at the brilliant average annual rate of 4.2 percent, with an import coverage (E_A/I_A) of 408 percent (Table 10.3). This growth was stimulated by large programs of public irrigation, successful technological change, and favorable price policies for agriculture.[10] In the subsequent decade, however, this growth rate fell to 2.2 percent, and the import coverage fell to 280 percent as increasingly massive volumes of food grains were imported. This poor aggregate performance was caused by attempts at controlling inflation through cheap food policies and overvalued exchange rates that led to falling real prices for producers of staple foods.

The aggregate slowdown, however, masks highly uneven crop performances. While the area planted in corn and beans fell, the area in luxury and export products grew rapidly. This is the case for sorghum (animal feed), meat, dairy products, and fruits and vegetables. The area planted in sorghum, for instance, increased by 35 percent between 1969 and 1977. These crops and activities are basically produced by the larger farmers with irrigated land and favorable access to credit. Under the demand pull of social disarticulation, Mexican agriculture thus became increasingly dependent in food grain imports and bankrupted large segments of the peasantry unable to shift to the irrigated, capital-intensive booming-sector crops. The result was large-scale abandonment of small farms, rapid urban migration, high levels of unemployment, and inadequate nutritional standards for many in spite of a satisfactory overall economic growth.[11] Displaced peasants were, however, absorbed in a rapidly growing urban economy and by employment opportunities in the United States.

LIBERALIZATION: THE TRANSITION FROM IMPORT-SUBSTITUTION INDUSTRIALIZATION TO NEOLIBERALISM

We consider here the cases of Chile and Argentina and occasionally Uruguay, where the transition to neoliberalism occurred through the military coups of 1973 in Chile and Uraguay and of 1976 in Argentina.

Output and Trade

The impact of liberalization on output and trade may be explored by fitting log-linear trends for the main agricultural commodities of these countries over the period 1967-1979 for Chile and 1967-1978 for Argentina, with multiplicative dummy variables for the postcoup periods. Tables 10.4 and 10.5 indicate the commodities and variables for which there exist statistically significant differences in compound growth rates between the pre- and postcoup periods. The results show that the patterns of production and trade changed significantly with economic liberalization. In Chile, the shift to comparative advantages was marked by a positive increase in production after a long decline under late ISI. Under open economy conditions, with no institutional rents, the pattern of production changed markedly with a significant increase in the export of fruits, vegetables, and wine, although wheat production was stagnant. The transition to NL also accelerated overall agricultural growth in Argentina and created an export boom in a variety of oilseeds (Table 10.5). It is thus obvious that the transition to NL was favorable to agriculture in general and particularly to the sectors with strong international comparative advantages—fruits and vegetables in Chile and oilseeds in Argentina.

These changes in output and trade were the result of domestic policy changes rather than of changes in international price levels. Argentina, for example, was specializing in oilseeds precisely at a time when international oilseed prices were declining relative to those of other crops that Argentina trades. Openness to the international market was increasing precisely when the market was turning unfavorable. We may then conclude that a significant part of the increase in trade and the change in trade patterns occurred in response to the transition from ISI to NL.

Table 10.3 Mexico: Agricultural Growth and Food Security

Units	Whole period 1959–1983 Average growth rate[a]	Early Import Substitution Industrialization 1959–1968 Average level[f]	Average growth rate[a]	Late Import Substitution Industrialization 1969–1977 Average level	Average growth rate[b]	Import Substitution Industrialization cum Dutch 1978–1979 Average level	Average growth rate[b]	Import Substitution Industrialization cum SAM 1980–1982 Average level	Average growth rate[b]	Debt crisis 1983 Average level	Average growth rate[c]
All agriculture	2.9*	76	4.2*	97	2.2+	119	−4.2+	126	0.4+	131	c
Cereal											
Production (Q) (millions of metric tons)	4.2*	10	7.6*	14	2.7+	17	−21.1+	22	2.2	25	
Net exports (millions of metric tons)		0.6		−1.4		−3.0		−5.8		−8.5	
Dependency[d] (%)		−7		8		15		21		25	
Corn											
Area (millions of hectares)	0.2	7.1	3.0*	7.2	.0+	6.4	−26.9+	7.0	−12.6+	8.4	
Production (millions of metric tons)	2.6*	7.5	7.7*	8.5	−0.3+	9.5	−29.7+	12.0	−4.7+	13.9	
Net exports (millions of metric tons)	0.5	−6.0	−0.8	7.5	−1.0	10.0	−2.4	15	−4.7	25	
Dependency[d] %											

Sorghum									
Area (millions of hectares)	12.2*	0.3	27.9*	3.3	1.4+	6.3	6.9	1.5	−7.2+	1.9
Production (millions of tons)	12.8*	0.8	28.0*	2.1	−11.4+	4.1	−7.4	5.2	.0+	6.4
Agricultural exports (E_A) (millions of dollars)	7.2*	544	1.8	912	10.9+	1,875	18.9	1,543	−10.8+	
Agricultural imports (I_A) (millions of dollars)	17.0*	144	−9.3	521	26.2+	1,184	26.4	2,807	−23.8	
$I_A - E_A/E^e$ %	−38		−21		−9		7			
E_A/I_A %	−9.9*	408	11.1	280	−17.1+	159	−7.6	57	12.8	

[a]The symbol * indicates growth rates significantly different from zero.
[b]The symbol + indicates growth rates significantly different from rates in late Import Substitution Industrialization period.
[c]Blanks indicate no data available.
[d]Dependency is measured by $(I - E)/(Q + I - E)$.
[e]E indicates total country exports.
[f]1974 − 1976 = 100

Q = Production
E = Exports
I = Imports

Source: UN, Food and Agriculture Organization, *Production Yearbook* and *Trade Yearbook* (Rome: UN Food and Agriculture Organization, various issues).

Table 10.4   Chile: Agricultural Growth and Food Security

	Whole period 1967–1983 Average growth rate[a]	Late Import Substitution Industrialization 1967–1973 Average level[f]	Late Import Substitution Industrialization Average growth rate[a]	Transition to Neoliberal Authoritarianism 1974–1979 Average level	Transition to Neoliberal Authoritarianism Average growth rate[b]	Neoliberal Authoritarianism cum Dutch 1980–1982 Average level	Neoliberal Authoritarianism cum Dutch Average growth rate[b]	Debt crisis 1982–1983 Average level	Debt crisis Average growth rate
All agriculture	1.5*	92	−1.8*	102	1.4+	111	3.6	112	c
Cereal									
Production (Q) (thousands of metric tons)	−0.9	1,767	−3.7	1,697	1.8	1,579	−9.6	1,642	
Net imports (thousands of metric tons)	7.9*	645	16.7*	1,029	−0.1+	1,449	−4.7	1,370	
Dependency[d] (%)	6.3*	26	15.3*	38	−1.1+	48	2.8	46	
Availability per capita (kilograms)	0.0	261	0.1	259	−0.7	268	−8.8+	258	
Wheat									
Production (thousands of metric tons)	−3.4*	1,179	−4.8	988	.7	767	−19.8	800	
Net imports (thousands of metric tons)	8.3*	441	8.3	828	−0.6	1,030	−3.7	1,158	
Dependency[d] (%)	7.3*	27	7.8	45	−0.6	58	7.0	59	
Availability per capita (kilograms)	−0.7*	173	−1.4	173	−1.7	159	−12.3+	168	
Fruit and vegetable exports (millions of dollars)	22.4*	21	7.6*	108	27.9+	261	10.7		
Agricultural exports (millions of dollars)	21.0*	35	3.4	182	26.6+	382	0.3		
Agricultural imports (millions of dollars)	10.3*	215	11.7*	447	−0.4+	698	−19.4+		
Agricultural balance of trade (millions of dollars)	4.2*	−316	13.0*	−265	−13.8+	−316	46.7+		
$I_A - E_A/E^e$ (%)	−7.3*	18	10.9*	11	−23.2+	8	−36.3+		
E_A/I_A (%)	10.5*	18	−8.2	44	26.5+	56	20.3		

[a] The symbol * indicates growth rates significantly different from zero.

[b] The symbol + indicates growth rates significantly different from rates in late Import Substitution Industrialization period.

[c] Blanks indicate no data available.

[d] Dependency is measured by $(I - E)/(Q + I - E)$.

[e] E indicates total country exports.

[f] 1974–1976 = 100

Q = Production
E = Exports
I = Imports

Source: UN, Food and Agriculture Organization, *Production Yearbook* and *Trade Yearbook* (Rome: UN Food and Agriculture Organization, various issues).

Table 10.5 Argentina: Agricultural Growth and Food Security

	Whole period 1967–1983	Late Import Substitution Industrialization 1967–1973		Transition to Neoliberal Authoritarianism 1974–1979		Neoliberal Authoritarianism cum Dutch 1980–1982		Debt crisis 1982–1983	
	Average growth rate[a]	Average level[f]	Average growth rate[a]	Average level	Average growth rate[b]	Average level	Average growth rate[b]	Average level	Average growth rate
All agriculture	2.6*	90	1.2*	110	4.5	117	–1.3	123	–6.5
Total cereals (millions of metric tons)	3.1*	21	3.6*	24	5.9	25	9.1	32	–12.5
Soybeans (thousands of metric tons)	39.6*	166	45.4*	1,532	64.0	3,657	0.9+	3,950	–10.1
Sunflower (thousands of metric tons)	4.7*	924	–3.1*	1,195	19.4+	1,447	–6.3	2,140	15.0[d]
Agricultural imports (millions of dollars)	11.2*	164	13.4*	240	15.2	584	1.4	281[c]	
Agricultural exports (millions of dollars)	12.0*	1,759	9.6*	3,802	22.2	5,819	6.8	4,883[c]	
E_A/I_A %	0.8	11.1	–3.7*	15.8	6.9	10.1	5.4	17.4[c]	

[a] The symbol * indicates growth rates significantly different from zero.
[b] The symbol + indicates growth rates significantly different from rates in late Import Substitution Industrialization period.
[c] 1982 only.
[d] Blanks indicate no data available.
[e] 1974–1976 = 100

E = Exports
I = Imports

Source: UN, Food and Agriculture Organization, *Production Yearbook* (Rome: UN Food and Agriculture Organization, various issues).

Domestic Price Effects

It logically follows that, if liberalization policies result in significant increases in the import of certain crops, those crops must have previously had a certain amount of protection from foreign competition through the complex set of policies typical of the import-substitution period. In Table 10.6, for Argentina a crop price index deflated by an input price index is given, thus providing an indication of terms of trade; for Chile, in Table 10.7, we give deflated price indices for various crops.

It is evident from these tables that the precoup ISI policies effectively prevented producers of many crops, especially of traditional grains, such as wheat, corn, and oilseeds, from capturing the rents that would have accrued to them from the international boom in crop prices in the early to mid-1970s. In Argentina, for example, the real price of wheat was stagnant between 1972 and 1974, whereas in the international market it increased by at least 60 percent. The purchasing power of the crops listed generally doubled between the lowest year in the precoup period and the highest point after the coups, usually after a year or two. The same pattern may be discerned in Chile. The last year of the Allende government certainly seems to have put a squeeze on agriculture. Here, real prices were declining remarkably, whereas on the international market they were peaking.

Apparently not all crops were equally discriminated against during the populist-ISI period. Note that corn is the most "peasant-based" grain in Chile. The protection for corn was greater than for wheat or rice in Chile. Thus, it is clear that ISI policies were relatively more favorable to some crops than to others: There was a class basis to these policies as well. This difference in protection was probably the net result of a complex set of policies rather than of conscious policy manipulation. We are justified in concluding that ISI price policies before the coups resulted in a severe "rent squeeze" on agriculture, especially for the larger-scale farmers. This rent squeeze was quite sharp and greatly intensified in the period just prior to the coups.

Furthermore, it is clear, both from the turnaround in output as well as from the increased prices, that rent was at least partially restored after the coups, especially considering that by then international prices were declining. A rent squeeze on agriculture is one of the problems the coups were meant to re-

Table 10.6   Argentina: Terms of Trade for Agriculture (1965–1969 = 100)

	1973	1974	1975	1976	1977	1978	1979	1980
Wheat	91	81	57	63	108	112	90	86
Corn	88	76	41	73	95	91	71	70
Linseed	129	137	100	184	132	104	194	70
Sunflower	112	99	44	157	164	140	104	66

Source: Banco Ganadero de Argentina, *La Producción Rural Argentina* (Buenos Aires: The Banco, various issues).

Table 10.7   Chile: Indices of Real Output Prices (1965 = 100)

	1970	1971	1972	1973	1974	1975	1976	1977
Wheat	88	88	71	15	55	65	94	87
Corn	94	90	79	107	61	52	89	60
Beans	131	107	76	83	37	75	128	61
Grapes	149	125	131	102	104	171	171	186
Apples	149	117	140	122	79	146	120	118

Source: J. Bengoa et al., "Capitalismo y Campesinado en el Agro Chileno," Grupo de Investigaciones Agrícolas, No. 1, Santiago, 1979.

solve. This process, in turn, helps identify more clearly the class basis of the dictatorships. If we assume that the coups were at least partly motivated by the rent squeeze in the last years of ISI and that this rent squeeze was caused largely by the huge difference between the frozen internal prices and the booming international prices, then the liberalization of trade onto a declining market is understandable if no less unfortunate in hindsight. The opening up seems to have come too late to have had a profound and long-lasting beneficial effect on agriculture.

Monetary Policy Effects

Monetary and exchange-rate policies have been crucial in determining the fate of agriculture before and after the NA coups. Much of the rent squeeze we have alluded to can be explained in terms of the large-scale overvaluation of exchange rates common in the period immediately preceding the coups. In Table 10.8, we show the official rate as a percentage of the black market rate in each of these countries. The exchange rate regimes in these countries were extremely complex. In Chile in 1971, for example, there were at least fifteen official exchange rates. It is sometimes difficult to know which ones applied to agriculture, especially because, at least in Argentina, a certain proportion of the foreign exchange proceeds could be traded in at a certain rate and the rest at a different rate, and these proportions changed frequently.

   In spite of the problems, these measurements seem to account for the stagnation of national prices during a period when international prices were increasing quickly. In Argentina, for example, the real price of wheat was stable between 1972 and 1974, whereas on the international market it rose about 60 percent. But the peso was about twice as overvalued in 1974 as in 1972. Similarly, the price of wheat on the world market declined significantly between 1974 and 1977; but inside Argentina it hardly changed. During this period, the overvaluation of the peso declined significantly over two years so that local prices could remain stable even as world prices tumbled. We may conclude that the exchange-rate phenomenon was one of the most, if not the most, important factors in explaining agricultural performance under NA.

Table 10.8   Measures of Official Exchange - Rate Distortion

	Argentina		Chile	
	Tradable exports	Nontradable exports	Tradable exports	Nontradable exports
1970	0.90		0.50	
1971	0.50		0.40	
1972	0.40		0.15	(precoup)
1973	0.45		0.40	0.95 (postcoup)
1974	0.20		1.00	
1975	0.25		0.95	
1976	0.75	1.00	0.90	
1977	0.90	1.00	0.90	
1978	0.90	1.00	0.90	
1979	0.70	0.80	0.80	
1980			0.75	

Sources: G. Steve, ed., *Pick's Currency Yearbook* (New York: Pick Publishing Corporation, 1981); E. Muchnik and C. Zegers, "El Sector Agropecuario Chileno, 1974–1980: Análisis de Tendencias y Perspectivas," Catholic University, Department of Agricultural Economics, Santiago, Chile, 1980; and Comisión Económica Para la América Latina (CEPAL), *Economic Survey of Latin America, 1979* (Santiago, 1981), pp. 214 and 511.

Global Income Effects and the Market for Wage Goods

Another important determinant of the performance of agriculture is the dynamism of the national market. It is possible that the declines in either national income or the income of the masses reduce the local market for food crops at the same time that the liberalization policies reduce the protection on these crops from international competition. Thus, a double blow is dealt to the producers of these crops. Table 10.9 shows index numbers for per capita real total income of wage earners.

Although it is clear that the story is not the same in all countries, several features stand out. In the years of populism prior to the NA coups, labor incomes gained significantly. In Argentina the gains were only slightly greater than the average, whereas in Chile they were radical indeed. In Uruguay they were about equivalent to the average gain. Unfortunately, we do not have postcoup labor income data for Argentina. From Chile and Uruguay, however, it is evident that the level of income of the wage earners was cut much more than was average income. In fact, at least in one country, Uruguay (which is the only one for which complete data were available), average income had begun to increase to unprecedented levels while labor incomes were still declining.

In conclusion, it seems that the market for mass consumption goods had stagnated. In Argentina, at least, part of the export expansion may be understood as an attempt to replace the greatly reduced domestic market. But, in general, it is likely that the impact of changing foreign demand or of changes in the transmission of foreign demand to national producers via such factors as exchange rates was more important than the general income-induced local demand effects.

Credit Policies

The application of monetarism, by definition, implies highly restricted money supplies, at least in relation to inflationary expectations. If inflation actually slows down and expectations lag behind reality, then real rates of interest will tend to reach extremely high levels. Thus, monetarism would imply scarce and expensive credit. Furthermore, the free-market ideology suggests that no sector should be especially favored by making credit available to it at rates lower than those for other sectors. Thus, in effect, the policies here are quite opposite to those prevailing during ISI, when abundant credit was used as institutional rents to compensate particular productive and social sectors for the lack of economic incentives. One of the results of relying on credit expansion as a permanent stimulatory policy is the inflation that the neoliberal policies tried to break. Table 10.10 gives real interest rates for funds loanable to agriculture.

Naturally, under these circumstances, the amounts borrowed by agriculture declined substantially. In Chile, in the 1965-1973 period, agriculture captured between 20 to 34 percent of the credit in the economy, whereas its contribution to GDP was about 9 percent. But in the postcoup period, the participation in credit declined to about 9 percent of total credit, which is about equal to its participation in GDP. In the precoup period, agriculture was clearly more subsidized by the artificially low interest rates than was any other sector. It has been calculated[12] that in some years the credit subsidy reduced the implicit taxation caused by overvalued exchange rates and discriminatory tariffs by some 40 percent. Not all subsectors within agriculture have been as negatively affected, however. Some farmers, especially capitalist farmers with good connections to the credit markets, were able to borrow in dollar-denominated terms with rates of interest about seven points above those in international credit markets at the time when the international rates were very low. Fruit pro-

Table 10.9 Real Per Capita Total Income (PCI) and Labor Income (Labor I)

Year	Argentina PCI	Labor I	Chile PCI	Labor I	Uruguay PCI	Labor I	
1967	100	100	100	100	100	100	
1968	104	100	101	104	101	95	
1969	108	103	102	105	107	104	
1970	108	107	105	113	111	107	
1971	110	111	114	145	109	109	
1972	112	105	112	150	105	89	
1973	114	118	106	101	103	91	(precoup)
1974	120	122	109	92	112	100	(postcoup)
1975	116	121	93	79	114	97	
1976	112		95	79	119	95	
1978	110		109		127	89	
1979	122		116		137	88	

Source: International Monetary Fund, *International Financial Statistics* (Washington, D.C.: (IMF, various issues).

duction, which is highly capitalistic and has boomed, captured increasing amounts of the credit that was available.

In Uruguay, credit supply was relatively withdrawn from the peasant and/or family-farm sectors. This is shown by the data in Table 10.11, which give the flows of credit from official sources to various subsectors of agriculture as percentages of the total flow of agricultural official credit to all sectors.

Thus, in general, we may conclude that, after the imposition of NA, credit ceased to be a source of subsidy to agriculture. The decline in credit subsidy to the small-farm sector appears to have been greater. And it is the sectors that have benefited the most from trade liberalization (because of their comparative advantages) that have been hurt the least by the generalized withdrawal of credit as a source of subsidy.

Welfare Effects of NA in Agriculture

Now that we can be certain that the neoliberal policies had very definite effects on agricultural production and trade, we can attempt to discern which social groups benefited from these changes. A starting point is to identify the social basis of production of the various crops in order to map output performance onto the class distribution of policy-induced benefits.

In Chile, according to the 1976 census, the production of fruits and rice expanded quickly, and production of these crops was dominated by large farms. On the other hand, of the crops originating in smaller farms, only beans showed significant growth in output and exports. Unfortunately, we do not

Table 10.10   Real Interest Rates

Year	Chile	Uruguay
1967	−2.4	
1968	−6.3	
1969	−4.7	
1970	−8.1	
1971	−3.4	
1972	−57.0	
1973	−80.9	
1974	−64.8	
1975	13.7	
1976	64.2	22.1
1977	57.2	33.8
1978	42.3	−10.2
1979	16.9	42.2
1980	12.2	46.7

Sources: For Chile: E. Muchnik and C. Zegers, "El Sector Agropecuario Chileno, 1974–1980: Análisis de Tendencias y Perspectivas," Catholic University, Department of Agricultural Economics, Santiago, Chile, 1980, Table 8, p. 124. For Uruguay: Luís Macadar, *Uruguay, 1974–1980: ¿Un Nuevo Ensayo de Reajuste Económico?* (Montevideo: Estudios CIMVE, 1982).

Table 10.11   Flows of Agricultural Credit in Uruguay (percentages)

	1975	1976	1977	1978
Family farm crops	21	12	8	9
Other crops	79	88	92	91

Source: CIEDUR, "La Agricultura Familiar Uruguaya en El Marco de Una Nueva Política Económica" (Montevideo, 1982), Table V-23.

have the right kinds of data for Argentina, so we cannot determine accurately the social basis for crop products. In any case, the most significant trend in Argentine agriculture after the coup was the remarkable expansion in oilseeds, especially soybeans; and it is clear that soybeans are not produced anywhere in Latin America by peasants, at least not where soybeans are becoming an important crop. Certainly, in the case of Chile, we can claim that within agriculture the distribution of the benefits from liberal policies is highly skewed away from the family farms. Not only has the relative position of small farms worsened, but the absolute level of income in the small-farm crops appears to be basically stagnant.

For peasants, the difficulty of shifting their resources to the booming sectors (capital-intensive fruit production) implied that they were trapped in the lagging sectors. Their land thus became increasingly concentrated in commercial farms. Limited employment opportunities in agriculture, as well as in the rest of the economy that was suffering from lack of protection, did not offer sufficient employment opportunities as had occurred under ISI. The result was rapid impoverishment of peasants.

The shift from late ISI to NA further entrenched social disarticulation as the force of economic growth in these countries. It reinforced two of the models' essential supporting variables: The provision of cheap labor and cheap food. Where a peasantry exists (a feature of Chile), this social group has often been identified with the provision of these functions. The peasantry can deliver cheap labor to the balance of the economy by ensuring the reproduction and maintenance of part of the labor force outside of the wage economy, and wages paid to semiproletarianized peasant workers can be below the total cost of subsistence. It can also deliver cheap food, as its production costs need not allow for profits and rents nor for implicit wages equal to those paid on the labor market. In functional terms, the peasantry is thus the ideal social basis for disarticulated accumulation. In Chile, impoverishment of the peasantry, as a result of the deepening of the NA model, has thus been identified as *"campesinizacion pauperizante"* (impoverished peasant class increasing in size).[13] The peasant spheres are reproduced and enlarged, and their functions as purveyors of cheap food and cheap labor are increased. Poverty increases as their land base deteriorates, the terms of trade turn against them, unemployment deepens, and rural wages fall. There is a functional space for peasants under NA, but the functions they perform imply deterioration of their economic conditions.

These data indeed support the interpretation that there has been both *campesinización* and impoverishment. In Chile, the number of peasant farms increased by 35 percent between 1965 and 1979,[14] and many of these farms incorporated an increasingly larger number of families. Impoverishment may be deduced from the facts that the prices of peasant products such as wheat, potatoes, beans, and corn fell in real terms about 20 percent between 1965-1972 and 1974-1979.[15] Real rural wages also fell by about 20 percent between 1970 and 1979. Total agricultural employment remained about constant between 1975 and 1978 in spite of an expansion of the fruit sector. With urban migration essentially stopped, this implied that per capita employment opportunities dropped. The nature of employment opportunities also changed dramatically with a sharp fall in permanent employment; with increased demand for seasonal labor, employers were allowed to minimize both fixed labor costs and the potential demands of organized labor. The result was increased employment uncertainty for the landless and the marginal farmers.

In Uruguay, the long-run tendency, even before 1973, was toward a decline in the productive potential of the small-farm sector regardless of whatever changes there may have been in the number of farms in the sector. Total production by the small-farm sector was some two to three times larger in the early 1960s than in the mid-1970s, and land productivity was two to fives times higher in the earlier period. The most important measure is labor productivity, which was some three times higher in the early 1960s. These trends hold for field crops and tree crops, but a reverse trend is observed in vegetable production.[16]

The period 1970-1980 saw a stabilization in the tendency for a decline in the number of small farmers and the amount of land they control. Thus, in Uruguay, we are also justified in talking about a process of both peasantization and immiserization: The number of small farms is stable or even, perhaps, increasing, but the income produced in these farms is declining. The decline has been particularly severe since 1978. Between 1973 and 1978, the decline in protection to small farms resulting from generalized ISI preferences—such as low interest rates, government intervention in marketing, etc.—was offset by the favorable effects of liberalization, such as the existence of more realistic exchange rates. But after this period, exchange rates tended to become as overvalued as during ISI, and the forms of protection that ISI had provided were no longer there.

Thus, there is little doubt that the NA model had a dismal impact on rural welfare, producing both peasantization and impoverishment. This outcome was, of course, never in doubt, as it is an integral feature of accumulation under social disarticulation; and the model was to be judged, therefore, by its impact on growth and not on social welfare. What appears to be the case, however, is that the model went beyond functional needs in terms of ensuring cheap labor and cheap food requirements: Instead of the function of *campesinización pauperizante* (impoverished peasant class increasing in size), application of the model created the contradiction of "*pauperización campesinizante* (growing impoverishment of the peasant class)."[17]

In effect, the two requirements of cheap food and cheap labor no longer necessarily implied a functionalization of the peasantry. Cheap food was largely ensured through food imports, which doubled between 1970 and 1980; they became cheaper toward the end of the period because of the overvalued exchange rates made available by foreign borrowing. Peasant production was displaced by cheap imports and its contribution to food security relegated to a minor role. At the same time, repression and unemployment tended to ensure cheap labor. With urban unemployment reaching 70 percent in some particular slums, the rural poor had no place to go but to cling to their peasant status. Cornered between the expansion of capitalist agriculture, which creates little new employment, and lack of migration opportunities, many of the rural poor are found in the ranks of marginal peasants. By contradiction more than by function, poverty has been the cause of the permanence of peasants under neoliberal authoritarianism.

AGRICULTURE UNDER DUTCH DISEASE

There was a return to large overvaluation of the exchange rate in most Latin American countries during the late 1970s under two types of circumstances: a booming export sector, as with oil in Mexico (1978-1982) and Ecuador (1975-1982); and a booming international debt, as in Chile and Argentina. In both cases, the income created by the booming sector led to rising demand and increasing prices for nontradable goods, typically construction and services, but also perishable or bulky agricultural products such as fresh milk and vegetables. Simultaneously, a plentiful supply of foreign exchange allowed the exchange rate not to be devalued in spite of domestic inflationary pressures. The result was a rising real exchange rate and falling real prices for tradable goods, such as domestic industry and imported foods as cereals.

If this Dutch disease occurs under late ISI (as during the Mexican oil boom) and if export revenues accrue to the state, this oil rent can be used to selectively protect and subsidize particular sectors of tradables. The non-protected tradable sectors decline under both transfer of resources to the booming and nontradable sectors (resource effect) and under pricing through overvalued exchange rates (spending effect[18]). In 1978 and 1979, corn was not protected, with the result that the area planted in corn (1979) was 76 percent below the average for 1969-1971; and imports in 1980 were nearly three times larger than in 1978.

The oil boom thus brought to a crisis stage the steady deterioration of Mexican staple food production that began in 1968 with the imposition of cheap food policies to control the inflationary effect brought about by rapid economic growth. Concerns with food security and with the plight of dryland corn producers, who were abandoning their plots of land in large numbers, led to initiation of the Mexican Food System Program (SAM) in 1980. This program transferred large subsidies—in the form of farm-level price supports and input subsidies for corn and beans—to the agricultural sector to compensate for overvalued exchange rates. Total cost of subsidies over three years was $10.9 billion.

Combined with favorable weather in 1981 and 1983, the program was able to increase corn production in 1981-1983 by 25 percent over what it had been in 1978-1980 and to reduce imports from 3.1 million tons in 1981 to 0.2 million tons in 1982 (Table 10.3). It is not clear, however, what share of this increase in production originated in peasant versus capitalist farms. If, as case studies show, better prices induced a shift in resource allocation toward corn in capitalist farms, it is quite likely that the SAM program may have reduced absolute poverty but also increased social differentiation. In 1983, however, with the change in administration and austerity policies imposed by the end of both the oil and debt booms, the SAM program was abandoned as Mexico shifted to a neoliberalism forced by a crisis in the balance of payments.

When the Dutch disease occurs under neoliberalism, as it did in Chile and Argentina under the massive buildup of international debt between 1979 and 1982, the impact on the tradable goods sector can be much more devastating. In both countries, devaluations were insufficient to compensate for domestic inflation, and the exchange rate became massively overvalued until the debt crisis of 1983.

This was particularly evident in Chile, where the Chicago doctrine of the "monetary approach to the balance of payments" (the school of economic thought advanced by Milton Friedman and his associates at the University of Chicago) froze the exchange rate for three years between June 1979 and June 1982. The domestic rate of inflation cumulated to 91 percent during this period, the real exchange rate fell by 25 percent, and the international debt doubled. By 1979, all protective tariffs had been brought down to a uniform 10 percent, and real interest rates peaked at levels as high as 30 to 40 percent. Thus, under neoliberal Dutch disease, tradable agricultural commodities were again under the same exchange rate disadvantage as under ISI but this time without the compensations offered by institutional rents.

The impact on wheat production was severe. Production in 1980-1982 was 22 percent below the average for 1974-1979, and imports were up by 24 percent in 1980-1981 (Table 10.4). External dependency in 1982 reached 60 percent for wheat, 43 percent for corn, 51 percent for sugar, and 91 percent for edible oil. The growth of fruit and forest product export revenues was not sufficient to make up for the cost of increasing food imports. The agricultural balance of trade thus deteriorated 93 percent in nominal dollars between 1979 and 1981, while the coverage of agricultural imports by agricultural exports fell from 53 percent to 46 percent. The balance of agricultural trade remained negative but improved subsequently because of the sharp fall in imports associated with deindustrialization and recession.

Because wheat is produced to a significant extent by small farmers—the Mapuche Indians, in particular—whereas fruit production is a highly capital-intensive activity, the dichotomy between declining and booming sectors worsened inequality in the distribution of income among producers. With unemployment reaching 20 percent, migration opportunities were severely reduced, and real rural wages in 1979-1981 were 20 percent below the 1970-1971 level. In addition, permanent workers hired on commercial farms were increasingly replaced by seasonal workers in response to labor legislation and labor antagonisms created by the land reform process before 1973. Application to agriculture of the neoliberal model cum Dutch disease thus increased social differentiation, deepened duality between commercial and peasant farming, and created massive impoverishment among small farmers and landless workers resulting from the combined economic crisis in staple food production, declining urban migration opportunities, and rising rural unemployment. Once more, the rural poor were trapped in declining activities in agriculture and had few opportunities to gain access to land or to employment.

AGRICULTURE IN THE DEBT CRISIS

Easy indebtedness during the 1970s and through 1981 came to an abrupt end as interest rates were rising and the terms of trade for Latin America deteriorated. This crisis unveiled the magnitude of the disequilibria created by a period of debt-led growth. During this period, the cities were increasingly being fed by cheap imports and food subsidies (Mexico) financed by debt, while domestic agriculture-producing tradables were being assaulted by a combination of resource and spending effects. Indebtedness had crept into agriculture as well. The immediate impact of the crisis, with both massive devaluations of the exchange rate and austerity programs, was thus principally a selective paralysis of debt-ridden producers and sharp increases in food prices for consumers.

Although it is yet difficult to place a judgment on the complex consequences on agriculture of adjustment to the crisis, the following seem to be some key changes:

1. Under the pressure of debt-service obligations, many Latin American countries have rediscovered the importance of their agricultural sectors as sources of foreign exchange. The result is to reinforce the long-standing bias in favor of export crops and against food crops. An improved ability to finance agricultural imports through agricultural exports was also obtained in 1982 in Chile, Mexico, and Brazil as imports fell more rapidly than exports as a consequence of domestic recessions.

2. Austerity policies imposed by the debt crisis forced elimination of subsidies in countries that had not yet implemented neoliberal policies (Mexico and Brazil); devaluation of land prices and rising cost of debt in dollar terms

made difficult further access to loans (Chile). In Chile, the 100 percent devaluations of 1982-1983 increased the stock of outstanding debt by no less than 45 percent. Defaulting on outstanding debts by up to 50 percent of farmers and general decapitalization of the sector are the main bottlenecks to reactivation of the tradable sector. Farmers who are in sufficiently good credit standing can take advantage of the partial debt renegotiations offered by the state and take fresh loans by mortgaging crops. For some 70 percent of the farmers, however, access to new loans is not possible and indebtedness remains a major bottleneck to increasing production.

3. After a marked decline in the terms of trade for tradable agricultural commodities in Chile between 1979 and 1982, the year 1983 marked a significant recuperation. This was the result of continued devaluations at rates equal to domestic inflation; an increase in protective tariffs from 10 to 20 percent; and minimum prices for wheat, corn, rice, and sugar. Even though fertilizer prices have increased by the same amount as wheat and corn prices, nominal wages have remained constant, allowing production prices to trail behind product prices. For commercial agriculture, the terms of trade (relative to crop-specific indices of production cost) have increased by 50 percent in wheat and 45 percent in corn. For export crops, basically fruits, devaluation makes Chilean products more competitive even though depressed international prices and stricter quality control limit Chilean exports. In all cases, producers who are in good credit standing and already involved in international markets are able to take advantage of better terms of trade. By contrast to the previous period, producers of nontradables, such as milk (protected by tariff), and livestock (trade prohibited by hoof-and-mouth disease) face stagnant domestic markets.

4. The social impact of the crisis has been devastating on small farmers and the landless. With 34 percent unemployment, urban migration has been brought to a halt, and the agricultural sector has to retain the full 2.3 percent annual increase in population it generates. This implies, in particular, an accumulation in agriculture of young people (the traditional migrants) with few economic opportunities. The peasantry thus increases in members, not as a symptom of its competitive success with commercial agriculture but as that of a cornered population with insufficient economic opportunities either through access to land or to employment. In addition, rural slums are rapidly spreading in the countryside as a result of increased landlessness because of the undoing of the land reform, reduced urban migration, dismissal of permanent workers, and shift to seasonal employment of nonresident workers.[19]

Structural adjustments to the crisis thus have been disproportionately borne by the family farmers who lost access to land, permanent workers whose real wages have fallen sharply, peasants who do not have access to credit to reactivate production, landless workers whose seasonal employment opportunities have declined, and low-income urban consumers for whom sharply rising food prices have deteriorated real incomes.

CONCLUSIONS

Our analysis of Latin American agriculture since the mid-1960s shows that it has been subjected to a variety of sharply contrasted economic and political conditions over a short period of time. We contrasted, in particular, the performance of agriculture under late ISI, the transition to neoliberalism, Dutch disease conditions under both ISI and NL, and the debt crisis with stabilization policies. Our results reveal two surprising conclusions: one about agriculture under ISI and the other about agriculture under the practice (not the theory) of neoliberalism.

It now seems clear that the agrarian ideology of the proponents of NL was based on a misunderstanding of the effects of ISI on agriculture. It had been thought that ISI policies had been overwhelmingly disfavorable to agriculture in general. But as we have shown, the removal of those policies did not have a sustained, generalized, positive impact on agriculture. The logical explanation is that ISI policies did not necessarily have only negative effects on agriculture because of extensive institutional rents channeled to specific products and social groups. There were government marketing mechanisms that may have depressed prices, but they also stabilized them. There was customs disprotection, but there was also highly favorable credit policy. Increasing incomes for the working class created buoyant markets for the outputs of wage-goods producers, particularly nontradables. And, even though peasants would rarely shift their resources to economic activities benefiting from institutional rents (export crops in Brazil, sorghum in Mexico), rapid employment creation in the urban economy provided opportunities for gainful reallocation of peasant labor.

This is not to say that ISI policies were favorable to agriculture. The point is that probably they were less unfavorable than the monetarists have argued and that, in any case, the effects of the policies were by no means generalizable to the sector as a whole. A crop-specific analysis reveals a tendency for ISI to be less unfavorable and, in some cases, actually to favor crops produced by peasant producers and in family farms. This is in keeping with what is known to be the class basis of ISI.

Also, the structural context in which neoliberalism was being applied differed significantly from pure theory, and even the authoritarian political leaders have been unwilling to allow the economies to be fully determined by free market forces. Thus, the structural constraints discovered and explained by the advocates of ISI have been reasserted, and, even under NL, there was a return of inflation, overvaluation, rising debt, and massive unemployment. Structural constraints, such as imperfection in capital markets speculation, and refusal of cash holders to lower their inflationary expectations quickly enough, were not considered important in the monetarist world. These imperfections led to extraordinarily high and stable interest rates in spite of complete openness to international capital. The monetarist policies ended discriminating not against the inefficient but against those with no access to international credit. When the pressure from these and other structural constraints made itself felt again, it was in an economic environment that had been stripped of the institutions that ISI policies had erected as a response to the constraints. Thus, there was overvaluation but without the benefit of compensating institutional rents. By the late 1970s, the list of agricultural subsectors benefited by NL had become small indeed.

In terms of theoretical implications, our analysis of agricultural development under ISI and NL in dualistic agrarian economies has shown that there exists a variety of paths that peasants may follow in adjusting to new economic situations, paths that are far from the postulate of perfect mobility in the reallocation of resources. Indeed, in only rare situations are peasants able to turn their land to the production of growing sector activities. By comparing how peasant land and labor are reallocated in lagging and growing sectors, we show in Table 10.12 some of the paths followed. This allows us to rediscover some of the major theoretical categories that have characterized different positions in the debate on the role and future of peasants in the development of capitalism as well as in the explanation of the causes of rural poverty.

These categories are: (1) peasants' resources trapped in the lagging sector (functional dualism with peasants fulfilling the role of purveyors of cheap food on the basis of self-exploitation); (2) semiproletarianization (functional dualism with peasants as suppliers of cheap labor); (3) migration and labor absorption in the growing urban sector, which represents the archetype of Lewis-type growth; (4) land expropriation with surplus labor, which creates the impoverishing status of cornered peasantries; (5) peasant modernization when peasants are able to shift their production to growing-sector activities representing the ideal of modernization theory; and (6) proletarianization, whereby peasants become landless workers following the classical model of social differentiation. Table 10.12 recalls some of the determinants of each of these paths encountered in historical analyses and identifies the most typical country examples for each case.

We derive three sets of policy implications from these results. First, any definition of a new development strategy that goes beyond ISI and NL should retain the most advantageous aspects of each model to reach greater efficiency, stability, and equity while avoiding the pitfalls that each has revealed. From neoliberalism, the main teaching to be retained is that prices matter for an efficient allocation of resources; foremost among these is an equilibrium exchange rate. Yet, the concrete experience of neoliberalism has also shown that getting the prices right is necessary but far from sufficient. This is due to the fact that the structure of much of agriculture does not correspond to monetarist postulates: Traditional agriculture is neither stationary nor efficient; labor, land, and capital markets tend either to fail or to be ridden with serious distortions; resource allocation is significantly affected by the organization of production and the distribution of wealth; opportunities for producers to respond to price

Table 10.12 Paths of Adjustment to Neoliberal Opening in a Dualistic Economy

Peasant land \ Peasant labor	Lagging sector	Growing sector
Lagging sector	(1) *Trapped resources:* Functional dualism cheap food Lack of access to complementary resources Lack of employment opportunities *Examples:* Wheat in Chile under Neoliberal Authoritarianism Corn in Mexico under debt crisis	(2) *Semi-proletarianization:* Functional dualism cheap labor Growing sector in agriculture *Example:* Sorghum in Mexico under Import Substitution Industrialization (3) *Migration:* Lewis-type growth Growing sector: urban or abroad Land abandoned or concentration in lagging sector *Examples:* Northeast Brazil under Import Substitution Industrialization Mexican migration to United States
Growing sector	(4) *Expropriation:* Cornered peasantries Unfavorable resource competition and terms of trade effects Bankrupted peasants lose control over land that concentrates in growing sector Lack of employment opportunities *Examples:* Chilean land reform sector under Neoliberal Authoritarianism and Dutch disease	(5) *Peasant modernization:* Modernization theory Peasants in growing sector *Examples:* Food crops: Mexican SAM and nontradables Brazil Export crops: Chile EET (6) *Proletarianization:* Social differentiation Peasants employed in agricultural or urban sectors Land concentration in growing sector *Example:* Southeast Brazil under Import Substitution Industrialization

incentives require complementary public investments in research, education, information, infrastructure, etc.; and agriculture is destabilized by international and domestic fluctuations—in financial markets in particular.

From ISI, the main lesson to be retained is the essential role of the state in promoting rapid, sustained, and equitable growth. Beyond the delivery of public services (such as research, education, information, and infrastructure), an active role of the state will be required to (1) identify and promote sectors with international comparative advantages, as an active and flexible external sector will be needed to meet debt obligations and import capital goods; (2) manage the distributional aspects of growth through technological options, asset redistribution, and sectoral and social investment priorities; and (3) define strategies of income and food security to both stabilize consumption levels and submit the gains from trade to the requirements of equitable growth. Agricultural policy, in particular, cannot be reduced to a by-product of macroeconomic policy but must be the object of sectorally and socially specific interventions.

Second, the history of Latin American agriculture, particularly since 1970, is that of the cyclical dominance of specific sectors, usually export or luxury oriented, and the political ascendency of their main beneficiaries. By contrast to the postulates of the theory of comparative advantages, reallocation of resources toward the growing sectors of agriculture is highly imperfect; and peasants, in particular, have rarely been able to benefit from growing sector opportunities. With the rest of the economy unable to provide economic alternatives to the mass of peasants sufficiently rapidly, large segments of the population are trapped in lagging sectors that are eventually severely affected by resource competition with the growing sector and by cheap food policies and Dutch disease.

There are basically five approaches that may be followed to remedy this situation: (1) Assist peasants to shift their resources to the growing sectors; (2) increase the productivity of peasant labor in staple foods production through rural development projects; (3) protect the food items that compete with peasant production (Mexican SAM); (4) create additional employment in the growing sectors and in the rest of the economy; and (5) increase the degree of peasant household food self-sufficiency.

Third, in the current context of continued debt crisis, exhaustion of the ISI model (both inefficiencies and inequities), and serious limits to export-led growth because of unfavorable international market conditions, reactivation of the Latin American economies should be sought, initially at least, in a program of import substitution in wage foods. If this program is implemented through small-farmer or cooperative structures, it can create a broad-based domestic market for industrial wage goods with strong linkages and multiplier effects. This would provide the starting point for a socially articulated development strategy. This development model could find political support in the large informal sectors that have emerged as a symptom of the social failures of both late ISI and NL growth.

NOTES

1. Alain de Janvry, *The Agrarian Question and Reformism in Latin America.*

2. Raúl Prebisch, *Transformacion y desarrollo: La gran tarea de la América Latina*; Celso Furtado, *Obstacles to Development in Latin America*; and, Albert O. Hirschman, "The Political Economy of Import Substitution Industrialization in Latin America."

3. Albert O. Hirschman, "The Political Economy of Import Substitution Industrialization in Latin America."

4. Henry J. Bruton, "The Import-Substitution Strategy of Economic Development: A Survey."

5. W. Arthur Lewis, *The Theory of Economic Growth.*

6. Aldo Ferrer, "El monetarismo en Argentina y Chile;" R. Villareal, "Monetarismo e ideología: De la mano invisible a la mano militaria;" and, A. Foxley, "Experimentos neo-liberales en América Latina."

7. Theodore W. Schultz, ed., *Distortions of Agricultural Incentives.*

8. Gervasio Rezende, "Price of Food and the Rural Poor in Brazil, 1960-80."

9. Ibid.

10. Andrew Burst and Eduardo Segarra, "An Analysis of Mexican Agricultural Price Policies."

11. David Barkin, "Mexican Agriculture and the Internationalization of Capital."

12. Universidad Católica de Chile, Departamento de Economía Agraria, "El sector agropecuario chileno, 1974-1980: Análisis de tendencias y perspectivas."

13. Jamie Soler Crispi, "El agro chileno después de 1973: Expansión capitalista y campesinización pauperizante."

14. Lovell Jarvis, "Small Farmers and Agricultural Workers in Chile, 1973-1979."

15. Crispi, "El agro chileno."

16. CIEDUR, "La agricultura familiar Uruguaya en el marco de una nueva política económica."

17. Crispi, "El agro chileno."

18. See Max W. Corden, and J. Peter Neary, "Booming Sector and Deindustrialization in a Small Open Economy."

19. Rigoberto Rivera and M. Elena Cruz, *Pobladores rurales: cambios en el poblamiento y el empleo rural en Chile.*

11

W. Ladd Hollist

The Politics of Hunger in Brazil

Hunger and malnutrition in Brazil have increased in the 1980s, continuing a two-decade-long deterioration of food entitlements of the poor. Fortunately, officials of President José Sarney's government, installed in March 1985, have chosen to discuss the problem publicly, reversing the practice of previous, military-led regimes. For example, in May 1986 a prominent official of the Brazilian Ministry of Planning openly estimated that more than 50 percent of all Brazilians consume the equivalent of only one nutritious meal or less per day. He and others in government observed that the food problem is not new, but that it may now have assumed crisis proportions.[1]

In the 1970s, Brazil's food problem worsened dramatically. Fernando Homem de Melo reports that from 1967 to 1979 the availability of "domestic foods" consumed by the poor and destitute in Brazil, calculated in terms of daily per capita caloric supply, declined by an average of 1.34 percent each year.[2] According to a survey conducted for the World Bank[3] and reported by the International Food Policy Research Institute, 58.3 percent of all Brazilian children under eighteen years of age were considered malnourished by 1975; 37.2 percent (almost 20 million children) suffered from first-degree malnutrition, 20.2 percent (more than 10 million children) from second-degree malnutrition, and at least 0.9 percent (447,000 children) from third-degree malnutrition.[4]

As disheartening as these data are, hunger and malnutrition have actually increased in the 1980s. Homem de Melo calculates that in comparison to 1977, per capita production of domestic foods (rice, beans, corn, manioc, and potatoes) declined 15.1 percent by 1984, for an average decline of 1.94 percent per year. That the agricultural system of Brazil could have produced increasing amounts of foods typically consumed by the poor is evident from the fact that per capita production of exported agricultural commodities (soybeans, oranges, tobacco, cocoa, cotton, and peanuts) increased by an average of 13.3 percent from 1977 to 1984. Per capita production of sugarcane used to produce alcohol as a fuel substitute for gasoline increased by 74.8 percent during this period.[5]

Relative to a 1975 estimate that two-thirds of the Brazilian people were then undernourished, George Martine and Ronaldo Coutinho Garcia now argue that such estimates must be considered too optimistic for the 1980s[6]. Similarly, Elisio Contini, coeditor of the prestigious journal *Revista de Economia Rural,* and Antonio de Freitas Filho, a coworker at EMBRAPA (Empressa Brasileira de Pesquisas Agrarias), an arm of the Brazilian central government that promotes agricultural research and development, contend that the "food situation of the vast majority of the Brazilian population, that already was deficient and critical, has worsened tremendously in the mid-1980s."[7] Freitas Filho and Contini, drawing upon work by Fernando Homem de Melo[8] and Peliano, Castro, Martine, and Garcia,[9] estimate that if the average daily supply of calories and proteins per capita in 1975 was indexed at 100, by 1982 that index was 87 for calories and 91 for proteins. They further contend that the economic downturn of 1983 through at least the spring of 1986 probably has further increased the hunger and malnutrition that increasingly plagues the Brazilian poor.[10]

Evidence clearly suggests that despite twenty years of significant economic growth—making Brazil the eighth largest economy in the Western world, with an estimated gross national product of "310 billions of dollars,"[11]—a majority of Brazilians find themselves less able now than in the mid-1960s to obtain their basic food requirements. Food security continues to elude them, as per capita supplies of staples consumed by the poor have declined and their capacity to buy food likewise has diminished.[12]

Fortunately, the Sarney administration seems more willing and able to directly address the problems of hunger and poverty in Brazil than was President João Figueiredo (1979-1985) or other military-backed regimes. It is possible that Sarney and his associates may be engaging in rhetoric to placate their opposition without being committed to effecting change that will significantly benefit Brazil's poor and hungry. However, after interviewing several of these officials, I prefer to think that they are sincere in their belief that Brazil has little long-term future as a political and economic power unless it can feed its poor and elevate their standard of living. Nonetheless, the Sarney administration recognizes that, to retain its power to govern, it cannot radically reject the interests of productive landholders, industrialists, and bankers even if it were to choose to do so. To rapidly and comprehensively reverse policies that have benefited these interests is to risk losing the power to govern in Brazil's now more democratic but still elite-dominated society. Consequently, the challenge confronting the Sarney administration is to identify policies that can effectively reduce hunger and poverty without unduly threatening the government's ability to stay in power.

In this chapter I explore policy strategies that have been advanced to feed the hungry and to enrich the poor in Brazil. Brazilian scholars or government functionaries are the authors of each of the policy recommendations that I consider. My purpose is to assess whether strategies that have been advanced are politically possible and whether they are likely to achieve the desired outcome: to reduce hunger and poverty.

RECOMMENDATIONS OF THE INSTITUTO DE ESTUDOS POLÍTICOS E SOCIAIS

Of the several suggestions for policy changes, none has received more attention from government officials than those offered by the Instituto de Estudos Políticos e Sociais headed by Hélio Jaguaribe.[13] In advancing their recommendations, Jaguaribe and his associates have been particularly sensitive to the political risks that attend the Sarney government's move toward democracy.

In 1983, the institute determined that "military authoritarianism" in Brazil was coming to an end and that the nation would soon be entering a "democratic phase." Desiring to promote democracy, the institute began to assess under what conditions it might become viable in a country like Brazil. They feared that the often repeated cycle of authoritarianism, populism, and authoritarianism that has occurred in many Latin American countries, including Brazil,[14] might again be repeated. They recognized the possibility that democracy in Brazil could again generate populist tendencies and demands that would exceed society's short-term ability to respond.[15] Faced with such disparity between expectations and growing demands, the middle classes might panic, fearing the loss of new found perquisites—an apartment and a Volkswagen—and again support military intervention. After all, in 1964, for similar reasons, they had supported military intervention to advance Western values and to thwart the dangers of communism and organized labor. Confronted with this possibility, the institute attempted to determine under what institutional conditions it might be possible to secure democracy in Brazil.[16]

Important political interest groups in Brazil have not, in the 1980s, shifted much in favor of the interests of the poor, the landless, and the hungry, but they have shifted their support away from the military. The economic miracle for which the military dictatorship had claimed responsibility fell upon hard times during the global recession of the late 1970s and early 1980s. Moreover, democracy had found a place in the philosophical views of many industrialists, bankers, and large commercial farmers by this time, altering the political views of the people who in 1964 had supported military intervention. Against this backdrop, José Sarney commissioned Jaguaribe's institute to conduct its study.

In advancing its case, the institute cites data that amply demonstrate the severity of poverty in Brazil and the deepening food crisis. Jaguaribe summarizes the institute's findings by concluding that "no country in the world has such an extraordinary and unacceptable gap between its economic indicators and its social indicators."[17] Counting upon Brazil's apparent yearning for democracy and asserting that nothing threatens this prospect as much as these crisis conditions, Jaguaribe's institute advanced a "Paradigm for Brazil in the Year 2000," or a plan for "A New Social Pact." The plan hopes to transform Brazil's social condition (increase the incomes of the poor, reduce hunger, and improve social services) by the year 2000 to a condition comparable to that presently enjoyed by people in the southern area of Europe, most notably Greece and Italy.

In advancing its policies the institute noted that the military dictatorship (1964-1985) has had favorable effects on the process of industrialization. It further concluded that the industrialization effort has resulted in an economy with efficient capacity to generate jobs and, at least since the mid-1970s, to efficiently produce food. Nevertheless, despite such gains, a severe "food deficit," on the order of 40 percent,[18] has arisen. Faced with a woefully inadequate supply of food and growing demand, the price of food has increased phenomenally. The price increase has been so dramatic that the institute estimates that even if minimum salaries were doubled or tripled, low-income families would still be hungry and malnourished. The food deficit, the institute suggests, is the product of a crisis of production.

Jaguaribe and his associates link two developments in the past ten to fifteen years to this growing crisis. First, as a result of Brazil's large and increasing foreign debt, exports of agricultural commodities have been promoted to the detriment of food production. Second, the necessity to find a substitute for gasoline, preferably from a renewable source, has led to the "alcohol program." This program has triggered a marked increase in sugarcane production. As a result of these two developments, fertile land that previously was used to grow food increasingly has been employed to produce export crops and sugarcane. Consequently, the per capita production of food in Brazil has declined. The food crisis, although regrettable, is the unfortunate product of reasonable policy adjustments that Brazil has been required to take in the face of extraordinary circumstances: high-priced oil and the need for export growth to allow Brazil to service its foreign debt. The negative consequence, an extraordinary food deficit, now must be redressed.

By couching the source of Brazil's food crisis in these terms, and by suggesting that the solution is to increase food production, the arguments and recommendations advanced by the institute are made less threatening politically than they otherwise might be. Furthermore, by asserting that the prospects for democracy in Brazil may be dimmed unless the food deficit is reduced and hunger is lessened, the institute provides motivation for powerful economic interests in Brazil to support its recommendations. In terms of political acceptability, these arguments and associated recommendations receive high marks.

Upon this foundation, Jaguaribe and his colleagues advance short-term, medium-term, and long-term recommendations. In the short term, they suggest that Brazil should import food and distribute it at low prices. Food should be given to the most destitute. In the medium term, Brazil must increase its food production. Government policy should stimulate food production through the guarantee of minimum food prices and support for the transportation of food to market. The institute suggests that with such support significant increases in food production can be achieved in two to three years. Food producers should aspire to achieve rates of growth in excess of population growth, roughly 2.5 percent. In the long term, growth of food production should approach 5 percent per year to allow the government to accumulate stocks to be used during periods of unfavorable harvests and to allow for the net export of basic foods.[19]

The institute relies upon a simple premise for the success of its recommendations: Relatively modest increases in incentives to producers will result in significant growth of food production. Whereas this assumption seems plausible, it is doubtful that Brazil's food problem can be satisfactorily addressed with such modest adjustments. The arguments and recommendations are relatively safe politically, but the prospects for success, while not unimaginable, are suspect. An integrated policy package seems to be required to achieve the desired objectives.

POLICY RECOMMENDATIONS OF FERNANDO HOMEM DE MELO

Fernando Homem de Melo, perhaps Brazil's most respected agricultural economist, offers such a policy package. Like Jaguaribe, he is sensitive to present political realities; he does not blame past military governments for present problems. Rather, he is careful to minimize the possibility that his analysis and recommendations may alienate the military and its influential supporters. I mention two illustrations of his political sensitivity. First, Homem de Melo notes that in 1979, during the Figueiredo administration, Delfim Netto, then the minister of agriculture, advocated increased production of rice, beans, corn, milk, and meat. The government recognized the food problem and established an "agricultural priority;" it pledged to reduce the food deficit. The government, Homem de Melo observes, did not achieve *desempenho,*—the redemption or discharge of the pledge—but it did express determination to commence the process of change.[20] Second, in explaining why the food crisis deepened in the 1980s, Homem de Melo carefully chooses his words. Rather than analyzing policy mistakes, he analyzes "variables" that interfered with the attainment of the desired goal. He rightly senses that variables are less sensitive to criticism than are former political leaders, particularly when most of the variables are seen to be affected by international developments over which governments are presumed to have little control.

He cites five variables that have contributed to Brazil's worsening food crisis. They are: (1) a technological disequilibrium among agricultural production for export, the production of sugarcane, and the production of domestic foods (rice, beans, corn, manioc, and potatoes); (2) an exchange policy, particularly since February 1983, that has provided strong incentives for exports;[21] (3) declining international prices for Brazil's exports in the 1980s; (4) the expansion of the production of sugarcane for making alcohol, as a substitute fuel, in the late 1970s through the mid-1980s, with the likely prospect that production will be expanded further during the rest of the 1980s; and (5) the severe recession that has confronted Brazil since 1981. Let me briefly elaborate each point.

In his 1983 book, _O Problema Alimentar no Brasil,_ Homem de Melo convincingly shows that technical innovation in agriculture has been concentrated in either crops destined for export or in sugarcane used in alcohol production. Moreover, little research and development has been conducted in the north, northeast, and Amazon regions of Brazil; research in agriculture has largely focused on improving yields of crops in the richer, southern areas of the country. Only very recently has meaningful research been conducted to enhance the production of rice and beans in Brazil, and that is still well behind efforts to develop improved technologies for sugarcane and crops targeted for export. Research on other domestic foods (corn, manioc, and potatoes) is even less advanced.

In discussing the second variable, Homem de Melo largely concurs with Jaguaribe's stated reasons for Brazil's repeated currency devaluations throughout the 1980s: to increase exports. He laments that the exchange rates have been unduly favorable to exports since 1983. In elaborating his third point, Homem de Melo cites data indicating that world prices for cotton, peanut oil, soybeans, cocoa, and coffee declined significantly between 1980 and 1984. For example, soybeans, one of Brazil's principal products in terms of income generation and cultivated areas, experienced a price drop from $335 per ton in November 1980 to $195 per ton in October 1982, a reduction of 42 percent.[22] He further observes that these declines were accompanied by a second "oil price shock" in 1979/80 and a "financial shock" produced by a marked increase in international interest rates. Together, these developments increased pressures on Brazil to augment its total exports in order to recoup the income lost to lower export prices and to obtain the increasingly needed foreign exchange to service its foreign debt. The resulting opportunity cost to the production of domestic foods, he concludes, has been significant.

He views the fourth variable, the dramatic increase in the production of sugarcane for Brazil's alcohol program, in terms similar to those advanced by Jaguaribe's institute. He adds, however, that the cost of producing a barrel of alcohol has been extremely high—between $79 and $91 (in 1981 dollars). He notes that perhaps steps could be taken to reduce Brazil's reliance on alcohol as a fuel substitute. He suggests that oil could be emphasized more now that international prices are lower and that Brazil has made some significant finds. Natural gas can perhaps be further developed. Conservation and investment in electricity also might be pursued. He concludes that the cost of energy thus may actually decline and that fertile lands presently used for the production of sugarcane could be returned to the production of domestic foods.[23]

Finally, Homem de Melo examines the recession that since 1980 has resulted in a substantial decline in per capita income and a reduction in the standard of living for virtually all Brazilians.[24] In discussing this per capita income loss, he observes that at least some of the decline may be attributed to economic adjustments that Brazil has been required to make to deal with its external debt crisis. He cites estimates prepared by L. M. Lopes that the "real transfers" of wealth from Brazil to its debtors increased from 2.4 percent of its GNP in 1983 to 5.2 percent of its GNP in 1984.[25] The impact on per capita income was obviously significant.

Although Homem de Melo's discussion of variables that explain the increases in Brazil's food deficit in the 1980s is more elaborate and hence potentially more damning of past governments than are the arguments advanced by Jaguaribe, in most circles his views are considered reasonable and relatively moderate. Note that Homem de Melo links four of the five variables to international developments. The international economy controlled by multinational corporations and foreign commercial banks, not the government, is left to assume the greater part of the blame for present difficulties. Hence, political opposition that might have arisen in response to Homem de Melo's candid discussion of Brazil's food shortages is diffused. His position is perhaps more vulnerable to political criticism than is Jaguaribe's position, but it would appear to be relatively safe politically.

From this understanding of Brazil's food problems, Homem de Melo offers an integrated policy package[26] intended to increase the production of domestic foods and thereby lessen hunger and malnutrition in Brazil. His overarching recommendation is that regionally focused technological innovation relevant to the production of domestic foods (rice, beans, corn, manioc, and potatoes) needs to be accentuated. This can be achieved by expanding and partially redirecting the work of EMBRAPA to allow it to pursue technological innovations in domestic food production. He reasons that such technological advances can increase yields with resulting increases to the incomes of food producers and eventual reductions in the price of food to consumers. Through this process, the income of relatively poor, small farmers will increase and these gains will result in a higher standard of living for them and increased productivity of labor that otherwise would be underutilized. The condition of the rural poor will improve and economic growth will be stimulated.

As a further incentive to increase domestic food production, with benefits both to the small farmers who produce domestic foods and to poor rural and urban consumers, Homem de Melo recommends five other policy adjustments. First, Brazil's agricultural credit policies should be altered to favor food producers. He notes that from 1979 to 1984 the volume of credit available to agricultural operations declined by 54 percent. Moreover, interest rates increased. In light of this marked decline, he argues that credit must be differentially extended with priority given to food producers. The recommendation rests upon the need for increased food production and the fact that producers of cash crops for export already benefit from favorable exchange rates and producers of sugarcane receive other subsidies. He hastens to add that such differentiated credit support to food producers eventually could be reduced.

Second, Homem de Melo advocates that minimum prices that are compatible with the need to achieve increases in the production of basic foods consumed by the majority of the population should be established. He recommends that prices should be fixed for three years, with price adjustments at the end of this period based on increases in productivity and augmented stocks of domestic foods. The intention is to stabilize prices received by producers of domestic foods. The need for food price stability, he asserts, is evident in the fact that of the six agricultural goods that experienced significant price instability between 1948 and 1976, five were domestic foods (manioc, beans, potatoes, onions, and rice).[27] Homem de Melo argues that this policy is also justifiable on theoretical grounds: (1) Food producers face more risks relative to price levels and to price fluctuations than do producers of sugarcane and cash crops for export; (2) the small farmers who produce domestic foods are more risk averse than larger farmers; and (3) stable prices for domestic food products also favor the consumers.

Third, he suggests that even with increases in food production that may come from technological innovation, the area planted in domestic foods should be expanded. He suggests that emphasis should be placed on increased cultivation on small- and medium-sized farms. He argues that to achieve this end, credit should be targeted to promote such expansion, that experimental stations in diverse ecological settings should be supported, that the infrastructure for transport and storage of domestic foods should be improved, and that these farmers should receive effective technical and financial assistance.

Fourth, as part of a larger tax reform, indirect taxes[28] incident to the commercialization of food production and distribution should not be levied on low-income families. He recommends that those foods on which low-income families (those having two minimum salaries or less) expend 50 percent or more of their total income should be exempted. Doing so would be consistent with principles of progressive taxation. Surely, he concludes, such a tax change would be consistent with principles that should guide an anticipated wider tax reform effort.

Fifth, and finally, Homem de Melo argues that whereas far-reaching subsidization of food consumption as a means of redressing Brazil's food crisis is not desirable in the long run, the present crisis suggests the need for immediate action. He agrees with the position taken by Per Pinstrup-Andersen and Harold Alderman in a study conducted by the International Food Policy Research Institute, whose director is John W. Mellor.[29] They reason that "subsidies are only a means to maintain low food prices for consumers. Improving efficiencies in food production through technological change, infrastructure development and increased use of production inputs, along with improved efficiency in commercialization, offers more opportunity to reduce consumer prices without ad-versely affecting producers." They go on to argue that efforts should be made to increase the incomes of the poor to allow them to purchase food and other necessities that, in the long run, will improve the poor's welfare. In the mean-time, they conclude, "consumer food subsidies should be seen as an important way, although temporary, to assure that the poor are able to acquire sufficient food to satisfy their basic needs while the capacity to purchase food and other necessities is being developed."[30]

Consistent with this view, Homem de Melo recommends that consumer food subsidies should be provided, but that they should be restricted to only six to eight food items—rice, beans, corn, manioc, potatoes, milk, and perhaps meat (pork and chicken, but not beef)—that are consumed, on occasion, by low-income families. The purpose is to aid the truly destitute. He advocates that the consumer price subsidy on wheat, which in 1984 had an estimated cost of $400 million to $500 million, should not have been given as it favored not only the poor but also families with relatively high incomes. He concludes that the cost of any such subsidy needs to be monitored carefully; however, in the short term, consumer price subsidies on basic foods should be adopted.

The reader may have observed that Homem de Melo's analysis and policy recommendations, although significantly more detailed, are generally consis-tent with those advanced by Hélio Jaguaribe and the Instituto de Estudos Políticos e Sociais.[31] As such, they seem to be relatively safe in a political sense. The opportunity costs of Homem de Melo's recommendations, for producers of sugarcane and export crops, are more readily apparent. So also is the relative deemphasis of government support for industry-led economic growth that these policies imply. Homem de Melo's criticism of shifts in the international economy, perhaps suggesting that Brazil should rely less on international eco-nomic dealings (foreign investment and finance) to fuel its economic ad-vances, is similarly more developed than such insights were in Jaguaribe's work. Some will take issue with him on this count, but as Brazil's decision in February 1987 to furlough the payment of interest on its foreign debt seems to indicate, Homem de Melo's views now could be considered quite moderate in Brazil.

Moreover, it would appear that in 1987 the pinch of Brazil's economic re-cession and the food deficit is affecting some of the middle-class families, who until now were little touched by increasing food prices. Probably to such families, Homem de Melo's analysis and recommendations would appear to be increasingly credible. Finally, the prospect that the food crisis, if left unat-tended, could undercut Brazil's attempt to become a major political and eco-nomic power established on democratic principles, would also make Homem de Melo's policy package appear increasingly tolerable. Under present circum-stances, a policy like this would seem to be relatively acceptable, although not easy to implement.

But what about the prospect that such a policy package will lessen hunger, malnutrition, and poverty? The possibilities for improvement, if such a policy package were adopted, seem good. I argue that the prospect for success for Homem de Melo's recommended policies is much greater than for the less-developed recommendations advanced by Jaguaribe. As production increases, prices of domestic foods should decline, enhancing the ability of the poor to buy food. Productivity and producer incomes should increase as new investments are made to the production of domestic foods. The extent of the improvement obviously will depend upon the extent of the commitment of resources and the degree to which all parts of the policy package are implemented. However, even modest resource commitments to domestic food production should result in commendable growth. And when initial resource investments are met with relatively impressive production gains, momentum favoring further implementation of the policy package should build.

ADVOCATES OF LAND REFORM

Many Brazilian scholars, government officials, and reformers who have studied Brazil's chronic poverty and present food crisis concur that adopting such a policy package would be a plus. Many urge rapid adoption of such policies. However, many of these same observers lament that in the absence of comprehensive land reform far too many Brazilians will still remain hungry and destitute. To them, Homem de Melo's recommendations are a step in the right direction, but are not far-reaching enough—such policy implementation must be coupled with land reform.

The logic behind such a comprehensive reform policy differs from that advanced by Jaguaribe and Homem de Melo. Rather than describing the problem in terms of a "food deficit" caused by inadequate production of "domestic foods," those who advocate land reform generally suggest that these are but symptoms of enduring inequalities and injustices. The overwhelming concentration of wealth and productive assets, particularly land, in the hands of so few Brazilians, it is argued, assures the perpetuation of poverty and hunger even when aggregate production (GNP) grows significantly. Hunger is a product of poverty, and poverty is a product of the unequal distribution of income, land, and other productive assets.

At the risk of being redundant, it is important to note that staunch advocates of land reform do not define Brazil's problem in terms of a "food deficit" and the need for increased production of domestic foods. To them, the problem is hunger. They would agree with the argument advanced in the first paragraph of Chapter 2 of this book, in which Keith Griffin contends that "there is no world food problem, but there is a problem of hunger in the world. Food and hunger are, of course, related, and it is tempting to argue that an increase in food output will lead to a reduction in hunger, malnutrition, and starvation. But, alas, the connection is not so straightforward or so simple. Indeed, many cases can be found [Brazil] in which hunger has increased, or failed to diminish, despite a rise in per capita food supplies."

In Brazil, income and land are unequally distributed, with observable connections to chronic poverty and hunger. Indeed, available data suggest that income and land are more severely concentrated in Brazil than in any country for whom the World Bank reports such data. In 1972, the World Bank studied income distribution in Brazil and reported that the poorest 20 percent of the population received only 2 percent of the nation's total household income. By contrast, the richest 10 percent of the population received nearly 51 percent of household income. Moreover, the bottom 60 percent of the population earned only 16.4 percent of total household income.[32]

Despite Brazil's rapid economic growth since the time of this 1972 study, it appears highly unlikely that income inequality has lessened. Citing the 1978 National Household Sample Survey and later estimates, Peter T. Knight and Ricardo Moran in 1981 observed that "for the past 20 years the richest 10 percent of families have been receiving over 50 percent of the income, while the poorest 40 percent have received well under 10 percent."[33] In 1986, Hélio Jaguaribe reported that the richest 1 percent of the population received the same percentage of Brazil's total income (13 percent) as was received by the poorest 50 percent of the population.[34]

When we recognize that approximately seven out of ten families receive two minimum salaries or less per month, and that more than the value of one minimum salary is required to purchase sufficient food to meet the essential, monthly food requirements of one adult man, we quickly see that many are poor and few are rich in Brazil.[35] The crisis of hunger in Brazil, then, is the product of inadequate, low incomes received by the majority of Brazilians. To redress hunger, the incomes of the poor must increase; increasing the incomes of the poor, the argument continues, requires that income be transferred from the rich.

Of course, an even more direct objective of advocates of land reform is to reverse the centuries-old and increasing concentration of land in Brazil. Unlike trends in any other nation, land distribution is fast becoming more unequal. In 1972, 1 percent of Brazil's agricultural properties occupied 45.2 percent of the cultivable land. As remarkable as that land concentration was then, by 1978 that proportion had increased to 48.7 percent. Small properties held by 50 percent of the propertied rural households covered only 4.2 percent of the cultivable land in 1972, and by 1978 that proportion had declined to 2.8 percent.[36]

Given the increased emphasis on sugarcane and agricultural production for export beginning in the 1970s and continuing through the 1980s, it is reasonable to estimate that land has become even more concentrated since 1978. Further evidence of this likelihood can be found in estimates of the number of people who have migrated from rural areas to the cities in the past ten years. Estimates range from 900,000 per year[37] to 1.5 million per year.[38] It would appear that agribusiness, with its emphasis on production of agricultural commodities for export and on sugarcane production, has displaced rural labor from the land as it has mechanized its activities and expanded the total area cultivated for those purposes. Growing unemployment and underemployment also reflect this development.[39]

The essence of land reform is to reduce the unequal distribution of land and income so that chronic poverty and the worsening food crisis might be lessened. Advocates consider it essential to solving the problem, as opposed to treating the symptoms of present crisis conditions. For greatest effect, it should be coupled with policy changes such as those advocated by Homem de Melo and Jaguaribe. It envisions comprehensive social, political, and economic changes. It is not a policy that weak governments can pursue without fear of being severely challenged by the politically and economically powerful interest groups in Brazil. The Catholic Church seems to support land reform in Brazil, but large landholders, major industrialists, and most commercial bankers either worry about or forthrightly oppose such far-ranging changes. At best, land reform in Brazil is a high-risk political venture.

When I arrived in Brasília in May 1986 for interviews with government officials, I was uncertain about the strength of the Sarney regime. Faced with near-catastrophic economic developments, it seemed that the government had increased its public support with the announcement of a major price freeze and the creation of a new currency, the cruzado. However, like other outside observers with long acquaintance with Brazil I suspected that the New Republic was yet very fragile.

Given these expectations I was surprised by the enthusiasm with which recommendations for land reform were being discussed in Brasília and in many parts of the country. Major newspapers and news magazines regularly reported plans that were being formulated. The 1964 Estatuto da Terra[40] (Land Statute) had been resurrected as the basis for transferring underutilized and noncultivated rural properties to small farmers who would actually work the land. Displeasure was widely expressed for property owners who held land simply for purposes of speculation; most agreed that such land must be put to productive use. The Plano Nacional de Reforma Agrária (National Plan for Agrarian Reform) had been decreed by the Sarney administration on 10 October 1985. Leaders of relevant committees in both houses of the Brazilian legislature expressed the need for land reform and the hope that it could be accomplished despite some potentially formidable opposition. A major speech advocating comprehensive land reform, given in August 1985 by Nelson Ribeiro, then the head of the new Ministry of Agrarian Reform and Development and acting director of INCRA (Instituto Nacional de Colonização e Reforma Agrária, the National Institute for Agrarian Colonization and Reform), was being widely read and favorably discussed.[41] By May 1986 some regional offices of INCRA had prepared preliminary recommendations, including indications of what lands should be transferred.[42]

Closer inspection of the details of the proposed land reform revealed why it could be so boldly endorsed without immediately triggering strong opposition. First, most of the directors of the regional offices of the agency of government charged with implementing land reform, INCRA, perceived (in personal interviews) that Ribeiro's speech and the decreed national plan for agrarian reform would prove to be little more than rhetoric. Second, the land initially scheduled for transfer was of poor quality, widely dispersed, located in areas accessed by substandard roads, and largely dependent upon irregular rainfall. Land was not to be confiscated; owners were to be compensated at a negotiated value of the land.[43] As an example of the more ambitious regional plans, consider the one prepared for the state of Bahia by José Carlos Arrute Rey, regional director of INCRA.[44] Beginning in the summer of 1986, Arrute Rey planned to commence the transfer of 85,809 hectares of land to landless farmers. Of this land, nearly 70,000 hectares would require irrigation in order to be productive. Antonio Balbino, the owner of Sertaneja, a 54,000-hectare, unirrigated area targeted for transfer, had actually proposed the deal to Arrute Rey. The transfer was attractive enough to induce his cooperation.

As conservative as plans for these initial land transfers were, it was not long until, first, sporadic and, later, well-organized opposition appeared among large landholders. Old social and political coalitions emerged anew to rebut the potentially far-ranging implementation of land reform.[45] Indicative of the strength and influence of the opposition, by early 1987 discussion of land reform had all but disappeared from the newspapers, news magazines, and the conference rooms of ministries and legislative bodies in Brasília. As in the 1960s, land reform had again proved politically improbable.

CONCLUSION

Elsewhere I have argued that in Brazil social change beneficial to the poor and the hungry has been very difficult to achieve.[46] Such change has proved particularly difficult during the twenty-one-year period of military-led governments (1964-1985). Indeed, the social circumstance of the poor in Brazil has notably worsened during this period, despite rapid economic growth. Hunger and malnutrition also have become worse since the mid-1960s.

With others, I have considered that the recent political opening that brought the Sarney administration to power holds some promise that the condition of the poor and hungry in Brazil now might be improved. Evidence suggests that such improvements have become important to some influential members of the present government. However, the power required for the government to implement policies to this end is likely not as secure as seems to be required to implement a comprehensive reform policy, including land reform.

I believe that major land reform, coupled with policies such as those advocated by Homem de Melo, is required to dramatically reduce poverty and
hunger in Brazil. However, it appears that if pursued such an effort might not
only evoke strong opposition against land reform but may also jeopardize policy changes that could lessen, albeit less dramatically, poverty and hunger in
Brazil. Whereas policies advocated by Homem de Melo may not be ideal, they
may be possible. As John Mellor argued at the conference that precipitated this
book, if achievable, land reform may be beneficial to the usually landless, rural
poor. However, if land reform cannot be achieved politically, then other
strategies with admittedly less promise for the poor but greater political acceptability should be pursued. Hopefully, Fernando Homem de Melo's proposals
will prove sufficiently acceptable politically to be adopted. So as not to jeopardize that possibility, perhaps the strident advocacy of land reform should be
softened. The politics of hunger in Brazil seem to suggest this course of action.

NOTES

1. This information was gathered by the author in May 1986 during several interviews with government officials in Brasília, Brazil.
2. See Fernando Homem de Melo. *Prioridade Agrícola: Sucesso ou Fracasso?*,
Tables 1 and 2, pp. 3, 4.
3. See Peter T. Knight, Dennis Mahar, and Ricardo Moran, "Health, Nutrition, and
Education," p. 61.
4. See Cheryl Williamson Gray, "Food Consumption Parameters for Brazil and
the Application to Food Policy." First-degree malnutrition is defined as 76-90 percent of
the median standard weight for age, second-degree malnutrition as 61-75 percent, and
third-degree as less than 60 percent.
5. See Homem de Melo, *Prioridade Agrícola,* p. 195.
6. See George Martine and Ronaldo Coutinho Garcia, "Mudanças Tecnológicas e
Sociais na Agricultura: A Panela de Povo em Tempo de Crise."
7. Antonio de Freitas Filho and Elisio Contini, "Análise da Situação Nutricional e
das Políticas Alimentares no Brasil."
8. See Fernando Homem de Melo, *O Problema Alimentar no Brazil.*
9. See A.M.M. Peliano, C. de M. Castro, George Martine, and Ronaldo Coutinho
Garcia, *O Problema Alimentar Brasileiro: Situação Atual, Perspectivas e Proposta de
Políticos.*
10. See Freitas Filho and Contini, "Análise da Situação Nutricional e das Políticas
Alimentares no Brasil."
11. This figure for GNP in 1985/86 ("produto bruto") is from a study commissioned by José Sarney, president of Brazil, and conducted by the Instituto de Estudos
Políticos e Sociais. The estimated GNP per capita for 1986 is in excess of $2,000. See
Hélio Jaguaribe, "Conferência do Professor Hélio Jaguaribe," p. 8. According to this
study, it is conceivable that Brazil could become the fifth largest economy in the Western world by the year 2000. Data published by the World Bank generally confirm this
observation. According to its *World Development Report 1985,* from 1965 to 1983

Brazil's GNP grew more than thirteen-fold to more than $254 billion. However, according to data published in World Bank, *World Development Report 1986,* p. 185, in 1984 Brazil's GNP had declined to only $187 billion. Although troubling, the reported dollar value of Brazil's gross national product in 1984 is somewhat misleading unless we remember that during this period the value of the Brazilian currency (cruzeiro) relative to the dollar plummeted dramatically. With the dramatic economic reforms of the Sarney regime, referred to as the "Plano do Cruzado," the cruzado being Brazil's new currency, the Brazilian currency has been strengthened. Hence, in the spring of 1986 Jaguaribe estimated that the dollar value of Brazil's GNP was "310 billions of dollars."

12. As further support for these claims, note the dramatic decline in purchasing power of perhaps 70 percent of the Brazilian population during the past two decades, but most particularly in the mid-1980s. In 1981, 17.9 million people age ten or more only received up to one minimum salary. Under Brazilian law, a minimum salary should be sufficient for two adults and two children to have food, housing, transportation, health, and education. Calculations made in January 1983 indicated that a minimum salary was then insufficient to provide the minimum food necessities of a single adult person. It was estimated that a laborer earning a minimum salary, for which he was required to work 240 hours per month, actually had to work 263 hours to purchase just his essential, monthly food ration. Martine and Garcia also estimated in 1983 that seven out of ten laborers earned only two minimum salaries or less. See Martine and Garcia, "Mudanças Tecnológicas e Sociais na Agricultura." In 1986, the Instituto de Estudos Políticos e Sociais estimated that one-third of the Brazilian families earn one minimum salary or less, with another one-quarter earning between one and two minimum salaries. In terms of the total population, 65 out of 100 Brazilians earn no more than two minimum salaries, which destines them to live in extraordinary poverty plagued with hunger and malnutrition. See Jaguaribe, "Conferência do Professor Hélio Jaguaribe," p. 7.

13. The description presented here of the strategy advanced by Jaguaribe's institute is based on two unpublished manuscripts. Both manuscripts are actually transcripts of a "Conference with Hélio Jaguaribe" that was attended by prominent government officials and university scholars. "Conferência do Professor Hélio Jaguaribe" is Jaguaribe's presentation to the conference. "Para Um Novo Pacto Social" is a transcription of debates between Jaguaribe and the conference participants. The conference was held under the auspices of IPEA and IPLAN, two government-funded research and policy analysis organizations. Each manuscript is dated 24 April 1986. These manuscripts are not yet published, but copies are available from Ladd Hollist.

14. See David Collier, ed., *The New Authoritarianism in Latin America,* and Guillermo A. O'Donnell, *Modernization and Bureaucratic-Authoritarianism: Studies in South American Politics.*

15. Populism last gained prominence in Brazil from 1960 to 1964 during the brief presidencies of Janio Quadros and João Goulart. This populist period was followed by the military intervention of 1964 that lasted for twenty-one years. See Peter Flynn, *Brazil: A Political Analysis,* pp. 190-307.

16. See Instituto de Estudos Políticos e Sociais, *Brasil, Sociedade Democrática.*

17. See Jaguaribe, "Conferência do Professor Hélio Jaguaribe," p. 8.

18. Ibid., p. 14.

19. Whereas the specifics of Jaguaribe's arguments and recommendations differ from those advanced by John Mellor, similarities are evident. See John W. Mellor, *The*

New Economics of Growth: A Strategy for India and the Developing World, and Chapter 3 in this book.

20. See Homem de Melo, *Prioridade Agrícola.*

21. Again, like Jaguaribe, Homem de Melo understands the justifications for Brazil's policy to promote exports and sugarcane production in the late 1970s and in the 1980s. He too judges those policies to be reasonable, although disadvantageous in terms of the resulting disincentives to the production of domestic foods.

22. See Homem de Melo, *Prioridade Agrícola,* p. 168.

23. Ibid., p. 169.

24. Homem de Melo cites E. L. Bacha, "Uma Proposta para a Retomada do Crescimento Econômico," in estimating that between 1980 and 1984 the average standard of living for the Brazilian population declined 17 percent.

25. See L. M. Lopes, "Transferências v. Investimentos," p. 6.

26. For a more complete discussion of the following policy recommendations, see Homem de Melo, *Prioridade Agrícola,* pp. 163-200.

27. Ibid., p. 175.

28. Indirect taxes include such commercial taxes as the ICM (Imposto de Circulação de Mercadorias), a tax on merchandise; the IPI (Impostos Sobre Produtos Industrializados), a tax on industrial products; and FUNRURAL (Fundo Rural), a tax collected to help agricultural projects.

29. See Chapter 3.

30. See Per Pinstrup-Andersen and Harold Alderman, "The Effectiveness of Consumer Food Subsidies in Reaching Rationing and Income Transfer Goals," p. 26, as cited in Homem de Melo, *Prioridade Agrícola,* p. 192.

31. Homem de Melo's position is also consistent with those advanced by John W. Mellor (Chapter 3) and Cheryl Christensen (Chapter 4).

32. See World Bank, *World Development Report 1984,* p. 273.

33. See Peter T. Knight and Ricardo Moran, "Bringing the Poor into the Growth Process: The Case of Brazil," p. 22.

34. See Jaguaribe, "Conferência do Professor Hélio Jaguaribe," p. 7.

35. See Martine and Garcia, "Mudanças Tecnológicas e Sociais na Agricultura," and Jaguaribe, "Conferência do Professor Hélio Jaguaribe," p. 7.

36. *Latin American Economic Report,* 29 August 1980, p. 34.

37. See Paul Rabello de Castro, *Barões e Bóias-Frias: Repensando a Questão Agrária no Brasil.*

38. See Jaguaribe, "Conferência do Professor Hélio Jaguaribe," p. 16.

39. In 1983, 9.8 million people, or 19.3 percent of the work force, were unemployed. If the trend manifest between 1980 and 1983 has continued, then an estimated 13.1 million people, or 23.6 percent of the work force, were unemployed in 1986. See Martine and Garcia, "Mudanças Tecnológicas e Sociais na Agricultura," p. 27. Combined estimates of unemployed and underemployed laborers often exceed 40 percent of the work force.

40. See Ministério da Reforma e do Desenvolvimento Agrário, Instituto Nacional de Colonização e Reforma Agrária (INCRA), *Estatuto de Terra.*

41. See Nelson Ribeiro, "O Estatuto da Terra e o Problema Fundiário," a speech presented at the Commercial Federation of the State of São Paulo, 1 August 1985, and reprinted as the first item in a series, Coleção Reforma Agrária, of the newly established Ministry of Agrarian Reform and Development.

42. For example, see Ministério da Reforma e do Desenvolvimento Agrário, Instituto Nacional de Colonização e Reforma Agrária (INCRA), e Governo do Estado da Bahia, *Plano Regional de Reforma Agrária*. This effort in Bahia was supervised by José Carlos Arrute Rey, the regional director of INCRA, in Salvador, Bahia. I have a copy of the Preliminary Version of this regional plan.

43. Of course, landholders targeted for land reform considered nominal, speculation-inflated prices to be "fair" indications of the value of their land. Such prices were consistently higher than the actual worth of the land when used for agricultural production.

44. See Ministério da Reforma e do Desenvolvimento Agrário, Instituto Nacional de Colonização e Reforma Agrária (INCRA), e Governo do Estado da Bahia, *Plano Regional de Reforma Agrária*.

45. For a discussion of social and political coalitions that persist among large landholders, major industrialists, and major commercial bankers, see Florestan Fernandes, *Reflections on the Brazilian Counter-Revolution*.

46. See W. Ladd Hollist, "Dependency Transformed: Brazilian Agriculture in Historical Perspective."

F. LaMond Tullis

12

Cocaine and Food: Likely Effects of a Burgeoning Transnational Industry on Food Production in Bolivia and Peru

After Peru's newly elected president, Alán García, shocked international bankers in 1985 by setting his own terms for debt repayments,[1] some might have thought him capable of additional international mischief. While his country despairingly looks for ways to earn foreign exchange in order to service its debts and import needs, García affirms that "the only raw material that has increased in value is cocaine" and that "the most successful effort to achieve Andean integration has been made by the drug traffickers."[2] Peru earns a lot of money from the cocaine traffic; it could earn a lot more. Indeed, with three or four years' preparation, the country singlehandedly could supply the entire international market for the drug. That could go a long way toward retiring a weighty international debt.

Potential profits and debt repayment possibilities notwithstanding, García has proclaimed and initiated an impressive war on drug traffickers. At the same time he holds his international creditors at bay by the threat of de jure debt default and by moralizing that although drug trafficking is a grave crime injurious to his nation's and the world's health, "it is an equally grave crime against humanity to raise interest rates, lower the prices of raw materials and squander economic resources on technologies of death while hundreds of millions of human beings live in misery or are driven to violence."[3]

In 1987 García's war on drug traffickers is mirrored to some small extent by Bolivia's new posture. The similarities are recent. In the early 1980s Bolivia's highest governmental and military leaders were preeminent in the international narcomafia.[4] Being traffickers themselves, they were reluctant to move against the trade. Although Bolivia's new intermittent resolve on drug trafficking and its new IMF-prescribed fiscal and monetary policies have reduced the country's cocaine-induced annual inflation rate from over 20,000 percent to near 10 percent (March 1987),[5] the country nevertheless continues to live on a black-market cocaine economy and continues not to be able to satisfy its international creditors.

International pressure has helped Bolivia to stiffen its official resolve against cocaine; a belated realization of the drug traffick's undesirable domestic social and political effects has further hardened that resolve. In February 1986, the country was the first ever to have all its U.S. foreign aid cut off over drug-trafficking issues. Among other irritants, in 1985 the United States had generously funded a crop eradication program to destroy 10,000 acres of coca bushes whose leaves produce the alkaloids from which cocaine is processed; the Bolivian eradication teams had managed to use the money but destroy only 150 acres of bushes. U.S. Senator Jake Garn and others had tirelessly attempted to bring Bolivia into line by threatening a foreign-aid cut-off.[6] But the country had taken little practical notice even though its official protestations, following the demise of its narcotrafficking military leaders, were acceptable. Bolivia's earnings from cocaine far exceeded the $100 million in additional aid the United States had offered. The country's cocaine economy could not, it was said, withstand a substantial reduction in the drug's traffic without suffering enormous social and political stress. On the other hand, Bolivia could, the argument continued, cripple along without foreign aid. That view began to change when aid was actually cut off and when a new public realization emerged that Bolivia had several increasingly serious social and political problems to face that were potentially much more explosive than the conventional ones it had historically experienced. Thousands of the country's teenagers, having begun to smoke "coca paste," were becoming not only lastingly disabled but a permanent liability to the nation; also, the growing power of the "narco state-within-a-state," buttressed by private armies better equipped than the country's own military, threatened the very existence of the Bolivian national state. In July 1986 Bolivia's president called for, and received, American troops to help combat the flourishing cocaine trade.[7]

Cocaine trafficking is a many-sided issue involving moral, physiological, economic, political, and social considerations. My interest is in food, principally in its production and consumption by low-income rural families in lesser-developed countries. What effect does the cocaine trade have on basic food production in Bolivia and Peru? Given widespread malnutrition, especially in Peru, I have wondered about the extent to which malnutrition and the cocaine trade may walk hand in hand.

I have attempted to address the first of these issues—the possible effect of the cocaine trade on basic food production—by examining cocaine's global production trends and economic transactions; by establishing the extent to which Bolivia and Peru provide feeder stocks for the trade; by showing the coinciding decline in per capita food production, particularly in Peruvian basic foods; by examining the cocaine traffic's probable contribution to that decline through food crop displacements, agricultural labor displacements, increased food imports, and commodity competition; and, finally, by suggesting features of the international political economy that could alter the traffic's impact on food production. Arguments concerning the extent and nature of the second issue—the cocaine trade's probable links with malnutrition—must await a subsequent paper.

COCAINE TRAFFIC

In 1985 through 1987, U.S. imports of cocaine garnered as much press coverage as the controversial and increasingly emotion-laden issue of the importation of automobiles, steel, and computer chips from Japan and other Pacific Basin countries.[8] In international contraband, cocaine has now replaced marijuana as U.S. public concern number one.[9] The cocaine industry transacted $16 billion to $30 billion worth of tax-free business in 1980,[10] probably more than $58 billion in 1984 (see the discussion of estimates in this chapter's appendix), and perhaps as much as $80 billion in 1985 and $83 billion in 1986.[11] The estimated world-wide financial transactions in cocaine for 1986 exceeded the reported 1984 gross domestic product of eighty-eight of the world's market economy countries (see Figure 12.1), and the transactions for 1987 continue apace.

The drug affects the lives of perhaps 20 million Americans either as traffickers, consumers, or victims of its crime-laden means of distribution.[12] Millions more are affected in the taxes they pay to interdict the drug, care for its addicts or their children, and provide law enforcement to combat its associated crime and governmental corruption. Because Americans demand the substance in ever-increasing amounts[13] (see Figure 12.2), both the financial impacts and short-term financial transactions are likely to grow, even in the face of increased drug-law enforcement efforts.[14]

PRINCIPAL SOURCES OF COCA, COCAINE'S AGRICULTURAL INGREDIENT

South America is the principal supplier of cocaine.[15] Traditionally, Peru and Bolivia have supplied 90 percent of the agricultural raw materials used in its production, and Colombia has done 75 percent of the processing and trafficking business.[16] These figures are now in flux because Peruvian and Bolivian traffickers are beginning to compete with Colombians in processing and distribution; Colombians, in turn, are starting to grow their own agricultural raw material for the product; and, tighter drug-law enforcement programs in Colombia and Peru are forcing many traditional traffickers into Ecuador, Brazil, Argentina, Mexico, Nicaragua, and Cuba to conduct their business.[17] A few processing plants have even been set up in Florida.[18] The resulting mix, in 1984, shows Peru and Bolivia still producing 90 percent of (increased) production, but Colombia now appearing to do only 54 percent of the processing (see Table 12.1); presumably the trafficking mix has begun to change as well, involving more and more Bolivians and Peruvians.

Figure 12.1   Street Value of Global Cocaine Trade Compared to Gross Domestic Product of 88 Countries

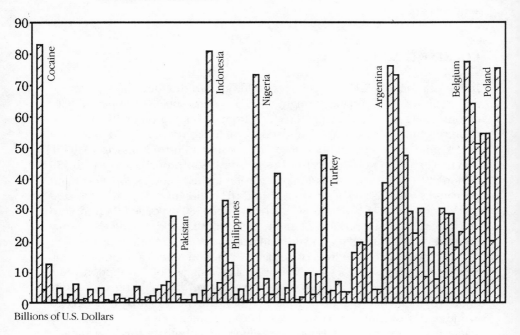

Billions of U.S. Dollars

Country GDP figures are for 1984. Cocaine estimate is for 1986.

Sources: Based on "Method Three," appendix, this chapter, and World Bank, *World Development Report, 1986,* pp. 184–185.

Cocaine also affects people in the countries of its origin. The usual social costs apply there, too, and in ever-increasing measures.[19] But beyond these and other liabilities are many perceived benefits—foreign exchange earnings, enhanced rural incomes in some areas, more buoyant (or perhaps just less catastrophic) national economies, and, of course, stunning opportunities for local politicians (even national ones in Bolivia) to enjoy the Midas touch by turning their public trusts into private gains.[20] Not unexpectedly, some governments and judges have been reluctant to enforce either their own laws on illegal drugs or lend much support to international conventions on drug trafficking to which they are signatories.[21] Numerous other, more resolute, judges and politicians have been assassinated.

Cocaine, or cocaine hydrochloride,[22] is processed from coca leaves, which grow on bushes. As an agricultural crop, coca has always had commercial value, for it is used as a flavoring for soft drinks (after drug alkaloids have been removed) and as raw material in licit medical drug manufacturing, and—in spite of educational efforts to break a 2,000-year-old Andean South American habit—

it is still chewed by over 3 million Peruvians and Bolivians who annually consume about 28,000 tons.[23] But it is with the exploding demand for illicit drugs that the planting and harvesting of coca has in recent years undergone dramatic expansion in Bolivia and Peru; and cultivation has now spread (although with an inferior genetic product[24]) into Colombia, Ecuador, Brazil's Amazon basin, and even Argentina.[25] In some areas the expanded production has replaced traditional food crops and has bid up labor costs in traditional agriculture.

The cultivation of coca for export on such a vastly expanded basis is an understandable reaction to international market demand. In this, coca cultivation is not unique and simply adds an additional crop to already expanding Latin American agricultural exports (such as soya from Brazil and livestock and animal products from Mexico).[26] But trade expansion in coca, soya, or livestock cannot be explained adequately by referring simply to international market demand. Other factors have been at work, too. Brazil and Mexico have had explicit investment, credit, tax, and support policies favoring capital-intensive production of soya and livestock exports for foreign exchange earnings. Likewise, through 1983 Peru had an implicit and Bolivia an explicit export promotion policy on coca. For Peru the situation was almost total "benign ne-

Figure 12.2   Tons of Cocaine Entering the United States, 1978–1985

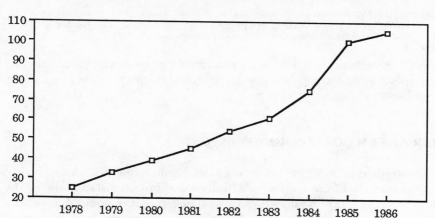

Sources: Figures for 1980 and 1984 are extrapolations. Figures for 1978 and 1979 are from Armstrong and Vallance, "U.S.-Bolivia Relations Further Strained." The 1981, 1982, and 1983 figures are the high estimates from the National Narcotics Intelligence Consumers Committee, *Narcotics Intelligence Estimate,* p. 17. (Alan Riding, in "Shaken Colombia Acts at Last on Drugs," gives figures for 1981 as 50 tons; 1982, 58 tons; and 1983, 69 tons.) The 1985 figure is advanced by several observers: William D. Montalbano, "Latins Push Belated War on Cocaine"; Dan Williams, "Mexico a Funnel for U.S.-Bound Cocaine"; and Lee May, "Cocaine-Effect of Life in America." The Select Committee on Narcotics Abuse and Control thought the 1985 tonnage to be more than 100 (see U.S. House of Representatives, Latin American Study Missions Concerning International Narcotics Problems, p. 7). The 1986 figure is from U.S. Department of State, Bureau of International Narcotics Matters, "International Narcotics Control Strategy Report," March 1987.

Table 12.1   Cocaine and Coca Production, 1984 (Metric tons)

	Coca Production	%	Cocaine Production	%
Argentina			6	3
Bolivia	49,200	41	47	26
Brazil			8[a]	4
Colombia	11,680	10	99	54
Ecuador	895	1	1[b]	0.5
Panama			1[a]	0.5
Peru	56,820	48	22[c]	12
Totals	118,595	100	184	100

[a] The estimates for Brazil and Panama are based on the assumption that seizures represented about 10 per cent of production. Three cocaine labs were destroyed in Brazil, one in Panama.

[b] The report lists production at less than 1 per cent of the total.

[c] There are no reliable estimates for Peru. However, domestic consumption of cocaine is estimated to be 10 metric tons. And although seizures were only 120 kilograms, the estimated retiring potential in 1984 was 68.6 metric tons. Thus the figure of 22 metric tons is purely speculative but more accurate than listing nothing at all given that in 1984 at least 119 Peruvian cocaine-processing labs were destroyed by drug-law enforcement agencies. See U.S. Department of State, Bureau of International Narcotics Matters, "International Narcotics Control Strategy Report, Mid-year Update," August 1, 1985, mimeo, pp. 47–50.

Source: U.S., Department of State, Bureau of International Narcotics Matters, *International Narcotics Control Strategy Report 1985*, pp. 37, 52, 59, 75, 90, 109, and 117–118. See also Appendix, this chapter, for discussions on coca production.

glect"[27] of well-known international contraband, whereas for Bolivia it was active sponsorship and collaboration, at the highest government levels, with drug traffickers.[28]

COCA AS A MAJOR COMMODITY EXPORT

The estimated value for 1984 of the coca leaf, cocaine paste, and cocaine hydrochloride exports from Peru were $1 billion and from Bolivia $2 billion.[29] In Bolivia, cocaine export values dwarf any other export commodity or combination of commodities, thus making the Bolivian economy exceptionally dependent on the cocaine trade (see Figure 12.3). Considering that these figures do not enter into either country's national accounting system, they are truly striking.

Even with the considerable financial slippage resulting from income concealed abroad,[30] it is estimated that $500 million are returned each year to each of these national economies,[31] amounting in 1984 to $29 per capita for Peru and $84 per capita for Bolivia. Although these additions constitute only 3 percent of Peru's gross domestic product, they amount to a gigantic 17 percent for Bolivia. The impact is so great on Bolivia that "narco-dollars," it is said, were and remain the only thing keeping the country afloat economically.[32] A measure of that desperate relationship is associated with Bolivia's halting steps in 1984 and 1987 to reduce its drug trafficking. In 1984 its army occupied the Chaparé region, where nearly a third of the world's coca leaf grows, and drove the drug dealers out. A regional depression set in immediately, understandably enough, but in addition, the Bolivian peso's value fell in one day to 30 percent of its former value.[33] The U.S.-sponsored "helicopter raids" of mid-1986 produced similar economic disturbances. Until late 1986 the country had the world's highest inflation rate. Bundles of bills made up routine retail transactions.

For Bolivia and Peru, coca production may now be thought of as a major commodity export either substituting for or adding to other conventional exports, and it has become a big foreign exchange earner. In reality, many Latin American countries have established explicit "export-substitution" agricultural policies in order to enhance their foreign exchange earnings. Thus whether by policy default or design, the new Peruvian and Bolivian exports are filling a widely felt need for hard-currency earnings.

Figure 12.3   Major Legal and Illegal Commodity Exports from Bolivia and Peru, 1982 and 1984

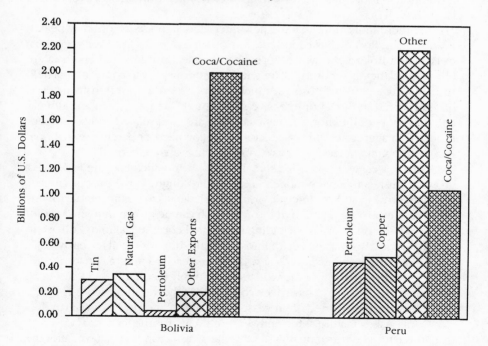

Sources: The Inter-American Development Bank's *1984 annual report,* pp. 126, lists each country's highest three commodity exports as a percentage of total exports. The Organization of American States (*Statistical Bulletin of the OAS, 1984,* Table A-10, pp. 48–51), and the World Bank (*World Development Report 1984*) list the dollar value of the aggregate commodity exports. Extrapolations were made for petroleum for 1980–1983.

COCA PRODUCTION TRENDS IN PERU AND BOLIVIA

Conventionally, most export-substitution agriculture from Latin America is characterized by capital-intensive technologies geared to produce products meeting international market standards. Increasingly, this type of agriculture is also characterized by a concentration of land—or its effective control[34]—in the hands of fewer and fewer people or companies.

For very complex reasons, agricultural export-substitution policies and the practices they foster, at least in countries inadequately concerned at a policy level with food production for domestic consumption, have been accompanied by several unfortunate if unintended consequences: a deterioration in domestically consumable food production; a rise in basic food costs or a reduction in their availability; and falling nutritional standards among the poor and "ultra poor."[35] Given policy inclinations among most of Latin America's contemporary elite, and given the class nature of most of their societies, some people see capital-intensive agricultural export trends as a substantial cause in the deterioration of food standards among lower income groups almost everywhere in the region.[36]

Are there indications that the new international trade in coca may be having a similar effect on basic food production (and perhaps food consumption) in Peru and Bolivia, the world's principal coca-leaf producers?[37] The data are elusive, and the matter does not lend itself easily or safely to conventional field research. Yet any casual observer quickly recognizes that vast transformations have occurred in the labor-intensive agricultural sectors of Peru and Bolivia, and that some of the most dramatic changes are coca related and are neither reported in aggregate official statistics nor recognized, apparently, in national income accounts, at least as far as export earnings are concerned.

Coca leaves, which provide the alkaloids from which cocaine is derived, grow on bushes in a wide range of soils. Interestingly, in the proper climate, coca will grow in soils so infertile or mineral laden as to be unsuitable for any other cash crop.[38] And, although the coca bush can be grown in many areas of the world, the only varieties yielding substantial cocaine alkaloids still are in South America. Bolivia and Peru, almost the only suppliers until the early 1980s when Colombia's and Ecuador's new plantings reached minimal maturity, still provide over 89 percent of the world's coca supply (see Table 12.1). About 25 percent of recent harvests have been consumed in the traditional coca-chewing way,[39] the balance exported or processed for licit and illicit international trade.

Coca bushes mature sufficiently in three years for the leaves to be picked from three to six times annually—an excellent cash cropping pattern. After the bushes have matured, almost no cultivation is required, although initial planting and periodic harvesting are decidedly labor-intensive. With hardly any additional labor requirements, the leaves render in cash income more per hectare than other small-farmer cash crops usually planted (see Table 12.2).[40] A peasant family can easily work one or two hectares.

Table 12.2 Comparative Income per Hectare of Labor-Intensive Agriculture in Peru and Bolivia

	Bolivia-Chaparé[a]				Peru-Huallaga[a]	
	1979[b]	1983[c]	1984[d]	1986[e]	Aug. 1984[f]	Late 1985[g]
Coca	$1,285	$4,400	$8,000	$10,000	$4,400	$2,600
Oranges	837					
Bananas	378					
Rice	168					
Cassava	40					
Corn	25					
Cacao						450

[a]The areas included are the upper Huallaga Valley in Peru and the Chaparé area of Bolivia, scenes of rapid coca production expansion. Soil fertility and climatic suitability are best in these regions for coca. In the Chaparé, 2,650 kilograms/hectare yields are assumed in production estimates. See U.S. Department of State, Bureau of International Narcotics Matters, "International Narcotics Control Strategy Report 1985," p. 52. The yields for the upper Huallaga Valley are probably comparable to those in the Chaparé. Other areas yield as low as 800 kilograms/hectare. The figures in this table assume 2,000 kilograms/hectare, except that the figures for 1979 are taken as cited.

[b]These data, and the only comparative crop data I have found other than for cacao, are from A. Gaston Ponce Caballero, *Coca, Cocaína, Tráfico,* p. 71.

[c]Assumes $2.20/kilogram to the farmer (S. Cohen, "Recent Developments in the Abuse of Cocaine," U.N., *Bulletin on Narcotics* 36, p. 6, considered coca-leaf values to be $2,000/metric ton).

[d]Assumes $4.00/kilogram (Joel Brinkley, "Bolivia Drug Crackdown Brews Trouble.")

[e]Storer Rowley, "It Is Legal to Grow, Sell Coca Leaf in Bolivia."

[f]Government interdiction efforts ceased, ending a depression in the area, when Peruvian army troops entered the valley in the wake of *Sendero Luminoso's* raid on a U.S.-sponsored crop-substitution and coca-eradication project. Figures assume a recovery to the 1983 price of $2.20/kilogram.

[g]William D. Montalbano, "Coca Valley: Peru Jungle Surrealism."

In 1986 over 100,000 hectares of coca were cultivated in Peru and an additional 45,000 in Bolivia.[41] From the traditional coca-growing areas in the Bolivian Yungas and the Peruvian eastern uplands near Cuzco, production has now expanded into the fertile lands of Bolivia's Chaparé and Peru's Huallaga Valley (see map, Figure 12.4). In Bolivia, first cocaine processing and now coca production have also entered the isolated Beni where there are fewer roads and more airstrips per capita than perhaps anywhere else in the world—2,000 airstrips for 300,000 inhabitants.[42] (Surely the Beni is a smugglers' paradise. Its principal narco-king, Roberto Suárez, offered to pay off two-thirds of Bolivia's national debt of over $3 billion if Bolivia's new civilian government would call off its U.S.-financed drug-law enforcement squads.)[43] In Peru's upper Huallaga Valley, over 14,000 small farmers and their families cultivate roughly 35,000 hectares. Many farmers are recent immigrants from the mountains, where they used to grow corn and potatoes.

Figure 12.4 Principal Coca-Growing Regions of Bolivia and Peru

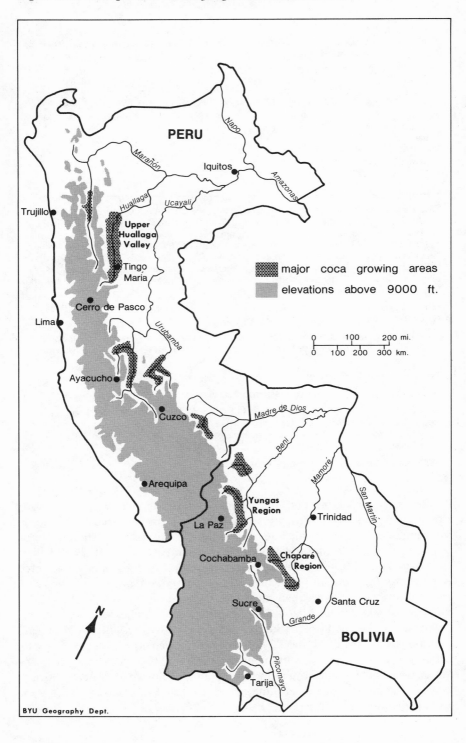

Although *cocaine* trafficking is illegal in both Peru and Bolivia, *coca-leaf* growing, until very recently, has not been. True, for more than a decade in Peru, and now in Bolivia, a small farmer has needed a government license for his bushes in order to cultivate them legally, but until recently licensing was not enforced. In Bolivia, until August 1983, there were no restraints on production although, at the insistence of the United States, a form of bush licensing came under discussion and has now been adopted.[44] Nevertheless, Bolivian coca-bush laws are not enforced very much and Peru's only slightly more. Thus Peruvian and Bolivian peasants have, on the whole, been free to sell on two markets and have increasingly risked participation in a third: (1) the traditional chewing market (government monopoly in Peru), in which producer incomes compare favorably with those deriving from other cash crops; (2) the intermediate-dealer, drug-trafficking market, in which grower income is considerably higher but crop confiscation and eradication is a danger; and (3) intermediate manufacture of coca paste by farmer-owned "cottage industries" that require low-level technology (a jungle hideout, some heavy-duty sheet plastic and forty liters of kerosene and other minor ingredients will do).[45] The paste is then sold to processors, usually from Colombia, or directly on domestic urban markets to increasing numbers of young Colombians, Peruvians, and Bolivians who mix it with tobacco and smoke it.[46]

EFFECTS OF THE INTERNATIONAL COCAINE TRADE ON FOOD PRODUCTION FOR DOMESTIC CONSUMPTION

In considering international market impacts on local food production, there are obvious initial differences between exporting, say, soya from Brazil, beef from Mexico, and coca and cocaine products from Peru and Bolivia. Soya production in Brazil, for example, has been characterized as marginalizing labor through capital-intensive technology and land concentration,[47] thereby contributing to a reduction in many Brazilians' ability either to grow or to pay for food. The same argument has been made regarding Mexico's beef export industry.[48] Coca production, on the other hand, along with its initial (but not final) processing, is very labor-intensive; frequently uses lands unsuitable for any other agricultural purpose;[49] is carried out in remote, not easily accessible, areas; improves small-farmer incomes; and gives local economies a boost as regional per capita income rises. Indeed, in this regard and at this level, the coca industry does almost all that the "current view"[50] on rural and agricultural development in lesser-developed countries calls for: It is labor-intensive, decentralized, growth-pole oriented, cottage-industry promoting, and foreign exchange earning.[51] If the coca industry were completely licit and high returns to the growers held, it could be the final answer to rural development in economically stagnating areas. Even under mixed licit-illicit marketing conditions, coca growing heavily infuses capital into backwater areas, turning frontier towns into regional shopping centers and improving employment at many levels.[52] Of course, the social and political costs deriving from the illicit trade and the mind-altering effects of the refined drug understandably dampen many people's enthusiasm for the crop.[53]

Beyond these general "rural development" interests, the likely effect of the coca/cocaine trade on food production and availability is best examined through specific categories of activity and circumstance.

Food Crop Displacement

Elsewhere in Latin America (for example, Brazil and Mexico), new patterns of agricultural trade responding to international markets have pushed small farmers from the land. On the other hand, in Bolivian and Peruvian areas that are geographically, climatologically, and strategically suited for coca production, small farmers are courted by practical and economic incentives to stay on their land (or to in-migrate) and to grow coca.

Coca production favors small plot, labor-intensive agriculture. Thus, in coca-growing areas, displacement of small farmers as a consequence of a new export crop does not occur nearly as much as elsewhere in Latin America. Moreover, as long as market conditions prevail that invite labor in-migration and impose high practical risks on traffickers and processors, neither small-plot cultivation nor labor-intensive methods will likely be disrupted. Aside from the hand labor required to harvest the leaves, any motivation for capital investment in new technological field production methods is low. A large, physically prominent, capital-intensive layout invites drug-law enforcement raids. Beyond that, current governments, although happy to confiscate every capital-intensive processing laboratory they have found, have been reluctant to "confiscate" their small-farmer peasants, although they have begun to be a bit more aggressive in enforcing their coca bush licensing laws. Thus small-plot, labor-intensive coca production fosters a kind of supply stability for traffickers and processors that would be lost if changes were made in field production technology. Capital will not be forthcoming to change that technology, and small coca farmers, especially in the more remote areas, will be more or less "safe" in the use of their land.

With higher incomes from their new coca cash crop, small farmers purchase much of their food supplies on the open market and spend relative fortunes on the material amenities of life they can now afford. If these people suffer nutritionally, it is not for lack of money to buy food—at least when the coca market is "up." (Drug interdictions that force traffickers and intermediate dealers temporarily underground bring the market down from time to time.)

Nevertheless, accompanying the economic improvements that reach deeply into rural coca-growing areas is a current (perhaps temporary) negative impact on national food production and possibly a negative impact on nutrition levels among lower economic classes. The economic incentives that keep labor-intensive farmers on their land push them to shift more and more of their production away from food crops to a cash-income exportable—coca. Thus, it is not surprising that in the coca-growing regions there has been a decline in food production even though real food prices there (and therefore better income potential for cash-crop food producers) reportedly have risen.

Both the decline in production and the rise in prices seem natural enough. As returns from labor invested in coca are one and a half to fifty times better than for other cash crops (see Table 12.2), we might expect peasants to spend their efforts growing coca.[54] Food prices usually rise when regional food deficits must be satisfied by food imports from food-surplus areas.[55] Primitive roads, regional isolation, the relative bulkiness of food, and the risks associated with its perishableness all combine to add considerable transportation costs and additional overhead to meet demand in coca-growing regions.

In the wake of lower food production and higher food prices in coca-growing regions, people not in the coca trade, or those unable to profit from it, must surely be affected nutritionally or at least be inconvenienced. A sure sign of some difficulty is that *Sendero Luminoso* guerrillas working in Peru's upper Huallaga Valley since late 1984 have ordered coca growers to plant food in addition to their coca.[56]

If a country produces a food surplus or has a food import capability, in-country food transfers to coca-growing regions would not appear to have a marked impact on food prices in areas producing the marketable surplus. The coca regions would disproportionately bear the increased costs of transportation, handling, and risk; they can afford it. On the other hand, if a national food shortfall or even a barely adequate national food supply exist, shipments at inflated prices to supply the coca economy would likely bid up food prices everywhere else. If price hikes or supply shortfalls were not met by favorable national food imports or food aid, a deleterious condition would result—reduced food intake among the poor or ultra poor whose real incomes are marginal, static, or declining. I discuss the food import issue later. As for food aid, the compelling evidence suggesting a difficult food shortage condition is presented in Figure 12.5. For the period 1974 to 1984, cereals food aid per capita increased by more than 900 percent to Bolivia and nearly 350 percent to Peru. Ordinarily, food aid is not sent to food-surplus countries.

In Bolivia and Peru, the actual condition is further clarified, partially at least, by looking at per capita food production trends since coca growing began to accelerate in the late 1970s and also at patterns of national food imports and exports. If per capita food production is falling while real prices rise (even in spite of "price controls"), then we might expect the worst, particularly if basic foods are affected significantly. Also, an increase of food imports over exports would further suggest that food production and, perhaps, basic nutrition are being adversely affected.

The aggregate data as of 1984 (the most recent more or less reliable data I have found) show both Peru's and Bolivia's per capita food production de-

Figure 12.5   Food Aid in Cereals to Bolivia and Peru (kilograms per capita)

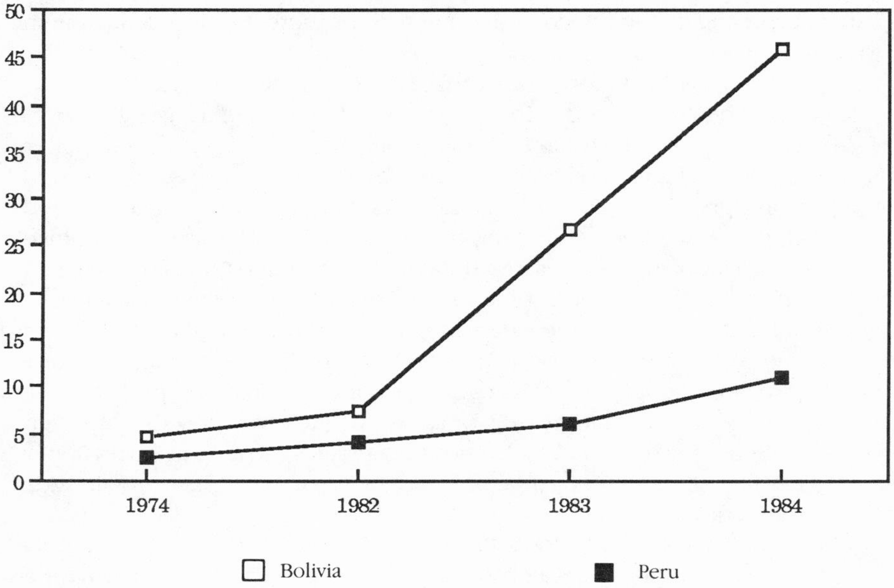

Source: Table 12.5

teriorating, especially since coca production expanded (see Figure 12.6). Evidence from other sources indicates that since 1981 per capita food production in these countries has deteriorated remarkably.[57] Significantly, per capita production of potatoes and cassava, basic staples for the rural poor, show significant long-term declines (Figures 12.7 and 12.8). Per capita production of wheat, maize, and rice have held fairly steady in the two countries.

It is true that this general deterioration in basic food production parallels the countries' gradually worsening economies (see Figure 12.9). And, in 1983 the disasterous *El Niño* (cyclical warming of the Humboldt current) produced weather-related catastrophes in the two countries. Thus, declines in per capita food production cannot be attributed to crop displacements resulting from coca production alone. However, that per capita food production is falling and that coca growers can and do bid up food prices surely suggest a difficult problem for those whose incomes remain marginal. In Peru, where nutrition data are available, the level of malnutrition among the bottom two economic quintiles of the population has risen markedly since 1980.[58]

Aggregate food production has fallen, and although the causes are no doubt many—weather, government policies, overall state of the national economy—coca, through crop-displacement patterns, is very likely one of those causes.

Labor Displacement

A principal component of the per capita decrease in overall food production is the decline in *basic* food production, especially in Peru. This adds further to the suspicion that the international trade in coca and cocaine affects food production almost everywhere in Peru and Bolivia. Traditional food-producing labor is migrating from ancestral homes to coca-growing areas and, in so doing, has reduced the availability of labor (supply, skills, or desire) at home, however underemployed such labor may have been on an annual basis. Since

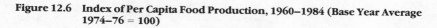

Figure 12.6   Index of Per Capita Food Production, 1960–1984 (Base Year Average 1974–76 = 100)

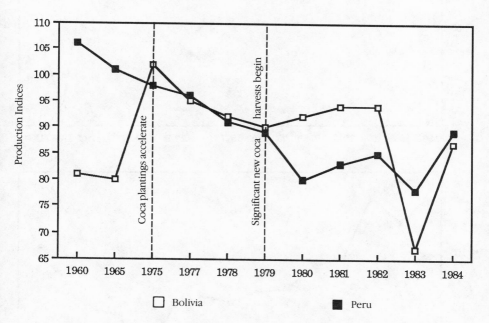

Sources: UN, Economic Commission for Latin America and the Caribbean (ECLA), *Statistical Yearbook for Latin America 1984*, pp. 608–609; and, UN, Food and Agriculture Organization (FAO), *1984 Production Yearbook* 38:77. ECLA lists the 1960 and 1965 figures in reference to base year average 1961–1965 = 100. For the figure presented here these figures have been deflated by twenty-four points for Bolivia and inflated by two points for Peru in order that they may be compared to base year average 1974–1976 = 100. ECLA listed the 1970 figures in reference to base year average 1969–1971 = 100. These figures have been deflated by fourteen points for Bolivia and inflated by four points for Peru so that they may also relate comparatively to the base year average of the rest of the data represented by this figure. The 1984 entry for Bolivia was calculated from aggregate indices listed by FAO, *1984 Production Yearbook* 38:77, and were deflated by 20 points for per capita comparability with base year average 1974–1976 = 100. The 1984 entry for Peru, calculated as was Bolivia's 1984 entry, was deflated by 21 points for similar comparability.

Figure 12.7   Potato Production in Bolivia and Peru, 1960–1984 (kilograms per capita)

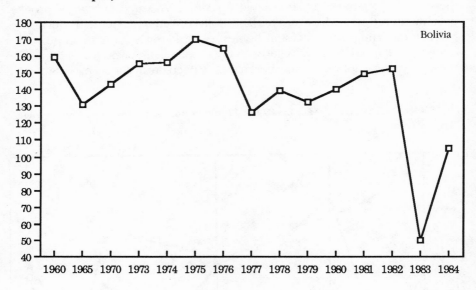

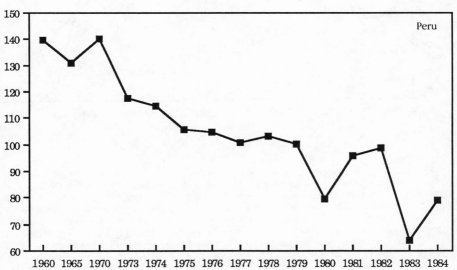

Sources: Table 12.3 and 12.4, this chapter.

Figure 12.8   Cassava Production in Bolivia and Peru, 1960–1984 (kilograms per capita)

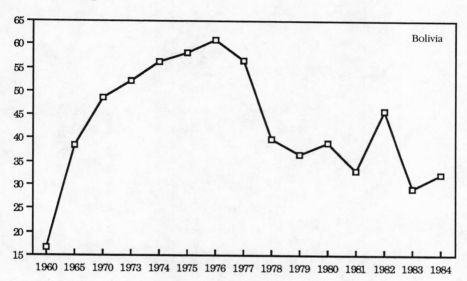

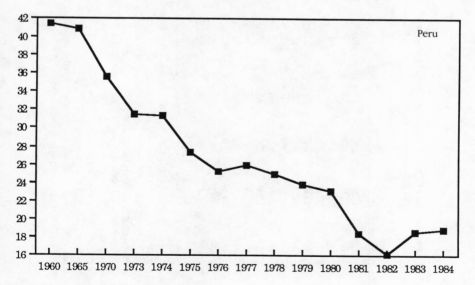

Source: Tables 12.3 and 12.4, this chapter.

Table 12.3   Production of Basic Foods in Bolivia, 1960–1984

Year	Wheat[a] TMT[c]	Wheat[a] Kg/cap[c]	Maize[a] TMT	Maize[a] Kg/cap	Rice[a] TMT	Rice[a] Kg/cap	Cassava[a] TMT	Cassava[a] Kg/cap	Potatoes[a] TMT	Potatoes[a] Kg/cap	Population[b]
1960	68	17.9	248	65.3	40	10.5	63	16.6	605	159.2	3.8
1965[d]	60	14.0	248	57.7	44	10.2	165	38.4	562	130.7	4.3[e]
1970[f]	48	10.4	291	63.3	80	17.4	223	48.5	660	143.5	4.6[g]
1973[h]	57	12.1	276	58.7	67	14.3	245	52.1	730	155.3	4.7
1974[h]	62	12.9	277	57.7	83	17.3	270	56.3	749	156.0	4.8
1975	62	12.7	305	62.2	127	25.9	285	58.2	834	170.2	4.9
1976[h]	70	14.0	342	68.4	113	22.6	305	61.0	824	164.8	5.0
1977	56	10.8	305	58.7	112	21.5	294	56.5	659	126.7	5.2
1978	57	10.8	337	63.6	89	16.8	211	39.8	738	139.2	5.3
1979	68	12.4	378	68.7	76	13.8	201	36.5	730	132.7	5.5
1980	60	10.7	383	68.4	95	17.0	219	39.1	786	140.4	5.6
1981	67	11.6	504	86.9	101	17.4	191	32.9	867	149.5	5.8
1982	66	11.2	450	76.3	86	14.6	271	45.9	900	152.5	5.9
1983	37	6.1	336	55.1	61	10.0	179	29.3	303	49.7	6.1
1984	69	11.1	489	78.9	194	31.3	200	32.3	650	104.8	6.2[i]

[a] Unless otherwise indicated, data are from U.N., Comisión Económica para América Latina y el Caribe, *Anuario estadístico de América Latina,* 1984:609–629.

[b] From James W. Wilkie and Adam Perkal, eds., *Statistical Abstract of Latin America* 24 (1985):75.

[c] Thousands of metric tons; kilograms per capita.

[d] 1964–66 Average. U.N., Comisión Económica para América Latina y el Caribe, *Anuario estadístico de América Latina,* 1978:389–95.

[e] 1964–66 average.

[f] 1969–71 average. See note [d] above.

[g] 1969–71 average.

[h] U.N., Comisión Económica para América Latina y el Caribe, *Anuario estadístico de América Latina,* 1981:609–29.

[i] Population estimates based on trends through 1983.

Table 12.4 Production of Basic Foods in Peru, 1960–1984 (global metric tonnage and average kilograms per capita)

Year	Wheat[a] TMT[c]	Wheat[a] Kg/cap[c]	Maize[a] TMT	Maize[a] Kg/cap	Rice[a] TMT	Rice[a] Kg/cap	Cassava[a] TMT	Cassava[a] kg/cap	Potatoes[a] TMT	Potatoes[a] Kg/cap	Population[b]
1960	146	14.6	442	44.2	358	35.8	414	41.4	1398	139.8	10.0
1965[d]	145	12.4	558	47.7	339	29.0	478	40.9	1533	131.0	11.7[e]
1970[f]	125	9.3	605	45.1	539	40.2	477	35.6	1877	140.1	13.4[g]
1973[h]	123	8.4	599	41.0	483	33.1	460	31.5	1713	117.3	14.6
1974[h]	127	8.5	606	40.4	494	32.9	469	31.3	1722	114.8	15.0
1975	126	8.1	635	41.0	537	34.6	424	27.4	1640	105.8	15.5[i]
1976[h]	127	8.0	726	45.7	570	35.8	402	25.3	1667	104.8	15.9
1977	115	7.2	734	45.9	587	36.7	414	25.9	1616	101.0	16.0
1978	104	6.3	590	36.0	468	28.5	410	25.0	1695	103.4	16.4
1979	102	6.0	621	36.7	560	33.1	403	23.8	1695	100.3	16.9
1980	77	4.5	453	26.2	420	24.3	400	23.1	1380	79.8	17.3
1981	119	6.7	587	33.0	712	40.0	327	18.4	1705	95.8	17.8
1982	101	5.5	625	34.3	765	42.0	295	16.2	1796	98.7	18.2
1983	75	4.0	583	31.2	770	41.2	347	18.6	1193	63.8	18.7
1984	88	4.6	576	30.2	1134	59.4	361	18.9	1515	79.3	19.1[j]

[a] Unless otherwise indicated, data are from U.N., Comisión Económica para América Latina y el Caribe, *Anuario estadístico de América Latina,* 1984:609–629.

[b] From James W. Wilkie and Adam Perkal, eds., *Statistical Abstract of Latin America* 24 (1985):75.

[c] Thousands of metric tons; kilograms per capita.

[d] 1964–66 Average. U.N., Comisión Económica para América Latina y el Caribe, *Anuario estadístico de América Latina,* 1978:389–95.

[e] 1964–66 average.

[f] 1969–71 average. See note [d] above.

[g] 1969–71 average.

[h] U.N., Comisión Económica para América Latina y el Caribe, *Anuario estadístico de América Latina,* 1981:609–29.

[i] Extrapolation.

[j] Population estimates based on trends through 1983.

Figure 12.9   Per Capita Gross Domestic Product, Bolivia and Peru, 1960–1985 (In 1984 U.S. dollars)

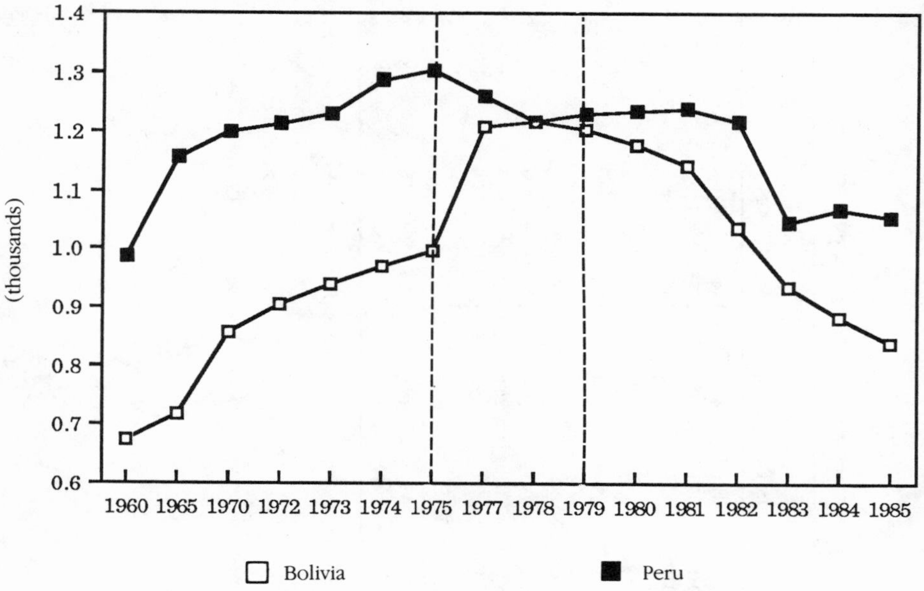

Bolivia   ■ Peru

Sources: For 1979 through 1985, Organization of American States (OAS), *Statistical Bulletin of the OAS* 8:1–2 (January–June 1986):30–31; for 1960 through 1978, OAS, *Statistical Bulletin* 2:1–2 (January–June 1980):30–31. Gross Domestic Product is calculated in 1978 dollars in volume 2, 1984 dollars in volume 8. Figures given in 1978 dollars were brought to a 1984 equivalency by multiplying, in the case of Bolivia, 1978 dollars by 2.41 and, in the case of Peru, by 1.236.

the beginning of the increased international demand for coca in the late 1970s, peasants by the thousands have flocked to coca-growing regions to seek their fortunes. As a result of the out-migration, labor costs for traditional food growing in many traditional food-growing regions have risen.[59] Small farmers accustomed to hiring seasonal labor for traditional growing, or even trading work, are less able to do so. They plant less, and they harvest less.

When those who have spent their lives growing basic foods arrive in coca-growing regions, they have little incentive to return to food growing. Rather, they set about doing the task for which they arrived—integration into the cocaine trade as growers, couriers, hired field hands, property squatters or owners, members of private armies, coca-paste processors, hawkers, provisioners, petty merchants, sharks. This is how it must have been in California during gold-rush days, when fortune-seekers of a dozen nationalities built new towns almost overnight.[60]

Inasmuch as the traditional food-growing areas "specialize" in *basic* foods and therefore produce the bulk of production in those categories, and inasmuch as those foods are showing a net decline,[61] and inasmuch as labor out-migration and consequent rising labor costs appear to be significant in that decline, and inasmuch as food aid to compensate for shortfalls has risen markedly, we may say that coca cropping probably not only displaces food crops but also displaces food-producing labor in ways that result in less food per capita being grown on a national basis. All these transformations are inexorably tied in small and large ways to the fortunes, or misfortunes, of the international political economy of cocaine.

Food Imports

The export of food implies, in theory at least, a food surplus. Its import implies something less than national food self-sufficiency. When increased imports are associated with declining indices of food production and rising levels of food aid,[62] and when these are associated with evidence of increasing levels of domestic malnutrition, it is reasonable to assume that the country is suffering a food availability dilemma. In the case of Bolivia and Peru, the dilemma is made more manifest by the fact that the respective governments are trying to conserve foreign exchange.

The data show food imports per capita rising dramatically during the nine-year period from 1974 to 1983 (Figure 12.10). The significant jump between 1982 and 1983 is probably due mostly to the havoc of *El Niño* on crop production. Still, even with the drop in imports noted for 1984, the temporal trend from 1974 is upward and, in the case of Peru, significantly so. Anecdotal evidence suggests that Bolivian and Peruvian food imports over exports have in-

Table 12.5 Food Aid and Food Imports in Cereals (metric tons and kilograms per capita)

			Bolivia		
	Imports	Kg/cap	Aid	Kg/cap	Population
1974	207	43.0	22	4.6	4.8
1982	293	49.7	44	7.5	5.9
1983	415	68.0	164	26.9	6.1
1984	320	51.6	284	45.8	6.2
			Peru		
	Imports	Kg/cap	Aid	Kg/cap	Population
1974	637	42.5	37	2.5	15.0
1982	1524	83.7	76	4.2	18.2
1983	1772	94.8	111	5.9	18.7
1984	1205	63.1	207	10.9	19.1

Sources: World Bank, *World Development Reports,* 1984, 1985, 1986, pp. 228, 184, and 190.

Population figures, from which per capita calculations were made, come from James W. Wilkie and Adam Perkal, eds., *Statistical Abstract of Latin America* 24:75.

creased in recent years. Diverse sources have noted heavy food imports coming into Peru.[63]

The problem with utilizing food trade data as a proxy for estimating food surpluses and deficits is that governments and businesses do not always engage in trade on the basis of a country's nutritional needs. Many times governments encourage exports not only of surpluses but also of basic foods even when there may be a serious national shortfall.[64] In any event, although no hard evidence seems available,increased food imports have been noted.[65] Surely these must be partly in response to declining domestic production per capita, especially in basic foods. Insofar as they are, the coca trade appears to be part of the cause.[66]

Market Competition

If until now the international political economy of coca has had a negative impact on Bolivian and Peruvian food production for domestic consumption even though it has functioned in some sense as a "rural developer," the same results cannot be expected to hold indefinitely. Coca has the prospect of a precipitous decline in price and, therefore, a substantial reduction in its attractiveness as a cash crop. One of the factors in this is increased competition among

Figure 12.10   Food Imports in Cereals, 1974–1984 (kilograms per capita)

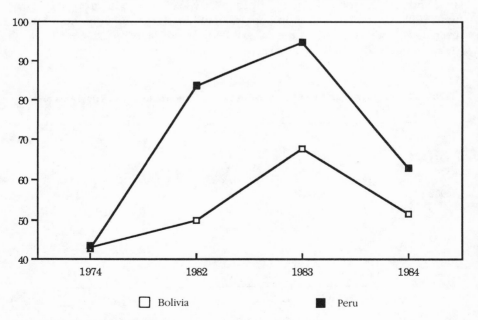

Source: Table 12.5, this chapter.

coca growers. Too much coca is being grown for long-term market price stability (assuming the whole world does not become addicted to cocaine). Not only has coca-leaf growing spread to new regions of Peru and Bolivia, but it has spilled over into Colombia, Ecuador, and Brazil. The annual harvest—and the cocaine that is made from it—is thought to have exceeded 1984 market demand (at prevailing prices) by some forty-five tons.[67]

In the third quarter of 1984 this excess availability caused a precipitous decline in cocaine prices—from $60,000 per kilogram to $28,000 per kilogram, for example, in New York City. Although the price in major U.S. consumer cities rose again in 1985 to $35,000 per kilogram, the increase is attributed to better drug-law enforcement efforts at detecting, interdicting, and destroying cocaine (rather than coca), particularly in Colombia. The new cooperation of Colombian, Bolivian, and Peruvian authorities has contributed to these results.

As competition in the coca-leaf market has increased, there are indications that prices being offered growers have peaked and may have begun to decline. Accompanying the decline is a certain amount of intragrower rivalry that could become violent in some areas as disputes arise regarding producers' market shares. (Of course, to the extent that current government crop-eradication forces are successful in "maintaining a balance" by destroying as many hectares as are planted elsewhere, prices may not decrease at all, for spreading production would be neutralized by coca-crop eradication.)

In the face of increased producer competition that may not be offset by crop eradication, coca-leaf prices will most surely fall and the incentive for growing the leaves be reduced. Many growers may look once again to alternative cash crops that are less volatile, less prone to booms and busts, less risky. Food growing might once again interest them, particulary if the "price is right." The more successful the efforts to interdict cocaine (but not the efforts to eradicate coca-leaf production per se), the more pronounced will be this tendency, as traffickers take their pick from the multitude of growers. But governments will also need national food policies in place for small farmers that do something other than control the prices farmers can command for their labors.

FEATURES OF THE INTERNATIONAL POLITICAL ECONOMY THAT COULD ALTER COCA'S IMPACT ON FOOD PRODUCTION

Crop Eradication

Under pressure and financial incentive from the United States, anti-drug-trafficking forces in Bolivia, Colombia, Peru, and Ecuador have stepped up their endeavors to interdict the cocaine traffic that has drawn so much small-farmer interest. Although notable successes have been advertised, it is still thought that only 10 to 15 percent of the traffic is being intercepted. So the United States has increasingly raised pressure on Latin American governments to deal with cocaine as a "source" problem—by U.S. interpretation, this is, in part, a "grower" problem.

Peruvians have become a little more serious about enforcing their coca-leaf licensing laws, and although they still emphasize going after the traffickers rather than the growers,[68] they have already destroyed thousands of hectares of coca bushes in the upper Huallaga Valley. As for the Bolivians, they were forced in 1983 to enact legislation empowering the government to license and supervise coca-leaf production, but with a few notable exceptions, they have not enforced any of their drug laws much.

On the whole, both Bolivia's and Peru's crop-eradication programs have been insufficient to reduce coca-leaf harvests even in the areas where the countries have concentrated their eradication efforts—Peru's upper Huallaga Valley and Bolivia's Chaparé. Aside from logistics, part of the problem is the lack of political and implementational will. Digging up peasants' coca bushes is a dangerous occupation. Eradication-team employees have been killed in Peru. In January 1986, 17,000 Bolivian coca leaf farmers laid seige to a camp of 245 narcotics officers at Ivargazama, a village in Bolivia's tropical Chaparé region.[69] Anti-drug efforts have been reduced or withdrawn in areas of "confrontational violence." It is not surprising that coca plantings are expanding in Peru and Bolivia as well as in Ecuador, Colombia, and even Brazil. Ironically, in Bolivia, a new link-up road under construction between Santa Cruz and Cochabamba is further facilitating Chaparé drug traffic.[70]

Assume that U.S. pressure and money and new Peruvian and Bolivian political resolve actually combine to make a significant dent in coca-leaf production in the Bolivian Chaparé and Peruvian upper Huallaga Valley. Success would be accompanied by a number of interesting events, including the following: Coca-growing would be driven, more and more, on to marginal, isolated lands in the Amazonic uplands, where the leaf of the climatically suited Epadú plant renders only 20 to 25 percent in alkaloids relative to the coca bushes of the upper Huallaga valley and the Chaparé. The growers who migrate with the trade might reap profits, but their work would be harder, their productivity lower, and life's amenities less. Moreover, the risk of crop seizure or plant destruction would always exist. Many growers would not make that sacrifice or continue with the risks and would leave coca production as the "law" and its associated violence became more severe. Beyond these considerations, and regardless of the outcome of the cocaine battle, highly fertile lands would thereby be made available for alternative crops, and the growing of food might qualify. Improved national production could thereafter be expected.

Crop eradication follows a U.S. policy that is funded quite handsomely. Its success depends on international cooperation and a domestic political will that seems to be emerging in Peru and perhaps even in Bolivia. Nevertheless, assuming that it eventually does, to replace coca crops with food crops will require incentives. One such incentive is a U.S.-funded crop-substitution program now in operation in the Chaparé and upper Huallaga Valley.

Subsidized Crop Substitution

Crop Substitution is designed to get peasants to grow crops—any crop—other than coca. It is U.S.-sponsored, U.S.-financed, and it has the elegance of "program integration" (seeds, equipment, subsidies, credit, indemnification, extension services, wells, roads) in every way but one. The price is not right. Although peasants may be paid one-time compensations of $300 per hectare to move out of coca leaves[71] and into, say, rice or bananas or cacao, or any of eighty commercializable plants adapted to the humid, semitropical areas,[72] the price they obtain for their substituted agricultural product may be less than one-tenth their earnings from coca, and the peasant has to destroy a very valuable investment to make such a change.

Beyond the pricing considerations, there is considerable uncertainty in other-than-coca markets. For example, in Tingo María (Peru's upper Huallaga Valley), the government sponsored a rice substitution program at a guaranteed price (a government marketing board would buy the harvest). But at harvest time the government had insufficient cash and offered to pay the farmers over a five-year period (with no interest) for their crop. The farmers did not plant rice the following year. Then the government introduced sesame seeds into the region, but no one knew where to sell them.[73] Farmers know where to sell coca leaves, and they know about how much they will earn from them. The price is more or less stable, the market predictable (so far), and a cash crop can be sold from four to six times a year.

Hardly any farmer will accept a crop-substitution program on the basis of 1987 production and marketing economics. The only way to get small farmers to do so would be to introduce considerably more risk for them into coca transactions than now exist, and perhaps the only way to do that would be to engage in considerably more eradication efforts.

"Legalizing" Cocaine

Whatever the outcome of the hotly contested debate on decriminalizing drug traffic in the United States[74] (the moral and ethical implications for an entire society are substantial), at some point people may consider the enforcement battle lost, as they did with alcohol, and antidrug efforts may more or less cease. Such a development, whatever its unfortunate side effects, could have some interesting consequences—it could put most drug traffickers and small-time processors out of business, and it could lower coca-producer incomes sufficiently to motivate small Bolivian and Peruvian farmers to shift into other crops such as food.

Without entering into a detailed discussion of critical assumptions were decriminalization to occur, we might start with a simple, reasonable set: The price of cocaine would drop appreciably; demand for cocaine would be fairly elastic (dramatic decrease in price would result in sizeable increases in the amount consumed); there would be no appreciable change in processing technology; no exceptional tariffs on cocaine imports; no exceptional special taxes (as on cigarettes); no limitations on quantity imported; no appreciable change in the labor-intensive nature of coca growing; and little likelihood of a cartel strategy to control production quantities.

Accepting these assumptions as a basis for analysis, demand for cocaine would increase because people inhibited by illegality and high price would be drawn into the market when those factors no longer applied. Prices would be lowered dramatically because production would be rationalized in the "open," inefficient trafficking patterns would be avoided, numerous intermediate dealers would be cut out, expenses of avoiding interdiction and maintaining private standing armies would be eliminated, and other costs of marketing and distribution would be reduced or eliminated.

Feeding a "normal" transnational agricultural export market would bring prices paid to growers to a "clearing house" rate, and those prices would probably drop sufficiently from their present level to make alternative crops, on economic considerations alone, attractive once again. Ironically, legalizing the physiological and psychological subversion of U.S. society would probably mean that low-income Peruvians and Bolivians would eat better because more basic food would likely be grown and probably at a more affordable price.

Coca-leaf production has been exceptionally profitable relative to food crops because it has been associated with a high-risk industry laden with cash and short of raw product that has been willing to pay whatever price needed to be paid. This exceptional profitability hinges on not oversupplying the market, on cocaine's illegality (which produces such vast sums of money), and, until now, on the relative low risk for small farmers in producing the raw product. Should any of these factors change, peasants would likely go back to growing their food and marketing a surplus for urban markets.

But they will be different peasants, having entered a money economy as never before and tasted a style of life they will be loathe to abandon. Watch out for political events in Bolivia and Peru in the wake of any decline in coca-leaf profitability.

Designer Drugs

In 1985, synthetic heroin produced in local chemical laboratories surfaced for the first time in the United States, in California. Synthetic heroin has the same effects as natural heroin but, for any given quantity, is several thousand times stronger. People with requisite skills are now working on a synthetic cocaine. The technology exists to fabricate virtually unlimited numbers of synthetic drugs, many of them from cheap and readily available raw materials.[75] If such a synthetic cocaine is produced, there will be little need for Bolivian or Peruvian coca. The market for that raw material will collapse rather quickly; there will be considerable "negative incentives" for peasants to move back to food crops.

Imaginative governments, however, will not return to policies that, historically, have disadvantaged peasant farmers (such as price controls on basic foods and deleterious credit policies,[76] but will move to incorporate small farmers in a rural-urban alliance that holds promise for all a country's citizens.

NOTES

1. García initially declared that his country would make debt repayments only as a fixed percentage of exports (no exports, no payments) and followed with an announcement that Peru, not the bankers, would set interest rates on the outstanding debt.

2. William D. Montalbano, "Latins Push Belated War on Cocaine."

3. Ibid.

4. See, as illustrative testaments, Diehl Jackson, "U.S. Drug Crackdown Stalls in Bolivia"; "Bolivia: Coke and Black Eagles"; Joel Brinkley, "Rampant Drug Abuse Brings Call for Move Against Source Nations"; Everett G. Martin, "A Little Cattle Town in Bolivia is Thriving as a Financial Center"; Scott Armstrong and Karia Vallance, "U.S.-Bolivia Relations Further Strained as Cocaine Smuggling Charges Fly"; and, "Fighting the Cocaine Wars."

5. *The Economist,* 14 March 1987, p. 63.

6. UPI release published in *Provo Herald* (Utah), 29 March 1985.

7. Widespread press coverage began worldwide as soon as the operation started, and it garnered considerable internal opposition in Bolivia even from main-line politicians ("violation of our sovereignty"). Within two months of the troops' being withdrawn, the cocaine business bounced back. See Marlise Simons, "Bolivia Cocaine Trade Revives after G.I.'s Go."

8. Coverage began systematically with a six-part front-page series in the *New York Times,* 9-14 September 1984, followed in early 1985 by cover-page feature articles in popular newsmagazines (*Newsweek,* 25 February 1985; and *Time,* 25 February 1985), and culminating in late 1985 with an extensive four-part series in the *Los Angeles Times* (1, 2, 3, and 4 December 1985). *The Miami Herald* ran an extensive four-part series on the "Colombian connection" in its editions of 8, 9, 10, and 11 February 1987.

9. Marijuana, the earlier drug "mainstay," continues to be used widely, but starting in the late 1970s cocaine usage began to grow spectacularly. So many people now use cocaine that a wide range of U.S. federal officials say it has become the most serious drug problem the United States has ever faced (Brinkley, "Rampant Drug Abuse"). Cocaine-related hospital emergencies grew from less than 3,000 in 1979 to over 7,000 in 1983 (Joel Brinkley, "The War on Narcotics: Can It Be Won?"). It is estimated that every day 5,000 additional Americans experiment with cocaine for the first time (James Liber, "Coping with Cocaine," p. 39).

10. The $16 billion figure comes from Armstrong and Vallance, "U.S.-Bolivia Relations Further Strained," p. 5. The $30 billion figure is from S. Cohen, "Recent Developments in the Abuse of Cocaine," p. 6.

11. See "method three," appendix, this chapter. For a discussion on pricing see Cohen, "Recent Developments in the Abuse of Cocaine."

12. Cocaine usage among the general U.S. population grew approximately 12 percent in 1983, with about 70 percent more cocaine entering in that year than in 1981.

More than 20 million Americans—and many more world-wide—are now estimated to have tried the drug, and at least a million are addicted (*National Narcotics Intelligence Estimate,* as cited by Brinkley, "Rampant Drug Abuse." See also Liber, "Coping with Cocaine," p. 48.

13. Suggesting here that Americans "demand" the drug rather than that Latin Americans "supply" it gets to the heart of a trafficking issue hotly discussed at the highest levels. The official U.S. position is that the cocaine problem is a supply issue ("supply-side economics"?) (Alan Riding, "Drug Region in Peru Booming Again"); that narcotics control is a responsibility of Latin American governments under international treaties, and that these governments should deal with it as a matter of international obligation and concern (U.S. Department of State, Bureau of International Narcotics Matters, "International Narcotics Control Strategy Report 1985", p. 14; U.S., House of Representatives, *A Report of the Select Committee on Narcotics Abuse and Control,* hereafter *Report*). Until 1984, however, Latin Americans viewed the U.S. problem strictly as a demand problem. In this the Mexicans, for example, concluded that there was an inherent contradiction in U.S. policy on drugs because the Americans viewed the matter simply as a supply problem beyond its borders rather than a demand problem at home, as exemplified by members of congress coming to meet U.S. drug traffickers (presumably their constituents) being released from Mexican jails to do their prison terms in U.S. jails in the exchange procedures elaborated in the early 1980s (Marshall Ingwerson, "Heated U.S.-Mexico Rhetoric Belies 'Strong' Relations"). Thus, well into 1984 there was hardly any resolve in any of the countries (other than Mexico) to tackle the domestic drug production problem. All this changed with the murder on 30 April 1984 of Colombia's justice minister, Rodrigo Lara Bonilla, by gunmen in the pay of drug barons and the murder in Mexico of U.S. drug agent Enrique Camareno Salazar. The killings have awakened many Latin American governments to what narcotics have been doing to their own societies. In Colombia, the government agreed, for the first time, to extradite criminals to the United States; no longer did people boast of going to cocaine barons' parties; judges were more discreet in what they took (Riding, "Shaken Colombia Acts at last on Drugs"; and *Newsweek,* 25 February 1985, p. 14). In Peru, the new regime of Alán García has launched impressive interdiction efforts in collaboration with Colombia (Juán de Onís, "Latin Nations Uniting in War on Cocaine"). On the other hand, many responsible observers have now come to the conclusion that the "war on drugs" will be lost unless the United States addresses the demand side of the market and goes after users as well as traffickers so as to discourage consumption (Liber, "Coping with Cocaine," p. 48).

14. In 1984, there was some indication of a nominal decrease in drug abuse in the United States. Brinkley "The War on Narcotics" quoted Dr. William Pollin, director of the National Institute on Drug Abuse, as saying that the "turnaround in drug use may already be under way." Before 1979, increases in drug use seemed to parallel increases in availability. However, whereas availability of cocaine increased between 1982 and early 1984, use patterns seemed not keep up as evidenced by a plunging price from $60,000/kilogram to $28,000/kilogram (*New York Times,* 9 September 1984, p. 12). This is a difficult matter to confirm on the price issue alone, however, because by February 1985 prices had risen to $35,000/kilogram. Although some thought the price rise was caused by interrupted supplies, it might also have been caused by more demand. However, more teenagers, according to polls, consider cocaine harmful, and slightly fewer of them are using it (*New York Times,* 14 September 1984, p. A12). Nevertheless, aggregate U.S. demand continues to increase (see Figure 12:2).

15. Before 1980, 47 percent of cocaine seized in the United States originated in South America, principally Colombia. By 1984, the South American share of the market had risen to 95 percent, and of that amount 75 percent originated in Colombia, 10 percent in Peru, and 10 percent in Bolivia. See Armstrong and Vallance, "U.S.-Bolivia Relations Further Strained," for 1980 and Riding, "Shaken Colombia Acts at Last on Drugs," for 1984. In Canada in 1982, 85 percent of the seizures were from only three South American countries. Of that 85 percent, 67 percent came from Colombia, 18 percent from Bolivia, and 15 percent from Peru (Stamler et al., "Illicit Traffic and Abuse of Cocaine," p. 51).

16. The National Narcotics Intelligence Consumers Committee, *Narcotics Intelligence Estimate,* p. 18. *Time,* 25 February 1985, p. 28, lists the percentage at 80.

17. Since Colombia finally decided in 1984 to go after its traffickers and processors (Riding, "Shaken Colombia Acts at Last on Drugs") its drug control agents, working in collaboration with the U.S. Drug Enforcement Agency, have made several spectacular seizures. One was at a compound deep in the Colombian Amazon, 400 miles southeast of Bogotá, named Tranquilandia, a self-contained community with 1,000 employees (including electricians, plumbers, waiters, and cooks) and all life's amenities plus a 3,500-foot airstrip for commerce and pleasure travel. Agents found there nineteen laboratories capable of processing 300 tons of cocaine a year. Police poured the fourteen tons of cocaine they found (worth over $280 million in Colombia—figured at $20,000/kilogram) into the nearby Yari river (*Time,* 25 February 1985, p. 26). Information on additional successes (and failures, too) may be found in the following: Riding, "Drug Region in Peru Booming Again"; "Drug Raid in Peru Nets Four Colombian Officers"; Everett G. Martin, "High Drama in the Jungles of Peru: Fight Against Cocaine is a Tangled-up Affair"; Jonathan Cavanagh, "Peru Rebels Threaten U.S. Drug Program"; Martin, "A Little Cattle Town"; Juán de Onís, "Colombia Cracks Down but the Marijuana Gets Through Them"; F. Raul Jeri, "Coca-Paste Smoking in Some Latin American Countries: A Severe and Unabated Form of Addiction"; Stamler et al., "Illicit Traffic and Abuse of Cocaine"; "Fighting the Cocaine Wars"; U.S., House of Representatives, *Report;* Jackson, "U.S. Drug Crackdown Stalls"; Hoge Warren, "Bolivians Find a Patron in Reputed Drug Chief"; Joel Brinkley, "Vast, Undreamed-of Drug Use Feared"; "U.S. Suspends Drug Fight in Peru as Deaths from Attack Reach 19"; Joel Brinkley, "Bolivia Drug Crackdown Brews Trouble"; Joel Brinkley, "In the Drug War, Battles Won and Lost"; Marshall Ingwerson, "Agents Targeted in Growing Drug War: Heightened Violence May Reflect Smugglers' Desperation"; "Cocaine: The Evil Empire"; Ingwerson, "Heated U.S.-Mexico Rhetoric"; Francisco Ortiz Pinchetti, et al., *La Operación Condor;* Warren Richey, "U.S. Praises Colombian Government for Drug Crackdown"; Charles Lane, "Peru Steps up War on Cocaine Industry"; U.S. Department of State, Bureau of International Narcotics Matters, "Strategy Report: Midyear Update"; Montalbano, "Latins Push Belated War on Cocaine;" Ingwerson, "Anti-cocaine Push Escalates"; and, Onís, "Latin Nations Uniting in War on Cocaine." A general treatment of drug-law enforcement is by Caffrey, "Counter-Attack on Cocaine Trafficking." The developments in Cuba are reported by Remos, "Cuba's Drug Trafficking Bank"; the case is argued vigorously by George Shultz, "The Campaign Against Drugs: The International Dimension."

18. Ingwerson, "Anti-cocaine Push Escalates."

19. As services have developed in Latin American countries to supply this demand, social and political fallout have begun to strain the fabric of the societies and have caused untold misery to individual drug users who have found novel ways to use the

coca alkaloids, including mixing coca paste with their tobacco. See Cohen, "Recent Developments"; Jeri, Proceedings of the Inter-American Seminar, Chapter 6; Ponce Caballero, "Coca, Cocaína, Trafico"; Cagliotti "La Taxicomanía de la Coca"; Gutiérrez-Noriega and Zapata Ortiz, *Estudios Sobre la Coca y la Cocaína en el Perú*; and Briceño P., *Los Drogas en el Perú*. A general clinical treatment of the effects of cocaine is Chapter 8 in Ashley, *Cocaine,* but his more or less "clean bill" must be counterbalanced. See Jeri "Coca-Paste Smoking in Some Latin American Countries."

20. The anecdotes on government corruption are astonishing (judges, for example, are being offered, and accepting, several hundred thousand dollars to vacate the trials of minor traffickers; in the early 1980s the highest national leaders in the Bolivian government and military jumped into the "trough" for all they could get). For illustrative material, see "Bolivia: Coke and Black Eagles," *Newsweek,* 23 November 1981; Martin, "A Little Cattle Town in Bolivia"; Armstrong and Vallance, "U.S.-Bolivia Relations"; "Fighting the Cocaine Wars," *Time,* 25 February 1985; Warren, "Bolivians Find a Patron"; Brinkley, "Rampant Drug Abuse"; Riding, "Shaken Colombia"; "Cocaine: The Evil Empire," *Newsweek,* 25 February 1985; Riding, "Bolivia Drug Crackdown"; and, Montalbano, "Latins Push Belated War."

21. In March 1961, a UN conference completed a draft of the Single Convention on Narcotic Drugs that codified nine previous international narcotic conventions that different nations had agreed to between 1912 and 1953. In addition to getting everything into one document, the 1961 convention established for the first time provisions governing the cultivation of the coca bush and cannabis plant, similar to what had been provided for opium production by the Protocol of 1953 and carried forward in the Single Convention. In 1964 Peru ratified the convention, as have other Latin American countries (U.S. House of Representatives, A Report of the Select Committee, 1984, pp. 18, 19, and 22). The only country with which the United States has normal diplomatic relations that is not bound by such a formal agreement is Jamaica (Treaster, "Jamaica, Close U.S. Ally").

The U.S. House of Representatives team that visited Latin America in 1983 was exceedingly exercised at Bolivia's and Peru's failure to live up to, or even to attribute much importance to, their Single Convention agreements (U.S. House of Representatives, A Report of the Select Committee, 1984).

22. The technical terms and laboratory characteristics of cocaine are discussed by Morales-Vaca, "A Laboratory Approach to the Control of Cocaine in Bolivia."

23. The consumption figures come from U.S. Bureau of International Narcotics Matters "International Narcotics Control Strategy Report 1985" pp. 52, 53, 117, and 118. The report lists Peru with 3 million coca chewers, Bolivia with 450,000.

24. There are twenty-six varieties of coca with an alkaloid content running from 0.5 to 2.5 percent. The coca in Peru and Bolivia is the best quality; that in Colombia and Ecuador renders fewer alkaloids. The Epadú plant, suitable for the Amazon River basin of Colombia and Brazil, renders even less (U.S. House of Representatives A Report of the Select Committee, 1984, p. 18; and *Time,* 25 February 1985, p. 32).

25. Drug expansion in Argentina is predominately for export. Argentina records lower drug abuse per capita than does either the United States or Europe, and there is widespread revulsion there regarding illicit drug use. (See U.S. Department of State, Bureau of International Narcotics Matters, "Strategy Report, Midyear Update," p. 35).

26. Fernando Homen de Melo, "Unbalanced Technological Change and Income Disparity in a Semi-open Economy: The Case of Brazil"; Steven E. Sanderson, *The Trans-*

formation of Mexican Agriculture: International Structure and the Politics of Rural Change; and, Steven E. Sanderson, "The Emergence of the 'World Steer': International and Foreign Domination in Latin American Cattle Production."

27. Peru was carrying out negligible drug-law enforcement, financial transactions were not being monitored, and coca-bush licensing laws were not being enforced.

28. "Bolivia: Coke and Black Eagles," *Newsweek,* 23 November 1981; and Martin, "A Little Cattle Town."

29. The Peruvian estimates vary from $850 million (U.S. House of Representatives, A Report of the Select Committee, 1984, p. 20) to $1 billion (Martin 1984). *Time* and *Newsweek* both list Bolivia's 1984 gross at $2 billion (issues of 25 February 1984, pp. 31 and 18 respectively). Martin considered Bolivia's 1983 gross to be $1.5 billion.

30. High-rise apartments in Panama and Miami and bank accounts in Switzerland.

31. For Peru, the estimate is reported in Jackson, "Model Anti-Drug Drive Fails"; for Bolivia, see Martin, "A Little Cattle Town."

32. "Bolivia: Coke and Black Eagles," *Newsweek,* 23 November 1981.

33. Brinkley, "Bolivia Drug Crackdown"; Riding, "Shaken Colombia Acts."

34. The increasing practice of large food companies not owning land outright but contracting with local providers for agricultural inputs still constitutes effective large-company control over land in that incomes so derived accrue to those who can grow for an international market and make the capital investment necessary to do so, and they are told what they can and cannot do to make that income.

35. Michael Lipton, *Why Poor People Stay Poor,* distinguishes between the "poor" and the "ultra poor," the latter defined as those spending 80 percent or more of their income on food.

36. Perhaps the best illustration is Sanderson, *The Transformation of Mexican Agriculture.*

37. Colombia is omitted from consideration at the coca-leaf production level because its forte has been processing, although recently it has also begun to grow coca. Refer to Table 12.1 for relative production figures.

38. Department of State, Bureau of International Narcotics Matters, "Strategy Report 1985," pp. 71 and 111.

39. Cohen "Recent Developments." See also, U.S. House of Representatives 1984:20.

40. The general rule of thumb is a factor of ten, that is, coca income is about ten times better than for the next best crop (See Montalbano, "Coca Valley: Peru Jungle Surrealism"). In reality the ratios range from double to fifty times as much (see Table 12.2). No small wonder, then, that it is difficult to persuade peasants to adopt a different crop and cropping pattern, especially when in the upper Huallaga Valley rubber, bananas, coffee, and cacao have all had boom and bust cycles. Nevertheless, the climate and soil are suited to a wide variety of crops.

41. U.S. Department of State, Bureau of International Narcotics Matters, "Strategy Report 1985," pp. 52 and 117 reported the Peruvian hectareage to be 60,000, and that for Bolivia to be 35,000. In 1984 an additional 15,000 hectares of the crop were being grown in Colombia, primarily in the southern and eastern departments of Cauca, Guaviare, Meta, Vaupes, and Caqueta (ibid., p. 61). The 1986 figures, based on one hectare producing, on the average, one metric ton of coca leaves per annum, come from U.S. Department of State, Bureau of International Narcotics Matters, "International Narcotics Control Strategy Report", March 1987, p. 24.

42. Martin, "A Little Cattle Town."

43. "Bolivia Leader Starts a Fast," *New York Times,* 27 October 1984.

44. National Narcotics Intelligence Consumers Committee, *Narcotics Intelligence Estimate,* p. 22. See also U.S. Department of State, Bureau of International Narcotics Matters, "Strategy Report, Midyear Update 1985," p. 24.

45. Riding, "Shaken Colombia Acts."

46. Ibid.

47. Fernando Homem de Melo, *O Problema do Alimentar do Brazil,* and "Commercial Policy, Technology, and Food Prices in Brazil."

48. Sanderson, *The Transformation of Mexican Agriculture.*

49. U.S. Department of State, Bureau of International Narcotics Matters, "Strategy Report, 1985," pp. 71 and 111.

50. F. LaMond Tullis, "The Current View on Rural Development: Fad or Breakthrough in Latin America"; and, Robert L. Ayres, *Banking on the Poor.*

51. Ironically, this is precisely the mix, in legitimate agriculture and small-scale industry, that John W. Mellor called for in his path-setting book *The New Economics of Growth: A Strategy for India and the Developing World.*

52. In Bolivia bankers go out to backwater areas to trade for coca-dollars (Martin, "A Little Cattle Town"). In Tocache, a tiny town north of Tingo María in Peru's upper Huallaga Valley, one auto dealer reported selling 27 vehicles on a Sunday afternoon (Jackson, "Model Anti-Drug Drive Fails").

53. Physiological effects are discussed in Cohen, "Recent Developments," and Jeri, "Coca-Paste Smoking." The unfortunate political and social side effects are discussed in Riding, "Shaken Colombia Acts" and Montalbano, "Latins Push."

54. The assumption of course, is that although peasants may be prone to "risk-minimizing" as opposed to "profit-maximizing" behavior, they are still motivated to earn increased incomes when they believe they can. For discussions of "moral economy" and "political economy" views of the peasantry, see Forest D. Colburn, "Current Studies of Peasants and Rural Development: Application of the Political Economy Approach," pp. 437-449, and Samuel L. Popkin, *The Rational Peasant: The Political Economy of Rural Society in Vietnam.* In any event, it is noted in a number of sources (although quantitative figures are hard to find) that in many parts of Bolivia, Colombia, and Peru, the coca plant has displaced the fruits, grains, tea, cocoa, and coffee that used to be cultivated. See, for example, Jeri, "Coca-Paste Smoking," p. 24, who cites as his sources Cagliotti, "La Economía de la Coca," pp. 161-165, and Árias-Ramírez, "Uso de Estupefacientes."

55. An important discussion on food supply and food production issues that affect pricing is by James W. Wilkie and Manuel Moreno-Ibáñez, "New Research on Food Production in Latin America."

56. Cavanagh, "Peru Rebels Threaten U.S. Drug Program."

57. Cynthia McClintock, "After Agrarian Reform and Democratic Government: Has Peruvian Agriculture Developed?"

58. Ibid.

59. One Bolivian rancher (presumably more) could not run cattle anymore because of the labor costs (Martin, "A Little Cattle Town"). In Peru in 1984 migrant farm workers were paid less then $3 a day to work in rice fields but could make $16 a day picking coca leaves (Jackson, "Model Anti-Drug Drive Fails"). In Bolivia, wage rates in 1983 tripled for field hands to $10 a day. If peasants got into processing coca leaves into an intermediate product—coca paste—they could earn $50 a night. Prisoners were even

let out of jail at night to make paste out of leaves—to the benefit, presumably, of their wardens (Martin, "A Little Cattle Town"). For further discussions on this point, see Brinkley, "Bolivia Drug Crackdown"; Riding, "Drug Region in Peru"; and U.S. Department of State, Bureau of International Narcotics Matters, Strategy Report, 1985, p. 71. The distortions continued in 1986. Bolivian *pisadores* ("coca stampers") could earn from $10 to $17 a night—the monthly salary of a public employee. See Susanna Rance, "Bolivia: Coca Trade Warps Economy, Way of Life."

60. See the demographic discussion in Tullis, "California and Chile in 1851."

61. The aggregate data do not give regional information on this matter, but anecdotal evidence gives the impression that the phenomenon is probably widely spread.

62. F. LaMond Tullis, "Food Aid and Political Instability."

63. McClintock, "After Agrarian Reform."

64. Wilkie and Moreno-Ibáñez, "New Research on Food Production."

65. McClintock, "After Agrarian Reform."

66. Insofar as this line of argument holds, it is therefore ironic that U.S. food aid to Bolivia and Peru helps to underwrite the cocaine trade!

67. Assumes international demand to be 120 tons per annum and production 165 tons per annum net of interdiction. About 45 tons per annum may have been stockpiled. Cohen ("Recent Developments," p. 6) concludes that in 1983 there was a worldwide demand of 80 tons, supplies of 130 tons, and 50 tons stockpiled.

68. One of the best illustrations from 1985 came in November, when squadrons from the Peruvian National Police Force staged airborne raids throughout Peru's upper Huallaga Valley. They dynamited forty of the valley's fifty-seven clandestine airstrips, destroyed 2,000 pounds of coca paste worth almost $500 a pound, destroyed forty-eight facilities for processing the paste, burned more than 7,000 pounds of raw coca leaves and 55,000 pounds of partially processed leaves. But coca-leaf production continues to increase in the valley, with latest U.S. estimates at over 40,000 hectares (Lane, "Peru Steps Up War," p. 11). Onís, "Latin Nations Uniting" reported on the combined Colombian-Peruvian Operation Condor. Intelligence had located an airstrip sixty miles from the Peruvian border that seemed promising (six small airplanes were in bay there). The operation led to the discovery of six cocaine laboratories, including a modern "super-laboratory" in the process of installation. "It had a 300 horsepower generator, steel vats, pumps, and centrifuges capable of producing up to 300 kilograms of cocaine a day." Under the shade of the treetops was a rest house for pilots with a large sign reading, "Welcome to Carpanalandia." Coca-leaf production, in spite of crop eradication, continues apace.

69. "Bolivian Coca Farmers End Seige Against Drug Officers' Camp," *Deseret News* (Utah), 12 January 1986.

70. Onís, "New Bolivian Road."

71. Lane, "Peru Fights Drug Traffic."

72. Crop diversification information may be found in U.S. House of Representatives, *Report,* pp. 40-45.

73. Martin, "High Drama."

74. See Liber ("Coping with Cocaine"), who gives an insightful review of Steven Wisotsky's "Exposing the War on Cocaine: The Futility and Destructiveness of Prohibition," *Wisconsin Law Review,* 1983. Wisotsky, who offers one of the most articulate arguments in support of decriminalizing cocaine, also raises a number of objections to his own proposal, among them that it has no chance of being enacted, that society is not

ready for it, that the British failed in decriminalizing heroin, and that more people, unfortunately, would become cocaine users.

75. Armstrong, "'Designer' Drugs Threaten."
76. Tullis, "Current Views on Rural Development," pp. 232-236.

APPENDIX

Determining the Global Value of Cocaine Trade Transactions

Four general ways, all imputational and subject to substantial error, may be used to calculate the global street-value transaction price of cocaine. These calculations use (1) the estimated foreign-exchange earnings for the principal countries times 10 to 15, the drug's estimated value added sold by the gram in the United States, Canada, and Europe (this does not consider value-added differentials in the respective countries or other cost factorings); (2) extrapolations from drug seizures in the countries of destination, assuming that about 10 percent of the traffic is interdicted and then multiplying the balance by prevailing retail cocaine prices; (3) assumptions about country-specific coca-leaf production, global value-added capabilities, successful manufacture and transport net of interdiction and other losses, and then multiplying the result by prevailing destination prices of cocaine; and, (4) production estimates of refined cocaine and the amount marketed net of interdiction and stockpiling.

Method 1

Using the rule of 10 (ten times foreign exchange earnings), the destination price becomes $80 billion; the rule of 15 raises it to $120 billion. Using this method and these assumptions, street-value transactions of cocaine amounted to between $80 billion and $120 billion in 1984.

Table 12.A1   Estimated Foreign Exchange Earnings from Cocaine Traffic (Billions of U.S. dollars)

		1984[a]	1983[a]
Peru		1[b]	
Bolivia		2[c]	1.5[d]
Colombia		5[c]	
	Total	8 bil.	

[a] These figures are not net returns to the economy of the respective countries because traffickers conceal fifty percent or more of their gross income abroad.
[b] Everett G. Martin, "High Drama in the Jungles of Peru," p. 1.
[c] *Time,* 25 February 1985, p. 31.
[d] Everett G. Martin, "A Little Cattle Town in Bolivia is Thriving as a Financial Center."

Method 2

As of this writing, figures for the second method based on seizures are not available, except for Canada, and those appear to be erroneous.[1]

Method 3

The third method renders a figure not inconsistent with the first. It starts with estimated coca-leaf production, as in Table 12.A2.

Accounting for coca-leaf losses, seizures, and consumption, the following emerges for 1984:

If, in 1984, 74,000 tons of coca leaves were available for illegal trade, those from Bolivia and Peru rendered about 785 tons of coca paste (@1.25 percent alkaloid content) and those from Colombia and Ecuador about 83 tons (@0.75 percent),[2] for a total of 868 tons. While a trained and skilled technician using basic equipment can produce cocaine hydrocloride from high quality coca paste directly on a 1:1 or 1:1.1 basis, in practice much of the coca paste is neither that pure nor many of the technicians working in small-scale factories that efficient. Assuming a 3:1 ratio (the worst reported was 4:1) on the average, the available cocaine hydrocloride would be about 289 tons. Because of enhanced drug enforcement efforts, especially in Colombia, but also in other Latin American countries and the U.S., assume that 50 percent of the available product was either destroyed or stockpiled.[3] Then supplies on the black market may have exceeded 145 metric tons. The value of this tonnage at the February 1985 wholesale prices in Miami ($35,000/kilo; assumed to be representative worldwide) amounts to more than $5 billion or, when cut to 25 percent (up from 12

Table 12.A2 Estimated Coca Leaf Production in Metric Tons (mid-range estimates)

	1986	1985	1984	1983
Peru	107,500	95,200	56,820	45,000
Bolivia	48,460	47,200	49,200	38,000
Colombia	12,600	12,400	11,680	11,215
Ecuador	1,000	895	895	
Total	169,560	155,695	118,595	94,215

Sources: The 1983 and 1984 figures are from U.S. Department of State, Bureau of International Narcotics Matters, "International Narcotics Control Strategy Report, 1985," p. 4. Production estimates are stated post-eradication but have not been discounted for loss, domestic consumption, or seizures. The 1985 and 1986 figures are from the above bureau's March 1987 report, p. 24.

All estimates are subject to considerable uncertainty. The Department of State's figures tend to be lower than others' estimates. For example, in September 1986 the Bolivian senate released a report estimating coca-leaf production in 1985 at 174,163 metric tons, over three times the State Department's figure for the same year. (See Roger Atwood's report for Reuter News Agency, "Cocaine Business Still Booming, Reports Bolivia.")

Table 12.A3   Availability of Coca Leaf for Illicit Trade, 1984 (metric tons)

	Bolivia	Peru	Colombia	Ecuador
Harvested	49,200	56,820	11,680	895
Loss	4,930	5,680	584	50
Seizures	500	42		42
Chewing	14,000	14,000	500	
Flavoring and Pharmaceutical	2,000	2,000		
Available for Illicit Trade	27,770	35,098	10,596	530
Total, four countries = 73,994 metric tons				

Source: U.S. Department of State, Bureau of International Narcotics Matters, *International Narcotics Control Strategy Report, 1985:* data for Bolivia, p. 52; Peru, p. 117; Colombia, p. 74; Ecuador, p. 90. The seizures in Bolivia were listed at 10 percent, clearly too high for the prevailing narcotics interdiction activity there in 1984. I have arbitrarily listed Bolivia's seizures at 500 tons, an amount I believe to be closer to the mark.

percent in 1980)[4] and sold at $100/gram on the retail market, $58 billion.

Using the *1986* estimates at constant ratios of loss and seizures, the value rises 43 percent to nearly $83 billion.[5]

Method 4

Using cocaine production estimates from a Department of State publication and reasonable extrapolations where those estimates are not present, and assuming 10 percent interdiction in the countries of destination, the figures in Table 12.A4 emerge. With 10 percent interdiction, 165 tons may have been available for sale. The value at the February 1985 wholesale rate in Miami of $35,000/kilogram would be nearly $6 billion or, when cut to 25 percent (up from 12 percent in 1980) and sold at $100/gram on the street, $66 billion.

Table 12.A4   Cocaine Production, 1984 (metric tons)

Countries	Cocaine Production
Argentina	6
Bolivia	47
Brazil	8
Colombia	99
Ecuador	1
Panama	1
Peru	22
Total	184

Source: Table 12.1

According to a 1985 statement by U.S. Vice President George Bush, head of President Ronald Reagan's South Florida Task Force on drug interdiction, the illicit drug trade brings in about $100 billion a year.[6] When Marijuana, heroin, and other illegal drugs are added to the $66 billion on cocaine derived from this estimate, the figure is probably not far from the mark.

NOTES TO THE APPENDIX

1. Stamler, et al., "Illicit Traffic and Abuse of Cocaine," p. 46.

2. There are 26 varieties of coca with an alkaloid content ranging from 0.5 percent to 2.5% percent The coca leaves in Peru and Bolivia are the best quality; those grown in the Colombian and Ecuadorian highlands render less. Although the Epadú plant (natural to the Amazon river basin of Colombia and Brazil) is, in 1987, being increasingly exploited, it renders even less (around 0.25 percent). See U.S., House of Representatives, International Narcotics Control Study Missions to Latin America and Jamaica, August 6-21, 1983, and Hawaii, Hong Kong, Thailand, Burma, Pakistan, Turkey, and Italy, January 4-22, 1984, *A Report of the Select Committee on Narcotics Abuse and Control,* p. 18, and *Time,* 25 February 1985, p. 32.

3. After a period of price declines in the U.S. (indicating an abundance of the crop entering the country) that saw the wholesale price drop in Los Angeles from over $60,000 a kilogram in 1982 to $30,000 in 1984 (See *New York Times,* September 9, 1984, p. 12), the price plummeted even further in Miami to $23,000 per kilogram. In the last six months of 1984, however, wholesale prices rose 35 percent, to $35,000 per kilogram in Miami. (See *Time,* "Fighting the Cocaine Wars.") The wholesale price in Los Angeles in early 1987 was quoted at $37,500 per kilogram (see "Nearly 1 Ton of Cocaine Is Impounded in L. A.").

4. UN, Division of Narcotic Drugs, *Bulletin on Narcotics,* p. 6.

5. U.S. Department of State, Bureau of International Narcotics Matters, "International Narcotics Control Strategy Report," March 1987.

6. *Time,* 25 February 1985, p. 27.

Part 5

Development and Food Security in the Middle East

Alan Richards

13

Food Problems and State Policies in the Middle East and North Africa

One of the most serious problems facing the Middle East and North Africa (MENA, hereafter) is the region's growing inability to feed itself. The food problems of this region are, however, markedly different from those of sub-Saharan Africa, with its falling per capita agricultural production, or of South Asia, with its extraordinarily high levels of human misery. Rather, the problem is one of the rising imbalance between consumption and domestic production, a gap that constituted the Achilles' heel of the oil boom of the 1970s. Despite slackening oil prices and (for many) declining export revenues, this "food gap" has continued to grow. Rapidly escalating effective demand and sluggish domestic supply response have made MENA the least food-self-sufficient region in the world. Food security consequently dominates discussions of food policy in the region.

In this chapter, I make two principal arguments. First, the imbalance between demand and domestic supply will continue for the foreseeable future. Second, this disequilibrium has generated, and will continue to generate, substantial private and public responses that are transforming agriculture and rural society throughout the region. During the decade of the oil boom, the interaction of the trade position, the internal class structure, and the behavior of governments and farmers yielded a "model," or schema, of agricultural development and rural change in the region. This model is now under (varying)

A previous version of this paper was prepared for the International Fund for Agricultural Development and grew out of ideas discussed at a workshop held at IFAD and sponsored by the Social Science Research Council. I have benefited from discussions with the workshop participants and from comments from audiences at Harvard, MIT, Princeton, and the University of California-Berkeley. I would especially like to thank Gouda Abdel-Khaleq, Alain de Janvry, Charles Issawi, Atul Kohli, Samuel Morley, Samir Radwan, and Kutlu Somel. Of course, responsibility for the views expressed in this chapter falls to no one but myself.

degrees of pressure in the region; such pressures lead to additional responses, which in turn generate change in the region's political economy of food.

I intend to conclude with some assessment of the consequences of the current phase of austerity for the small farmers and landless of the region. I am particularly concerned with the impact of austerity on entitlements to food.[1] Despite the social importance of small farmers, and notwithstanding the high internal rates of return for projects designed to assist them, all too often governments have sharply reduced such programs. Although the entitlements of some rural groups improved during the decade of the oil boom, the current phase of austerity threatens rural entitlements as opportunities for emigration narrow, whereas urban entitlements are threatened by the budgetary need to cut consumer subsidies. I also argue that the combination of austerity with the overriding desire to increase domestic food output is contributing to further differentiation of the peasantry.

THE FOOD GAP: THE IMBALANCE OF
DEMAND AND DOMESTIC SUPPLY

The broad outlines of the food situation are not in dispute. All of the estimates of demand-supply balance in the region predict a continuing growth of the food gap, the difference between demand and domestic supply.[2] All agree that demand will continue to grow rapidly, whereas supply response faces serious natural, economic, and political constraints. On the demand side, the U.S. Department of Agriculture estimates that the cereal consumption of capital importers in MENA grew by roughly 4 percent per year from 1970 to 1979; the Arab League estimates the rate of growth of demand for food at 6.5 percent per year. Nabil Khaldi finds a somewhat lower rate of growth of consumption of 3.9 percent for the whole period from 1966-1970 to 1976-1980; from 1973 to 1980, total staples consumption grew at 4.8 percent for the region as a whole.[3] Consumption of livestock products has grown faster still; consumption of meat grew by 6.8 percent, milk by 5.1 percent, and eggs by 8.5 percent for the region as a whole for 1973-1980.[4] Consumption of fruits and vegetables also soared.

Such information does not provide direct information about changes in the nutritional status of the population. However, because the rates of growth of consumption were well above rates of population growth (see Table 13.1), growth would have to have been extremely disequalizing for there to have been no improvement in the nutritional status of the average resident of the region. As we shall see below, this is most obviously true for urban residents, whose entitlements to food are guaranteed by the state; in some countries, the rural situation is much less favorable. Other indicators, such as the improvement in life expectancy at birth, indicate that the growth of food demand and consumption is broadly based (see Table 13.2). However, the variance is very wide across countries; for some, such as the Sudan, the food situation for large groups of people is desperate.[5] And of course, however rapid the growth process, it always leaves behind some very poor (and therefore hungry) people.[6] The numbers on the growth of consumption do provide evidence on the challenge facing domestic suppliers of food.

There are three determinants of demand growth: population growth, per capita income growth, and the income elasticity of demand.[7] Population growth is often stressed to the exclusion of all other factors, especially in the popular press. However, even for cereals, much of the growth in demand has been caused by expansion of per capita incomes (see Table 13.3). Rapid population growth did make a substantial contribution to increased demand for food. All population growth rates exceed 2 percent per year and many are considerably higher. Apart from sub-Saharan Africa, MENA has the highest rate of population growth of any region in the world. Further, fertility in the region is considerably higher than what might be expected, given the levels of income;[8] poor health conditions in the rural areas and low levels of female literacy and

Table 13.1   Growth Rates, the Middle East and North Africa, 1970–1982 (percent per annum)

	Population	Per capita GDP	Index of food production per capita 1980–82 (1969–1971=100)	Agricultural output	Value added in agriculture	Cereal imports 1974–82
Sudan	3.2	3.1	87	4.1	3.7	19.8
People's Democratic Republic of Yemen	2.2	n.a.	92	n.a.	n.a.	7.4
Yemen Arab Republic	3.0	5.5	93	3.6	5.0	15.8
Egypt	2.5	5.9	85	3.0	3.1	6.8[a]
Morocco	2.6	2.4	84	0.1	0.5	9.6
Turkey	2.3	2.8	115	3.2	3.3	−10.6
Tunisia	2.3	4.7	128	3.6	4.4	14.1
Syria	3.5	5.3	168	10.0[b]	9.1[b]	2.9
Jordan	2.5	6.8	70	0.2	3.0	17.0
Algeria	3.1	3.5	75	3.9	3.1	9.3
Iran	3.1	n.a.	111	n.a.	n.a.	5.3
Iraq	3.5	n.a.	87	n.a.	n.a.	2.3
Oman	4.3	1.5	95	n.a.	n.a.	17.0
Libya	4.1	−1.7	127	10.5	9.4	4.1
Saudi Arabia	4.8	5.0	n.a.	5.6	5.2	30.1
Kuwait	6.3	−4.2	n.a.	5.5	n.a.	18.4
United Arab Emirates	15.5	n.a.	n.a.	n.a.	n.a.	9.5

[a]If food aid is included, the rate is 8.2 percent per annum.

[b]Figures are for 1970–80.

Source: World Bank, *World Development Report 1984* (New York: Oxford University Press, 1984).

Table 13.2   Percentage Decline in Longevity Shortfall, 1960–1977

Country	Percentage Change[a]
Sudan	17
Egypt	24
People's Democratic Republic of Yemen	25
Yemen Arab Republic	24
Morocco	24
Jordan	27
Tunisia	28
Syria	28
Algeria	27
Turkey	34
Iraq	26
Iran	18
Saudi Arabia	n.a.
Libya	30

[a]Percentage change in the difference between maximum life span of 80 years old and life expectancy at birth.

Source: Calculated from data in World Bank, *World Development Report* (New York: Oxford University Press).

status generally doubtless contribute to this situation.

Such population growth rates would pose a challenge in themselves. But the task was compounded during the decade of the oil boom by the very rapid growth of incomes. For five countries, incomes have grown faster than 5 percent per year, a doubling of incomes in fifteen years. Further, as the numbers used in Table 13.1 are for GDP, which excludes remittances, the estimates for countries such as the Yemen Arab Republic (YAR) are underestimated. There can be no doubt that per capita incomes advanced swiftly in the region during the past decade.

The impact of such income growth upon food demand depends, of course, on the specific foodstuff. Even for cereals for direct food consumption, income growth accounted for roughly 25 percent of the growth of consumption in the region. Cereal demand as a whole grew much more rapidly, largely as a result of the soaring demand for feed for animals. By far the largest impetus to the increased derived demand for feed and to the growth of direct demand for such "luxury" products as meat, fruit, and vegetables came from the expansion of incomes resulting from the oil boom (see Table 13.3).

Such a situation implies that even if population growth decelerates markedly, and even if the food subsidies that receive so much attention were withdrawn, the demand for food in the region would continue to increase rapidly. Only if economic growth in the region were to collapse would the rate of growth of demand decelerate markedly. Even a collapse of oil prices might not lead to a collapse of growth, as the investments made during the past decade have only now begun to pay off. Even the grim conjuncture of an "oil-price-led economic collapse" would still leave a large gap between current consumption and domestic production. Food consumption is highly inelastic downwards: governments are likely to cut everything else (except national defense) before they reduce the nation's (urban) food supply. We may conclude that there is unlikely to be any reduction in the food gap coming from the demand side.

Let us now look at the domestic supply response. First of all, it should be noted that few countries (and especially those with the natural social constraints to agricultural growth as face most MENA countries) could have met

Table 13.3   Sources of Growth of Consumption of Food, by Commodity Group and Region, 1973–1980 (percents)

A. Staples

	For Food		For Feed		All Uses	
	g	%y	g	%y	g	%y
Region	3.6	25	6.8	60	4.8	44
Oil X	5.1	39	9.4	67	6.2	50
Labor X	3.3	30	8.1	72	4.5	49
M.F.P.	2.8	7	5.4	36	4.2	38

B. Cereals

	For Food		For Feed		All Uses	
	g	%y	g	%y	g	%y
Region	3.6	25	6.9	61	4.9	45
Oil X	5.1	39	9.4	67	6.2	52
Labor X	1.6	n.a.	8.3	72	4.7	51
M.F.P.	2.7	4	5.6	54	4.3	40

C. Animal Products

	Total		Chicken		Milk		Eggs	
	g	%y	g	%y	g	%y	g	%y
Region	6.8	60	14.0	81	5.1	47	8.5	68
Oil X	12.7	76	20.8	85	9.3	66	7.8	60
Labor X	4.6	50	8.8	74	4.6	50	6.4	64
M.F.P.	4.1	37	10.1	74	3.1	18	9.8	73

g = growth of consumption

%y = percent of growth of consumption caused by income growth, using the formula g = n + y*e, n = population growth rate, y* = income growth rate, and e = income elasticity of demand.

Oil X (oil exporters) are: Algeria, Iran, Iraq, Kuwait, Libya, Oman, and Saudi Arabia; population growth rate = 3.1 percent.

Labor X (labor exporters) are: Egypt, Jordan, Lebanon, Yemen Arab Republic, and People's Democratic Republic of Yemen; population growth rate = 2.3 percent

M.F.P. (major food producers) are: Afghanistan, Cyprus, Morocco, the Sudan, Syria, Tunisia, and Turkey; population growth rate = 2.6 percent.

Population growth rate for the region = 2.7 percent.

Source: Calculated from data in Nabil Khaldi, *Evolving Food Gaps in the Middle East/North Africa: Prospects and Policy Implications,* IFPRI Research Report No. 47 (Washington, D.C.: International Food Policy Research Institute, December 1984).

such a rate of growth of consumption from domestic supply alone. For example, for the entire century from 1860 to 1959 Japanese agricultural output never grew faster than 2.2 percent per year. During the twentieth century, the agricultural output of the United States never exceeded 4 percent growth per year. Even highly protected, subsidized Dutch agriculture grew at "only" 4.3 percent per year from 1970 to 1982. Among Third World agricultural production success stories, Taiwanese agricultural growth was some 3.5 percent both before and after World War II. Mexican agricultural output expanded by 4.7 percent per year during the period of extensive irrigation investment in its northwest, 1940-1953. Such a rate was not sustainable, however, and has since fallen to roughly 3 percent.[9]

Indeed, by international standards, Middle Eastern agricultural output has grown relatively respectably. According to the World Bank, the average annual rate of growth of agricultural output was some 2.3 percent, 3 percent, and 1.8 percent for low-income, middle-income, and industrialized market economies, respectively, during the decade 1970-1980.[10] As a glance at the column for agricultural output of Table 13.1 shows, many Middle Eastern countries have performed better than this.

However, when we turn to a regional comparison, a somewhat different picture emerges. From 1961 to 1977 food production in MENA grew 2.5 percent per year, less rapidly than that of Latin America (3.22 percent) or Asia (2.78 percent) but higher than food production growth in sub-Saharan Africa (1.6 percent).[11] It is important to note that MENA countries' agricultural sectors have lagged primarily in relation to their own rates of growth of demand; the problem is not one of stagnation or retrogression, as is often the case in sub-Saharan Africa.

Increasing yields play an increasingly important role in expanding domestic supplies. For the two decades of the 1960s and 1970s, some 55 percent of the growth in food output was the result of increased yields, whereas extension of the cultivated area explains the remaining 45 percent. During the era of the oil boom (1973-1980), some 88 percent of output growth was caused by higher yields.[12] Apart from the Sudan and perhaps some areas of Iraq, little potentially cultivable, but uncultivated, land remains in the region. Consequently, the rate of expansion of the cultivated area during the past generation (1.1 percent) will continue to decline. Further growth of output in the region can only come from increasing land productivity. The region has shifted from "extensive" to "intensive" growth. The difficult and expensive process will continue to involve the state deeply and will both require and stimulate considerable rural social change.[13]

The aggregate data presented so far conceal important differences among countries and among crops. As the columns in Table 13.1 for index of food production per capita and agricultural output show, the range of country performance is wide indeed. Agricultural performance is only weakly linked to overall economic growth during the 1970s; countries with rapid overall GDP growth rates have included agricultural success stories such as Syria and relative failures such as Morocco.

The growth of production of different crops has also varied widely. Using Food and Agricultural Organization (FAO) data, we find that the output of "luxury" foods such as fruits, vegetables, poultry, and livestock products has usually increased more rapidly than production of wheat, the staple cereal of the region. Chicken production grew faster than wheat production in nine of fourteen countries, vegetable production grew faster in ten of fourteen, and fruit production grew faster in seven of fourteen. This underscores the argument that the challenge to agriculture in the region is meeting demand growth, spurred by rising incomes.

Surely much of such increases in "luxury" food production is simply the result of the working of Engel's Law (see glossary) and the higher-income elasticity of demand for horticultural and livestock products. Additional factors, such as price and credit policies, may also contribute. However, such trends not only do little to reduce the food gap, but actually increase it via the derived demand for imported feed. Further, if relatively prosperous farmers disproportionately produce the higher value crops, income gaps among farmers may increase.

One final point concerning supply response deserves mention. It will be noticed that the data in Table 13.1 indicate that food production has been declining as a percentage of total agricultural production in four countries—namely, Egypt, the Sudan, YAR, and Algeria.[14] These countries are following a "food second" strategy.[15] For Egypt and the Sudan, the explanation lies in the expansion of cotton output. For Egypt, this makes much sense; the country clearly has no comparative advantage in small grains and cannot in any case hope to feed its population exclusively through domestic production. This explanation is much less obvious for the Sudan. In the YAR, there is much evidence for the substitution of qat (*Catha edulis*) for sorghum, whereas in Algeria wine production explains the phenomenon. Without much more information on the size of holdings, the pattern of labor inputs, the structure of agricultural labor markets, relative price trends, and so forth, it is impossible to say whether this trend has improved or worsened food security or hunger in these countries.

SUPPLY CONSTRAINTS

Meeting the challenge of rapidly rising food demand from domestic production encounters a series of natural and socioeconomic constraints. The natural constraints are rather obvious. As roughly 80 percent of the agricultural area is rain fed, inadequate and undependable water supplies limit domestic supply response. The main source of food insecurity both globally and in the MENA region is fluctuations in domestic production, not price instability. Many countries face a high probability that production will fall at least 5 percent below trend in any one year. Planners must find supplementary foreign exchange to buy "unusual" (that is, 5 percent above trend) amounts of food four years out of ten. The problems posed by the natural environment are underscored by the devastating impact of the recent drought in the Maghreb and in the Sudan.

The social constraints are no less severe. We may divide such constraints into three groups, each the inheritance of a particular historical period. These are, roughly speaking, the constraints of urban bias and bimodalism (the ancien régime and plantation-like or large-farm agriculture), the effects of import-substituting industrialization policies (the era of nationalism and populism), and the affliction of the Dutch disease (the period of the oil boom). Urban bias has deep roots in the region. With a few exceptions, regimes have always been based in the cities and have neglected or abused the rural areas. Such bias persists, whether measured by rural-urban income gaps, differences in education and health indicators, or the pattern of taxes and subsidies.[16]

Land tenure systems also constrain the growth of agricultural output in the region. There is by now a large literature that criticizes the impact of a bimodal distribution of farms for both equity and efficiency of the farm sector. The combination of a large number of small farmers exploiting large, modern farms and of the large majority of the peasants seeking out a subsistence living on dwarf holdings either retards the growth of land yields or, at a minimum, biases the direction of agricultural growth against the interests of the rural majority.[17] The absence of linkages between industry and agriculture and the distortions in factor and input markets are usually cited as among the most significant unfortunate results of such a land tenure system.

The gross inequalities evident from the data in Table 13.4 are the fruits of the ancien régime in the region—that is, the period of colonial rule and influence and its immediate aftermath. The process could be characterized as the "premature spread of private property rights in land."[18] European colonists or modernizing indigenous regimes imposed private property rights in Egypt, Iraq, Algeria, Iran, and Syria. Urban-based landlords, whether wealthy merchants as in Syria or court favorites as in Egypt, accumulated large tracts of land because of their connections to state power. Just as in Latin America, the region consequently developed gross inequalities in the distribution of land ownership. This process was especially marked in the Maghreb, with its history of settler colonialism. In Morocco, some 75 percent of farmers hold less than five hectares each, accounting for some 25 percent of the cultivated area.[19]

It is interesting that the country in the region in which agriculture has performed best—Turkey—has had a very different experience. In Turkey a centralizing state continually sought to reduce the power of large landlords in the countryside lest such local potentates challenge the prerogatives of the Ottoman bureaucracy. The republican regime continued this tradition. As a result, unimodal farm systems (many small farms) are the rule in the most productive

Table 13.4   Gini Coefficients[†] of Farm Size

Country	Gini Coefficient
Syria	.461 (1970)[a]
Egypt	.601 (1961)[b]
	.460 (1974)[b]
	.550 (1979)[b]
Turkey	.629 (1960)[c*]
Morocco	.640 (1960)[c]
	.588 (1981)[d]
Iran	.624 (1960)[d]
Tunisia	.645 (1961)[d]
India	.585 (1960)[d]
Pakistan	.631 (1960)[d]
Republic of Korea	.195 (1960)[d]
Senegal	.399 (1960)[d]
Taiwan	.401 (1960)[d]
Mexico	.747 (1960)[d]
Brazil	.831 (1960)[d]
Kenya	.822 (1960)[d]
Colombia	.868 (1960)[d]
Peru	.935 (1960)[d]
Chile	.933 (1960)[d]

Sources:

[a]Calculated from data in Raymond Hinnebusch, *Party and Peasant in Syria* (Cairo: American University in Cairo Press, 1980).

[b]Egyptian Ministry of Agriculture, 1961, 1975, 1979, unpublished data.

[c]World Bank data as cited in R. Albert Berry and William Cline, *Agrarian Structure and Productivity in Developing Countries* (Baltimore: Johns Hopkins University Press, 1979), pp. 38–39.

[d]Irrigated sector as reported in Saad Eddin Ibrahim, *Population and Urbanization in Morocco* (Cairo: American University in Cairo Press, 1980).

[†]See glossary for definition of Gini coefficient.

[*]Using data from 1970, the Turkish Gini becomes .480. Calculated from data in Oddvar Aresvik, *The Agricultural Development of Turkey* (New York: Praeger, 1978), p. 37.

areas of Turkey.[20] It is unsurprising that the benefits of the Green Revolution have been widely shared in Turkey, whereas in the Maghreb, the bias of credit systems, and so forth, has generated a more concentrated pattern of benefits.[21]

Land reforms undertaken during the past generation modified, but failed to transform, this picture. Although land reforms succeeded in breaking up the largest estates and in eliminating much of the political power of their former owners, many peasants either received no land at all (for example, in Egypt only 12 percent of the peasantry received land) or received parcels too small for subsistence (in Iran, 75 percent of peasants got such dwarf parcels). The landless class remained large; in 1970 about one-third of the rural population in the region was landless.[22] Throughout the area, the upper strata of the peasantry benefited most from land reform.

The administration of land reforms often created additional obstacles. Confiscating land proved easier than redistributing it. Especially in Iraq, delays in redistribution, failures to provide credit and other complementary inputs, and the lack of trained rural cadres undermined agricultural production. Too often, governments removed large landowners, who often had also supplied credit and seed, without replacing them with anything else.[23] More successful reforms, like those in Egypt, created cooperatives to supply inputs and to tax outputs of farmers. Better-off farmers usually dominated such cooperatives. The resulting rural class structure has been characterized as a "kulak-bureaucrat" system, although some have argued that the former are far more potent than the latter. The rural societies of the region are not entirely polarized, however. There are several intermediate strata who are often linked to their richer neighbors through various social and economic ties.[24] Further, the uncertainty surrounding the transfer of property rights and decision making exacerbated the difficulties of land reforms in both Iraq and Iran.

The regimes that instituted land reforms also embarked on ambitious programs of import-substituting industrialization. Such policies, which remain in place in many countries in the region, constitute the second set of social constraints to agricultural growth. For example, Egypt, which had no alternative source of investible surplus, used the cooperative system to shift the terms of trade against agriculture ostensibly to increase the rate of investment.[25] The resulting bias against the agricultural sector that resulted from such "macro-price" policy has been extensively documented.[26] In addition, the stress on industrialization led to a very low share of the total public investment being allocated to agriculture.

It should be noted here that *some* source of investible funds is, after all, necessary. Only if some alternative source is available can a country that wishes to accelerate its growth rate *avoid* a net outflow of resources from the agricultural sector. Turkey, whose agricultural performance has been among the best in the region in the past generation, illustrates this point. The Menderes government reversed the Ataturkist policy of maintaining unfavorable terms of trade for agriculture. Some argue that the government sought to expand the domestic market for industrial goods by a policy of raising rural incomes.[27] The fact that Turkish peasants can and do vote in elections ensured that governments of quite different ideological stripe have maintained this favorable policy stance toward agriculture. During the critical period of policy reversal, the 1950s, external funds, largely U.S. foreign aid, eased the transition. The combination of abundant nonagricultural sources of funds with peasant political leverage joined to create a favorable policy environment for the only agricultural sector of the region to generate net grain exports.

Most other countries of the region have not enjoyed such a conjuncture. Among Arab regimes, only the Syrians' social origins and political base lie in the countryside. It may not be accidental that Syria's agricultural performance has been among the best in the region. Many regimes did acquire an alternative source of foreign exchange—oil revenue (or remittances, in turn dependent on oil money). However, it is well known that the inflow of oil wealth was a "very mixed blessing"[28] for oil exporters' agricultural sectors. Although there are somewhat different versions of the Dutch-disease argument, all focus on the shift in the terms of trade against tradables (including, of course, agriculture) and in favor of nontradables (services and construction) as the real exchange rate appreciates.[29] This may be explained as the result of the rate of inflation in the oil states exceeding that of their principal trading partners, the OECD (Organization for Economic Cooperation and Development) nations. On the other hand, differential supply elasticities may be stressed.[30] The shift in these relative prices leads to an outflow of resources from tradables into nontradables; consequently, agricultural (and industrial) growth suffers.

It seems, however, that the problems of the Dutch disease have been overrated. According to the World Bank, oil-importing middle-income countries' agricultural sectors grew at 2.8 percent per year from 1970 to 1982, whereas oil-exporting, middle-income countries' agricultures grew at 3 percent. High-income, oil exporters' agricultures grew at 5.6 percent. At the national level, some oil exporters' agricultures have performed quite well, as the data in Table 13.1 show. They seem to have survived the Dutch disease, largely because the state intervened directly to counteract the shift in the terms of trade against agriculture. This was done both by launching investment projects and by either directly subsidizing agricultural inputs (e.g., Saudi Arabia) or by shifting agricultural price policies that had formerly taxed agriculture heavily (e.g., Egypt).[31]

States had rather more difficulty coping with the second effect of the oil boom. The rise of urban incomes, and especially the increase in construction wages due to the building boom accompanying the surge in government revenues, stimulated rural-to-urban migration. In accordance with increasing evidence that the rural male agricultural labor supply is relatively unresponsive to wage increases,[32] the withdrawal of rural labor led to rapid escalation of farm wages.[33] Given food imports, domestic prices did not rise so fast, catching farmers in a "profit squeeze." Cries of "labor shortage" were heard throughout the region.

Because appropriate technologies were unavailable to many farmers, the outflow of rural labor stimulated by the oil boom further weakened the supply response of domestic agriculture. In come cases, the outflow of labor led to a decline in rural infrastructure, as terraces were abandoned in the YAR and falaj irrigation systems decayed in Oman and Iran. Responses to the "labor shortage" have ranged from labor imports to increased female participation in farm work to mechanization. None, however, has relaxed the labor constraint dramatically.

STATE RESPONSES

Food Imports

The first state response to the imbalance of demand and domestic supply was to accelerate food imports (see the column for cereal imports in Table 13.1). This was attractive both politically and economically. There were four economic reasons or components of the food import boom. First, as mentioned earlier, domestic production was (and is) highly unstable due to erratic rainfall. Second, the barter terms of trade moved sharply in oil exporters'/food importers' favor. In 1970 a barrel of oil would buy roughly a bushel of wheat, but by 1980 the same barrel would purchase six bushels. Although oil prices have fallen since 1980, wheat prices have also fallen, and the relative price ratio still stands at roughly six to one. Third, most MENA countries had ample supplies of foreign exchange; the balance of payments did not constrain food imports during the 1970s. Finally, in some countries urban consumer tastes shifted away from local grains toward bread wheat, a crop that was often ill suited to local ecological and economic conditions. Thus Yemenis and Sudanese shifted away from sorghum and millet, North Africans away from couscous made from durum wheat, and rural Egyptians abandoned maize flour; all replaced these local foodstuffs with imported wheat flour and bread.[34]

Increased reliance on food imports was also politically attractive for governments in the short run. First, they really had no choice in the short run if consumption was to rise. Second, food imports afford the government with a high degree of political control over strategic urban food supplies. It is much easier for a government to control and allocate food that arrives at one or a few ports than to collect grain from thousands of local markets in the countryside. Because most governments subsidize urban food consumption, and because urban food supply is a national security issue, governments were, and are, reluctant to rely exclusively on private grain traders to supply cities with food. Money spent on imported food has, of course, an opportunity cost; usually investment is reduced as a result of the use of imports to stabilize food consumption.[35] Reliance on food imports also exposes a country to substantial risks should foreign exchange availability decline, as the cases of Tunisia and Morocco illustrate. But in the 1970s, the forces favoring increased imports were overwhelming.

The levels of food dependency shown by the data in Table 13.5 prompted widespread alarm in the region. The risk of a politically motivated food embargo became almost an obsession with many government planners. However, the effectiveness of the "food weapon" has probably been overrated. First, the U.S. agricultural lobby constitutes a powerful domestic force against restricting grain exports to attain political goals. Second, the weapon is ineffective because of the fungibility of grain and multinational scope of the grain trade. Number 2 Hard Red Wheat is Number 2 Hard Red Wheat, whether it comes from North America or Argentina. There is evidence that just as the multinational oil companies restructured their global oil flows to evade the Arab embargo of that commodity to the United States and the Netherlands in 1973, so did the grain multinationals evade the U.S. wheat embargo of the Soviet Union after the invasion of Afghanistan. Finally, many countries in the region have diversified their sources of food. As Table 13.6 shows, relatively few countries depend heavily on the United States (the only potential embargoer).

However, heavy reliance on food imports undeniably carries political risks. Three countries of the region purchase at least 20 percent of their total food supply from the United States: Egypt (25 percent), Israel (34 percent), and Morocco (20 percent). Furthermore, for highly strategic *wheat supplies* the percentage is even higher in some cases: Egypt gets nearly 50 percent of all wheat and wheat flour from the United States. It is clear that a cutoff to Egypt would be catastrophic; the small size of the country relative to the world market implies that the U.S. farm lobby would be less opposed to a politically motivated boycott there than to a similar action against the (much larger) Soviets. Second, the effectiveness of the weapon varies directly with the tightness of the market; a conjuncture of relatively high wheat prices with a politically motivated boycott would probably face less U.S. domestic opposition.

Third, giving, rather than withholding, food aid is commonly thought to be a more effective political instrument for the supplier.[36] The United States has extended food aid as part of "policy packages," in which the recipient makes concessions to U.S. strategic interests; for example, the Camp David Accords could be interpreted in this light. And, of course, few countries anywhere are willing to rely exclusively on comparative advantage and market forces in their food systems.

It is not surprising, therefore, that state reactions to the imbalance of domestic supply and demand for food have not been limited to increasing imports. These additional responses may be placed in two groups: changes in investment and technological policies, including input subsidies; and changes in

Table 13.5 Food Self-sufficiency Ratios for Selected Foods and Countries, 1970 and 1981

	Cereals		Vegetable oil		Meat		Sugar	
	1970	1981	1970	1981	1970	1981	1970	1981
Egypt	81	49	56	32	94	75	100	52
Morocco	94	60	51	16	100	100	36	55
Tunisia	61	54	100	99	98	84	10	0
Algeria	73	40	26	11	97	87	0	0
Libya	25	20	42	28	60	30	0	0
Iran	98	66	33	11	90	66	100	38
Iraq	91	47	15	4	98	44	0	0
Saudi Arabia	22	7[a]	0	0	38	27	0	0
Syria	73	84	100	90	100	75	17	24

[a]Saudi Arabia became self-sufficient in wheat in 1984.

Source: U.S. Department of Agriculture

Table 13.6   Agricultural Imports from the United States as a Percent of Total Agricultural Imports, 1983

	percent
Egypt	25.0
Morocco	20.3
Algeria	8.1
Tunisia	16.8
Libya	4.0
Turkey	15.2
Syria	3.0
Israel	34.0
Lebanon	9.2
Jordan	14.4
Iraq	11.8
Iran	<1.0
Saudi Arabia	7.0
Kuwait	4.4
United Arab Emirates	4.5
Qatar	3.1
Bahrain	4.8
Oman	2.6
People's Democratic Republic of Yemen	<1.0
Yemen Arab Republic	9.1

Source: U.S. Department of Agriculture

price policies. Such policy shifts have aimed at increasing domestic supply, but have all too often either ignored the mass of rural producers or have been at the expense of the long-term viability of agricultural production. As during the period of land reform, state action, by favoring some and disfavoring others, continues to contribute to peasant differentiation and class formation.

Investment Policies

As is so common in the less-developed countries, agricultural investment has suffered from relative neglect in MENA (see Table 13.7). Most countries in the region have allocated less than 20 percent of investment to agriculture.[37] It is likely that agriculture will require much larger sums in the future, as the necessity to expand irrigation will probably raise the incremental capital-to-output ratio.

Some governments have recognized this problem during the past five years. Saudi Arabia has made a major effort to expand domestic food production; agricultural project loans in 1982 exceeded $1.18 billion. Algeria has recently reoriented its investment priorities toward its woefully lagging agricultural sector. But many countries have done relatively little.

Existing investment projects are also marred by a bias in favor of those farmers who are already relatively well-off. Such favoritism has both political and administrative roots. Richer farmers have much better access to the state; it is also easier for the very limited extension services and government agents to reach a small number of large farmers than a large number of small farmers. These tendencies are reinforced by the food security fear. The governments' main concern is to increase production; they believe, rightly or wrongly, that a "wager on the strong" is the way to close the food gap. This may be seen in three specific areas: irrigation investment, input subsidies, and in efforts to promote specialty crops and livestock production. Should such responses prove successful, the Middle East and North Africa would run the risk of replicating the Latin American situation: rapid agricultural output expansion coupled with persistent rural poverty.

There are two biases implicit in irrigation investment in most MENA countries: a bias in favor of relatively wealthy farmers *within* irrigated areas and a bias against the rain-fed zones where most of the total (and especially the poor) population live. It is well known that if irrigation is introduced or expanded into an already highly dualistic agrarian system, the existing inequalities will be reinforced.[38] This may be reflected in the design of agricultural development projects themselves. In Morocco, for example, a sugarcane project in the Gharb was designed to use highly mechanized, capital-intensive harvesting techniques, rather than try to employ the seasonal labor of villagers in the adjacent higher (rain-fed) areas.

Such biases are not merely the result of the distribution of political power and influence. Given the focus on closing the food gap, and given the link between irrigation and increased yields, governments understandably push irrigation. They consequently neglect the rain-fed areas, where usually some 80 percent of the rural population lives. For example, in Morocco, 57 percent of all agricultural investment goes to expanding irrigation; the corresponding figures in Algeria and Tunisia are 45 percent and 43 percent, respectively. Such allocations persist despite evidence that the internal rates of return on rain-fed

Table 13.7 Share of Agriculture in Public Investment, According to Development Plans, 1975–1980

Country	% Share
Iraq	23.6
Yemen Arab Republic	14.2
People's Democratic Republic of Yemen	35.0
Jordan	5.2
Syria	23.9
Egypt	3.5
Sudan	22.6
Libya	17.6
Saudi Arabia	0.9
Tunisia	11.9
Algeria	11.0
Morocco	16.3

Source: Yusif A. Sayigh, *The Arab Economy: Past Performance and Future Prospects* (New York: Oxford University Press, 1982), p. 116.

agricultural projects exceed those of irrigation: For example, the World Bank has estimated that in Morocco the rate of return for the "more favorable" rain-fed areas was some 20 percent whereas that of irrigated areas was roughly 7 to 12 percent.[39]

In addition to the link between increased yields and irrigation, governments also neglect rain-fed areas because of the lack of knowledge of how to raise productivity and incomes under such conditions. It is by now widely realized that a "farming systems" approach is essential to designing successful small-farmer projects in dry areas. But such an approach requires slow, patient accumulation of considerable socioeconomic data. Recommendations may run against powerful rural social groups' interests (for example, if small farmers have more and better livestock, their family members may insist on higher wages for work on nearby large farms). Government engineers can rightly argue that they *know* how to build a dam, and although the evidence in favor of small-farmer farm systems projects accumulates, the engineers' case typically persuades the planning ministry. Professional training and inclination thus reinforce political biases in shaping investment programs.

But governments of the region will neglect the rain-fed sector at their peril. We have seen that demand for livestock products is growing extremely rapidly; most, by far, of such products are produced by small farmers under rain-fed conditions. In 1982, the government of Egypt introduced a new variety of cotton that matured later than the former varieties, overlooking the fact that the majority of harvesters (children) would be in school by the time the new variety matured. Consequently, the crop suffered substantial losses. The relative lack of adequate small-farmer projects has also contributed to the rural exodus to the cities and to the ecological destruction (especially deforestation) that is undermining irrigation systems in both Tunisia and Morocco.

In short, the numbers of people involved, the initial rates of return, and the need to maintain existing irrigation systems all lend support to a strategy that stresses the role of small farmers in rain-fed areas. So far, however, despite the efforts of international agencies such as the International Foundation for Agricultural Development (IFAD) and the International Center for Agricultural Research in Dry Areas (ICARDA) to promote such activities, all too little has been done.

Some of the attempts to expand production via irrigation have had unfortunate ecological consequences. Sometimes this is a case of purchasing output now at the expense of output in the future. Of course, this phenomenon is hardly limited to MENA or indeed to the less-developed countries. But the problem is acute. Salinity plagues much of Egyptian and Syrian land because adequate drainage was not provided when irrigation was expanded. Despite ten years of effort and substantial funding from the World Bank, a majority of Egyptian land still suffers from some degree of salinity. Libyan and Saudi Arabian agricultural expansion has been criticized as "water-mining" agriculture. In some areas of the Gafara coastal plain in Libya, the water table fell at a rate of

five meters per year; many hydraulic scientists believe that the coastal resources are now at serious risk as a result of excessively rapid expansion of
well irrigation.[40]

Price Policies

The second government domestic supply response to the food gap has been to
subsidize modern agricultural inputs. There exists a bewildering array of subsidies in the region, but low prices for fertilizers and tractors are especially
prominent. Saudi Arabia spent some $376.5 million in 1982/83 subsidizing in-
puts. In Egypt, tractors receive direct subsidies for purchase (credit subsidies)
and operation (cheap fuel), as well as indirect subsidies via price policies.[41] The
same situation prevails in North Africa and Syria. As Table 13.8 shows, tractor
and fertilizer use has increased dramatically in all countries. It is commonplace
that relatively prosperous farmers reap the lion's share of such subsidies. For
example, in the Gharb region of Morocco, farmers holding more than twenty
hectares each (less than 3 percent of the farmers) received almost all of the
government input subsidies for that area.[42]

Some argue that differentiation of farmers by crop mix is emerging in the
region. Small farmers are said to produce the staple cereal while their better-off
neighbors shift into such high-value crops as fruits and vegetables or enjoy government subsidies for modern poultry and feedlot operations. Governments
have promoted such activities because of soaring demand and the difficulties
that small farmers have faced in trying to increase livestock production. The
principal instrument has been output price policies. In order to guarantee

Table 13.8   Use of Modern Agricultural Inputs, 1970–1980

	Fertilizer[a]		Tractors[b]	
	1970	1980	1970	1980
Sudan	31	65	0.7	0.9
Yemen Arab Republic	1	35	0.4	0.7
People's Democratic Republic of Yemen	0	98	3.7	6.7
Egypt	1,282	2,324	6.3	9.3
Morocco	130	335	1.7	3.4
Tunisia	82	135	6.5	10.6
Turkey	166	412	4.2	17.2
Syria	67	220	1.6	5.3
Iran	76	359	1.3	3.8
Iraq	35	169	2.8	4.2
Algeria	174	320	0.1	6.4
Libya	64	374	0.2	8.0
Saudi Arabia	44	352	0.8	1.2

[a]Fertilizer use in kilograms per hectare of cultivated land.
[b]Tractor use per 1,000 hectares of cultivated land.

Sources: World Bank, *World Development Report 1983* (New York: Oxford University Press, 1983)
and UN, Food and Agriculture Organization, *Production Yearbooks* (Rome: FAO).

cheap food for the cities, governments have often pushed the price of the staple cereals below the international price. At the same time, transportation costs, local consumer preferences, and other aspects of "natural protection" have joined explicit government policy to raise livestock prices and, often, fruit and vegetable prices above international levels. Those with access to subsidized credit and those enjoying political favor have been able to abandon cereal growing for the more profitable crops. Small farmers have been less able to do this.[43]

This tendency is much more pronounced in some countries than in others. In Turkey, farmers in the same geographical area typically produce the same crops; in Egypt, many vegetable farmers hold relatively small farms, and most livestock products are produced on farms of two hectares or less. "Differentiation by crop mix" seems much less pronounced in the Middle East than in, say, Latin America.[44] It may be spreading, however.

Some governments have impeded the growth of output of cereals through their output pricing policies. Indeed, some believe that this is *the* cause of the food gap. The argument holds that if only governments could "get the prices right"—specifically, permit cereal prices to rise to international levels—the food gap would shrink dramatically. Although current pricing policies do indeed introduce significant distortions into many agricultural sectors in the region, correcting such biases will provide no panacea for agrarian problems. It remains to be demonstrated that *agricultural output as a whole* is elastic with respect to price: Most of the (relatively scarce) studies of aggregate agricultural supply response to shifts in the terms of trade find elasticities of around 0.2 or 0.3. *Individual crops* are indeed highly responsive, but the case for sectoral output is much less persuasive.[45]

But the reallocation of crops is a serious problem in its own right. In Tunisia, where nominal protection coefficients for cereals are less than 1, but those for livestock products, fruits, and vegetables are above 1, it is not surprising to find sluggish growth of cereal output. Similarly, Egypt in 1987 devotes nearly 25 percent of its extremely scarce land to growing food for animals! Saudi Arabia pays farmers at least six times the international price for wheat; it is not surprising that the Saudis now have a wheat surplus. But, at the same time, the barley area has declined and, therefore, animal-feed imports have soared.

These policies may simply accelerate a trend that we might expect anyway. After all, as incomes rise and demand shifts increasingly to high-value crops, farmers might be expected to shift into "semitradables," such as fresh fruit, vegetables, and livestock products. This may be conceived as part of the Dutch disease phenomenon, in which the agricultural sector itself is disaggregated by "degree of tradability."

As the Saudi case indicates, oil revenues can make it possible for governments to modify price policies that are unfavorable toward agriculture. At the same time as the food gap grew, taxing agriculture via price policies became less essential to provide funds for accumulation or to provide adequate food supplies for the cities. Consequently, governments who were worried about food security modified their policies. For example, farmers' tax burden has declined in Egypt, Saudi Arabia, Jordan, and Syria; in these last three countries, farmers now receive prices above international levels. Yet, so far, both Jordan and Syria remain heavily dependent on food imports. Improved price policies, although necessary, are no panacea for the agricultural problems of the region.

State policy toward agriculture during the oil boom thus presents a contradictory picture. On the one hand, oil and foreign exchange largesse has permitted decreased taxation of agriculture, made available additional investible funds for the sector, and, via labor emigration, raised real wages in rural areas. On the other hand, subsidy and investment policies, along with remaining price policies, have promoted social differentiation as larger farmers increasingly concentrate on high-value, often subsidized, "luxury" foods, while smaller farmers are left with the taxed field crops and/or are simply neglected.

MENA AGRICULTURAL DEVELOPMENT IN THE 1970S: THE RISE AND FALL OF A "MODEL"

The essence of the pattern of agrarian change in the region may be summarized as follows. Very strong growth of domestic demand for food, stimulated by population increase and especially the rapid increase of incomes during the decade, could not be met from local production because of natural and social constraints on domestic supply. Governments responded with increased imports and with programs of selective incentives for domestic producers. The ensuing "model" of agrarian change had the following elements: (1) abundant foreign exchange, directly or indirectly caused by the oil price revolutions of 1973 and 1979; (2) outflows of labor from the major agricultural producers; (3) accelerating imports to feed the cities; (4) input subsidies and specialty crop promotion for the larger farmers; (5) migration and (some) increased commercialization for small farmers and the landless;[46] (6) food subsidies for the urban population; and (7) some changes in the mode of finance of these subsidies, with a general tendency to take the funds for general tax revenues, now augmented by oil and aid, rather than to obtain the revenue by shifting the terms of trade against agriculture.

This model has come under considerable pressure in the early 1980s. Because the key to the process was foreign exchange largesse, the decline in such revenues has forced many governments to move toward austerity. Morocco, Tunisia, and Jordan have been forced to try to cut government spending and to promote exports. The North African countries face particular difficulties because the collapse of their export revenues from, for example, phosphates, remittances from workers in France, or light industrial products has combined with increased debt burden resulting from high U.S. interest rates and also with the devastating impact of a series of years of drought. The situation of the North African countries illustrates the "worse case" scenario from the food security point of view: declining foreign exchange *combined with* declining domestic production because of bad weather.[47]

Some countries have avoided this fate. There are few signs that Saudi Arabia has reduced spending on or incentives for agricultural production. Despite serious unsolved social and economic problems, Egypt's foreign exchange picture remains fairly healthy, permitting the regime to avoid implementing long-overdue policy reforms.[48] So long as foreign exchange revenues hold up, countries can continue to follow the model of the 1970s. But in cases such as Egypt's, this may simply make the day of reckoning even grimmer.

The ensuing "political economy of austerity" has a number of implications for the food systems of the region. There is a renewed emphasis on export crops to increase foreign exchange; yet, the largest nearby market, the EEC, is increasingly inaccessible with the accession of Greece, Spain, and Portugal to full membership. Government retrenchment seems to hit projects in rain-fed areas particularly hard. It is understandable that planners mainly wish to increase urban food supply; this means promoting irrigation projects and helping the relatively well-to-do farmers. And, of course, governments have reduced (or sought to reduce) outlays on consumer food subsidies.

THE IMPLICATIONS OF THE FOOD GAP, STATE RESPONSES, AND AUSTERITY FOR ENTITLEMENTS TO FOOD

What are the implications of the rise and fall of the "oil boom model" for entitlements to food? Here it is essential to distinguish between the rural and the urban situations, which are usually radically different in this region. In the rural areas, entitlements are, in the first instance, determined by access to land. We have seen that much of the best land in the region is held by relatively few farmers. There has been a substantial landless class in many countries in the region. Especially in the rain-fed areas, government neglect and disincentives, ecological degradation, and the patterns of land distribution have combined with harshly unfavorable weather to create disastrous conditions (such as in Morocco and the Sudan). In the Sudan, famine conditions prevail over large areas. In Morocco, the problem has usually been transferred to the cities, now inundated with drought refugees.

Elsewhere in the region, however, small farmers and landless agricultural workers have been able to improve their situations (at least temporarily) in two major ways: by renting in land and cropping intensively (a "commercialization strategy"); and/or by emigration. In Egypt, for example, very small farmers produce the bulk of dairy and livestock products. By renting in small parcels of land and cropping them very intensively, they manage to obtain sufficient food entitlements and, in some cases, even some additional income.[49]

Of course, such commercialization strategies are not open to most of the landless. Their position can improve only through an increase in rural real wages and employment. Their situation improved during the oil boom, as higher-paying jobs appeared either in construction in the major cities or in the oil-exporting countries (such as Egypt and the YAR). There is clear evidence of an increase in rural real wages during the 1970s, implying both a considerable outflow of labor stimulated by the oil boom and an improved entitlement position for those agricultural laborers remaining behind. At the same time, the response in cropping patterns, land yields, and, so far, the pattern of mechanization, seems to have favored an increase in the demand for agricultural labor. The shift to fruit and especially vegetables has raised the demand for labor in many cases; the need to rely on increased land yields also implies considerable potential for raising the demand for agricultural labor.

On the other hand, private farmers are rapidly mechanizing their operations, usually with extensive government subsidies to do so. Although there is no evidence that this pattern has yet reduced the demand for agricultural labor, there can be little doubt that eventually continued mechanization will have this effect. The slackening of oil exporters' demand for unskilled labor may leave the remaining rural poor in a very difficult situation, as the supply of labor in rural areas grows more rapidly than in the last decade, but the demand grows more slowly, because of past mechanization.

In the urban areas, food entitlements are largely determined by political conflict. Throughout the region, basic consumption needs are guaranteed by the state. Food-subsidy programs, often grossly untargeted, assure a minimum subsistence for the poor. In Egypt, for example, they provide 15 to 16 percent of the total income for the poorest 25 percent of the population.[50] Maintaining this guarantee is absolutely essential to the survival of the state, as any major cutback in subsidies will meet violent resistance.[51] As is well known, cutting urban consumer subsidies has provoked widespread political unrest. Food riots (or "IMF riots") have broken out at least seven times in the last eight years: in Egypt in 1977 and again in 1984; in Morocco in 1981 and again in 1984; in the Sudan in 1981 and 1985; and in Tunisia in 1984. Although hardly the cause of the overthrow of the Nimeiry regime, food-subsidy cuts did provide the spark to the initial protests. Governments have usually backed down rapidly in the face of such protests; food prices remain very low to consumers and the government deficit remains large.

In most of these countries, the "food riots" are really "equity riots": They are protests against how the gains of the decade of the oil boom have been shared. Governments have often added insult to injury when cutting subsidies by pointing to alleged waste in food consumption habits. Stories are rampant in Egypt of bread being fed to chickens or water buffaloes.[52] Stories of bread winding up in the Tunis rubbish dump are said to have convinced President Bourguiba to raise consumer prices there in early January 1984. But, of course, poor people waste very little; they cannot afford such a luxury. Claims to the contrary by members of the elite simply show how far they are removed from the realities of the daily lives of those whom they claim to represent. The poor may find such an allegation particularly insulting if the beneficiaries of oil boom growth have been flaunting their wealth. This seems to be the case in Egypt, Tunisia, Morocco, and, perhaps to a lesser extent, the Sudan. Poor residents of these countries apparently felt that those least able to afford it were being asked to shoulder the burden of austerity. In short, they found the cuts illegitimate. Given their dependence for food on a politically based entitlement, their behavior is understandable.

Such a perspective is reinforced by recognition that there have been several instances of cuts in consumption that did not provoke riots. In Egypt under Nasser, per capita grain consumption fell from 115 kilograms per year in 1966 to 72 kilograms per year in 1969/70. But because these cuts were widely shared, and because the cause of the austerity was the widely supported and evident need to fight the Israelis to regain the Sinai, people accepted such hardships. More recently, Algeria raised consumer food prices by some 30 percent, again without protest. The long, bitter war of national liberation and the strong political institutions in that country may mean that most citizens perceive the state as relatively legitimate. *Infitah*-style[53] growth has also been much less marked in Algeria than in the other Maghreb countries. It is notable that the Algerians combined the announced cut in subsidies with a program to target them to the poor and to finance them by taxing luxury consumption. The Tunisians began to implement a similar policy after the riots of 1984.

It is clear that internationally generated austerity threatens urban entitlements. Equally clear is that the urban poor in the Middle East and North Africa are unwilling to suffer alone. The IMF invariably recommends subsidy cuts, rather than tax increases. Yet it has been estimated, for example, that Morocco could pay for its entire food-subsidy bill simply by levying a tax of roughly 9 percent on the income of the land of the large farmers in irrigated areas.[54] This may merely be a realistic assessment by the IMF of the nature of political economy of Morocco, however. Many, if not most, of the differences between Moroccan and Algerian policies may be traced to different patterns of ownership of productive assets.

The entitlements of both the urban and the rural poor are threatened by the current austerity in the region. The extent of this austerity varies very much across countries. Morocco's situation is very different from Syria's or Egypt's. With the exception of the Sudan, large-scale famine is probably not a threat. Nor is it likely that urban entitlements (food subsidies) will be withdrawn; resulting budgetary deficits may be covered by collecting "strategic rent."[55] On the other hand, the process of social change under the twin spurs of the food gap and responses to this gap are likely to continue the process of social change in the countryside. Unless the MENA countries can adopt "equitable growth" strategies, the situation for those at the bottom of the social scale, especially in the rural areas, is likely to remain rather grim.

NOTES

1. The concept of entitlement is, of course, that developed by Amartya Sen, *Poverty and Famines: An Essay on Entitlement and Deprivation.*

2. See, for example, Ahmad Goueli, *Future of the Food Economy in the Arab Countries* (Arabic); UN, Food and Agriculture Organization, *Agriculture: Toward 2000*; and Nabil Khaldi, *Evolving Food Gaps in the Middle East/North Africa: Prospects and Policy Implications.*

3. One of the strengths of Khaldi's work is that he disaggregates this highly heterogeneous region into "oil exporters," "labor exporters," and "major food producers." These reported growth rates of consumption of staples of 6.2 percent, 4.5 percent, and 4.2 percent, respectively, from 1973 to 1980.

4. Khaldi, *Evolving Food Gaps in the Middle East/North Africa.*

5. Although most news accounts focus on the plight of Ethiopian and Eritrean refugees in eastern Sudan, the situation in the north and east of the country may be worse. No one knows how many people in these areas are threatened by starvation; journalistic estimates range around 5 million people. See, for example, Michael Prest, "Sudan on the Brink." It is notable that livestock prices have recently plummeted in the Sudan, usually a sign of distress sales by nomads; such price changes often presage famine. See Sen, *Poverty and Famines.* I am indebted to Samir Radwan for this information.

6. Cf. C. Peter Timmer et al., *Food Policy Analysis.*

7. The formula is $D = N + Y e$, where D = the growth of demand, N = population growth rate, Y = rate of growth of per capita incomes, and e = the income elasticity of demand. Cf. John Mellor and Bruce F. Johnston, "The World Food Equation: Interrelations Among Development, Employment, and Food Consumption."

8. See World Bank, *World Development Report 1984.*

9. The Mexican case, with its "once for all gains" from irrigation and the highly unequal sharing of the benefits of such growth would seem (unfortunately) to have parallels in the MENA region.

10. World Bank, *World Development Report 1983.*

11. John Mellor, "Food Prospects for the Developing Countries," p. 2.

12. Ibid.; Khaldi, *Evolving Food Gaps.*

13. Given the overwhelming evidence that small farmers' yields per unit of ground exceed those of larger farmers, the necessity of growth of output coming from higher yields suggests a policy emphasis on such farmers. Barriers in the political economy to the adoption of such a strategy are examined below.

14. Cf. the columns for population, index of food production per capita, and agricultural output in Table 13.1.

15. The reference is to Frances Moore Lappé and Joseph Collins, *Food First: Beyond the Myth of Scarcity.*

16. See the evidence presented in M. Riad El-Ghonemy, *Economic Growth, Income Distribution, and Rural Poverty in the Near East.*

17. Bruce Johnston and Peter Kilby, *Agriculture and Structural Transformation: Economic Strategies for Late-Developing Countries,* and Alain de Janvry, *The Agrarian Question and Reformism in Latin America.*

18. That is, the diffusion of individualistic tenure forms before the ratio of population to cultivated area has created conditions favorable to such institutional change.

19. World Bank, *Morocco: Economic and Social Development Report.*

20. See Tosun Aricanli, "Agrarian Relations in Turkey: State and Peasant Property—A Historical Sketch." Large landlordism persisted, and persists, in those regions more remote from central power, such as the Cukorova (southeast) region and the eastern areas of the country. However, unlike in Latin America, such landlords had relatively limited access to political power.

21. See, on Turkey, Ergun Ozbudun and Aydin Ulusan, eds., *The Political Economy of Income Distribution in Turkey.* On the Maghreb, see Irene Hauri, *Le projet cerealier en Tunisie: études aux niveaux national et local,* and Hendrik van der Kloet, *Inégalités dans les milieux ruraux: Possibilités et problèmes de la modernisation agricole au Maroc.*

22. World Bank, *Land Reform: A Sector Policy Paper.* Landlessness is by now less prevalent, largely as the result of migration patterns stimulated by the oil boom.

23. Cf. Eric Hooglund, *Land and Revolution in Iran 1960-1980.*

24. See, for example, Richard Adams, "Growth Without Development in Rural Egypt: A Local-Level Study of Institutional and Social Change."

25. Whether the actual result was an increase in investment is debatable. See, for example, Bent Hansen and Karim Nashashibi, *Foreign Trade Regimes and Economic Development: Egypt.*

26. On the concept of macro-prices (i.e. wages, interest rates, foreign exchange rates, and the rural-urban terms of trade), see Timmer et al., *Food Policy Analysis.* On the Egyptian case, see my review article, "Ten Years of *Infitah*: Class, Rent, and Policy Stasis in Egypt," p. 4, and the literature cited there.

27. Kutlu Somel, "Agricultural Support Policies in Turkey: A Survey of the Literature."

28. The phrase is from Jahangir Amouzagar, "Oil Wealth: A Very Mixed Blessing." A fuller analysis is available in his "Oil Exporters' Economic Development in an Interdependent World."

29. See, among others, Sweder van Wijnbergen, "Dutch Disease: A Disease After All?" Indeed, some authors (e.g., Gelb) define the real exchange rate as the relative price of tradables to nontradables. (Alan Gelb, "Capital Importing Oil Exporters: Adjustment Issues and Policy Choices.")

30. Tradables are supplied perfectly elastically to a "small country," whereas the elasticity of supply of nontradables such as construction is very much less than infinity.

31. This is consistent with the argument of Robert Bates, *Markets and States in Tropical Africa: The Political Basis of Agricultural Policies.* See also van Wijnbergen, "Dutch Disease." Whether such growth rates are ecologically sustainable will be discussed later.

32. Pranab K. Bardhan, "Employment and Wages in a Poor Agrarian Economy," p. 1, and Alan Richards, Philip Martin, and Rifaat Nagaar, "Labor Shortages in Egyptian Agriculture."

33. Implications of migration for entitlements are discussed later.

34. This last shift may have been partly the result of government policy: Food subsidies, mainly in the form of (largely imported) wheat flour, are not widely available in the rural areas. See Harold Allderman and Joachim von Braun, *The Effects of the Egyptian Food Ration and Subsidy System on Income Distrubution and Consumption.*

35. See, for example, Grant M. Scobie, *Food Subsidies in Egypt: Their Impact on Foreign Exchange and Trade.*

36. Mitchel B. Wallerstein, *Food for War—Food for Peace: United States Food Aid in a Global Context,* and Robert M. Hathaway, "Food Power."

37. Although there is a lively debate among economists on how much investment agriculture should receive, Raj Krishna has argued persuasively that agriculture should get at least 20 percent of investment. Krishna, "Some Aspects of Agricultural Growth, Price Policy, and Equity in Developing Countries."

38. See, for example, Cynthia Hewitt de Alcantara, *Modernizing Mexican Agriculture: Socio-Economic Implications of Technological Change, 1940-1970.*

39. World Bank, *Morocco: Economic and Social Development Report.*

40. J. A. Allan, *Libya: The Experience of Oil.*

41. See the essays in Alan Richards and Philip Martin, eds., *Migration, Mechanization, and Agricultural Labor Markets in Egypt.*

42. World Bank, *Morocco: Economic and Social Development Report.*

43. Cf. the argument in Mahmoud Abdel-Fadil, *Development, Income Distribution, and Social Change in Rural Egypt (1952-1970): A Study in the Political Economy of Agrarian Transition.*

44. On Latin America, see Alain de Janvry, *The Agrarian Question and Reformism in Latin America.*

45. See Krishna, "Some Aspects of Agricultural Growth," for the general argument; for a specific, detailed study, see Joachim von Braun and Hartwig de Haen, "The Effects of Food Price and Subsidy Policies on Egyptian Agriculture." They show that permitting all prices to move to international levels would likely lead to a reduction in Egyptian wheat production, given the strong "comparative disadvantage" that Egypt faces in that crop.

46. In Egypt, for example, small farmers have been able to take advantage of the protected livestock market. The menu of "survival strategies" for the landless and land-poor is admirably laid out by Samir Radwan, "Rural Labor Markets in Egypt."

47. The link of Moroccan and Tunisian currencies to the French franc combined with the precipitous rise in the dollar/franc exchange rate to raise the costs of food imports (denominated in dollars) even further.

48. See my review article, "Ten Years of *Infitah*."

49. See the essay in Richards and Martin, *Migration, Mechanization, and Agricultural Labor Markets in Egypt.*

50. Alderman and von Braun, *The Effects of the Egyptian Food Ration and Subsidy System.*

51. Some have also argued that guaranteeing consumption is part of a "bread and circuses" approach of many relatively unpopular MENA governments toward their populations: Unwilling or unable to offer meaningful political participation possibilities to their people, and (temporarily) awash in revenue, many states promoted consumption as a "diversion." (I am indebted to Roger Owen of Oxford for this observation.)

52. Such stories are very difficult to document, however. Alderman and von Braun's very thorough survey (*The Effects of the Egyptian Food Ration and Subsidy System*), covering every governorate, turned up no such evidence.

53. "Opening up" in Arabic; usually used to refer to partial liberalization of import trade in the 1970s, a process that stimulated the growth of a nouveau riche class.

54. Samir Radwan, personal communication.

55. See my "Ten Years of *Infitah*."

Bibliography

Abdel-Fadil, Mahmoud. *Development, Income Distribution, and Social Change in Rural Egypt (1952-1970): A Study in the Political Economy of Agrarian Transition.* Cambridge: Cambridge University Press, 1975.

Adams, Richard. "Growth Without Development in Rural Egypt: A Local-Level Study of Institutional and Social Change." Ph.D. diss., University of California, Berkeley, 1981.

Adelman, Irma, and Cynthia Taft Morris. *Economic Growth and Social Equity in Developing Countries.* Stanford: Stanford University Press, 1973.

Alderman, Harold, and Joachim von Braun. *The Effects of the Egyptian Food Ration and Subsidy System on Income Distribution and Consumption.* International Food Policy Research Institute (IFPRI), Research Report 45, (July 1984). Washington, D.C.: International Food Policy Research Institute.

Alagh, Y. K., and P. S. Sharma. "Growth of Crop Production: 1960/61 to 1978/79—Is It Decelerating?" *Indian Journal of Agricultural Economics* 35:2 (April-June 1980):104-18.

Ali, Salamat. "Off the Standby List." Far Eastern Economic Review 120:25 (June 23, 1983):74-75.

Allan, J. A. *Libya: The Experience of Oil.* London and Boulder, Colorado: Croom Helm and Westview Press, 1981.

Amouzagar, Jahangir. "Oil Exporters' Economic Development in an Interdependent World." IMF Occasional Paper 18, April 1983.

Amouzagar, Jahangir. "Oil Wealth: A Very Mixed Blessing." *Foreign Affairs* 60 (April 1982):814-835.

Anstey, Vera. *The Economic Development of India,* 4th ed. London: Longmans, Green and Company, 1957.

"Anti-Cocaine Push Escalates, But So Do Sales." *Christian Science Monitor,* 7 January 1986, p. 3.

Árias-Ramírez, J. "Uso de estupefacientes en Colombia." Address given at the International Conference on the Effects of Drug Abuse on Society, held at the Academia Nacional de Medicina, Bogotá, 27-30 September 1983.

Aricanli, Tosun. "Agrarian Relations in Turkey: State and Peasant Property—A Historical Sketch." Paper presented at SSRC/IFAD (Social Science Research Council/ International Foundation for Agricultural Development) workshop "The Food Problem and State Policy in the MENA Region," September 1984.

Armstrong, Scott. "'Designer' Drugs Threaten to Open a New Era in Drug Abuse." *Christian Science Monitor,* 19 June 1985, p. 1.

Armstrong, Scott, and Karia Vallance. "U.S.-Bolivia Relations Further Strained as Cocaine Smuggling Charges Fly." *Christian Science Monitor,* 14 August 1980, p. 5.

ARTI. *Sri Lanka and the International Food Crisis.* Colombo: Agrarian Research and Training Institute, 1976.

Ashley, Richard. *Cocaine: Its History, Uses and Effects.* New York: St. Martin's Press, 1975.

Atwood, Roger. "Cocaine Business Still Booming, Reports Bolivia," *Salt Lake Tribune* (Utah), 3 September 1986.

Ayres, Robert L. *Banking on the Poor*. Cambridge, Massachusetts: MIT Press, 1983.

Bacha, E. L. "Uma Proposta para a Retomada do Crescimento Econômico." *Economia em Perspectiva: Carta de Conjuntura*, no. 3 (June 1984).

Baden-Powell, B.H. *Land Revenue and Tenure in British India*, 2nd ed. Oxford: Clarendon Press, 1913.

Balakrishnan, N. "Industrial Policy and Development Since Independence." In K. M. de Silva, ed., *Sri Lanka: A Survey*. Honolulu: University Press of Hawaii, 1977.

Balassa, Bella. *Adjustments to External Shocks in Developing Countries*. World Bank Staff Working Paper No. 472. Washington, D.C.: World Bank, July 1981.

Balassa, Bella. "Policy Responses to External Shocks in Sub-Saharan African Countries." *Journal of Policy Modeling* 5:1 (1983):77-105.

Banco Ganadero de Argentina. *La Producción Rural Argentina*. Buenos Aires: Banco Ganadero de Argentina (issued periodically).

Bandarage, Asoka. *Colonialism in Sri Lanka: The Political Economy of the Kandyan Highlands, 1833-1886*. Berlin and New York: Mouton, 1983.

Bangladesh. *Master Survey of Agriculture in Bangladesh (Seventh Round, Second Phase): Report on Land Utilization, Acreage under Principal Crops, and Production thereof, Marketing of Selected Crops, and Use of Fertilizer, Irrigation and Insecticide in Bangladesh during 1967-68*. Dacca: Government of Bangladesh, November 1972. Reprint.

Bardhan, Pranab K. "Employment and Wages in a Poor Agrarian Economy." *American Economic Review* 69 (March 1979).

Bardhan, Pranab K. *Land, Labor and Rural Poverty: Essays in Development Economics*. Delhi: Oxford University Press, 1984.

Bardhan, Pranab K. *The Political Economy of Development in India*. Oxford: Basil Blackwell, 1984.

Bardhan, Pranab K. "The So-Called Green Revolution and Agricultural Labourers." Unpublished. 1970.

Barkin, David. "Mexican Agriculture and the Internationalization of Capital." University of California, School of Social Sciences, Research Report No. 68. Irvine, 1980.

Barraclough, S. *Agrarian Systems in Latin America*. Lexington, Massachusetts: Lexington Books, 1973.

Bates, Robert. *Markets and States in Tropical Africa: The Political Basis of Agricultural Policies*. Berkeley: University of California Press, 1981.

Bates, Robert. "The Maize Crisis of 1979/80: A Case Study." (mimeo, 1985).

Bell, Clive, and Pinhas Zusman. "A Bargaining Theoretic Approach to Cropsharing Contracts." *American Economic Review* 66:4 (1976):578-588.

Bengoa, J., J. Crispi, M. E. Cruz, and C. Leiva. "Capitalismo y campesinado en el agro chileno." Grupo de Investigaciones Agrícolas, No. 1, Santiago, 1979.

Bihar, Aulna. *Problems of Small Farmers of Losi Area (Purmea and Saharsa Districts)*. Patna, Binar: Secretariat Press.

Bjorkman, James Warner. "Health Policy and Politics in Sri Lanka: Developments in South Asian Welfare State." *Asian Survey* 25(5) (May 1985):537-552.

"Bolivia: Coke and Black Eagles." *Newsweek,* 21 November 1981.

"Bolivia Drug Crackdown Brews Trouble." *New York Times,* 12 September 1984.

"Bolivia Leader Starts a Fast." *New York Times,* 27 October 1984.

"Bolivian Coca Farmers End Seige Against Drug Officers' Camp." *Deseret News* (Utah), 12 January 1986.

Bonner, Raymond. *Weakness and Deceit: U.S. Policy and El Salvador.* London: Hamish Hamilton, 1984.

Bornschier, Volker. "Multinational Corporations and Economic Growth: A Cross-National Test of the Decapitalization Thesis." *Journal of Development Economics* 7(2) (June 1980):191-210.

Bornschier, Volker; Christopher Chase-Dunn; and Richard Rubinson. "Cross-National Evidence of the Effects of Foreign Investment and Aid on Economic Growth and Inequality: A Survey of Findings and Reanalysis." *American Journal of Sociology* 84:3 (November 1978):651-683.

Brass, Paul R. "Institutional Transfer of Technology: The Land Grant Model and the Agricultural University at Pantnagar." In *Science, Politics, and Agricultural Revolution in Asia,* Robert S. Anderson, Paul R. Brass, Edwin Levy, and Barrie M. Morrison, eds. Boulder, Colorado: Westview Press, for the American Association for the Advancement of Science, AAAS Selected Symposia Series, 1982.

Braun, Joachim von, and Hartwig de Haen. "The Effects of Food Price and Subsidy Policies on Egyptian Agriculture." Washington, D.C.: International Food Policy Research Institute, Research Report No. 42, November 1983.

Briceño P., Carlos Alberto. *Las drogas en el Perú.* Lima, Peru: Talleres SESATOR, 1983.

Brinkley, Joel. "Bolivia Drug Crackdown Brews Trouble." *New York Times,* 12 September 1984, A1.

Brinkley, Joel. "In the Drug War, Battles Won and Lost." *New York Times,* 13 September 1984, p.1.

Brinkley, Joel. "Rampant Drug Abuse Brings Call for Move Against Source Nations: Supply Soars as Traffic Corrupts Government." *New York Times,* 9 September 1984, p. 1.

Brinkley, Joel. "Vast, Undreamed-of Drug Use Feared." *New York Times,* 23 November 1984.

Brinkley, Joel. "The War on Narcotics: Can It Be Won?" *New York Times,* 14 September 1984, p. A12.

Brown, Dorris D. *Agricultural Development in India's Districts.* Cambridge: Harvard University Press, 1971.

Brown, Lester. "The Green Revolution, Rural Employment and the Urban Crisis." Pearson Conference Document No. 35. Columbia University Conference on International Economic Development, Williamsburg, Va. and New York, 15-21 February 1970.

Bruton, Henry J. "The Import-Substitution Strategy of Economic Development: A Survey." *The Pakistan Development Review* 10:2 (Summer 1970):123-146.

Burfisher, Mary. "Food Production Recovers From Drought." In *Sub-Saharan Africa Stiuation and Outlook Report.* Washington, D.C. U.S. Department of Agriculture Economic Research Service, July 1986.

Burst, Andrew, and Eduardo Segarra. "An Analysis of Mexican Agricultural Price Policies." *Revista Ensayos* 6:1 (January 1982):1-54.

Caffrey, Ronald. "Counter-Attack on Cocaine Trafficking: The Strategy of Drug Law Enforcement." In UN, Division of Narcotic Drugs, *Bulletin on Narcotics* 36:2 (1984):57-64. Special issue on cocaine.

Cagliotti, Carlos Norberto. "La economía de la coca en Bolivia," *Revista de la Sanidad de las Fuerzas Policiales* 42 (Bolivia, 1981):161-165.

Cagliotti, Carlos Norberto. "La toxicomanía de la coca." Appendix 9 of Amado Canelas Orellana and Juán Carlos Canelas Zannier, *Bolivia, coca cocaína: Subdesarrollo y poder político*. Cochabamba, Bolivia: Editorial Los Amigos del Libro, 1983, pp. 467-468.

Callaghy, Thomas M. *The State-Society Struggle: Zaire in Comparative Perspective.* New York: Columbia University Press, 1984.

Cardoso, Fernando Henrique, and Enzo Faletto. *Dependéncia y desarrollo en América Latina.* México: Siglo XXI, 1969.

Castro, Paulo Rabello de. *Baroés e Bóias-Frias: Repensando a Questão Agrária no Brasil.* Rio de Janeiro: Sindicato Nacional dos Editores de Livros, 1982.

Cavanagh, Jonathan. "Peru Rebels Threaten U.S. Drug Program." *Wall Street Journal,* 10 August 1984.

Central Bank of Ceylon. *Annual Report.* Colombo. Published annually.

Central Bank of Ceylon. *Consumer Finance Survey.* Colombo, 1984.

Central Bank of Ceylon. *Economic Performance in the First Half of 1983.* Colombo, 1984.

Central Bank of Ceylon. *Review of the Economy.* Colombo. Published annually.

Chenery, Hollis. *Structural Change and Development Policy.* New York: Oxford University Press for the the World Bank, 1979.

Christensen, Cheryl. "World Hunger: A Structural Approach." *International Organization* 32:3 (Summer 1978):745-74.

Christensen, Cheryl, Lawrence Witucki, and Michael Lofchie. "Agricultural Development in Africa: A Comparison of Kenya and Tanzania." Paper prepared for the Curry Foundation, August 1986.

Christensen, Cheryl, and Lawrence Witucki. "State Policies and Food Scarcity in Sub-Saharan Africa." In F. LaMond Tullis and W. Ladd Hollist, eds., *Food, the State, and International Political Economy.* Lincoln: University of Nebraska Press, 1986, pp. 37-73.

Christensen, Cheryl, Arthur Dommen, Nadine Horenstein, Shirley Pryor, Peter Riley, Shahla Shapouri, and Herb Steiner. *Food Problems and Prospects in Sub-Saharan Africa.* Washington, D.C.: U.S. Department of Agriculture, Economic Research Service, November 1981.

CIEDUR. "La agricultura familiar uruguaya en el marco de una nueva política económica." Montevideo (mimeographed), 1982.

Clarke, Thurston. *The Last Caravan.* New York: G.P. Putnam's Sons, 1978.

"Cocaine: The Evil Empire," *Newsweek,* special report, 25 February 1985.

Cohen, S. "Recent Developments in the Abuse of Cocaine." In UN, Division of Narcotic Drugs, *Bulletin on Narcotics* 36:2 (1984):3-14.

Colburn, Forrest D. "Current Studies of Peasants and Rural Development: Application of the Political Economy Approach." *World Politics* 34 (1982):437-449.

Collier, David, ed. *The New Authoritarianism in Latin America.* Princeton, N.J.: Princeton University Press, 1979.

Corden, W. Max, and J. Peter Neary. "Booming Sector and De-Industrialization in a Small Open Economy." *Economic Journal* 92:368 (December 1982): 825-848.

Corea, Gamani. *The Instability of an Export Economy.* Colombo: Marga Institute, 1975.

Crispi, Jamie Soler. "El agro chileno despues de 1973: Expansión capitalista y campesinización pauperizante." Grupo de Investigaciones Agrícolas. Santiago, July 1980.

Crunden, Robert M., Manoj Joshi, and R.V.R. Chandrasekhar Rao, eds. *New Perspectives on America and South Asia.* Delhi: Chanakya Publications, 1984.

Cummings, Ralph W., Jr.; Robert W. Herdt; and Susanta K. Ray. *Policy Planning for Agricultural Development: The Indian Example.* Delhi: Tata McGraw-Hill Publishing Co., 1979.

Dahanayake, P. A. S. "Growth and Welfare: Some Reflections on the Effects of Recent Development Policy Reforms in Sri Lanka." CBC *Staff Studies* 9 (April/September 1979).

Dantwala, M. L. "The Problem of a Subsistence Farm Economy: The Indian Case." In Clifton R. Wharton, Jr., ed., *Subsistence Agriculture and Economic Development.* Chicago: Aldine Publishing Company, 1969, pp. 382-386.

DeWilde, John C. *Agriculture, Marketing, and Pricing, in Sub-Saharan Africa.* Los Angeles: UCLA African Studies Center, 1984.

Dinham, Barbara, and Colin Hines. *Agribusiness in Africa.* London: Earth Resources Research Ltd., 1983.

Dorner, Peter. *Land Reform and Economic Development.* Middlesex, England: Penguin Books, 1972.

"Drug Raid in Peru Nets Four Colombian Officers." *New York Times,* 2 August 1983, p. A7.

D'Silva, Brian. *Sudan: Policy Reforms and Prospects for Agricultural Recovery After the Drought.* Washington, D.C.: U.S. Department of Agriculture, Economic Research Service, September 1985.

Dumont, Rene. *False Start in Africa.* Translated by Phyllis Nants Ott. New York: Praeger, 1969.

Economist. 14 March 1987.

Edirisinghe, Neville. "Preliminary Report on the Food Stamp Scheme in Sri Lanka: Distribution of Benefits and Impact on Nutrition." Washington, D.C.: International Food Policy Research Institute, 1985.

Eicher, Carl K., and Doyle C. Baker. *Research on Agricultural Development in Sub-Saharan Africa: A Critical Survey.* MSU International Development Paper No. 1. East Lansing: Michigan State University, Department of Agricultural Economics, 1982.

El-Ghonemy, M. Riad. *Economic Growth, Income Distribution, and Rural Poverty in the Middle East.* Rome: FAO, September 1984.

Faaland, Just, and J. R. Parkinson. *Bangladesh: The Test Case of Development.* London: C. Hurst and Company, 1976.

Farmer, B. H., ed. *Green Revolution? Technology and Change in Rice-Growing Areas of Tamil Nadu and Sri Lanka.* London: Macmillan, 1977.

Farmer, B. H. *An Introduction to South Asia.* London and New York: Methuen, 1983.

Farmer, B. H. *Pioneer Peasant Colonization in Ceylon: A Study in Asian Agrarian Problems.* London: Oxford University Press, 1957.

Fernandes, Florestan. *Reflections on the Brazilian Counter-Revolution.* Armonk, N.Y.: M. E. Sharpe, 1981.

Ferrer, A. "El monetarismo en Argentina y Chile." *Comercio Exterior* 31:1 (January 1981): 3-13 and 31:2 (February 1981):176-192.

"Fighting the Cocaine Wars," *Time,* 25 February 1985, pp. 26-34.

Fitch, Robert, and Mary Oppenheimer. *Ghana: End of an Illusion.* New York and London: Monthly Review Press, 1966.

Flynn, Peter. *Brazil: A Political Analysis.* Boulder, Colo.: Westview Press, 1978.

Food and Agricultural Organization (FAO). See UN, Food and Agricultural Organization.

Foxley, A. "Experimentos neo-liberales en América Latina." *Estudios Cieplan* 7 (March 1982).

Franke, Richard W., and Barbara H. Chasin. *Seeds of Famine: Ecological Destruction and the Development Dilemma in the West African Sahel.* Montclair, N.J.: Allanheld, Osmun and Co., 1980.

Frankel, Francine R. *India's Green Revolution: Economic Gains and Political Costs.* Princeton, N.J.: Princeton University Press, 1971.

Freitas Filho, Antonio de, and Elisio Contini. "Análise da Situação Nutricional e das Políticas Alimentares no Brasil." Manuscript, EMBRAPA, 1986.

Freund, W. M., and R. W. Shenton. "'Vent-For-Surplus' Theory and the Economic History of West Africa." *Savanna* 6:2 (December 1977):191-195.

Frykenberg, Robert Eric, ed. *Land Tenure and Peasant in South Asia.* New Delhi: Orient Longman, 1977.

Furtado, Celso. *Obstacles to Development in Latin America.* Translated by Charles Ekker. Garden City, N.Y.: Anchor Books, 1970.

Gavan, James D., and Indrani Sri Chandrasekera. *The Impact of Public Foodgrain Distribution on Food Consumption and Welfare in Sri Lanka.* International Food Policy Research Institute (IFPRI), Research Report 13 (December 1979). Washington, D.C.: International Food Policy Research Institute.

Gelb, Alan. "Capital Importing Oil Exporters: Adjustment Issues and Policy Choices." World Bank Staff Working Paper No. 475 (August 1981).

George, P. S. *Public Distribution of Foodgrains in Kerala: Income Distribution Implications and Effectiveness.* International Food Policy Research Institute (IFPRI), Research Report 7 (March 1979). Washington, D.C.: International Food Policy Research Institute.

Ghatak, Subrata, and Ken Ingersent. *Agriculture and Economic Development.* Baltimore: Johns Hopkins University Press, 1984.

Goldsmith, Edward, and Nicholas Hildyard. *The Social and Environmental Effects of Large Dams.* Vol. 1. Overview. Camelford, Cornwall, U.K.: Wadebridge Ecological Centre, 1984.

Goueli, Ahmad. *Future of the Food Economy in the Arab Countries* (Arabic). Khartoum: Arab Organization for Agricultural Development, 1979.

Gray, Cheryl Williamson. "Food Consumption Parameters for Brazil and the Application to Food Policy." International Food Policy Research Institute Report 32, Washington, D.C., September 1982.

Griffin, Keith. "Communal Land Tenure Systems and Their Role in Rural Development." In Sanjaya Lall and Frances Stewart, eds., *Theory and Reality in Development: Essays in Honor of Paul Streeten.* London: Macmillan, 1985.

Griffin, Keith. "Efficiency, Equality and Accumulation in Rural China: Notes on the Chinese System of Incentives." *World Development* 6:5 (May 1978):603-607.

Griffin, Keith. *International Inequality and National Poverty.* London: Macmillan, 1978.

Griffin, Keith. *Land Concentration and Rural Poverty.* 2nd ed. London: Macmillan, 1981.

Griffin, Keith. *The Political Economy of Agrarian Change. An Essay on the Green Revolution.* Cambridge: Harvard University Press, 1974; 2nd ed. London: Macmillan, 1979.

Griffin, Keith. "Socialism from the Grass Roots: Accumulation, Employment and Equity in Ethiopia." Addis Ababa, ILO (JASPA), September 1982.

Griffin, Keith., ed. *Institutional Reform and Economic Development in the Chinese Countryside.* London: Macmillan, 1984.

Griffin, Keith, and Jeffrey James. *The Transition to Egalitarian Development: Economic Policies for Structural Change in the Third World.* London: Macmillan, 1981.

Grindle, Merilee S. *Politics and Policy Implementation in the Third World.* Princeton, N.J.: Princeton University Press, 1980.

Guardian (Manchester and London), 25 February 1985.

Gunasekera, H. M. "Foreign Trade of Sri Lanka." In K. M. de Silva, ed., *Sri Lanka: A Survey.* Honolulu: University Press of Hawaii, 1977, pp. 172-191.

Gunatilleke, Godfrey. "Participatory Development and Dependence: The Case of Sri Lanka." *Marga Quarterly Journal* 5 (3) (1978).

Gutierrez-Noriega, Carlos, and Vicente Zapata Ortiz. *Estudios sobre la coca y la cocaína en el Perú.* Lima, Perú: Ministerio de Educación Pública, Ediciones de la Dirección de Educación Artística y Extensión Cultural, 1947.

Gwatkin, Davidson R. "Food Policy, Nutrition Planning and Survival: The Cases of Kerala and Sri Lanka." *Food Policy* 4:4 (November 1979):245-258.

Haggard, Stephen. "The Politics of Adjustment: Lessons from the IMF's Extended Fund Facility." *International Organization* 39:3 (Summer 1985):505-534.

Halfani, Mohamed S., and Jonathon Barker. "Agribusiness and Agrarian Change." In Jonathon Barker, ed., *The Politics of Agriculture in Tropical Africa.* Beverly Hills, Calif.: Sage Publications, 1984, pp. 35-63.

Halliday, Fred, and Maxine Molyneux. *The Ethiopian Revolution.* London: Verso, 1981.

Hansen, Bent, and Karim Nashashibi. *Foreign Trade Reqimes and Economic Development: Egypt.* New York: Columbia University Press, 1975.

Hathaway, Robert M. "Food Power." *Foreign Service Journal,* December 1983, pp. 24-29.

Hauri, Irene. *Le projet cerealier en Tunisie: études aux niveaux national et local.* Geneva: United Nations Research Institute for Social Development, 1974.

Hazell, Peter. "Sources of Increased Variability in the World Cereal Production Since the 1960s." *Journal of Agricultural Economics* 36:2 (May 1985):145-159.

Hazell, Peter, and Ailsa Roell. *Rural Growth Linkages: Household Expenditure Patterns in Malaysia and Nigeria.* Research Report 41. Washington, D.C.: International Food Policy Research Institute, 1983.

Herring, Ronald J. "Economic Liberalization Policies in Sri Lanka: International Pressures, Constraints and Supports." In William Glade, ed., *State Shrinking: A Comparative Inquiry into Privatization.* Austin: Institute of Latin American Studies, 1986.

Herring, Ronald J. "The Janus-Faced State in a Dependent Society: Determinants of Shifts in Sri Lanka's Development Strategy." Paper presented at the American Political Science Association's annual convention, New York, 1981.

Herring, Ronald J. *Land to the Tiller: The Political Economy of Agrarian Reform in South Asia.* New Haven and London: Yale University Press, 1983; Delhi: Oxford University Press, 1983.

Hewitt de Alcantara, Cynthia. *Modernizing Mexican Agriculture: Socio-Economic Implications of Technological Change, 1940-1970.* Geneva: United Nations Research Institute for Social Development, Report No. 76.5, 1976.

Heyer, Judith, Pepe Roberts, and Gavin Williams, eds. *Rural Development in Tropical Africa.* London: Macmillan, 1981.

Hicks, Norman, and Paul Streeten. "Indicators of Development: The Search for a Basic Needs Yardstick." *World Development* 7 (5) (June 1979):567-580.

Hirschman, Albert O. "The Political Economy of Import Substitution Industrialization in Latin America." *Quarterly Journal of Economics* 82:1 (February 1968): 1-32.

Hogendorn, J. S. "Economic Initiative and African Cash Farming: Pre-Colonial Origins and Early Colonial Developments." In Peter Duignan and Lewis Gann, eds., *Colonialism in Africa, 1870-1960,* Vol. 4 of *The Economics of Colonialism.* Cambridge: Cambridge University Press, 1975, pp. 283-328.

Hogendorn, J. S. "The Vent-For-Surplus Model and African Cash Agriculture to 1914." Savana 5, 1 (June 1976):15-28.

Hollist, W. Ladd. "Dependency Transformed: Brazilian Agriculture in Historical Perspective." In Charles Doran, George Modelski, and Cal Clark, eds., *North-South Relations: Studies of Dependency Reversal.* New York: Praeger Publishing, 1983, pp. 157-186.

Homem de Melo, Fernando. "Commercial Policy, Technology, and Food Prices in Brazil." *Quarterly Review of Economics and Business* 23:1 (1983):58-78.

Homem de Melo, Fernando. *O Problema Alimentar no Brasil: A Importância dos Desiquilíbrios Tecnológicos.* Rio de Janeiro: Editora Paz e Terra, 1983.

Homem de Melo, Fernando. *Prioridade Agrícola: Sucesso ou Fracasso?.* São Paulo, Brazil: Livraria Pioneira Editora, 1985.

Homem de Melo, Fernando. "Unbalanced Technological Change and Income Disparity in a Semi-open Economy: The Case of Brazil."

Hooglund, Eric. *Land and Revolution in Iran 1960-1980.* Austin: University of Texas Press, 1982.

Huq, M. Ameerul, ed. *Exploitation and the Rural Poor: A Working Paper on the Rural Power Structure in Bangladesh.* Comicca, Bangladesh: Bangladesh Academy for Rural Development and Samabaya Press, 1976.

India, Administrative Reforms Commission. *Report of the Study Team on Agricultural Administration,* Volumes 1 and 2, Annexures. Delhi: Manager of Publications, 1967.

India, Expert Committee of Assessment and Evaluation, Department of Agriculture. *Report on Intensive Agricultural District Programme, 1961-63.* New Delhi: Manager of Publications, 1964.

India, Ministry of Food and Agriculture. *Agricultural Legislation in India.* Volume 6: *Land Reforms—Reforms in Tenancy,* Delhi: Ministry of Food and Agriculture, 1955. (Includes Bihar Tenancy Act of 1885. In the nineteenth century this was known as the Bengal Tenancy Act and its provisions applied to the Permanent Settlement region as a whole.)

India, Ministry of Food and Agriculture. *Report of the Indian Delegation to China on Agricultural Planning and Techniques.* Delhi: Manager of Publications, 1956.

India, Ministry of Food and Agriculture and Ministry of Community Development and Cooperation. *Report on India's Food Crisis and Steps to Meet it.* Delhi: Government Press, 1959.

India, Planning Commission. *Implementation of Land Reforms: A Review by the Land Reforms Implementation Committee of the National Development Council.* New Delhi: Planning Commission, Government of India Press, 1966.

Ingham, Barbara. *Tropical Exports and Economic Development: New Perspectives on Producer Response in Three Low-Income Countries.* London: Macmillan Press, 1981.

Ingwerson, Marshall. "Agents Targeted in Growing Drug War: Heightened Violence May Reflect Smugglers' Desperation." *Christian Science Monitor,* 26 March 1985, p. 3.

Ingwerson, Marshall. "Anti-cocaine Push Escalates, But So Do Sales," *Christian Science Monitor,* 7 January 1986, p. 3.

Ingwerson, Marshall. "Heated U.S.-Mexico Rhetoric Belies 'Strong' Relations." *Christian Science Monitor,* 27 March 1985, p. 3.

Inter-American Development Bank. *Annual Report 1984.* Washington, D.C.: IDB, February 1985.

Instituto de Estudos Políticos e Sociais. *Brasil, Sociedade Democrática.* Rio de Janeiro: Livraria José Olympio, 1983.

International Labour Office. *Matching Employment Opportunities and Expectations: A Programme of Action for Ceylon.* Imprimeries Populaires, Vol. 1, *Report;* Vol. 2, *Technical Papers.* Geneva, 1971.

International Labour Organisation (ILO). *Poverty and Landlessness in Rural Asia.* Geneva: International Labour Office, 1978.

International Monetary Fund. *Government Finance Statistics Yearbook.* Vol. 4. Washington, D.C.: IMF, 1980.

International Monetary Fund. *Government Finance Statistics Yearbook.* Washington, D.C.: IMF, various issues.

International Monetary Fund. *IMF Survey* 6:23 (1977).

International Monetary Fund. *International Financial Statistics.* Washington, D.C.: IMF, various issues.

International Monetary Fund (IMF). *World Economic Outlook, April 1985.* Washington, D.C.: IMF, 1985.

Isenman, Paul. "Basic Needs: The Case of Sri Lanka." *World Development.* 8 (3) (March 1980):237-258.

Jackson, Diehl. "Model Anti-Drug Drive Fails in Peru." *Washington Post,* 29 December 1984, p. 1.

Jackson, Diehl. "U.S. Drug Crackdown Stalls in Bolivia." *Washington Post,* 23 January 1984, p. 1

Jaguaribe, Hélio. "Conferência do Professor Hélio Jaguaribe." Transcript of a presentation to a meeting of IPEA and IPLAN, Brasília, Brazil, 24 April 1986.

Jaguaribe, Hélio. "Para Um Novo Pacto Social." Transcript of a presentation to a meeting of IPEA and IPLAN, Brasília, Brazil, 24 April 1986.

Jannuzi, F. Tomasson. *Agrarian Crisis in India: The Case of Bihar.* Austin: University of Texas Press, 1974.

Jannuzi, F. Tomasson. "Land Reform in Bihar, India: The Agrarian Structure in Bihar." In *Land Reform in India,* AID Spring Review of Land Reform, June 1970, 2nd ed., Vol.1, Country Papers. Washington, D.C.: U.S. Agency for International Development, 1970, pp. 1-79.

Jannuzi, F. Tomasson, and James T. Peach. *The Agrarian Structure of Bangledesh: An Impediment to Development.* Boulder: Westview Press, 1980.

Jannuzi, F. Tomasson, and James T. Peach. *Bangladesh: A Profile of the Countryside.* Austin: University of Texas Center for Asian Studies, 1979.

Jannuzi, F. Tomasson, and James T. Peach. "A Note on Land Reform in Bangladesh: The Efficacy of Ceilings." *Journal of Peasant Studies* 6 (1979):342-347.

Jannuzi, F. Tomasson, and James T. Peach. *Report on the Hierarchy of Interests in Land in Bangladesh.* Washington, D.C.: USAID, 1977.

Janvry, Alain de. *The Agrarian Question and Reformism in Latin America.* Baltimore and London: John Hopkins University Press, 1981.

Jarvis, Lovell. "Small Farmers and Agricultural Workers in Chile, 1973-1979." Santiago: Organización Internacional del Trabajo, Programa mundial del Empleo, Programa Regional del Empleo para América Latina y el Caribe, working paper, September 1981.

Jayatissa, R. A. "Balance of Payments Adjustments to Exogenous Shocks During 1970-1981: The Case of Sri Lanka." *Central Bank of Ceylon Staff Studies* 12 (1) (April 1982):41-92.

Jayawardena, Lal. "Sri Lanka." In Hollis Chenery, et al., eds., *Redistribution with Growth: Policies to Improve Income Distribution in Developing Countries in the Context of Economic Growth.* London: Oxford University Press, 1974, pp. 273-279.

Jeri, F. Raul. "Coca-Paste Smoking in Some Latin American Countries: A Severe and Unabated Form of Addiction." In UN, Division of Narcotic Drugs, *Bulletin on Narcotics* 36:2 (April-June 1984):15-31. Special issue on cocaine.

Jeri, F. Raul, ed. *Cocaine 1980.* Proceedings of the Inter-American Seminar on Medical and Sociological Aspects of Coca and Cocaine. Lima, Peru: Pacific Press, 1980.

Johnson, D. Gale. "World Food Institutions: A 'Liberal' View." *International Organization* 32:3 (Summer 1978):837-854.

Johnston, Bruce, and Peter Kilby. *Agriculture and Structural Transformation: Economic Strategies for Late-Developing Countries.* London and New York: Oxford University Press, 1975.

Jones, William O. *Marketing Staple Food Crops in Tropical Africa.* Ithaca and London: Cornell University Press, 1972.

Kappagoda, Nihal, and Suzanne Paine. *The Balance of Payments Adjustment Process: The Experience of Sri Lanka.* Colombo: Marga Institute, 1981.

Kapuscinski, Ryszard. *The Emperor: Downfall of an Autocrat.* Translated by William R. Brand and Katarzyna Mroczkowska-Brand. London: Quartet Books, 1983.

Karunatilake, H. N. S. "The Impact of Welfare Services in Sri Lanka on the Economy." *Central Bank of Ceylon Staff Studies* 5(1) (April 1975):201-232.

Karunatilake, H. N. S. "The Public Sector in the National Economy." *Central Bank of Ceylon Staff Studies* 6(2) (September 1976):179-198.

Khaldi, Nabil. *Evolving Food Gaps in the Middle East/North Africa: Prospects and Policy Implications.* Washington, D.C.: International Food Policy Research Institute, December 1984.

Khan, Azizur Rahman, and Eddy Lee, eds. *Poverty in Rural Asia.* Bangkok: International Labor Organization, Asian Employment Programme (ARTEP), 1984.

Killick, Tony, ed. *The Quest for Economic Stabilization: The IMF and the Third World.* New York: St. Martin's Press, 1984.

Kloet, Hendrik van der. *Inégalités dans les milieux ruraux: Possibilités et problèmes de la modernisation agricole au Maroc.* Geneva: United Nations Research Institute for Social Development (UNRISD), 1975.

Knight, Peter T., Dennis Mahar, and Ricardo Moran. "Health, Nutrition, and Education." In International Bank for Reconstruction and Development, *Brazil: Human Resources Special Report.* Washington, D.C.: World Bank, 1979, Annex 3, p. 61.

Knight, Peter T., and Ricardo Moran. "Bringing the Poor into the Growth Process: The Case of Brazil." *Finance and Development* (December 1981).

Krishna, Raj. "Some Aspects of Agricultural Growth, Price Policy, and Equity in Developing Countries." *Stanford University Food Research Institute Studies* 18:3 (1982):219-260.

Kuznets, Simon. "Economic Growth and Income Inequality." *American Economic Review* 45:1 (March 1955):1-28.

Kyesimira, Yoeri. *Agricultural Export Development.* Nairobi: East African Publishing House, 1969.

Ladejinsky, Wolf. "Green Revolution in Bihar, The Kosi Area: A Field Trip." *Economic and Political Weekly* 4 (September 27, 1959):1-14.

Ladejinsky, Wolf. "The Green Revolution in the Punjab: A Field Trip." *Economic and Political Weekly* 4 (June 28, 1969): A73-A83.

Lakshman, W. D. "Income and Wealth Distribution in Sri Lanka: An Examination of Evidence Pertaining to the Post-1960 Experience." IDCJ Working Paper No. 16. Tokyo: International Development Center of Japan, 1980.

Lane, Charles. "Peru Fights Drug Traffic by Destroying Coca Crops." *Christian Science Monitor,* 27 November 1985, p. 22.

Lane, Charles. "Peru Steps Up War on Cocaine Industry." *Christian Science Monitor,* 11 December 1985, p. 11.

Lappé, Frances Moore, Joseph Collins, and David Kinley. *Aid as Obstacle: Twenty Questions About Our Foreign Aid and the Hungry.* San Francisco: Institute for Food And Development Policy, 1980.

Lappé, Frances Moore, and Joseph Collins. *Food First: Beyond the Myth of Scarcity.* New York: Ballantine, 1979. *Latin American Economic Report,* 29 August 1980.

Latin American Economic Report, 29 August 1980.

Lee, E. L. H. "Rural Poverty in Sri Lanka, 1963-1972." World Employment Programme Working Paper. Geneva: ILO, 1976.

Lee, Eddy. "Development and Income Distribution: A Case Study of Sri Lanka and Malaysia." *World Development* 5:4 (April 1977):279-289.

Lele, Uma. "Rural Africa: Modernization, Equity and Long-term Development." *Science* 211:6 (February 1981).

Lele, Uma. "Terms of Trade, Agricultural Growth and Rural Poverty in Africa." In J. Mellor and G. Desai, eds., *Agricultural Change and Rural Poverty: Variations on a Theme by Dharm Narain.* Baltimore: Johns Hopkins University Press, 1985.

Lewis, W. Arthur. "Economic Development with Unlimited Supplies of Labor." In A. Agarwala and S. Singh, eds., *The Economics of Underdevelopment.* London: Oxford University Press, 1970.

Lewis, W. Arthur. *The Theory of Economic Growth.* Homewood, Ill.: Richard Irwin, 1955.

Leys, Colin. *Underdevelopment in Kenya: The Political Economy of Neo-Colonialism, 1964-1971.* London: Heinemann, 1975.

Leys, Roger. *Dualism and Rural Development in East Africa.* Copenhagen: Institute for Development Research, 1973.

Liber, James. "Coping with Cocaine." *Atlantic Monthly,* January 1986.

Linear, Marcus. "The Tsetse War." *The Ecologist* 15(1/2):27-35.

Lipton, Michael. "Conditions of Poverty Groups and Impact on Indian Economic Development and Cultural Change: The Role of Labour." *Development and Change* 15:4 (October 1984):473-493.

Lipton, Michael. *Why Poor People Stay Poor: Urban Bias in World Development.* London: Temple Smith, 1977.

Livingstone, I., and H. W. Ord. *Agricultural Economics for Tropical Africa.* London: Heinemann, 1981.

Lofchie, Michael F., and Robert H. Bates. *Agricultural Development in Africa.* New York: Praeger, 1980.

Lopes, L. M. "Transferências v. Investimentos." *Informações.* Fundação Instituto de Pesquisas Econômicas, 58, University of São Paulo, (February 1985).

Macadar, Luís. *Uruguay, 1974-1980: Un Nuevo Ensayo de Reajuste Econômico?* Montevideo: Estudios CINVE, 1982.

Malenbaum, Wilfred. *Prospects for Indian Development.* London: George Allen & Unwin, 1962.

Manor, James, ed. *Sri Lanka in Crisis and Change.* London, Croom Helm, 1984.

Marga Institute. *An Analytical Description of Poverty in Sri Lanka.* Colombo: Marga Institute, 1981.

Martin, Everett G. "High Drama in the Jungles of Peru: Fight Against Cocaine is a Tangled-up Affair." *Wall Street Journal,* 20 March 1984, p. 1.

Martin, Everett G. "A Little Cattle Town in Bolivia Is Thriving as a Financial Center." *Wall Street Journal,* 17 February 1983.

Martine, George, and Ronaldo Coutinho Garcia. "Mudanças Tecnológicas e Sociais na Agricultura: A Panela do Povo em Tempo de Crise." Manuscript, 1983.

Mattis, Ann R. "An Experience in Need-Oriented Development." *Marga Quarterly Journal* 5:8 (Colombo, 1978):1-29.

Maxwell, Simon J., and Hans W. Singer. "Food Aid to Developing Countries: A Survey." *World Development* 7:3 (March 1979):225-246.

May, Lee. "Cocaine-Effect of Life in America." *Los Angeles Times,* 4 December 1985, p. 1

McClintock, Cynthia. "After Agrarian Reform and Democratic Government: Has Peruvian Agriculture Developed?" In LaMond Tullis and Ladd Hollist, eds., *Food, the State, and International Political Economy.* Lincoln: University of Nebraska Press, pp. 74-98.

McLaughlin, Martin M., and Overseas Development Council. *The United States and World Development: Agenda 1979.* New York: Praeger, 1979.

Meillassoux, Claude. "Development or Exploitation: Is the Sahel Famine Good Business?" *Review of African Political Economy* 1 (1974):27-33.

Mellor, John W. "Food Price Policy and Income Redistribution in Low-Income Countries." *Economic Development and Cultural Change* 27:1 (October 1978):1-26.

Mellor, John W. "Food Prospects for the Developing Countries." *American Economic Review* 73:2 (May 1983):239-243.

Mellor, John W. *The New Economics of Growth: A Strategy for India and the Developing World.* Ithaca, N.Y.: Cornell University Press, 1976.

Mellor, John W., and Bruce F. Johnston. "The World Food Equation: Interrelations Among Development, Employment, and Food Consumption." *Journal of Economic Literature* 22 (June 1984):531-574.

Mellor, John W., and G. Desai, eds. *Agricultural Change and Rural Poverty: Variations*

on a Theme by Dharm Narain. Baltimore: John Hopkins University Press, 1985.
Mellor, John W., Thomas F. Weaver, Uma J. Lele, and Sheldon R. Simon. *Developing Rural India: Plan and Practice.* Ithaca: Cornell University Press, 1968.
Miami Herald, 8, 9, 10, and 11 February 1987.
Ministério da Reforma e do Desenvolvimento Agrário, Instituto Nacional de Colonização e Reforma Agrária (INCRA). *Estatuto da Terra.* Lei no. 4.504, 30 November 1964.
Ministério da Reforma e do Desenvolvimento Agrário, Instituto Nacional de Colonização e Reforma Agrária (INCRA), e Governo do Estado da Bahia. *Plano Regional de Reforma Agrária.* Salvador, Bahia, Brazil: INCRA, 1985.
Minority Rights Group. *Eritrea and Tigray,* Report No. 5. London: Minority Rights Group, 1983.
Mockler, Anthony. *Haile Selassie's War.* Oxford: Oxford University Press, 1984.
Montalbano, William D. "Coca Valley: Peru Jungle Surrealism." *Los Angeles Times,* 2 December 1985, p. 1.
Montalbano, William D. "Latins Push Belated War on Cocaine." *Los Angeles Times,* 1 December 1985, p. 1.
Moon, Bruce E., and William J. Dixon. "Politics, the State, and Basic Human Needs: A Cross-National Study." *American Journal of Political Science* 29 (4) (November 1985):661-694.
Morales-Vaca, Mercedes. "A Laboratory Approach to the Control of Cocaine in Bolivia." In UN, Division of Narcotic Drugs, *Bulletin on Narcotics* 36:2 (April-June 1984):33-44. Special issue on cocaine.
Morris, Morris David, and Michelle B. McAlpin. "Measuring Welfare in South Asia." Paper distributed for the Social/Science Research Council (SSRC)/Indian Council of Social Science Research (ICSSR) Conference on South Asian Political Economy, New Delhi, December 12-16, 1980.
Morris, Morris David. *Measuring the Condition of the World's Poor: The Physical Quality of Life Index.* New York: Pergamon, Policy Studies, 1979.
Muchnik, Eusenia, and C. Zegers. "El Sector Agropecuario Chileno 1974-1980: Análisis de Tendencias y Perspectivas." Catholic University, Department of Agricultural Economics, Santiago, Chile, 1980.
Mukhoti, Bela. *The International Monetary Fund and Low-Income Countries.* FAER, Forthcoming.
Mulema, P. S. "Reflections on Uganda's Economic Performance." Kampala, S.N., 1983.
Myint, H. "The 'Classical Theory' of International Trade and the Underdeveloped Countries." *Economic Journal* 68 (June 1958):317-337.
Myint, H. "The Gains from International Trade and the Backward Countries." *Review of Economic Studies* 22 (1954):129-142.
Naik, K. C., and A. Sankaram. *A History of Agricultural Universities.* New Delhi: Oxford and IBH Publishing Company, 1972.
Nankani, Gobind. *Development Problems of Mineral Exporting Countries.* World Bank Staff Working Paper No. 354. Washington, D.C.: World Bank, 1979.
National Narcotics Intelligence Consumers Committee. *Narcotics Intelligence Estimate.* Washington, D.C.: Drug Enforcement Administration, U.S. Department of Justice, 1983.
"Nearly 1 Ton of Cocaine Is Impounded in L.A." *Salt Lake Tribune* (Utah), 25 March 1987.

Nelson, Douglas R. *The Political Structure of the New Protectionism.* World Bank Staff Working Paper No. 471. Washington, D.C.: World Bank, 1981.

New York Times, 9 September 1984, p. 12

Newsweek, 25 February 1985, special issue on drugs.

Nicholson, Norman K., John D. Esseks, and Ali Akhtar Khan. "The Politics of Food Scarcities in Developing Countries." In R. Hopkins, D. Puchala, and R. Talbot, eds., *Food, Politics and Agricultural Development: Case Studies in the Public Policy of Rural Modernation.* Boulder: Westview Press, 1979, pp. 261-305.

Oberst, Robert C. "Foodstamps and Government Nutrition Policy: The Battle over Basic Needs in Sri Lanka." Paper presented at the Conference on South Asia at the University of Wisconsin, Madison, Wisconsin, 1985.

Obeysekara, Jayasumana. "Revolutionary Movements in Ceylon." In Kathleen Gough and Hari P. Sharma eds., *Imperialism and Revolution in South Asia.* New York: Monthly Review Press, 1973, pp. 368-395.

O'Donnell, Guillermo A. *Modernization and Bureaucratic-Authoritarianism: Studies in South American Politics.* Berkeley: University of California Press, 1973.

Oliver, Henry M., Jr. *Economic Opinion and Policy in Ceylon.* London: Cambridge University Press, 1957.

Onis, Juan de. "Colombia Cracks Down but the Marijuana Gets Through Them." *New York Times,* 23 March 1979.

Onis, Juan de. "Latin Nations Uniting in War on Cocaine." *Los Angeles Times,* 3 December 1985.

Onís, Juán de. "New Bolivian Road May Become Cocaine Turnpike." *Los Angeles Times,* 2 December 1985.

Oram, Peter, Juan Zapata, George Alibaruho, and Shyamai Roy. *Investment and Input Requirements for Accelerating Food Production in Low-Income Countries by 1990.* International Food Policy Research Institute Research Report 10. Washington, D.C.: International Food Policy Research Institute, 1979.

Organization of American States (OAS). *Statistical Bulletin of The OAS.* Washington, D.C.: Published annually.

Ortiz Pinchetti, Francisco, Miguel Cabildo, Federico Campbell, and Ignacio Rodríguez. *La Operación Cóndor.* Mexico City: Proceso, 1981.

Oxfam. *Behind the Weather: Lessons to Be Learned: Drought and Famine in Ethiopia.* Oxford: Oxfam Public Affairs Unit, 1984.

Ozbudun, Ergun, and Aydin Ulusan, eds. *The Political Economy of Income Distribution in Turkey.* New York: Holmes and Meier, 1981.

Paiva, Ruy Miller. "Objetivos Econômicos da Reforma Agrária." *Revista Econômica Rural* 23, 3 (July/September 1985): 317-332.

Paulino, Leonardo A. *Food in the Third World: Past Trends and Projections to 2000.* Washington, D.C.: International Food Policy Research Institute, 1986.

Payne, Rhys. "Economic Development and Comparative Advantage." Los Angeles: UCLA Department of Political Science.

Peliano. A.M.M., C. de M. Castro, George Martine, and Ronaldo Coutinho Garcia. "O Problema Alimentar Brasileiro: Situação Atual, Perspectivas e Proposta de Políticas." CNRH/IPEA, Documento de Trabalho, no. 11, 1983.

People's Bank. *Economic Review.* Colombo: People's Bank, various issues.

People's Republic of China, State Statistical Bureau. *Statistical Yearbook of China.* Hong Kong: Economic Information Agency. Published annually.

Pick's Currency Yearbook. New York: Pick Publishing Corporation, 1981.

Pieris, G. H. *Basic Needs and the Provision of Government Services in Sri Lanka: A Case Study of Kandy District. World Employment Programme Research Working Papers.* Geneva: International Labour Organization, 1982.

Pinstrup-Andersen, Per, and Harold Alderman. "The Effectiveness of Consumer Food Subsidies in Reaching Rationing and Income Transfer Goals." International Food Policy Research Institute, Conference on Consumer-Oriented Food Subsidies, Chang Mai, Thailand, 1984.

Poleman, Thomas T. "Quantifying the Nutrition Situation in Developing Countries." *Food Research Institute Studies.* 18:1 (1981):1-58.

Ponce Caballero, A. Gastón. *Coca, cocaína, tráfico.* La Paz, Bolivia: Empresa El Diario, 1983.

Ponnambalam, Satchi. *Dependent Capitalism in Crisis: The Sri Lankan Economy, 1948-1980.* London: Zed Press, 1981.

Popkin, Samuel L. *The Rational Peasant: The Political Economy of Rural Society in Vietnam.* Berkeley: University of California Press, 1979.

Poulantzas, Nicos. *Political Power and Social Classes.* Translated by Timothy O'Hagan. London: New Left Books, 1973.

Prebisch, Raul. *Transformación y desarrollo: La gran tarea de la América Latina.* México: Fondo de Cultura Económica, 1970.

Prest, Michael. "Sudan on the Brink." *Middle East International* (London), 5 April 1985, pp. 12-14.

Prest, Michael, and Paul Vallely. "Drive to Resettle Refugees." *Times* (London), 27 February 1985, p. 6.

Provo Herald (Utah), 29 March 1985.

Radwan, Samir. *Agrarian Reform and Rural Poverty: Egypt, 1952-75.* Geneva: International Labour Organization, 1977.

Radwan, Samir. "Rural Labor Markets in Egypt." Paper presented to Social Science Research Council(SSRC)/International Foundation for Agricultural Development (IFAD) workshop, September 1985.

Rake, Alan. "Collapse of African Agriculture." *African Development* (London), February 1975.

Ram, Rati, and Theodore W. Schultz. "Life Span, Health, Savings and Productivity." *Economic Development and Cultural Change* 27:3 (April 1979):399-421.

Rance, Susanna. "Bolivia: Coca Trade Warps Economy, Way of Life." *Latinamerica Press,* 5 June 1986, p.5.

Remos, Ariel. "Cuba's Drug Trafficking Bank." *Washington Times,* 13 December 1985, p. 13.

Reutlinger, Shlomo, and Marcello Selowsky. *Malnutrition and Poverty: Magnitude and Policy Options.* World Bank Staff Occasional Papers, No. 23. Baltimore and London: Johns Hopkins University Press, 1976.

Rezende, Gervasio. "Price of Food and the Rural Poor in Brazil, 1960-80." Instituto de Planejamento Econômico e Social, Rio de Janeiro, January 1985.

Ribeiro, Nelson. "O Estatuto da Terra e o Problema Fundiário." Coleção Reforma Agrária, no. 1. of the Ministério da Reforma e do Desenvolvimento Agrário, Brasília, Brazil, 1985.

Richards, Alan. *Egypt's Agricultural Development, 1800-1980: Technical and Social Change.* Boulder, Colorado: Westview Press, 1982.

Richards, Alan. "Ten Years of *Infitah*: Class, Rent, and Policy Stasis in Egypt." *Journal of Development Studies* 20 (July 1984):323-338.

Richards, Alan, and Philip L. Martin, eds. *Migration, Mechanization, and Agricultural Labor Markets in Egypt.* Boulder, Colorado and Cairo: Westview Press and the American University in Cairo Press, 1983.

Richards, Alan, Philip Martin, and Rifaat Nagaar. "Labor Shortages in Egyptian Agriculture." In Alan Richards and Philip Martin, eds., *Migration, Mechanization, and Agricultural Labor Markets in Egypt.* Boulder, Colorado and Cairo: Westview Press and the American University in Cairo Press, 1983, pp. 21-44.

Richards, Peter, and Wilbert Gooneratne. *Basic Needs, Poverty and Government Policies in Sri Lanka.* Geneva: International Labor Organization (ILO) 1980.

Richey, Warren. "U.S. Praises Colombian Government for Drug Crackdown." *Christian Science Monitor,* 5 April 1985, p. 3.

Riding, Alan. "Bolivia Drug Crackdown Brews Trouble." *New York Times,* 12 September 1984, p. 1.

Riding, Alan. "Drug Region in Peru Booming Again." *New York Times,* 29 December 1984, p. 1.

Riding, Alan. "Shaken Colombia Acts at Last on Drugs." *New York Times,* 11 September 1984, p. 1.

Riley, Peter, and Margaret Missiaen. "An Analysis of Rising Grain Imports in Sub-Saharan Africa: The Outlook for Wheat and Rice." In *Sub-Saharan Africa Situation and Report.* Washington, D.C.: U.S. Department of Agriculture Economic Research Service, July 1985.

Rimmer, Douglas. "'Basic Needs' and the Origins of the Development Ethos." *Journal of Developing Areas* 15 (January 1981):215-237.

Rivera, Rigoberto, and M. Elena Cruz. *Pobladores rurales: Cambios en el poblamiento y el empleo rural en Chile.* Santiago, Chile: Grupo de Investigaciones Agrarias, Academia de Humanismo Cristiano, 1984.

Rowley, Storer. "It is Legal to Grow, Sell Coca Leaf in Bolivia." *Salt Lake Tribune* (Utah), 27 July 1986, p. A11.

Ruggie, John Gerara, ed. *The Antinomies of Interdependence: National Welfare and the International Division of Labor.* New York: Columbia University Press, 1983.

Ruttan, Vernon W. "The Green Revolution: Seven Generalizations. *International Development Review* 19:4(December 1977):16-23.

Ruttan, Vernon W. "Organizing Research Institutions to Induce Change: The Irrelevance of the Land Grant Experience for Developing Economies." University of Minnesota, Department of Agricultural Economics, 1968.

Sahn, David E. "An Analysis of the Nutritional Status of Pre-School Children in Sri Lanka, 1980-81." Washington, D.C.: International Food Policy Research Institute, 1983.

Sahn, David E. "Malnutrition and Food Consumption in Sri Lanka: An Analysis of Changes During the Past Decade." Washington, D.C.: International Food Policy Research Institute, 1986.

Saith, Ashwani. "Production, Prices, and Poverty in Rural India." *Journal of Development Studies* 17:2 (January 1981): 196-213.

Samarasinghe, S. W. R. de A. "Current Economic Policy: A Comment." Conference on Post-War Economic Development of Sri Lanka, Peradeniya, 16-20 December 1980.

Samarasinghe, S. W. R. de A. "Sri Lanka in 1982: A Year of Elections." *Asian Survey* 23:2 (February 1983):158-164.

Sanderatue, Nimal. "The Effects of Policies on Real Income and Employment." In *Sri Lanka: The Social Impact of Economic Policies During the Last Decade.* Colombo: UNICEF, 1985.

Sanderson, Steven E. "The Emergence of the 'World Steer': International and Foreign Domination in Latin American Cattle Production." In F. LaMond Tullis and W. Ladd Hollist, eds., *Food, the State, and International Political Economy.* Lincoln: University of Nebraska Press, 1986.

Sanderson, Steven E. *The Transformation of Mexican Agriculture: International Structure and the Politics of Rural Change.* Princeton, N.J.: Princeton University Press, 1986.

Schultz, Theodore W. "Effects of the International Donor Community on Farm People." *American Journal of Agricultural Economics* 62:5 (December 1980):873-878.

Schultz, Theodore W. *Transforming Traditional Agriculture.* New Haven: Yale University Press, 1964.

Schultz, Theodore W., ed. *Distortions of Agricultural Incentives.* Bloomington: Indiana University Press, 1978.

"Scientific Advances Lead to Era of Food Surplus Around World." *New York Times,* 9 September 1986, pp. 19-20.

Scobie, Grant M. *Food Subsidies in Egypt: Their Impact on Foreign Exchange and Trade.* Washington, D.C.: International Food Policy Research Institute, Research Report No. 40, August 1983.

Scott, James C. *The Moral Economy of the Peasant: Rebellion and Subsistence in Southeast Asia.* New Haven: Yale University Press, 1976.

Sen, Amartya. "Famines." *World Development* 8 (1980):613-621.

Sen, Amartya. *Poverty and Famines: An Essay on Entitlement and Deprivation.* New York and Oxford: Clarendon Press of Oxford University Press, 1981.

Sen, Amartya. *Resources, Values and Development.* Oxford: Basil Blackwell, 1984.

Shapouri, Shahla, Arthur J. Dommen, and Stacey Rosen. *Food Aid and the African Food Crisis,* FAER No. 221. Washington, D.C.: U.S. Department of Agriculture, Economic Research Service, June 1986.

Shastri, Amita. "Politics of Constitutional Development in South Asia in the Seventies: A Case Study of Sri Lanka." Ph.D. dissertation. New Delhi, Jawaharlal Nehru University, 1984.

Shaw, Timothy M. *Towards a Political Economy for Africa: The Dialectics of Dependence.* New York: St. Martin's Press, 1985.

Shawcross, William. *The Quality of Mercy: Cambodia, Holocaust and Modern Conscience.* London: Andre Deutsch, 1984.

Shepherd, Jack. *The Politics of Starvation.* New York and Washington, D.C.: Carnegie Endowment for International Peace, 1975.

Shepherd, Jack. "When Foreign Aid Fails." *Atlantic Monthly* 225:4(1985):41-46.

Shortlidge, Richard L., Jr. "University Training for Gramsevaks in India, An Example of Recurrent Education in a Low Income Country." Occasional Paper No. 67, Employment and Income Distribution Project, Department of Agricultural Economics, Cornell University, January 1974.

Shultz, George. "The Campaign Against Drugs: The International Dimension." U.S. Department of State, Bureau of Public Affairs, *Current Policy No. 611.* An address given before the Miami Chamber of Commerce, Miami, Florida, 14 September 1984.

Simons, Marlise. "Bolivia Cocaine Trade Revives after G.I.s Go." *New York Times,* 3 January 1987, p.1.

Singh, Shamsher. *Sub-Saharan Agriculture: Synthesis and Trade Prospects.* World Bank Staff Working Paper No. 608. Washington, D.C.: World Bank, 1983.

Skidmore, Thomas. "The Politics of Stabilization in Postwar Latin America." In James Mallor, ed., *Authoritarianism and Corporatism in Latin America.* Pittsburgh: University of Pittsburgh Press, 1971.

Somel, Kutlu. "Agricultural Support Policies in Turkey: A Survey of the Literature." *METU Studies in Development* 6 (1979):275-323.

Souza, Percival de. *Society, Cocaina.* Sao Paulo, Brazil: Traco Editora e Distribuidora, 1981.

Special Report. *Ecologist* 14:5/6 (1984):206-231.

Sri Lanka. "Budget Speech, 1981," by minister of Finance and Planning. Colombo: Ministry of Finance and Planning, 1980.

Sri Lanka. "The New Tax Policy." Speech of the minister of Finance and Planning in Parliament, 17 April 1979.

Sri Lanka, Department of Census and Statistics, Ministry of Plan Implementation. *Census of Agriculture, 1982.* Colombo: Ministry of Plan Implementation, 1982.

Sri Lanka, Department of Census and Statistics, Ministry of Plan Implementation. *Socio-Economic Indicators of Sri Lanka, 1983.* Colombo: Department of Census and Statistics, 1983.

Sri Lanka, Department of Census and Statistics, Ministry of Plan Implementation. *Sri Lanka Yearbook.* Colombo: Department of Census and Statistics, 1982.

Sri Lanka, Department of Census and Statistics, Ministry of Plan Implementation. *Statistical Pocket Book of the Democratic Socialist Republic of Sri Lanka.* Colombo: Department of Census and Statistics, 1983.

Sri Lanka, Ministry of Finance and Planning. *Public Investment, 1984-1988.* Colombo: Ministry of Finance and Planning, 1984.

Sri Lanka, Ministry of Finance and Planning. *Public Investment Programme, 1980-84.* Colombo: Ministry of Finance and Planning, 1980.

Sri Lanka, Ministry of Plan Implementation. "Evaluation Report of the Food Stamp Scheme." Colombo: Ministry of Plan Implementation, 1981.

Sri Lanka, Ministry of Plan Implementation. *Performance, 1980.* Colombo: Ministry of Plan Implementation, 1980.

Stamler, R.T., R.C. Fahlman, and S.A. Keele. "Illicit Traffic and Abuse of Cocaine." In UN, Division of Narcotic Drugs, *Bulletin on Narcotics* 36:2 (April-June 1984):45-55. Special issue on cocaine.

Stavenhagen, Rodolfo. *Social Classes in Agrarian Societies.* New York: Anchor Books, 1975.

Stepanek, Joseph F. *Bangladesh: Equitable Growth?* New York: Pergamon Press, 1979.

Subramaniam, C. *The New Strategy in Indian Agriculture: The First Decade and After.* New Delhi: Vikas Publishing House Private, 1979.

Sussman, Gerald E. *The Challenge of Integrated Rural Development in India: A Policy and Management Perspective.* Boulder, Colorado: Westview Press, 1982.

Thorner, Daniel. *The Agrarian Prospect in India.* Delhi: Delhi University Press, 1956.

Time, 25 February 1985.

Timmer, Peter C., Walter P. Falcon, and Scott R. Pearson. *Food Policy Analysis.* Baltimore: Johns Hopkins University Press, 1983.

Treaster, Joseph B. "Jamaica, Close U.S. Ally Does Little to Halt Drugs." *New York Times,* 10 September 1984.

Tullis, F. LaMond. "California and Chile in 1851 as Experienced by the Mormon Apostle Parley P. Pratt." *Southern California Quarterly* 68:3 (Fall 1985):291-307.

Tullis, F. LaMond. "The Current View on Rural Development: Fad or Breakthrough in Latin America." In W. Ladd Hollist and F. LaMond Tullis, eds., *An International Political Economy.* Boulder, Colorado: Westview Press, 1985, pp. 223-254.

Tullis, F. LaMond. "Food Aid, and Political Instability." In F. LaMond Tullis and W. Ladd Hollist, eds., *Food, the State, and International Political Economy: Dilemmas of Developing Countries.* Lincoln and London: University of Nebraska Press, 1986, pp. 215-238.

Tullis, F. LaMond. *Lord and Peasant in Peru: A Paradigm of Political and Social Change.* Cambridge, Mass.: Harvard University Press, 1970.

Tullis, F. LaMond. *Modernization in Brazil: Political Dueling Among Politicians, Charismatic Leaders, and Military Guardians.* Provo, Utah: Brigham Young University Press, 1973.

Tullis, F. LaMond. *Mormons in Mexico: The Dynamics of Faith and Culture.* Logan: Utah State University Press, 1987.

Tullis, F. LaMond, and W. Ladd Hollist, eds. *Food, the State, and International Political Economy.* Lincoln: University of Nebraska Press, 1986.

Turnbull, Colin M. *The Mountain People.* New York: Simon and Schuster, 1972.

UN, Comisión Económica para América Latina y el Caribe, (CEPAL/ECLA). *Anuario Estadístico de América Latina.* New York: United Nations, published annually.

UN, *United Nations Statistical Yearbook.* New York: United Nations, published annually.

UN, Division of Narcotic Drugs. *Bulletin on Narcotics*; special issue on cocaine. New York: UN, 1984.

UN, Economic Commission for Africa. *Survey of Economic Conditions in Africa.* New York: UN, 1973.

UN, Economic Commission for Latin America (ECLA/CEPAL). *Economic Survey of Latin America, 1979.* Santiago, 1981.

UN, Economic Commission for Latin America (ECLA/CEPAL). *Statistical Yearbook for Latin America.* New York: ECLA, published annually.

UN, Food and Agriculture Organization (FAO). *Agriculture: Toward 2000.* Rome: FAO, 1981.

UN, Food and Agriculture Organization (FAO). *Development Strategies for the Rural Poor: Analysis of Country Experiences in the Implementation of the WCARRD Programme of Action.* Economic and Social Development Paper No. 44. Rome: FAO, 1984.

UN, Food and Agriculture Organization (FAO). *The Fourth World Food Survey.* Statistical Series 11. Rome: FAO, 1977.

UN, Food and Agriculture Organization (FAO). *Production Yearbook.* Rome: FAO, various issues.

UN, Food and Agriculture Organization (FAO). *Socioeconomic Indicators Relating to the Agricultural Sector and Rural Development.* Rome: FAO, 1984.

UN, Food and Agriculture Organization (FAO). *State of Food and Agriculture, 1984.* Rome: FAO, 1985.

UN, Food and Agriculture Organization (FAO). *Trade Yearbook.* Rome: FAO, various issues.

UN, Food and Agriculture Organization (FAO), Relief and Rehabilitation Commission.

Early Warning System Meher (Main) Crop Season Synoptic Report, 1984 Crop Season. Addis Ababa, January 1985.

UN, Food and Agriculture Organization (FAO), Relief and Rehabilitation Commission. *Review of the Current Drought Situation in Ethiopia.* Addis Ababa, December 1984.

UNESCO. *Agricultural Education in Asia: A Regional Survey.* Paris: UNESCO, 1971.

Universidad Católica de Chile, Departamento de Economía Agraria. "El sector agropecuario chileno, 1974-1980: Análisis de tendencias y perspectivas." Santiago: 1980.

U.S. Agency for International Development (AID). *Blueprint for Development: The Strategic Plan of Action of the Agency for International Development.* Washington, D.C.: AID, n.d.

U.S. Agency for International Development (AID). *Pricing, Subsidies and Related Policies in Food and Agriculture.* Washington, D.C.: AID, November 1982.

U.S. Department of Agriculture, Africa and Middle East Branch, International Economic Division, Economic Research Service. *Food Problems and Prospects in Sub-Saharan Africa: The Decade of the 1980s.* Foreign Agricultural Research Report No. 166. Washington, D.C.: U.S. Department of Agriculture, 1981.

U.S. Department of Agriculture, Economic Research Service. *Food Needs and Availabilities, 1985: Update.* Washington, D.C.: USDA/ERS, November 1985.

U.S. Department of Agriculture, Economic Research Service. *World Agriculture: Outlook and Situation Report.* (March 1986).

U.S. Department of State, Bureau of International Narcotics Matters. "International Narcotics Control Strategy Report." Washington, D.C., February 1985 and March 1987, mimeo.

U.S. Department of State, Bureau of International Narcotics Matters. "International Narcotics Control Strategy Report: Midyear Update." Washington, D.C., 1 August 1985, mimeo.

U.S. House of Representatives, International Narcotics Control Study Missions to Latin America and Jamaica (6-21 August 1983) and Hawaii, Hong Kong, Thailand, Burma, Pakistan, Turkey, and Italy (4-22 January 1984). *A Report of the Select Committee on Narcotics Abuse and Control,* 98th Congress, 1st session. Washington, D.C.: U.S. Government Printing Office, 1984.

U.S. House of Representatives, Latin America Study Mission Concerning International Narcotic Problems (3-19 August 1985). *A Report of the Select Committe on Narcotics Abuse and Control,* 99th Congress, second session. Washington D.C.: U.S. Government Printing Office, 1986.

"U.S. Suspends Drug Fight in Peru as Deaths from Attack Reach 19." *New York Times,* 20 November 1984, p. 1.

Valdes, Alberto. "A Note on Variability in International Grain Prices." Paper prepared for IFPRI Workshop on Food and Agricultural Price Policy. Washington, D.C.: International Food Policy Research Institute, 1984.

Valdes, Alberto, and Panos Konandreas. "Assessing Food Insecurity Based on National Aggregates in Developing Countries." In Alberto Valdes, ed., *Food Security for Developing Countries.* Boulder, Colorado: Westview Press, 1981, pp. 25-51.

Vallely, Paul. "Ethiopians Admit Tigre Crisis." *Times* (London), 25 February 1985, p. 6.

Vallely, Paul. "Fear, Ethiopia's New Disease." *Times* (London), 16 February 1985, p. 80.

Vallely, Paul. "How Mengistu Hammers the Peasants." *Times* (London), 1 March 1985, p. 16.

Vallely, Paul. "Lack of Lorries Hinders Ethiopia Relief Work." *Times* (London), 20

February 1985.

van de Walle, Dominique. "Population Growth and Poverty: Another Look at the Indian Time Series Data." *Journal of Development Studies* 3 (April 1985):429-439.

Villareal, R. "Monetarismo e ideología: De la mano invisible a la mano militaria." *Comercio Exterior* 32:10 (October 1982):1059-1090.

Walinsky, Louis J., ed. *Agrarian Reform as Unfinished Business: The Selected Papers of Wolf Ladejinsky*. London: Oxford University Press, 1977.

Wallerstein, Mitchel B. *Food for War—Food for Peace: United States Food Aid in a Global Context*. Cambridge, Mass.: MIT Press, 1980.

Wanasinghe, Sydney. "The Hartal of August 1953." *Young Socialist* 2 (June 1980).

Warnapala, W. A. Wiswa. "Sri Lanka 1978: Reversal of Policies and Strategies." *Asian Survey* 19:2 (February 1979):178-190.

Warren, Hoge (1982). "Bolivians Find a Patron in Reputed Drug Chief." *New York Times,* 15 August 1982, p. 1

Warriner, Doreen. *Land Reform in Principle and Practice*. Oxford: Clarendon Press, 1969.

Wickramasinghe, Wimal. "The Faking of Foreign Trade Declarations." *Central Bank of Ceylon Staff Studies* 14:1 (April 1974):45-56.

Wickremeratne, L. A. "Planning and Economic Development." In K. M. de Silva, ed., *History of Ceylon*. Colombo: University of Ceylon, 1973.

Wickremeratne, L. A. "The Emergence of Welfare Policy, 1931-1948." In K. M. de Silva, ed., *Sri Lanka: A Survey*. Honolulu: University of Hawaii Press, 1977.

Wijesinghe, Mallory E. *The Economy of Sri Lanka, 1948-1975*. Colombo: Ranco, 1976.

Wijnbergen, Sweder van. "Dutch Disease: A Disease After All?" *Economic Journal* 94 (March 1984):41-55.

Wilkie, James W., and Manuel Moreno-Ibañez. "New Research on Food Production in Latin America Since 1952." In James W. Wilkie and Adam Perkal, eds., *Statistical Abstract of Latin America,* vol. 23. Los Angeles: UCLA Latin American Center Publications, 1984, pp. 734-781.

Wilkie, James W., and Adam Perkal, ed. *Statistical Abstract of Latin America,* vol 24. Los Angeles: UCLA Latin American Center Publications, 1985.

Williams, Dan. "Mexico, a Funnel for U.S. Bound Cocaine." *Los Angeles Times,* 3 December 1985.

Williamson, John, ed. *IMF Conditionality*. Washington, D.C.: Institute for International Economics, 1983.

Wiser, William H., and Charlotte Viall Wiser. *Behind Mud Walls 1930-1960*. Berkeley: University of California Press, 1963.

Wisotsky, Steven. "Exposing the War on Cocaine: The Futility and Destructiveness of Prohibition." *Wisconsin Law Review,* 1983.

World Bank. *Accelerated Development in Sub-Saharan Africa: An Agenda for Action*. Washington, D.C.: World Bank, 1981.

World Bank. *Annual Report*. Washington, D.C.: World Bank, 1980.

World Bank. *Coping with External Debt in the 1980s*. Washington, D.C.: World Bank, 1985.

World Bank. *The Economic Development of Ceylon*. Baltimore: Johns Hopkins University Press, 1952 and 1953.

World Bank. *Land Reform: A Sector Policy Paper*. Washington, D.C.: World Bank, 1975.

World Bank. *Morocco: Economic and Social Development Report.* Washington, D.C.: World Bank, 1981.

World Bank. *Poverty and Hunger: Issues and Options for Food Security in Developing Countries.* Washington, D.C.: World Bank, 1986.

World Bank. *Sub-Saharan Africa: Progress Report on Development Prospects and Programs.* Washington, D.C.: World Bank, 1983.

World Bank. *Toward Sustained Development in Sub-Saharan Africa: A Joint Program of Action.* Washington, D.C.: World Bank, 1984.

World Bank. *World Development Report.* New York: Oxford University Press. Published annually.

Wriggins, W. Howard. *Ceylon: Dilemmas of a New Nation.* Princeton, N.J.: Princeton University Press, 1960.

Zaman, M. A.. *Land Reform in Bangladesh to 1970.* Research Paper No. 66. Madison, Wisconsin: Land Tenure Center, 1976.

The Contributors

Cheryl Christensen was until 1986 chief of the Africa and Middle East Branch of the International Economics Division of the U.S. Department of Agriculture's Economic Research Service. She has since transferred to the Western Europe Branch of USDA. She and her colleagues have been instrumental in gathering the most credible data available concerning the food and economic crises that have faced sub-Saharan Africa. Her articles, "World Hunger: A Structural Approach (1978)," "Food Problems and Emerging Policy Responses in Sub-Saharan Africa (1982)" (with Lawrence Witucki), and "State Policies and Food Scarcity in Sub-Saharan Africa (1986)" (with Lawrence Witucki), have influenced academics and policymakers alike. She also contributed to *Africa's Agrarian Crisis* (1986), edited by Stephen K. Commins, Michael F. Lofchie, and Rhys Payne.

Keith Griffin is professor of economics and president of Magdalen College, Oxford University, England. An internationally recognized scholar and consultant in political and economic development, he is the author of numerous books, including *Institutional Reform and Economic Development in the Chinese Countryside* (1984), *The Political Economy of Agrarian Change* (1974, 1979, and 1983), *Growth and Equality in Rural China* (1981), and *Land Concentration and Rural Poverty* (1981). He is a frequent consultant to the International Labor Organization, the World Bank, the United Nations Research Institute for Social Development, the Food and Agricultural Organization of the United Nations, and to governments of countries such as Ethiopia, Ecuador, Morocco, Chile, Peru, Turkey, Pakistan, and Algeria.

Ronald J. Herring is associate professor of political science at Northwestern University. He is the author of *Land to the Tiller: The Political Economy of Agrarian Reform in South Asia* (1983). His articles have also appeared in *World Development, Journal of Peasant Studies, Peasant Studies, Pakistan Development Review,* and numerous edited volumes. He has received research grants from the National Science Foundation, the Social Science Research Council, the Lilly Endowment, the American Institute of Pakistan Studies, and the Ford Foundation.

W. Ladd Hollist is professor of political science and director of graduate programs in the David M. Kennedy Center for International Studies at Brigham Young University. When the conference that gave rise to this book was held, he was Visiting Milton R. Merrill Professor at Utah State University. He is coeditor of and contributor to *Food, the State, and International Political Economy* (1986), *An International Political Economy* (1985), and *World System Struc-*

334

ture: Continuity and Change (1981). His articles have been published in the *International Studies Quarterly, Journal of Politics, American Journal of Political Science, International Yearbook of Foreign Policy Studies,* and various edited books.

F. Tomasson Jannuzi is professor of economics and former director of the Center for Asian Studies at the University of Texas at Austin. He also is the director of the federally funded National Resource Center for South Asia at the university. Dr. Jannuzi's best-known academic work is his field research since 1956 in rural areas of South Asia, reported in his two books, *Agrarian Crisis in India: The Case of Bihar* (1974) and (with James T. Peach) *The Agrarian Structure of Bangladesh: An Impediment to Development* (1980) and in several articles. He is the former chairman of the board of the American Institute of Indian Studies, and he continues to serve as a trustee of that institute. Periodically he has served as a consultant to such organizations as the United States Agency for International Development in India and Bangladesh and the International Communications Agency (now United States Information Agency) for which he helped develop a Fulbright program for Bangladesh.

Alain de Janvry is professor of agricultural and research economics at the University of California, Berkeley. He has been a consultant for the Ford Foundation, the World Bank, the Rockefeller Foundation, the Organization of American States, and the United States Agency for International Development. His book, *The Agrarian Question and Reformism in Latin America* (1981), has stimulated much useful dialogue, as have also his numerous journal articles and publications in edited works.

Michael F. Lofchie is professor of political science and director of the African Studies Center at the University of California, Los Angeles. He has been a member of the board of directors of the African Studies Association and has served as chairman of UCLA's Council on Educational Development. Among his books are *Africa's Agrarian Crisis* (edited with Stephen K. Commins and Rhys Payne, 1986), *Agricultural Development in Africa* (with Robert Bates, 1980), *The State of the Nations* (1971), and *Zanzibar: Background to Revolution* (1965 and 1968). He has published regularly on Africa in *Journal of Modern African Studies, Comparative Politics,* and other peer-reviewed journals.

John W. Mellor is director of the International Food Policy Research Institute. He has served previously as chief economist of the U.S. Agency for International Development and at Cornell University, where he was professor of economics. He is the author of *The New Economics of Growth: A Strategy for India and the Developing World* (1976) and *The Economics of Agricultural Development* (1966, and winner in 1978 of an award by the American Agricultural Economics Association for a "publication of enduring quality") and is coeditor of three other volumes. He has served as a consultant to such agencies as the World Bank, the Food and Agriculture Organization of the United Nations, the Rockefeller Foundation, and the U.S. Agency for International Development. He has directed research projects in India, Bangladesh, Pakistan, Nepal, Thailand, the Philippines, Indonesia, Taiwan, and Chile. He is a fellow of the American Academy of Arts and Sciences and also of the American Agricultural Economics Association.

Alan Richards is associate professor of economics at the University of California, Santa Cruz, and he has also taught at the City University of New York, the University of Wisconsin, and Harvard University. He is the author of *Egypt's Agricultural Development, 1800-1980* (1982), *Development and Modes of Production in Marxian Economics: A Critical Evaluation* (1986), and numerous journal articles. From 1978 to 1981 he worked with Egyptian colleagues on a labor utilization survey in Sharkiyya governorate. The results of this work, and other contributions, appear in *Migration, Mechanization, and Agricultural Labor Markets in Egypt* (coedited with Philip L. Martin, 1983). As a member of the Joint Committee on the Near and Middle East of the Social Science Research Council, he organized a workshop on Food Policy in the Middle East, held by the International Foundation for Agricultural Development (IFAD) in Rome, 1984. He has traveled widely in the Middle East and North Africa, and presently he is collaborating on a book on the political economy of the Middle East.

F. LaMond Tullis is professor of political science and associate academic vice-president at Brigham Young University. He is the coeditor of and contributor to *Food, the State, and International Political Economy* (1986), *An International Political Economy* (1985), and other edited volumes. He is the author of *Lord and Peasant in Peru* (1970), *Politics and Social Change in Third World Countries* (1973), *Modernization in Brazil* (1973), and *Mormons in Mexico* (1987) and has published numerous articles on social mobilization and religious movements in Latin America. He spent 1983-1984 as a visiting fellow at the Institute of Development Studies, University of Sussex, and at the London School of Economics and Political Science. He has directed research projects in Peru and Mexico, has served as a consultant for the U.S. Agency for International Development, and is a member of the boards of editors of two journals.

Glossary

Bataidars and Bargadars: Bataidars and bargadars are actual tillers of the soil in the Permanent Settlement Region (see glossary below) who lack secure rights in land. They "take in" land for short periods from others (who have superior rights in land), usually on oral leases. They are rightly perceived as sharecroppers; their names signify that, in the general case, they are expected to give up at least fifty percent of their produce to those from whom they have "taken in" land. They are sometimes referred to as "tenants" of landlords. But, in Bangladesh, they have been denied that classification and are referred to only as sharecroppers.

Bengal Tenancy Act: The Bengal Tenancy Act (1885) applied to the Permanent Settlement Region. Its British authors were attempting to secure additional rights for persons (including sharecroppers) whose rights in land had largely been ignored at the time of the Permanent Settlement of 1793.

"Campesinización": A change leading to an increase in the number of peasant households. An example is a redistributive land reform that gives access to family farms to formerly landless households.

Comparative Advantage: A doctrine of classical economics specifying that specialization by nations in production for export of goods which they could produce more efficiently than other nations, while importing goods which in comparative terms can be more efficiently produced abroad, would benefit both trading partners when trade occurred. The problem is that the analysis is static, whereas planning must account for dynamic economic situations.

Debt Service Ratio: Ratio of debt service obligations (interest plus amortization) to total export earnings. Obligations on short-term credits and IMF transactions are typically excluded.

Dependent Welfare State: A configuration of public services and transfers which constitute a significant social wage, administered by the state and subject to periodic expansion and contraction through political mechanisms, located in a dependent political economy.

Distributive Justice: Distributive justice here refers to "modernizing" ideals articulated in the Indian subcontinent at the end of British colonial rule. The phrase is used generally as a means of specifying a goal of rural economic development that can be met only when steps are taken by government (e.g., by means of agrarian reforms, particularly those that redistribute "rights in land") to transform the traditional agrarian structure of a society—in the process attempting to ensure that sustained increases in production, if achieved, will be associated with improved distribution of the final product to persons (notably peasants now lacking secure rights in land or any land at all) who have been the historic victims of extractive, quasi-feudal systems of traditional agriculture (as in the Permanent Settlement Region of the subcontinent).

Dutch Disease: Macroeconomic and sectoral effects due to a large, sudden influx of foreign exchange, e.g., to the Dutch economy after large discoveries of natural gas in the North Sea. By its effects on the real exchange rate, it is held that such inflows reduce the profitability of tradeable goods, such as agricultural and industrial goods, in comparison with non-tradeables, such as services.

Engel's Law: Observation that the percentage of income which is spent on food declines as income rises.

Entitlements: Institutionalized rights to goods and services. Entitlement programs have the backing of public law and constitute a formalized social wage, hence are a defining characteristic of the welfare state.

Food Entitlement: Any socially sanctioned means of obtaining food, whether production on own land, exchange, gift from public or private sources, etc. Developed by Amartya Sen in his book, *Poverty and Famines.*

Functional Dualism: The traditional sector is functional to the growth of the modern sector through the delivery to that sector of cheap labor and cheap food based on self-exploitation of family labor.

Gini Coefficients: A gini coefficient is an aggregate numerical measure of income inequality ranging from zero (perfect equality) to one (perfect inequality). It is graphically measured by dividing the area between the perfect equality line and the Lorenz curve by the total area lying to the right of the equality line in the Lorenz diagram. The Lorenz curve is a graph depicting the variance of the size distribution of income from perfect equality. (See Michael P. Todaro, *Economic Development in the Third World,* 3rd ed., pp. 587,595.)

ICARDA: International Center for Agricultural Research in Dry Areas, located in Aleppo, Syria; member of the Consultive Group on International Agricultural Research.

Import Substitution Industrialization: A deliberate effort by government to replace industrial imports by domestic production. Typical instruments for this purpose include protective tariffs and import quotas on goods which compete with domestic industry and overvalued exchange rates to subsidize imports of noncompetitive imputs for industry.

Income Elasticity of Demand: The percentage by which the quantity demanded of a commodity increases for a one percent increase in income.

Incremental Capital to Output Ratio: The amount of investment required to raise output by one currency unit (e.g., the amount of investment needed to increase output by one dollar).

Infitah-style Growth: Proclaimed as policy after "infitah" (opening up) by the Sadat government in Egypt. More generally, it is a style of growth in the Middle East in which services, banking, and import trade grow rapidly, but sectors such as agriculture and industry, and popular incomes, lag.

Institutional Rents: Rents created by the state (e.g., through price-support programs, subsidized credit, protective tariffs, import licenses, and public investment projects) and distributed in civil society through the power structure of the political economy.

International Fund for Agricultural Development: An international lending agency funded by OECD and OPEC countries, headquartered in Rome and specializing in loans for small-farmer development in least developed countries.

IRR: Internal rate of return is the discount rate which makes the discounted stream of benefits of a project equal to the initial cost.

Kulak-Bureaucrat System: A characterization of rural cooperatives in the Middle East; holds that such cooperatives are dominated by rich peasants ("kulaks") and by government officials ("bureaucrats").

Lewis-Type Growth: Economic growth occurring in a dual economy with surplus labor and constant real wages. The modern sector is the key growth sector and produces investment goods and luxury consumption goods demanded by the capitalist and landlord classes.

Liberalization: The transition from an interventionist regime, such as import substitution industrialization, to a neoliberal economy. Liberalization includes the removal of trade barriers and elimination of price controls including those on interest and exchange rates.

Luxury Goods: Final consumption goods whose demand originates in the expenditure of profit and rent incomes.

Maliks: Maliks are persons in portions of the Permanent Settlement Region (i.e., Bangladesh) who enjoy (in a de jure sense) permanent occupancy rights to the land in their possession. The "permanent occupancy rights" are roughly the equivalent of "ownership" of the land in their possession. A malik may or may not be an actual tiller or cultivator of the land in his possession. Following the enactment of agrarian reform legislation in Pakistan (legislation now having the force of law in Bangladesh), some maliks are in fact ex-zamindars with "new names." Such maliks, regardless of the size of their landholdings, are often "absentee landlords" continuing—even in 1987—to function in an "extractive" relationship to cultivating peasants who do not have "permanent occupancy rights" in land.

Monetary Approach to the Balance of Payments: An anti-inflationary policy consisting of freezing the exchange rate based on the theory that domestic inflation is the sum of international price variations plus variations in the exchange rate. A fixed exchange rate in a fully open economy would, thus, limit domestic price increases to international inflation.

Neoliberal Authoritarian Model: A neoliberal economy managed under authoritarian forms of government implying, in particular, severe control over labor organizations and wage demands.

Neoliberalism: An economic doctrine that places markets as the driving force in the determination of prices and the allocation of resources. Typical neoliberal policies include free trade, balanced budgets, and equilibrium exchange rates.

Overvalued Exchange Rate: An exchange rate that is set at a level higher than its real value. The result is to cheapen imports and underprice exports in domestic currency while raising the price of exports on the world market. It tends to lead to deficits in the balance of payments and to the need for either devaluation or foreign exchange controls (rationing).

Permanent Settlement Region: The Permanent Settlement Region embraces the territory of the Indian states of Bihar and West Bengal, and parts of Orissa, and virtually all of the territory of contemporary Bangladesh. The term "Permanent Settlement" refers to the decision of the British in 1793 to settle lands with persons called zamindars (as defined below) as a means of satisfying the revenue needs of the East India Company.

Premature Welfarism: A notion derived from orthodox development theory assuming that the welfare state is appropriate only in advanced industrial societies; the appearance of an extensive welfare state in very poor societies is thus presumed to be "premature" in both and empirical and normative sense.

Proletarianization: Establishment of cash wage as the form of labor remuneration with freedom for the worker to choose his or her employer, by contrast to labor relations based on forced labor, sharecropping, or rents in labor services.

Raiyats: Raiyats are persons in portions of the Permanent Settlement Region who enjoy (in a de jure sense) permanent occupancy rights to the land in their possession. The "permanent occupancy rights" are roughly the equivalent of "ownership" of the land in their possession. A raiyat may or may not be an actual tiller or cultivator of the land in his possession. Following legislation to "abolish" zamindars in independent India, some raiyats are in fact ex-zamindars with new names. Such raiyats, regardless of the size of their landholdings, are often "absentee landlords" continuing—even in 1987—to function in an "extractive" relationship to cultivating peasants who lack "permanent occupancy rights" in land.

Rent: As noted above, a distinction can be made in the Permanent Settlement Region of South Asia between the terms rent and land revenue: rent was paid by peasants to zamindars. The zamindars, acting as agents or intermediaries of the state, then paid a share of the rent to the state; the state's share could then be classified as its land revenue.

Rent-seeking Behavior: Competition among individuals or groups to appropriate the rents (benefits) created by government restrictions on economic activity. An example of such behavior is to induce the government to impose price distortions which will benefit specific individuals or groups.

SAM (Mexican Food System): A program initiated by President López Portillo in Mexico to foment food self-sufficieny using price incentives, subsidized credit, and technical assistance and directed in priority to dry-land peasant producers.

Social Articulation: An economy where wage incomes create the bulk of final consumption and where the key growth sectors producing final consumption goods are the wage goods sectors. A rising real wage bill is, thus, necessary to absorb a growing output of the key sectors.

Social Disarticulation: An economy where investment demand, profit and rent incomes, or exports create the demand for the key growth sectors. The key growth sectors produce capital and intermediate goods, luxury consumption goods, and exports. In this case, a growing real wage bill is not necessary to absorb a growing output of the key sectors.

Social Wage: Income or in-kind equivalent in goods and services statutorily owed to specified members of society by virtue of their status as citizens of the country. For example, subsidized or free food typically provided in Sri Lanka supplemented market-derived earnings and was provided from the aggregate social surplus through the state. Free medical care and university education likewise are components of the social wage in Sri Lanka.

Special Drawing Rights (SDRs): This is an internationally recognized financial asset created by the International Monetary Fund (IMF) in 1970. Its purposes is to supplement gold, dollars, and other hard currencies in settling international balance of payments accounts.

Structural Dependency: Dependency generated and indicated by "hard" features of the internal economy and the position of the domestic economy in the international economic system; for example, the structure of exports, imports, sectoral distribution of employment, technology, inconvertible currency, debt. Structural dependency may be thought of as a combination of parameters, as opposed to short-term dependent situations which are conjunctural and "soft" residues of colonialism, such as cultural dependency.

Structural Dualism: An economy with a dual structure composed of a modern sector (with high labor productivity, wage relations, and profit as a return to capital) and a traditional sector (with low labor productivity, unpaid family labor, and no separate return to the different factors of production).

System of Revenue-Farming: The system of revenue-farming was one in which zamindars (landlords) acted as agents of the state in collecting rent from peasants, and transferred a share of the rent to the state the sum paid by the zamindars to the state in the British period was "land revenue" (revenue received by the state from its interests in land). The system of revenue-farming, then, was one in which landlords in no way functioned as farmers or "tillers of the soil."

Terms of Trade Index: Derived from the export price index (a weighted average of prices of all exported goods) divided by the import price index multiplied by 100. Usually standardized by setting the index at 100 for some particular year (e.g., 1970) so that changes in the terms of trade may be presented with a single number. Example: if the index is 100 in 1970, and 50 in 1980, a given level of exports will have one-half the purchasing power in terms of the same basket of imports in 1980 compared to 1970. The terms of trade in this example have deteriorated.

UNP: United National Party, one of the two dominant political parties in Sri Lanka (the other being the SLFP, or Sri Lanka Freedom Party, with which it regularly alternated in power until 1982). The UNP is a relatively pro-business party and the architect of the liberalization program, over which it still presides.

Urban Bias: Hypothesis that government policy systematically favors urban areas at the expense of rural areas. Associated especially with Michael Lipton, in his *Why Poor People Stay Poor,* 1977.

Wage Goods: Final consumption goods whose demand originates in the expenditure of wage income.

Zamindars: The Zamindars (landlords) were the tribute collectors of Mogul India. During the British period of Indian history the zamindars were classified as intermediaries between the state or ruling authority and the cultivating peasants. They were accorded secure rights in land by the British (over landholdings designated estates) and continued (as in the Mogul period) to act as agents of the ruling authority or state in collecting "rent" from peasants within their "estates."

Author Index

Subject Index

Africa, 67–136; absence of research on food crops in, 52; colonial economics in, 103–105; debt servicing in, 101–102; decline of terms of trade in, 113–116; decontrol of consumer and wholesale prices in, 92–93; devaluation of currency in, 79–81; drought in, 67; economic and food problems in, 68–75; economic institutions in, 86; effects of macroeconomic policies on inflation in, 94; erosion of foreign exchange earning capability in, 8; export taxation policies in, 80–81; external determinants of agrarian crisis in, 98–119; food and agricultural policy in, 5, 67–68, 70, 76, 78, 79; food crisis in, 4–5; food imports in, 69–70; food production declines in, 62, 67, 68–69, 122; foreign exchange in, 94; IMF constraints in, 83; institutional/structural policy agenda in, 82–83; interest rates in, 94; macroeconomic policies in, 79–80, 94; negative employment trends in, 100; policy reform agenda in, 76–83; policy reforms to alleviate food crises in, 67–68; pricing policy in, 76, 78; problems of debt servicing in, 101–102; stabilization programs in, 85; starvation in, 98; state patronage in, 85. *See also individual country names*

Agency for International Development (AID), 76

Agrarian reform, 7, 60, 156 (n. 15); in South Asia, 147

Agribusiness, in Brazil, 241

Aid, food, 24, 25, 55, 57; in Bolivia and Peru, 259–60, 279 (n. 66); in Ethiopia, 134–35; in MENA, 299

Aid, foreign, 28–29, 55–58, 100, 125–26, 166–68, 248, 259–60

Alcohol, use of as fuel substitute in Brazil, 235

Anstey, Vera, intellectual tradition deriving from, 153

Argentina, expansion of coca production in, 249, 250, 276 (n. 25)

Articulation, social, definition of, 198, 341

Asia. *See* South Asia and *individual country names*

Austerity: period of for small farmers and landless in the Middle East and North Africa (MENA), 288; policy of in MENA, 306; relationship of to debt crisis policies in Latin America, 223–24

Bangladesh, 7; famine in, 24

Bargadars, 146, 149, 337

Bataidars, 146, 149, 337

Belaúnde, Fernando, 197

Bengal Tenancy Act, 148, 337

Beni, 255

Bolivia, effects of cocaine on food production in, Ch. 12, passim; expansion of growing of coca in, 249–50, 254–57; export of coca from, 252–57; foreign aid cut off in, 248; governmental support of cocaine trade in, 247; inflation in, 247; international pressure to curb cocaine traffic in, 248; labor displacement in as result of cocaine trade, 261–67

Bonilla, Rodrigo Lara, 274, (n. 13)

Bourguiba, Habib ibn Ali, 307

Brazil, agribusiness in, 241; debt crisis in, 206; economic miracle in, 232; effects of international changes in food prices on production in, 235; elite-dominated society of, 231; expansion of area planted in, 237; expansion of export crops during neoliberal period in, 204; expansion of coca production in, 249;

About the Book

This book looks at the many internal and external factors that complicate the struggle against poverty and hunger in developing countries and examines strategies that have been advanced to redress these. The authors agree that the application of appropriate technologies could increase the availability of locally produced food with benefits for both farmers and food consumers. They conclude, however, that inappropriate government policies, social inequalities, excess emphasis on agricultural production for export and reliance on food imports, and foreign-financed industrialization impede efforts to provide food security in Africa, South Asia, Latin America, and the Middle East.